BACK TO THE ASYLUM

BACK TO THE ASYLUM

The Future of Mental Health Law and Policy in the United States

JOHN Q. LA FOND

MARY L. DURHAM

New York   Oxford
OXFORD UNIVERSITY PRESS
1992

Oxford University Press

Oxford   New York   Toronto
Delhi   Bombay   Calcutta   Madras   Karachi
Kuala Lumpur   Singapore   Hong Kong   Tokyo
Nairobi   Dar es Salaam   Cape Town
Melbourne   Auckland

and associated companies in
Berlin   Ibadan

Published by Oxford University Press, Inc.,
200 Madison Avenue, New York, New York 10016

Oxford is a registered trademark of Oxford University Press

Library of Congress Cataloging-in-Publication Data
La Fond, John Q.
Back to the asylum : the future of mental health law and policy
in the United States / John Q. LaFond and Mary L. Durham.
p. cm.   Includes bibliographical references (p.   ) and index.
ISBN 0-19-505520-9
1. Mental health laws–United States.
2. Mental health policy–United States.
I. Durham, Mary L.
II. Title.
KF3828.D87   1992
344.73'044—dc20   [347.30444]
91-42365

1 3 5 7 9 8 6 4 2

Printed in the United States of America
on acid free paper

To Evelyn, my wife,
for her love and friendship
J.Q.L.F.

To my parents, Alta and Lowell Durham,
whose intelligence, selflessness and hard work
inspired me
M.L.D.

ACKNOWLEDGMENTS

We owe many people a debt of gratitude for their assistance and support in helping us finally finish this venture. This book has been (too) many years in gestation. Only with the help of many colleagues and students over the years could we have persevered to the end.

Our respective employers, the University of Puget Sound School of Law and Group Health Cooperative of Puget Sound, have been extremely generous in allowing us to spend considerable time and energy on this undertaking. They have also provided us with wonderful support staffs and facilities. Both Dean James Bond of the law school and Dr. Ed Wagner of Group Health Cooperative Center for Health Studies have encouraged and sustained us throughout the process. The University of Puget Sound law school library staff, under the very able direction of Anita Steele, has been long-suffering in helping us gather our research sources. In particular, Faye Jones, Susan Kezele, Kelly Kunsch, and Bob Menanteaux have been resourceful and patient above and beyond the call of duty. An exceptionally capable group of secretaries have assisted in the preparation of (too many) manuscripts over the years. They include Genie Hoffman and Delia Wakefield, ably assisted by pinch hitters Nancy Ammons and Elizabeth Dorsett. Professor and Associate Dean Don Carmichael was very generous in letting us homestead in his faculty office while we noisily collaborated on the manuscript.

We also owe a special debt to a cadre of talented law students who served as invaluable research assistants over the years, including Kim Gaddis, Jodi McDougal, Katie Miller, Cheryl Nielson, Kim Padrow, Nina Rivkin, Ann Wakefield-Smith and David Wentzel.

Joan Bossert and Susan Hannan at Oxford University Press were enthusiastic supporters and constructive critics of our work. Linda Grossman, our copy editor, provided superb assistance in improving the work.

Other friends and loved ones missed us in our absence and tolerated us in their presence. Evelyn La Fond, Colleen Craig, Jim and Elizabeth Hunnicutt deserve special thanks for their indulgence in this process. We thank all of you.

PREFACE

Madness startles and provokes. There has always been a taut tension in American attitudes toward madness—at times oscillating between compassion and fear; at others, between tolerance and repression. Joseph Goldstein, professor of law, and Jay Katz, professor of psychiatry, write eloquently of this anxiety: "What must be recognized is the enormous ambivalence toward the 'sick' reflected in conflicting wishes to exculpate and to blame; to sanction and not to sanction; to treat and to mistreat; to protect and to destroy."[1] How we as a society react to madness tells us a great deal about our contemporary hopes, fears, and values.

There has recently been a clear pendulum swing in how society perceives and treats the mentally ill. From about 1960 to about 1980—a period we will call the Liberal Era—law and mental health policy strongly emphasized fairness to mentally ill offenders in assessing their criminal responsibility and permitted most other mentally ill individuals to live in the community, largely free of government interference. From about 1980 on—a period we will call the Neoconservative Era—there has been a noticeable reversal in these policies. Over this decade, the public clamored for the reestablishment of "law and order" by holding mentally ill offenders criminally responsible for their deviant behavior and by hospitalizing other disturbed citizens against their will. In short, there was growing pressure to return the mentally ill to the "asylum" of prisons and mental hospitals, a trend that continues to this day.

Our use of the term "asylum" is intended to be provocative. For some, a return to the asylum suggests a policy that responds to a humane desire to provide a caring and safe environment removed from the stress of the world for those in desperate need of help. From this viewpoint, the asylum is the "safe haven" for the mentally ill who simply cannot measure up to society's demands. For others, however, a return to the asylum suggests confinement in overcrowded and understaffed institutions in which society's outcasts are punished or warehoused for the convenience of the majority. From this view point, such institutions cannot be called hospitals because they do not provide treatment and cure. Instead, they are places that evoke images of the "snake

---

[1]J. Goldstein and J. Katz, *Abolish the Insanity Defense— Why Not?* Yale L.J. 72 (1963): 853–76, 854.

pits" of the past before the "enlightenment" of the mid-twentieth century. We have used this charged phrase in our work precisely because it forces the reader to confront these sharply different visions of the future. Society must make hard choices in how to cope with madness.

This book is about the pendular swings in mental health policy during the Liberal and Neoconservative eras and the legal reforms that are giving shape to a new consensus on how society should deal with the mentally ill. It is also about the larger social context that spawned these changes. We strongly believe mental health policy is driven by larger social and economic forces in American society, and these forces propel change in predictable directions— unless society takes positive steps to alter that course. Important decisions, including legislation and court decisions, will be influenced by this powerful social context.

There are those who will take issue with our use of two distinctive eras of mental health policy in the last half of this century. They will claim a consistent policy has generally stayed its course with only modest adjustments over the last several decades, and that we have simply overstated the case for a new cycle of reform. We disagree with this view but we also recognize that phases of reform are not neatly packaged in convenient intervals. In fairness to those who will take issue with our views, we acknowledge there are counterexamples that suggest continuity rather than change in policy. Nonetheless, we believe sufficient evidence has accumulated that clearly indicates a new direction for mental health policy—and it is quite different from that of the recent past.

The lives of hundreds of thousands of our most disabled citizens will be touched by the new laws implemented during the Neoconservative Era. Sufficient time has passed since the onset of this new era to permit a critical evaluation of the emerging strategies for controlling and caring for the mentally ill. And needless to say, the plight of the mentally ill in America raises profound questions for the country. Historically, new solutions to old problems invariably produce new problems. Moreover, economic resources for solving today's social problems are extremely limited; the needs of the mentally ill must compete with other societal needs, many of which generate much more public sympathy and support. We need to know if current mental health policy reforms are achieving society's goals, and if their costs are worth it. Thus, a hard look at these reforms is essential at this juncture to determine whether we should continue on this course or consider a mid-course correction.

Our analysis and conclusions will be controversial. Not all our readers will agree with the way we portray these issues or with our recommendations; we expect this. Any social commentary on public policy still undergoing transformation will be unable to escape criticism from those who interpret the evidence differently or from those who hold different values. Assessing mental health policy accurately and objectively is further complicated by society's fear of mental illness, which can cloud even the most well-intentioned judgments.

Nonetheless, we hope to shed more light than heat on these contentious questions. Psychiatrists and other mental health professionals may understand more fully the changing roles society is asking them to play. People from diverse backgrounds and political persuasions interested in mental health law and policy—including judges, lawyers, academics, policymakers, legislators, government employees, family members concerned about their disturbed loved ones, and others who come into contact with the criminal justice or public mental health systems—will find this book provocative and, more important, useful. Anyone concerned about the difficult public policy issues involving the mentally ill, such as the insanity defense or homelessness, will find this book a source of understanding and a stimulus for thoughtful reflection.

We have studied, taught, and written extensively on mental health law and policy for well over a decade. Throughout our respective professional careers as a law professor and as a medical sociologist, we have been especially interested in viewing this subject from an interdisciplinary perspective.

In this book, we examine how laws dealing with the mentally ill have changed dramatically during the last three decades. In particular, we examine whether law reform rests on sound empirical evidence and whether the neoconservative reforms have accomplished their intended effects or have been merely symbolic and even counterproductive.

Finally, we predict the future of mental health law and policy to the end of the twentieth century. There will surely be new problems to attend to and a need to rethink strategies that are in vogue. Addressing these issues now will help us prepare for the inevitable challenges of the future.

Tacoma, Washington   J. Q. L. F.
Seattle, Washington   M. L. D.
August 1991

CONTENTS

BACK TO THE ASYLUM

Introduction: The Pendulum
of Social Movements

> I do not see how any reasonably objective view of our mental hospitals
> today can fail to conclude that they are bankrupt beyond remedy.
> > Harry Solomon, president of the American Psychiatric
> > Association, addressing its members in 1958.[1]

> One of the basic functions fulfilled by state mental hospitals was, and in
> many instances continues to be, the provision of safety and security for
> individual patients needing refuge. That function is called "asylum." . . . I
> am . . . arguing in favor of the function of asylum, wherever it is provided.
> > Leona L. Bachrach, American Journal of Psychiatry, 1984.[2]

The sharply contrasting attitudes reflected in these quotations illustrate the
mercurial movement of mental health policy in the United States. Why has
policy shifted so precipitously in less than three decades?

The (admittedly) simple answer to such a complex question is that American society has changed dramatically during this same period. Mental health
policy is shaped not only by scientific and popular beliefs about mental illness,
but also by overarching values and social forces at work throughout society.
Current wisdom about the causes, consequences, and cures of mental illness
certainly guide our response to the mentally ill. But state legislators, hospital
administrators, government officials, and judges are also influenced in their
daily decisions by the political views of their constituencies. And the politics
of America has not stood still.

Admittedly, the history of American public mental health policy has not
been apocalyptic. As one respected historian who studies mental illness in
America has noted: "Public policies, more often than not, are evolutionary
in nature; only rarely do they emerge in some novel form following a cataclysmic event."[3] Only after specific changes aggregate over time do patterns
of reform emerge.

Gradual shifts of public attitudes toward the mentally ill took us from the
whipping posts, almshouses, and gallows of Colonial America to the construction of monolithic institutions for the insane in the late nineteenth and

3

early twentieth centuries. Each method of care, cure, or punishment was adopted with optimistic claims that the answer to the mystifying problem of mental illness had been found; yet each solution was eventually abandoned because it either made little difference or seemed to make matters worse.[4]

Even the most dramatic reforms in mental health policy of the twentieth century settled slowly into place, lacking a single cataclysmic cause. Programs providing outpatient treatment, halfway houses, and noninstitutional alternatives for prisoners and the mentally ill have been with us since the beginning of the twentieth century. But despite years of advocacy by many reformers, deinstitutionalization—the discharge of patients from psychiatric hospitals and the subsequent care of patients in the community—did not become the centerpiece of national policy until the 1960s and 1970s.[5]

Similarly, the neoconservative trends that are described in this book did not begin with any single event. Instead, they grew out of public disenchantment with policies that too readily excused mentally disordered criminals and severely limited involuntary hospitalization of the mentally disturbed.

To more fully understand why American mental health policy has evolved to its present state, we devote the remainder of this chapter to a review of the major historical trends of the twentieth century and how they have helped mold this policy.

The Progressives

Historians have referred to the period between 1900 and 1920 as the Progressive Era because so many strikingly new ideas, attitudes, and practices were introduced into virtually every aspect of American life.[6] The Progressive Era had an optimistic vision of the future and adopted strategies for change based on this optimism. According to noted historian David Rothman, the influence of Progressive reform principles and strategies persisted from 1900 through the early 1960s,[7] a view with which we concur.

During the Progressive Era and the years that followed, scientific discoveries and technological developments affected almost everyone. By the 1950s, the Great Depression of the 1930s and the deprivation of World War II had passed. Americans began to believe that science and technology would solve virtually all their major social problems, including poverty, hunger, and war. Adults who had lived through the Depression and the Second World War were now raising families in a nation which enjoyed shrinking unemployment and unaccustomed prosperity.

The explosion of scientific knowledge and technological advancement during the Progressive Era gave Americans unbounded confidence that they could change and improve the general condition of society. Progressives were champions of individual justice, rejecting outmoded notions that all people were alike and should be treated in a uniform fashion. Instead, they believed that each individual is a unique and complex product of environment as well as biology. Progressives were also willing to rely on a wide range of "experts" whose theories and practices might "cure" people with medical, mental, or moral problems. For them, the concept of rehabilitation was far more compatible with their new views of the world than the primitive concepts of custody and punishment.[8]

A striking feature of the Progressive Era was the unbounded trust the public placed in the benevolence of the state. Since the purpose of incarceration was to rehabilitate and cure, there were few qualms about enlarging the power of public officials to determine the fate of criminals and the mentally ill.[9] Indeterminate confinement in institutions and the absence of substantive and procedural protections for prisoners and patients were justified under the rubric of "treatment." Broad discretion was conferred on government agents on the assumption that state action benefited those who were incarcerated. Since the state was merely seeking to help and not harm, minimal scrutiny of state action was required.

At their own urging, psychiatrists became acknowledged as experts who could treat the mentally ill in prisons as well as in mental hospitals. Because confinement was for "therapy" and "rehabilitation," mentally ill offenders were institutionalized much longer than if they had been simply "punished" for their crimes. Confinement of mentally ill patients in mental hospitals was also open-ended, with discharge left to the discretion of hospital superintendents who had little to gain from discharging them.

The reforms of the Progressive Era resulted in an overwhelmingly paternalistic system of social control. Experts "diagnosed" what was wrong with each individual; the state decided what "treatment" was best; and wardens and hospital superintendents had the final word regarding every aspect of institutional life. A system which presumed only the best intentions for the care and rehabilitation of each individual had little need to respect the wishes or safeguard the rights of prisoners or patients.

Even after it became clear that institutions did not fulfill even the modest (let alone the grandiose) hopes of their founders, they continued in existence to serve a social control function for their communities.[10] The resulting disregard for personal liberties, even though well-intentioned, and the unforeseen consequences it wrought fanned the fires of the Liberal Era.

The Liberal Era

A brief but intense review of the complex set of events that shaped the Liberal and Neoconservative eras is crucial to understanding present policies toward the mentally ill. We do not intend to present a comprehensive history of these three decades—historians have already begun to apply their craft to that task.[11] Instead, we wish to provide an overview to refresh the reader's memory about these turbulent times. In doing so, we set the stage for why and in what context mental health policy and law took its particular direction.

Dynamic social, political, and economic forces shaped both the Liberal and the Neoconservative eras. By contrasting the values and ideology of one era with another, we gain a clearer vision of how mental health law and policy has evolved—and where it might be headed next.

We call the decades of the 1960s and 1970s the Liberal Era because of the emphasis placed on individual freedom and fairness to the individual—even at the expense of the community. The Liberal Era was a time of intense social upheaval. It was a moment in history when economic forces, social attitudes, and personal values converged to promote the extension of civil liberties, more tolerant attitudes toward disadvantaged groups, and a renewed penchant for social innovation and reform.

The Emergence of the "Great Society"

Many of the reforms of the Liberal Era were carried out as a direct reaction to social, economic, and political conditions that followed World War II.[12] By the middle of the twentieth century, affluence "was assumed to be a national condition, not just a personal standing."[13] With prosperity came a desire—indeed, an expectation—that virtually all Americans could achieve middle-class status through education and hard work. With the Protestant work ethic firmly in mind, the "affluent society"[14] of the 1950s gave little thought to Americans who could not get white-collar jobs, a house in the suburbs, and a new automobile.

During this same period, however, the U.S. economy grew very little and experienced two recessions, which were accompanied by an alarming increase in inflation.[15] By the early 1960s, inflation had slowed substantially and key segments of the economy, such as the steel industry, were able to regain strength in world markets. The economy began to show signs of recovery.

During the 1960 presidential campaign, candidate John Kennedy repeatedly declared it was time to "get America moving again." Under intense pressure from the civil rights movement to help minorities and the poor, Kennedy planned to stimulate the economy and achieve economic growth, providing jobs and economic opportunity for every citizen. Full employment, including jobs for those at the bottom of the economic ladder, would get the American economy on track. After Kennedy's assassination, President Lyndon Johnson extended this philosophy even further when he made an "unconditional war on poverty" his highest priority. Johnson chose the "Great Society" as the theme of his administration, claiming poverty would be eliminated if Americans put their hearts and minds to the task.

The philosophical underpinnings of the Great Society relied on two crucial assumptions. First, unless individual citizens were guaranteed the right to vote, go to school, and pursue jobs without discrimination, they could not achieve success in America. The absence of education, job training, and health care denied the poor "fair access to the expanding incomes of a growing economy."[16] Second, government had to play a crucial role in bringing about social change. It would do this by providing social and economic opportunities for the poor and protecting their individual rights through legislation, regulation, and judicial enforcement. To implement this agenda, the 89th Congress enacted an unparalleled spate of legislation, including federal aid to education, and the establishment of programs such as Medicare, low-income housing, Project Head Start, and manpower training.

In addition to these legislative initiatives, President Johnson appointed many federal judges who envisioned an activist role for the courts and began to reshape a host of institutional arrangements. Thus, the dynamics for profound and fundamental social change were set in motion. Law, in particular, was to be the primary instrument for this change.

The programs of the Great Society implicitly assumed that society created and maintained poverty, racism, and inequality. In Lyndon Johnson's words, "the Great Society rests on abundance and liberty for all. It demands an end to poverty and racial injustice." In launching a modern-day New Deal, Johnson undertook a venture intended to achieve genuine equal opportunity for all Americans.[17]

Social scientists told policymakers that what all disadvantaged groups shared was the lack of access to educational and economic opportunities.[18] This theory of "differential opportunity" claimed that if equal opportunities were given to everyone, the poor and disadvantaged would use those opportunities to break the cycle of poverty for themselves and their children. Without that break in social pathology, they would never take their rightful place in middle-class America.

The poor in America had become an "underclass" who lived within an affluent society but were not equal partners in it. Many people from poor neighborhoods and minority families had developed deviant adaptations to their social environment because they had few legitimate outlets for making a living. They committed crimes and became entwined in increasingly deviant lifestyles that led them to prison or social mayhem.

The Great Society promised opportunity to empower the individual and make society more just. Government was expected to help the downtrodden so that pervasive patterns of systemic discrimination would no longer be ignored.

There was a renewed optimism about solving a wide range of social problems. America had increasing confidence in its burgeoning technology and expertise as well as in its economic capacity to remedy many of the intractable social problems of the day. The technology for social and human engineering was readily available. It simply needed funding and implementation.

Social Protests and the Road to Reform

The reforms of the Liberal Era took place against a backdrop of turmoil and transition in virtually every corner of American society. Disenchanted with the status quo, many citizens insisted on basic changes in the nation's social structure. The most significant of these social protests was the civil rights movement.

The status of American blacks was perhaps *the* social inequity of U.S. society. Millions of black Americans were keenly aware they were not allowed to exercise many of America's rights. Laws divided blacks and whites. Among the injustices faced by American blacks were segregated schools and discrimination in housing and employment. Many black families lived in debilitating poverty—destroying the family and breeding crime. In fighting these abuses, nonviolent protests in the 1950s exploded into full-blown conflict during the 1960s, when civil rights activists demanded an end to institutional discrimination.

The civil rights movement represented a watershed of social change in the twentieth century, a social movement that historians now consider "a rare event in America"[19] because it initiated such "a radical shift in national social policy."[20] The specific demands for rights of blacks became transformed into a general concern for the individual rights of any who held minority status.

Eventually, the mentally ill were recognized as a special class of people who had been the target of discrimination and excessive social control. Mental health advocates set about to make sweeping changes in the mental health system.

Even as the Great Society urged a greater governmental role in social problems, there was a loss of confidence in the benevolence of the state, a major postulate of the Progressive Era. This loss of confidence was due to many reasons.

During the 1960s, the bitter battles of the Vietnam War—both abroad and at home—shook Americans' trust in government. Opposition to the U.S. military presence in Southeast Asia, the loss of American lives, and the extraordinary cost of fighting the war radicalized many college students against the war and against the authority of the U.S. government. The student movement galvanized around many of the same issues as the civil rights movement. Racism, poverty, and militarism were seen as fundamental flaws in American society, threatening its core.

Furthermore, elected officials seemed unwilling or unable to reform institutional arrangements that benefited the majority of their constituents at the expense of disenfranchised minorities. The abysmal failure of state and federal legislatures and executives to adequately protect the rights of minorities led many Americans to conclude that social change would have to originate from a different source of authority.

Widespread distrust of entrenched government bureaucracy activated citizens to seek protection in the courts rather than rely on the good faith of state legislators or other public officials. Minorities and disadvantaged groups of every description "discovered" the law as a powerful weapon in their quest for an open and just community.

The Role of the Courts

The civil rights movement was significant not only for the broad-based social change it brought about but also for the dramatic departure in social reform strategy it represented. To Progressives, courts and lawyers were the enemies of reform. The civil rights movement, however, was the first reform movement of the twentieth century to enthusiastically enlist the assistance of the courts in promoting its agenda for social change.[21]

Since the beginning of the twentieth century, the American Progressive tradition of social reform stressed legislative activity; courts and lawyers were generally seen as obstacles to Progressive social reform.[22] When the civil rights movement gathered strength in the South during the 1950s, however, it quickly became clear that the fears and prejudices of the majority were simply too strong and entrenched to obtain equality for racial minorities through the legislative process. The court system appeared the best—and perhaps only— effective instrument for achieving social equality.

Courts—now viewed as independent, accessible, and neutral—were a particularly suitable agent for social change.[23] They could serve as exponents of timeless, objective values devoid of vested interests, political agendas, and bureaucratic influence.[24] Thus, they could effectively criticize and modify the discriminatory practices of entrenched institutions.

Most important, American courts also had the special power to interpret the Constitution, the authoritative document of American government.[25] This charter guaranteed certain inalienable rights to individuals that could not be abrogated or violated by the government. Courts had the authority to define constitutional rights that would be binding both on other branches of government, including the legislative and the executive, as well as on the states. They could thereby protect individual rights from the improper exercise of power by the majority. As a pragmatic matter, test-case litigation in courts was the only hope on the otherwise dim horizon for systematically securing individual rights for blacks. The courts—especially federal courts—seemed the logical battlefield on which to wage a campaign for social justice. Judges adopted an activist role and stepped into places they had never been before.

The new jurisprudence of rights that emerged during the Liberal Era emphasized the inalienable rights of the individual, particularly as set forth in the Constitution. The role of the courts was to give practical substance to these rights. As constitutional scholar Owen Fiss remarked: "Adjudication is the process by which the values embodied in an authoritative legal text, such as the Constitution, are given concrete meaning and expression."[26] These newly articulated civil rights could even take precedence over the rights of the government and the community's need for security.

Along with others, Fiss argued that a new form of litigation, called "structural reform," had appeared during the Liberal Era.[27] This new form had two defining characteristics:

> The first is the awareness that the basic threat to our constitutional values is posed not by individuals, but by the operation of large-scale organizations, the bureaucracies of the modern state. Secondly, this new mode of litigation reflects the realization that, unless the organizations that threaten these values are restructured, these threats to constitutional values cannot and will not be eliminated.[28]

Courts, then, would implement constitutional values against large-scale bureaucratic institutions, including the state and federal government. Initially, courts were confident they possessed sufficient remedial capacities to bring about structural change. In particular, injunctions could provide prospective relief to aggrieved citizens by directing and monitoring wide-ranging modifications in institutions.

A small but growing activist bar nurtured by the NAACP (National Association for the Advancement of Colored People) and the ACLU (American Civil Liberties Union) was ready and willing to take the struggle for social justice into the courts. In one of the first test cases of a social movement being furthered by the judiciary, an authoritative decision by the U.S. Supreme Court in the historic case of *Brown* v. *Board of Education* (1954) declared that separate but equal public school systems violated the Constitution.[29] Against overwhelming odds, test-case litigation against intractable and pervasive discriminatory government policies had succeeded. The Supreme Court had used the Constitution to trump state and local legislation and systemic administrative practices. Structural change in this important aspect of society was ordered "with all deliberate speed."

Minorities had a firsthand demonstration of the power of the courts to initiate sweeping social change.[30] Flushed with success, the activist bar developed new theories and skills on behalf of other disadvantaged groups. In the 1960s, test-case lawsuits were filed on behalf of prisoners, handicapped children, the poor, women, and eventually the mentally ill.[31]

Courts handed down a veritable explosion of landmark decisions protecting personal liberty and individual autonomy. The Supreme Court issued opinions imposing newly recognized constitutional restraints on police and prosecutors. Indigent defendants were entitled to appointed counsel in many criminal trials, and police had to warn suspects of their right to silence and to having an attorney present during police interrogation.[32] *Roe* v. *Wade*, known widely as the Supreme Court case that gave women the constitutional right to terminate a pregnancy, also implied the constitutional right to make one's own medical treatment decisions.[33] Court decisions throughout the 1960s and 1970s strengthened the ordinary citizen's freedom from governmental control. Decisions were issued limiting when the state could intrude into the private lives of individuals.[34] Under the First Amendment, state authority to punish criminally those who used, or helped others to use, contraceptives[35] or to prohibit the publication and sale of sexually explicit material[36] was limited. Newspapers could print top-secret government documents in the middle of a war without prior restraint.[37]

Vagrancy laws, intact in many states for more than a century, were struck down under the due process clause of the Fourteenth Amendment as too vague and as interfering with individual liberty.[38]

Courts also struck down discriminatory laws that violated the Constitution's promise of "equal protection."[39] To remedy past discrimination, judges approved the concept of "affirmative action," which spelled out in great detail how public programs should operate to achieve equal opportunity.[40] Frequently, these programs imposed quotas on hiring or admission and created differential standards for selection and promotion. Other decisions guaranteed minority firms a specified percentage of government contracts.[41] All of these rulings were considered necessary both to rectify prior discrimination and to ensure continued minority participation in the economic life of the nation.

A generation of "public interest lawyers" who saw the law as a means of bringing about social change now emerged. They believed the "assembly-line justice"[42] meted out in state courts often violated due process for individuals. These young lawyers went to work for nonprofit legal service corporations to defend victims of institutional poverty and racism. They took advantage of the prevailing judicial activism to challenge existing institutions and to advance the political and economic rights of the poor.

The explosion of court decisions based on due process in this era was motivated in part by a growing distrust of the state and by a belief that government action often harms individuals. Safeguards against abuse and mistakes had been considered unnecessary and even counterproductive when citizens were confident that government had only their best interests at heart. For example, few of the safeguards found in criminal law applied to juvenile justice or intervention with the mentally ill because the state was considered to be acting as a beneficial caretaker. As legal scholar Nicholas Kittrie observed: "The noncriminal process professes the laudatory desire and policy of removing the criminal stigma from those either too young or too deficient medically or mentally to be forever branded."[43]

But Liberal Era courts became more willing to examine the actual consequences of seemingly benign state action and to acknowledge that mistakes could be made. In the 1967 *Gault* case, for example, the Supreme Court, while conceding the government's good intentions in dispensing with procedural formality in juvenile delinquency proceedings, nonetheless admitted that juvenile facilities actually harmed rather than helped many of those sent there.[44] Juvenile proceedings also stigmatized young people, damaging their reputation and self-image. Giving juveniles many of the due process protections given to adults in criminal trials would keep out of these facilities those who did not belong there.

To assure the fairness and accuracy of government decisions that might adversely affect individual rights, due process procedures—including written notice of the proposed government action, the right to the assistance of counsel, the opportunity to present evidence and to confront adverse witnesses, the right to appeal, and periodic review of official decisions—were widely adopted. The procedures were used in a variety of contexts, such as when challenging denial of welfare benefits and revocation of parole.[45]

In a related development of the Liberal Era, judges dramatically expanded their authority to shape public policy.[46] They did not stop at simply issuing orders to correct past violations of "rights"; they also set out to reform entire institutions through long-term monitoring of their orders, an endeavor previously considered off-limits for judicial action.[47] Perhaps as important, the Warren Court permitted greater accessibility to the federal court system.[48]

With a new theory of individual rights in place[49] and judges willing—
almost eager—to enforce these rights, judicial power seemed to be all-
encompassing. Federal courts became actively involved in the education of
schoolchildren, municipal and private employment policies, the administration of hospitals and mental institutions, and natural resources management.[50]
They set the minimum cell size in prisons, required the development of specific
discharge plans for patients leaving hospitals, placed a high school under
judicial control, and reorganized an entire city government.[51]

Too Much Freedom?

The courts took an active role in protecting the rights of individuals even if,
in many cases, the interests of the majority suffered. For example, according
to the Supreme Court's *Miranda* decision, prosecutors could not use confessions by criminals if the police had not advised them of their newly recognized
constitutional rights. This meant that even if some suspects had been "caught
in the act," unless they were informed of their so-called Miranda rights—the
right to remain silent and to request the help of a lawyer—they might not be
convicted and had to be released.

Starting in the late 1950s and throughout the Liberal Era, hundreds of
thousands of patients were released from the scandalously overcrowded
"warehouses" euphemistically called state hospitals.[52] Community treatment
on a voluntary basis became the primary strategy of providing for the needs
of the mentally disturbed. A new passion for civil liberties and a pronounced
distrust of government bureaucracy and coercion—together with fiscal pressures to reduce state expenditures—generated irresistible pressures to limit
the power of the state to hospitalize citizens against their will. Most states
passed laws to prevent involuntary hospitalization and unnecessary treatment
for the mentally ill, unless they were believed to be dangerous.

As a result, another important group of social misfits arrived on the scene
in growing numbers. Many people who led unusual or eccentric lifestyles were
left alone by these formal systems of social control because of a more tolerant
attitude toward individual differences and the promotion of individual rights.
During the Liberal Era, communities turned a blind eye to their presence as
long as they remained mostly invisible within the community. For the most
part, these people lived out-of-sight in urban skid rows, in rural areas, or
otherwise off the beaten path. It was not until the 1980s, when the swelling
ranks of the homeless generated a "crisis" of unprecedented proportions,
that politicians and the public took note.

Furthermore, mentally ill people who disrupted their neighbors could not
be detained unless they caused actual harm to themselves or others. Free at
home or on the streets, some continued to be a nuisance to their families and
neighbors; some committed serious crimes. The interests of the community
took a back seat to individual liberties.

Until recently, a majority of states in America, as well as the federal
government, permitted criminal defendants to use a very broad insanity defense to avoid conviction and punishment. By the 1980s, however, forgiveness

and treatment of mentally ill offenders gave way to calls for punishment and incarceration. Congress and many states passed laws to hold these offenders accountable for their crimes. Defenses based on mental illness have been severely constricted and, in some cases, abandoned altogether. Laws have been passed limiting the range and relevance of psychiatric testimony in criminal trials, and psychiatrists now receive a chilly reception in the criminal courtroom. In an unexpected decision, the Supreme Court has authorized states to confine insanity acquittees for life, even if they commit minor crimes such as shoplifting. (See Chapter 4, "The *Jones* Case.")

Parallel changes are also occurring in involuntary civil commitment of the mentally ill. The restrictive commitment laws of the Liberal Era prevented families from obtaining essential treatment for their disturbed loved ones. In hindsight, many observers now believe that the excessive protection of civil liberties created new legions of homeless mentally ill. For these unfortunate souls to be cared for in humane institutions and not be allowed to live in the shadow of the urban ghetto has become a pressing concern. Deinstitutionalization and civil libertarian commitment laws produced a new social reality that is generating powerful pressure to reinstitutionalize the mentally ill. Consequently, the Liberal Era's emphasis on voluntary treatment in the community has ironically been replaced by an increasing use of coercive hospitalizations and outpatient commitments.

These dramatic changes in mental health law and policy reflect the larger social movements occurring in the United States. The Liberal Era toleration of personal differences and protection of individual rights gave way in the 1980s to an abrupt shift in public sentiment and policy. To many, the rights of criminals and other dangerous persons threatened the rights of the community to safety. Tolerance for those who were different or dangerous evaporated almost overnight.

Why did America's vision of justice and care for the mentally ill shift its focus from the rights of the individual toward the protection of society? How did this transition take place? What difference will a readjustment of law and social policy make for the mentally ill and for us all?

The Great Society Promise Unfulfilled

By the end of the 1960s the American economy slowly began to unravel. Since World War II, Americans had controlled their own economic destiny and maintained a position of economic dominance in the world. Now accelerating unemployment, increasing business failures, and falling productivity were bringing an era of widespread prosperity to an end. As America's economic fortunes took a precipitous turn for the worse, jobs, affordable housing, and the amenities to which most people had become accustomed were becoming scarce.[53] Competition from foreign markets, such as Japan and other Pacific Rim countries, had many Americans running scared. Families who had taken pride in seeing each successive generation achieve greater social and economic status feared that their American dream was in jeopardy. "The problem [was] not simply that people [were] being laid off from jobs in large numbers. It [was] that the jobs themselves [were] evaporating. The industries in which these jobs were once found have packed up and left, and they are not being replaced by equivalent jobs."[54] A "lifeboat" mentality seized the public psyche, making many citizens afraid their seats would be given to someone else. Public support for liberal ideologies disintegrated rapidly. Increasingly, conservative values took center stage.

Moreover, many Americans began to feel that the social programs designed to provide income supports for millions of able-bodied citizens had backfired. Instead of providing job opportunities and economic independence, critics argued that welfare schemes threatened the motivation of millions of poor people to look for work, thereby creating a dependent "underclass." More and more Americans concluded that welfare recipients learned to depend on income maintenance and food stamps in lieu of finding gainful employment. The availability of welfare benefits created incentives for unemployment. In the eyes of many, social programs created rather than eliminated barriers to economic advancement for the poor. In Senator Daniel Patrick Moynihan's words: "The government did not know what it was doing. It had a theory. Or rather, a set of theories. Nothing more."[55]

This viewpoint reflected a widespread belief that many government social programs initiated during the Liberal Era were ineffective and sometimes produced unintended harm. Critics such as commentator Irving Kristol concluded that most social welfare programs had destroyed traditional American values of hard work and competitive advantage. According to this view, the 1960s had witnessed a crisis of values and morals that undermined the family, rejected religion, and devalued the Protestant work ethic.[56]

There was some legitimacy to this disgruntlement. As we shall see later, many of the ambitious promises of social reform made during the halcyon days of the Great Society were never met. In fact, crime rates soared, public assistance rolls grew, and new generations of welfare mothers were born. The public grew weary of what they believed were indulgent solutions to increasingly troublesome social problems.

Even the courts, bastion of Liberal Era reforms, faced the prospect that many decisions had unanticipated and undesirable ends. Liberal judges concluded there were inherent limits on the courts' ability to reform massive and recalcitrant public bureaucracies. Courts themselves had become bureaucratic in attempting to monitor local school systems, city governments, or psychiatric institutions.[57] To have any hope of being effective, judges had to appoint special masters and human rights committees, review reports and recommendations, and generally spend a great deal of time and energy keeping abreast of conditions in the institutions they were monitoring.[58] They also realized that, in a world of limited financial resources, articulating and enforcing rights for one group, such as institutionalized mental patients, usually meant less money spent on others not present or represented before the courts, such as the mentally ill who lived at home.[59]

We mark the end of the Liberal Era at the close of the 1970s. Welfare programs had failed to change the social prospects of the poor while heaping economic responsibilities for the disadvantaged on the middle class. Because citizens demanded more protection from dangerous individuals, public policy and law increasingly emphasized crime control. The Liberal Era's emphasis on each citizen's right to self-determination and minimal state interference was replaced by greater insistence on individual responsibility and account-ability for one's behavior. An ethic had emerged which called for "law and order" and a return of majoritarian values.

Ronald Reagan rallied the public with his presidential campaign promise that the federal government would no longer be a "monkey on people's backs" and that his "supply-side economics" would restore American individualism, competition, and personal pride. The election of Ronald Reagan was a broad mandate for conservative public policy and a roll call for those who believed that the Great Society had backfired.[60]

By the early 1980s, the values and social concerns of the general public had changed dramatically. The growing conservatism in America was reflected in electoral politics, appointments to the federal judiciary, and cutbacks in social welfare programs.

As the close of the twentieth century draws near, general disaffection with the elevation of individual rights over the rights of the majority has set the pendulum of social movement into motion once again.[61] The scene has been set for a "return to the asylum" so that society can keep close watch on those who are dangerous or cannot conform to the rigors of everyday life.

And so another era of reform has begun.

The Neoconservative Agenda

A distinct and powerful political outlook has emerged in the United States which is a direct reaction to the social philosophy and turbulence of the Liberal Era. While its tenets are not held universally by all of its adherents, neocon-servatism has begun to take on a characteristic shape. It seeks to reestablish stability and order. "Neo-conservatism tends to be respectful of traditional values and institutions: religion, the family, the 'high culture' of Western civilization."[62] Its catechism includes a return to conservative values fostering religion, the family, and other traditional institutions, and a strong allegiance to the power of the free market for remedying social problems and satisfying individual needs.

The return to religion was a predictable response to a desire for stability and institutional strength. Religion has frequently been viewed as a way to prop up a shaky social order[63] or as a patch to keep society from unraveling at the seams. Most important, religion stresses a public morality and a be-havioral prescription that imposes personal accountability and responsibility. While the political power of the self-described "moral majority" and the growth of conservative Christian groups have been two of the more obvious manifestations of the Neoconservative Era, a central hallmark of this religious revival is an insistence on individual responsibility.

Neoconservative allegiance to the free market system—particularly the private sector—expresses a corresponding preference for the autonomy and self-sufficiency of the individual. Neoconservatives object to bureaucratic interventions that provide what are viewed as "giveaways," such as welfare benefits and job training, for anyone but the most impoverished, "deserving poor"—the disabled or very old.[64]

The new era has rejected the concepts of affirmative action and its remedial tools, such as racial quotas for hiring and school enrollment. To neoconservatives, these cumbersome devices ignored individual merit.[65] As author Nathan Glazer stated in his book, *Affirmative Discrimination*: "Compensation for the past is a dangerous principle. It can be extended indefinitely and make for endless trouble."[66] Affirmative action contradicted a core belief that law should be applied consistently on the basis of personal qualifications instead of race, gender, or other social status. While many neoconservatives favored special efforts to seek out qualified minority candidates for job openings and to widen the applicant pool, they opposed institutionalized rules that would compel hiring through quotas or other similar measures,[67] thus minimizing bureaucratic intrusion. By 1989, a number of Supreme Court decisions had delivered a severe blow to civil rights activists supporting affirmative action. President George Bush vetoed the Civil Rights Act of 1990, ostensibly because of his objections to racial quotas.

From Opportunity to Morality

As noted earlier, liberals of the 1960s had viewed poverty and discrimination as impediments to the healthy functioning of American society. Income maintenance programs, food stamps, job training, early childhood education, and equal housing were seen as the mechanisms for breaking the cycle of poverty and constructing a Great Society. Liberal Era visionaries believed poverty could be virtually eliminated by a society devoted to the principles of equality, and government had a moral responsibility to assist individuals in reaching their potential by providing opportunities for success. Even the most disadvantaged citizen could get a handhold on the American middle class through the beneficence of government-sponsored programs.

But as social circumstances and values began to shift within American society, poverty came to be seen as a cultural and moral problem instead of an economic one. Neoconservatives became convinced that a redistribution of wealth could not successfully fight poverty.[68] According to Ronald Reagan, welfare destroyed "self-reliance, dignity, and self-respect."[69] A better life should not be a "gift" to the poor; it would have to be earned the old-fashioned way—through hard work! Thus poverty was cast primarily as a moral problem as opposed to one of missed opportunity; that is, able-bodied people did not have to be poor if they chose to work hard.

Crime, delinquency, and a whole raft of social problems emerged as proof of a growing "underclass" that was, by and large, weak, lazy, dishonest, and unwilling to help itself. No amount of public assistance could reverse these individual character flaws. Basic human weaknesses and dishonesty were simply exacerbated by paying people to choose idleness and dependency as an alternative to work.

The questioning of authority in the 1960s was replaced by a desire to restore authority in the 1980s. Ronald Reagan responded by promising to return America to a position of strength at home and abroad. In the words of two sixties radicals-turned-neoconservatives: "In the [New Left's] inchoate attack against authority, we had weakened our culture's immune system, making it vulnerable to opportunistic diseases."[70]

Law and Order

A new and radically different phase of public policy and legal reform has now become evident. A fearful public, inundated by reports of cascading crime rates, drug abuse, and gang warfare, and fearful of the homeless, the dangerous mentally ill, and other visible deviants, has demanded a new "war on crime." The resulting public insecurity has generated adamant demands for "law and order" and justice for victims. According to some, many lawbreakers were shielded from punishment and not given their just deserts. Neoconservatives cite rising crime rates as evidence that Great Society programs did not prevent crime—indeed, crime rates soared during the 1960s and 1970s.[71] By the 1980s, the call for a new balance was loud and clear: community security had to take precedence over individual rights.

Virtually all of the remedies to regain law and order emphasized the indispensable prerequisite of individual responsibility, an ethic reinvigorated by the Neoconservative Era. Citizens would be held accountable for their actions and given clear messages that there are personal and societal consequences for their behavior. The death penalty was reinstituted, and mandatory sentencing became part of the crime-fighting arsenal. Neoconservatives argued that the war on crime had to include long-term confinement to isolate troublemakers. The public supported self-defense and vigilantism, as exemplified by newsmakers like Bernard Goetz, who shot four possible assailants in the New York subway.[72]

Clearly, the Neoconservative Era manifested intense anger over "coddling" criminals at the expense of innocent victims. The war on crime required more convictions and more drastic measures if it was to have any hope of stemming the tidal wave of crime rising in America.

This mood clearly influenced the Supreme Court of the United States under the leadership of Chief Justices Warren Burger, and, later, William Rehnquist. The Supreme Court began to weigh the cost to society more heavily in the balance when it determined the constitutional rights of criminals.[73] In a number of cases, the Burger and Rehnquist courts limited the protection afforded criminal suspects by Liberal Era cases.[74] The Court majority plainly thought the community's interest in security and effective crime control had been crippled by the excessive deference given to individual rights during the Liberal Era.

On another front, Congress enacted a preventive detention law that permitted judges to keep a dangerous felon in jail until trial.[75] The Supreme Court upheld this statute against a court challenge that it violated the presumption of innocence contained in the Constitution.[76] Thus, in special cases, society was entitled to confine criminal suspects considered especially dangerous to prevent possible future crimes, even though the suspects had not even been convicted of the charged crime. In May 1989, President George Bush proposed an expanded crime-control package that included millions of dollars for the construction of new prisons and tougher penalties for lawbreakers.[77]

After a hiatus of four years, thirty-five states have passed death penalty laws; 148 convicted criminals have been executed as of July 1, 1991,[78] and thousands have been sentenced to death. The Supreme Court has revisited the abortion rights issue in *Webster* v. *Reproductive Health Services*.[79] This 5 to 4 decision held that a state's ban on the use of public facilities and employees to perform abortions is not prohibited by the Constitution nor by its prior decision in *Roe* v. *Wade*.[80] In 1991, the Supreme Court, by a 5 to 4 vote, also upheld federal regulations that prohibit all staff of family planning clinics that receive federal funding from discussing abortion with their clients.[81] Conservative forces have succeeded in barring federal funding of abortion and requiring that juveniles obtain parental approval prior to obtaining birth control or abortion.[82]

Court decisions praised during the Liberal Era for the active protection of individual rights now have been criticized in the Neoconservative Era. Judges have been charged with "creating" rights out of whole cloth, imposing their own views of wise public policy under the guise of constitutional adjudication, favoring individual rights at the expense of community interests, and improperly interfering in legislative and executive functions.[83]

The recent judicial backlash against affirmative action and busing illustrates how courts more readily protect majoritarian values and interests. In 1978 the Supreme Court ruled in *University of California* v. *Bakke* that the University of California had discriminated against Bakke, a white male, by denying him admission to medical school in favor of a less qualified minority applicant.[84] Other court decisions began to set boundaries on mandatory busing to achieve greater integration in public education.[85] Many who believe busing is educationally meaningless as well as politically and socially disruptive have applauded these decisions.[86]

In 1989 the U.S. Supreme Court announced a series of controversial decisions that made it more difficult for workers to prove and remedy discrimination. In *City of Richmond* v. *Cronson Company*, the Court struck down a city ordinance that required prime contractors on city construction projects to subcontract at least thirty percent of the dollar amount of each contract to minority businesses. The Court said local governments could not use an unyielding racial quota as a tool to remedy racial discrimination without first establishing with detailed evidence that discrimination actually exists.[87]

Fears that the Court had taken a sharp turn to the right on affirmative action were confirmed just a few months later in *Wards Cove Packing Company* v. *Atonio*, in which a bitterly divided Court tackled the use of statistics to prove employment discrimination.[88] In *Atonio*, nonwhite cannery workers in Alaska's salmon industry presented data that showed their companies employed mostly whites in higher-paying, skilled jobs, while nonwhites were generally relegated to lower-paying, nonskilled positions. The nonwhite workers claimed this disparity resulted from discriminatory employment practices. The Court called this use of internal work force comparisons "nonsensical" in ruling against the nonwhite employees.[89] On the heels of *Atonio* came *Martin* v. *Wilks*, which opened the way for white workers to attack court-approved affirmative action plans by filing reverse discrimination lawsuits.[90]

Critics of affirmative action charge that "reverse discrimination" gives unfair advantage to protected classes—including those who had not themselves been the victims of discrimination—at the expense of more qualified individuals. Moreover, it penalized those who have worked hard to accomplish valued personal and social goals, while rewarding those less deserving individuals who could not succeed on their own merits.[91]

Courts have also become more reluctant to interfere with state bureaucracies, including mental health systems, jails, and prisons. Federal courts have increasingly deferred to legislative judgments and relied on claims of expertise by mental health experts to decide what was best for institutionalized patients. The Supreme Court has also made access to federal courts more difficult for individuals and groups seeking to assert constitutional rights.[92] For example, class-action suits on behalf of the constitutional rights of a large group like confined mental patients received a chilly reception in many federal courts.[93] Not surprisingly, lawyers have become reluctant to pursue these kinds of cases. In short, the courts, with the blessing of the Supreme Court, have transformed themselves from anvils of change to anchors of the status quo. Why?

From 1980 to 1988, President Reagan appointed a large number of conservative judges to the federal bench, among them Sandra Day O'Connor, Anthony Kennedy, and Antonin Scalia, who is known for his hard law-and-order stance. There is some basis for concluding that this infusion of conservative judges has had some effect on judicial reluctance to strike down new legislation or to interfere with the operation of state agencies.[94]

As the nation's judiciary has become more conservative, the number of civil rights lawyers has also decreased. Not only are activist lawyers more likely to receive a cool reception in the courtroom, they also find it more difficult to find employment. President Reagan substantially reduced funding for the Legal Services Corporation during his eight years in office.[95] Moreover, conservative attitudes on college campuses and in law schools reflect the general political and social climate of the country.

The mentally ill also have been touched by this wider context. The clear trend today in mental health law is to return mentally ill offenders and other disturbed citizens to the "asylum" of either a prison or a hospital. The current wisdom holds that these individuals and—more important—society will be better off.

But so-called altruistic intervention to protect the mentally ill is a sword that cuts both ways. State intervention based on a need for treatment means taking care of people unable to care for themselves. But it is also a signal that the state wishes to put a stop to behavior beyond the boundaries of community tolerance. Civil liberties increasingly take a back seat to citizen safety in courtrooms, communities, and on the streets of American cities.

Community security has reemerged as a dominant social theme. This is manifest in countless ways. In subzero weather the homeless of New York City are transported against their will to shelters.[96] City councils propose quarantines for victims of AIDS.[97] An endless stream of "wars" are being launched, but the targets are new. The enemy is crime, homelessness, drugs, gangs, and AIDS.

In the Neoconservative age, if deviants do not seek "cures" voluntarily, the government may use coercion to protect the public against the threat they pose. "Prevention of harm" and "need for treatment" justify enlisting the expertise of "science" in the armamentarium of social control. "Cure" is no longer voluntary; instead, it is a coercive technique for controlling the behavior of out-of-control people. In adopting law and order and rejecting Liberal Era ideology, the Neoconservative Era has pushed the insanity defense and civil commitment reform to the forefront. Reemphasizing individual responsibility is once again the prerequisite to bringing American society back from the brink of chaos.

Difficult Choices

These turbulent periods of contrasting legal and social reforms strongly suggest that important philosophical and policy conflicts have not been resolved with finality, particularly with regard to the mentally ill. Should they be considered responsible and autonomous actors on life's stage, deserving of praise or blame for their actions? Or are they mere puppets dangling on broken strings? Do they know their own best interests and are they capable of pursuing them? Considered abstractly, the tension between punishment and treatment, between liberalism and paternalism, provokes impassioned controversy and debate.

When these questions arise in real-life cases, passion is more easily stirred and reason clouded. Should a disturbed young man who tries to assassinate the president of the United States to attract the attention of a movie actress be held criminally responsible for his violent act? Or should he be treated and released once he is no longer sick or dangerous? Should we permit an elderly bag lady to feed out of garbage cans and to sleep on cold city streets if she refuses our help? Or should she be forcibly brought to a psychiatric ward and given drugs intended to heal her mind? Although these are not easy questions, they demand answers.

Where does one turn for solutions? Do we have reliable information about mental illness and its impact on human behavior to provide the wisdom necessary for useful action? How we respond to these issues of responsibility and autonomy will determine whether many citizens spend time in a prison or in a mental institution, are cared for in supportive community facilities, or are simply left alone to fend for themselves.

This cauldron of contemporary controversy reflects deeply felt concern over the state of public safety and increased anxiety about personal security. The movement to abolish or restrict the insanity defense reflects a clear desire to strengthen the fight against crime. The mentally ill are seen by many as dangerous individuals who should be held accountable for their actions and imprisoned like any other criminal. Others consider society's lack of compassion for the homeless mentally ill a crime against desperate and defenseless people.

The rapid pace of law reform during the Neoconservative Era in both the criminal justice and mental health systems raises important questions of public policy. How many defendants actually raise the insanity defense and how many are successful? What happens to criminals who are acquitted by reason of insanity? Does a change in the way we define "insanity" make any difference? Are the mentally ill especially dangerous, justifying preventive detention? What happens when new laws make it easier to hospitalize the disturbed?

Our Agenda

Recent reforms holding mentally ill offenders more responsible and making involuntary hospitalization easier should not be viewed as unrelated events. They are integrally linked through the vision of the mentally ill that we share today. Parallels in the ideology and structure of reform in these two areas of law and policy should not come as a surprise when seen in the larger context of contemporary attitudes. In short, the insanity defense and civil commitment reforms may be viewed as a barometer of our changing attitudes toward the disadvantaged in general and the mentally ill in particular.

The more difficult challenge may be to recognize and accept the motives which underlie our social choices regarding the mentally ill. With the advantage of hindsight, historians have criticized the motives of Progressive reformers who became the "child savers,"[98] the parole officers, the healers of the mentally ill.[99] Thus, we must analyze the attitudes and values that motivate us today, along with the empirical evidence that is available to guide our decisions.

This analysis will require us to turn our attention to how law is used to implement mental health policy and whether it accomplishes its intended goals. We will assess the available empirical literature that measures the actual impact these legal reforms have had on the criminal justice system and on involuntary civil commitment in the real world to determine how much (or how little) we know about the intended as well as unintended consequences of these legal changes. In our view, the available empirical evidence clearly demonstrates that the insanity defense reforms have been mostly symbolic, satisfying the public outcry for change, but are otherwise of minimal practical consequence. In contrast, some civil commitment reforms have had significant impact, sometimes accomplishing their goals, while at other times arguably harming the very people they were supposed to help.

We will conclude with a critical evaluation of the present and future trends in mental health law and make recommendations about whether we should stay the course or modify our fundamental policy choices in light of what we now know.

1

Madness and
Responsibility

In the famous "Son of Sam" case in New York City, David Berkowitz initially claimed after his arrest in 1977 that he was compelled by the "demons in Sam Carr's dog" to kill young lovers while they were parked in their cars. Thus, he maintained he was legally insane and could not be convicted and punished for his carefully planned murders. After subsequently pleading guilty to these charges, he held a news conference in Attica prison and confessed he had invented the story about the demons.[1] David Berkowitz had tried to use the insanity defense to "beat the rap" for murder.

During the 1960s and 1970s, defenses based on mental illness, such as insanity and diminished capacity, expanded dramatically. They permitted more mentally ill offenders to escape conviction and punishment for their antisocial conduct. The dominant ideology held that these unfortunate individuals should not be considered responsible. They needed treatment, not punishment. Rehabilitation and speedy return of the mentally ill offender to the community were the hallmark goals of that period. In a sense, the "Son of Sam" case reflects the shift in public opinion.

In describing the major trends in both criminal law and the law of involuntary hospitalization which occurred during the last thirty years, we will place this pendulum swing of public policy into its historical and social contexts, using the Liberal and the Neoconservative Eras as useful reference points. We maintain that the mental health law reforms of the Liberal Era were an integral part of a broader agenda of progressive social reforms that marked that era, and the mental health law reforms of the 1980s are part of a larger pattern of neoconservative reforms that has been evolving since about that time. Though these phases of reform may not be as pronounced or as sharply delineated as we portray them, a strong case can be made for the usefulness of our demarcation. But first it is necessary to briefly describe the criminal law's assumptions about individual responsibility and the legal authority given to states to intervene in the lives of the mentally ill who have not committed crimes.

23

Mental Illness and Criminal Responsibility

The primary purpose of criminal law is to make the world a safe place in which all of us can go about our individual pursuits without fear of harm from others.[2] In our contemporary criminal justice system, legislative bodies enact statutes that forbid harmful conduct and authorize punishment for those convicted of violating these laws. The threat of serious sanction—loss of property, liberty, even life—is assumed to be an effective motivating force in shaping human conduct.

Although punishment is designed to deter harmful conduct and incapacitate or change those who commit crimes, it is not imposed on everyone who commits harmful acts. The moral basis of criminal law limits the use of punishment to those whom society considers truly blameworthy. Free will is the underlying premise of this system of social control. In general, any adult who intentionally commits an act forbidden by the criminal law is considered responsible for breaking the law and is subject to criminal process and sanction.[3]

Criminal law, however, provides limited opportunities for defendants to avoid criminal responsibility for their intentional harmful acts if they can show that, through no fault of their own, they did not choose to do wrong.[4] They may demonstrate that they lacked the knowledge essential to understand what they were doing or that they did not freely choose to act. The special excuse of insanity is based on this principle. Mentally ill offenders may avoid conviction and punishment if their mental illness was deemed serious enough at the time of the crime to impair important behavioral controls.[5] Until recently, every state in America and the federal government permitted this defense.

The rationale of the insanity defense is complex. Most judges and scholars have argued that the insanity defense is vital to maintaining the moral integrity of criminal law.[6] According to law professor Henry M. Hart, Jr., sentencing to prison or executing a seriously disturbed individual who, as a result of mental illness, is simply unable to understand the immorality of his action or to control his behavior does not further most of the purposes of punishment, including retribution, specific deterrence, and rehabilitation.[7] Punishing someone who lacks the essential element of free will is both ineffective and inhumane. A legally insane offender should not be convicted and sent to prison, but instead placed in a hospital for confinement and treatment until he or she is no longer mentally ill or dangerous.[8]

The assumptions embedded in this legal excuse are important ones to consider. First, there is such an entity as mental illness, which is beyond the control of any afflicted individual.[9] Second, mental illness interferes with normal human psychological activities, such as thinking and acting. Third, the impairment of these capacities diminishes an individual's ability to understand and direct his or her conduct. In short, the insanity defense accepts a causal connection between the existence of mental illness and the individual's law-breaking behavior.

But how do we decide if a person is indeed "insane"? Which "test" or legal rule should the law provide to juries or judges who must decide the difficult question of who is sane or insane? Until the mid–1950s, most jurisdictions used some version of the *M'Naghten* test of insanity, which traces its origin to the common law of early Victorian Britain. In 1843 England's House of Lords was asked to clarify the legal test of insanity in conjunction with the famous *M'Naghten* case. Daniel M'Naghten was a paranoid schizophrenic who thought the English Tory party was persecuting him. While under this delusion, he intended to kill the Tory British prime minister to stop his torment; however, he mistakenly shot the prime minister's secretary. Under the *M'Naghten* test, as it came to be known, a defendant may be determined legally insane if, as a result of mental illness at the time of the crime, he did not know what he was doing or was unaware that it was wrong.[10]

As we will see later in this chapter, it was fairly difficult under the *M'Naghten* insanity test for a criminal defendant to avoid conviction and punishment. And even if he was determined not guilty because of his mental condition, the "insane prisoner" usually spent more time in psychiatric facilities than he would have spent in jail if he had been convicted of the crimes charged.[11]

Mental Illness and Coercive Hospitalization

Up until the late 1960s, every state had involuntary civil commitment laws that allowed coercive, indeterminate hospitalization of the mentally ill at the request of virtually anyone.[12] This special use of public coercion may be exercised under two distinct types of state authority: police power and *parens patriae* power (literally, "parent of the country").

Under police power, the government is authorized to enact laws and regulations to protect the public health, safety, and welfare of its citizens.[13] It may take steps to prevent harm to the public, such as regulating conditions in the workplace, requiring that safe goods be sold to the public, or preventing the spread of disease.[14] In effect, coercive government action is permissible if future public injury is anticipated and can thereby be avoided.

States may use police power to enact laws empowering public officials to forcibly confine any citizen considered mentally ill and dangerous to others or to himself.[15] In modern times this special system of social control, which amounts to "preventive detention," has generally been applied almost exclusively to the mentally ill.[16] The criminal justice system assumes a citizen is innocent until proven guilty and generally will only incarcerate an individual who is convicted of a crime or to ensure an accused's presence at trial. In sharp contrast, the coercive mental health system confines a mentally ill person because a mental health expert predicts that, unless restrained, the mentally ill person will commit a dangerous act—such as committing suicide or assaulting an innocent person—sometime in the future.

Alan Dershowitz, a prominent scholar of mental health law, has characterized the criminal justice system as a "punishment-deterrent strategy" and the mental health system as a "prediction-prevention" strategy.[17] The former permits a citizen freedom until he commits a crime; the latter takes it away if someone thinks he might commit one. Of course, mistakes are inevitable in a system of preventive detention. Many people confined as dangerous would in fact not have done anything harmful if left alone.[18]

This special system of preventive detention rests on several crucial assumptions. First, the mentally ill are peculiarly prone to commit violent acts. Second, mental health experts can accurately determine who these dangerous people are.[19] Third, the mentally disturbed will not be influenced by the command of the criminal law and its threat of punishment.

Under its *parens patriae* power, the government can act on behalf of those unable to act competently in their own best interest.[20] For example, this *parens patriae* power enables the state to take custody of children who have no relatives able to raise them and to care for developmentally disabled citizens. It also permits the state to provide food, clothing, and shelter for those homeless who cannot take care of these essential needs themselves.

Many contemporary state statutes use the *parens patriae* power to assert government control over the mentally ill. These statutes authorize various agents of the government to involuntarily hospitalize mentally disturbed citizens if they cannot provide themselves with the basic necessities of life (such as nutrition and housing) or are unable to recognize their need for treatment.[21] In a celebrated case, Joyce Brown, a homeless woman living on the streets of New York City who supported herself by panhandling, was picked up by a Project Help psychiatric team during a 1988 cold weather emergency. She was committed involuntarily for care and treatment to Bellevue Hospital under the state's *parens patriae* power. Her case received national media attention and provoked heated controversy over whether she should be forcibly hospitalized or left alone. The laws authorizing *parens patriae* intervention assume mental illness so interferes with patients' rational decision-making abilities that someone else must make treatment decisions for them. Paternalism is the core justification.

The Legacy of the Progressive Era

The Progressive reform movement, which has influenced American criminology since the beginning of the twentieth century, stressed the rehabilitation and return of criminal offenders to society. By the end of that era, however, rehabilitation, though still an icon of the intelligentsia, had severely diminished in practical importance. Nonetheless, it left an indelible mark on the structure of the American corrections system.

Before the Liberal Era, most mentally ill offenders were processed though a criminal justice system that had precious few exits. If determined incompetent to stand trial,[22] an offender was sent to a mental health facility until he or she was considered fit to stand trial. Many of these criminals did not emerge from institutions for a very long time. If deemed incompetent to stand trial, they avoided punishment only if they successfully invoked the insanity defense. A successful insanity plea usually resulted in an indefinite commitment to a special ward in a psychiatric hospital, frequently run by the department of corrections, or to the psychiatric ward of a prison.[23]

Because almost every state and federal court used some version of the *M'Naghten* test for determining legal insanity, which made it quite difficult for defendants to establish this defense, many mentally ill offenders were convicted and sentenced to prisons like other convicted criminals.[24] Consistent with the Progressive emphasis on rehabilitation, the mentally ill inmates were released only when the professional staff were satisfied that the offenders had sufficiently recovered from their mental illness and no longer posed a threat to the community. Most served their full term in prison, and many were then simply transferred to a mental hospital for further treatment and safekeeping.

During this period, criminal law was seen primarily as an instrument of social control, and it underwent no dramatic changes. Its dominant purpose, as espoused by such noted legal scholars as Herbert Wechsler and Jerome Michael, was to prevent crime by inducing citizens to conform to the behavioral rules society imposed, thereby ensuring community safety.[25] Consequently, deterrence was an important goal of the criminal justice system. The threat of punishment—including imprisonment or even death—for those who might break the law was the ultimate weapon in society's arsenal of crime prevention. Punishment was forward-looking, seeking to influence the future behavior of the criminal and others who might be tempted to commit crimes. Whether it worked was difficult to tell.

Retribution, the notion that a person "is a responsible moral agent to whom rewards are due when he makes right moral choices and to whom punishment is due when he makes wrong ones,"[26] did not receive much support among policymakers and academics. As law professor Jerome Hall succinctly noted in 1971: "The salient 20th century fact about criminal law is widespread skepticism of punishment. . . . [R]etribution is sharply disparaged as, at best, a disguised form of vengeance."[27] Thus, punishment was not intended by the legal elite either to make a criminal pay for his crime or to atone for his misdeeds.[28]

Progressives had many theories about the causes of crime. As historian David Rothman has observed, some early Progressive reformers adopted the "enlightened" view that the causal sources of criminal behavior were outside the control of the individual. They felt that crime was bred by the poverty and ignorance that pervaded the ghetto environments in the rapidly expanding urban centers.[29] Other reformers believed the source of deviancy was internal—located in the psychology of the individual. In either case, the Progressive reform movement was extremely confident that scientific knowledge of human behavior had advanced sufficiently to enable society to change deviants and restore them as productive members of the community. But this required a broader range of strategies for preventing and controlling crime if the new learning was to make any difference in the real world.

The most immediate strategies for rehabilitation required structural changes in the corrections system (as opposed to changes in criminal statutes). Long sentences of fixed duration in harsh and austere state prison systems were ineffective leftovers from the Jacksonian era of American prison history. Those repressive institutions were now considered useless and even counter-productive for rehabilitation. If Progressives wished to cure crime, delin-quency, and insanity, they would need to understand the life circumstances of each offender. Real change in an offender's behavior would require case-by-case, therapeutic efforts to alter behavior and the life circumstances that produced the crimes in the first place.[30]

In order to respond to each case on its merits, the Progressive agenda required a corrections system with a wide range of dispositional alternatives that could be operated with broad discretion for the betterment of each individual. Those criminals who were amenable would be reformed and able to take their place in the community. Prisons were to become similar to hospitals, with therapy and training important institutional goals. Prison staff (which occasionally included a psychiatrist) would apply principles of behavior change and other scientific means of behavior control. The small number of inmates who could not be reformed but were still dangerous would be in-capacitated by keeping them in prison for a long time.[31] In either case, society would be made more secure and most offenders would benefit enormously as they became better human beings and responsible citizens.

To implement the emerging reform agenda, judges were given more choices than simply incarcerating a lawbreaker for a fixed term or imposing a suspended sentence. Thus were born the contemporary practices of pro-bation, parole, and indeterminate sentencing. If an offender was deemed suitable for release and rehabilitation in the community, a judge could order probation instead of incarceration for a convicted criminal, subject to varying degrees of supervision. The fate of an offender sentenced to custody would be largely in the hands of a parole board. If a convict's behavior within the institution—as judged by the custodians—manifested a pronounced change for the better, then the board might release him or her well before the maximum prison term was served. If, on the other hand, the inmate had not pleased his caretakers, he might find himself within prison walls for the max-imum term. Release depended not so much on what crime the offender had committed, but on who he or she was or would become while in prison.[32] Once convicted, offenders entered an almost timeless world.

Of course, this system of rehabilitation would need time—but here the time would be used to cure and not just incarcerate the deviant. How much time could not be known in advance. Custody and care had to be open-ended, since release did not turn on what a person had done in the past, but on future recovery. This would depend on the individual, the illness diagnosed, and the efficacy of treatment. Since the state was acting to benefit the indi-vidual, the scope of the state's power and the processes of commitment and release need not be carefully defined and rigidly controlled as they were in the criminal justice system.

The beauty of this open-ended approach was its seeming ability to serve different masters at the same time. As David Rothman put it: "In this way, the needs of justice and the aims of therapy, the welfare of the individual and the security of society would be satisfied."[33] This blend of science and compassion promised both a benefit to the individual and security for the community.

The Progressives did not focus their energy exclusively on the restoration of offenders after they became deviants. Reformers were convinced that the causes of crime, although complex and not yet fully comprehended, would eventually be identified and understood. They were confident that scientists would locate the causes of crime in heredity, genetics, or the environment. Given the prestige of science and medicine during the Progressive Era, it is easy to see why the new discipline of psychiatry began to acquire status and power. Despite the embryonic stage of its development, it made persuasive promises of its ability to diagnose, treat, and cure criminality.[34]

Despite the rhetoric and dominant ideology of Progressive Era reform, rehabilitation was not served in practice. Important participants, including prosecutors, wardens, and judges, saw to it that prisons served the security needs of society and jailers first.[35] Although there were psychiatrists on the staff of some prisons, their numbers were woefully few. If mentally ill criminals remained there, they would be treated much like any other prisoner. Without basic changes in the criminal law, most mentally ill offenders were swept into a criminal justice system poorly suited to meet their special needs.

In addition, expectations in the ability of experts to change prisoners for the better proved to be overly optimistic. Prevention of crime and rehabilitation of criminals require an understanding of the causes of deviancy if they are to be effective, and no clear-cut understanding was ever reached.

The Liberal Era: The Renaissance of the Rehabilitative Ideal

Despite the Progressives' historical failure to establish an effective system of rehabilitation, the Liberal Era was marked by an emphatic renaissance of the early Progressive Era goals of treatment and cure of social deviants. Although historians traditionally mark the end of the Progressive Era at the close of World War I, its influence on rehabilitation was felt for decades.[36] Yet another cycle of reform was clearly under way. Professor Francis Allen described this period as one which embodied what he calls the "Rehabilitative Ideal":

> It is assumed, first, that human behavior is the product of antecedent causes. These causes can be identified as part of the physical universe, and it is the obligation of the scientist to discover and to describe them with all possible exactitude. Knowledge of antecedents of human behavior makes possible an approach to the scientific control of human behavior. Finally, and of primary significance for the purposes at hand, it is assumed that measures employed to treat the convicted offender should serve a therapeutic function, that such measures should be designed to effect changes in the behavior of the convicted

person in the interests of his own happiness, health, and satisfactions and in
the interest of social defense.[37]

Thus, any criminal, whether mentally ill or not, needed therapy to "cure"
antisocial behavior. Instead of blaming or punishing deviants for their conduct, government in the Liberal Era would change the individual through
treatment. As Karl Menninger wrote in his 1968 book *The Crime of Punishment*: "The scientists and penologists I know take it for granted that rehabilitation—not punishment, not vengeance in disguise—is the modern
principle of control."[38]

Of course, innovative experiments in treatment programs for offenders
had been initiated before the 1960s. In 1951, for example, Maryland created
a special center to provide indeterminate treatment for selected recidivist
offenders.[39] Other states enacted legislation that provided for indefinite commitment of sex offenders as early as 1937; this rehabilitative movement crested
in the 1960s.[40] But in its early years the Liberal Era fostered renewed enthusiasm for preventing crime and treating an even broader range of offenders.
In the words of Nicholas Kittrie, the 1960s experienced the full blossoming
of the "therapeutic state."[41] Like the earlier Progressive movement, the therapeutic state would apply new scientific knowledge to prevent or control a
wide range of deviant behavior; but it would be more humane and caring
than the traditional criminal justice system had proven to be.[42]

Many social scientists claimed social engineering could dramatically change
both the self-image and behavior of large numbers of deviants and criminals.
Policymakers generally concluded that criminals, the poor, the mentally ill,
and other disadvantaged groups were victims of harsh, punitive environments.
Instead of punishing them, aggressive attempts should be made to understand
their unique circumstances and to avoid further discrimination and stig-
matization.

Disadvantaged lifestyle was bad enough, but a number of social scientists
argued that it was also important to minimize the stigma a label such as
"sick," "violent," "criminal," or "mentally ill" might inflict. These labels
were believed to be a powerful social force shaping an individual's self-image.
People so identified become segregated with their "own kind" and come to
believe the attributes assigned them by others are true; these social definitions
become a self-fulfilling prophecy as individuals conform to the stereotype by
behaving as "expected." Broader limits on state intervention would help guard
against unwarranted state labeling, while expanded due process protections
would minimize the likelihood that the state would make mistakes. The be-
neficent Great Society would heal the wounds inflicted by society on its hapless
victims, not punish them further.

If society had previously created perverse incentives to deviance, it could
now create positive motivations for conformity and success. Making allowance
for the unique circumstances of deprived individuals was an essential tool for
reintegrating these persons into the Great Society. Therapy, rehabilitation,
and prevention took precedence over assigning moral blame for personal

failure to conform. Deviance was transformed into a medical condition begging for therapy instead of a moral problem requiring condemnation. Human beings were viewed as products of their environment instead of individual artifacts of good or evil. Treatment and rehabilitation were not only possible but necessary for those who stepped over society's threshold of tolerance.

Themes of the Great Society programs were embedded in the repackaging of prisons. Disadvantaged offenders were given opportunities to change their lives and become productive citizens. Educational programs (including correspondence courses for advanced college degrees) sprang up in virtually all prisons. Inmates joined therapy or retraining groups to change their behavior and ready themselves for release. Halfway houses became common vehicles for staging the release of prisoners.

Therapists who might deliver the ministrations of social and medical engineering came from the ranks of physicians, social workers, psychologists, and criminologists. They expanded their treatment authority over more and more people at the margins of social acceptability, including alcoholics, drug users, sexual psychopaths, and child abusers. But, unlike the Progressives of the early twentieth century, Liberal Era reformers' growing faith in science and expertise took place within a social context that vehemently distrusted authority and encouraged individuals to "do their own thing." This proclivity for minimizing state intervention and protecting individual rights led to an interesting adaptation of an otherwise paternalistic and therapeutic model. Liberal Era reformers permitted coercive state intrusion, such as incarceration, parole, or inpatient therapy, but insisted that strict due process protections accompany it.

Increasingly, deviants were diverted to less restrictive treatment programs. Such programs implied "voluntariness" on the part of their participants (even though courts routinely ordered offenders to participate or be charged with crimes) and focused on treatment and rehabilitation. Because of their ostensibly voluntary and therapeutic nature, these diversionary programs often lacked the legal protections required by involuntary alternatives such as incarceration or hospitalization. Many forms of deviance became "medicalized"[43] and were dealt with through agencies other than the criminal justice system.

To implement the therapeutic state, criminal law had, as Kittrie put it, to be "divested" of its jurisdiction over many kinds of deviants, including alcoholics, drug addicts, and the mentally ill.[44] Newly ordained treatment experts laid claim to these fertile fields of state power. Once again, society believed the experts' claims of special competence and the efficacy of their cures. Major participants in the criminal justice system, already suffering from a systems overload of sorts, seemed glad to be rid of these marginal groups.

Thus, at the same time that procedural and substantive due process protections were narrowing the number of people who were confined for any length of time, less restrictive forms of social control, such as work release and therapy in lieu of confinement, were extended to a greater number of individuals. People who did not present a grave danger to themselves or others were usually passed over by formal systems of social control. The philosophy of deinstitutionalization and the *de jure* preference for less restrictive methods of social control minimized the loss of liberty while reducing the counter-productive effects of confinement. This gave the appearance of freedom and justice for all but a few hard-core deviants.

By the 1960s, there was deep concern about whether the mentally ill were being fairly treated under the law. New claims of successful treatment tech-niques and changing values regarding the poor and the disadvantaged led Americans to question their basic assumptions about free will and responsi-bility. Emerging theories of psychopathology influenced how criminal law determined personal responsibility, making the law more compassionate and willing to excuse from blame and punishment those unfortunates suffering from mental illness. Until this time, psychiatrists testifying in insanity cases were usually asked a few simplistic questions such as: "Was the defendant 'insane' at the time of the crime?" "Did he know what he was doing or the difference between right and wrong?" The law did not acknowledge that many psychiatrists found it difficult to give a simple "yes" or "no" answer to these questions. As a result of aggressive prodding by the psychiatric com-munity, the law was modified to expand what psychiatrists could tell the jury and to make their testimony even more influential in determining the guilt or innocence of criminal defendants.

One way to ensure that mentally ill offenders received the benefits of the therapeutic state was to enhance the chances for avoiding criminal respon-sibility and the resulting prison sentences. This would require essential changes in the formulation of the insanity test and expanded opportunities to use mental illness as a shield in criminal prosecutions. New interpretations of legal doctrine were needed to channel mentally ill offenders into mental health systems of care and control where they would receive appropriate treatment for their individual illness instead of punishment and neglect.[45]

The Power of Psychiatry

What brought about such abrupt and pervasive changes in how criminal law treated mentally ill offenders? Perhaps the most dominant influence was the blossoming of psychiatry as a relatively new science of human behavior. As America's faith in science and technology grew, so did faith in the specialists who would heal the sick minds of criminals and other deviants. Psychiatrists rose to the occasion by claiming their field of scientific knowledge had great potential for improving the human condition.[46] Psychiatry and its related fields of secular knowledge claimed to have developed novel insight into the reasons people behaved the way they did.

Simultaneously, psychoanalytic determinism became a dominant force in psychiatric thought. This theory hypothesized that human behavior was the product of prior life experiences or underlying mental illness and that, to a large extent, human action was not the product of knowledge and choice. In either instance, crime was frequently neither rational nor voluntary, but was caused by unconscious motives or by disease. Dr. Ralph Brancale, writing in 1958 for a symposium on sentencing, claimed:

> Criminality, like its prototype, delinquency, is a chronic process characterized by a disturbed behavioral reaction, the antisocial impulses of which, it is recognized, were developed to satisfy unmet and rather deep-seated instinctual needs. Criminal behavior is often as much a symptom of psychiatric illness as is a delusion in a paranoid individual or conversion paralysis in an hysterical patient. . . . [C]rime is not committed as much by choice as by compulsions, that it is not dominated by a rational process, but is rather inspired and motivated by unconscious pressures.[47]

This thesis was obviously inconsistent with the underlying assumption of then current criminal law that humans possessed free will and were therefore responsible for their intentional conduct. This innovative science posed significant challenges to the empirical assumptions criminal law had adopted about the cause and cure of antisocial behavior. It called into question the very notion of individual responsibility for any human action and required critical reassessment of what the purposes of punishment and the goals of the criminal justice system should be. This reexamination of human behavior opened up incredible new possibilities for the criminal justice system. There was now a perceived basis for believing experts possessed the knowledge to change people for the better. Rehabilitation of criminal offenders could and should—once again—become a realistic goal of the criminal justice system. Consequently, it made sense, both morally and in terms of society's own self-interest in preventing future crime, to modify the criminal law to permit experts to identify those offenders who were suitable candidates for therapy instead of punishment.

The Doubts Emerge

Psychiatrists themselves seemed ambivalent about what role, if any, they should play in the legal system. During the Liberal Era, most psychiatrists thought they should play a significant part in determining whether criminal offenders were held responsible and punished, or excused and sent to psychiatric institutions for treatment. But a few mental health professionals were more skeptical. They doubted whether psychiatry had anything special to say in a criminal trial. In their opinion, psychiatrists' primary task should be to assist the courts in deciding what should be done with an offender after conviction.[48]

Even if they had useful expertise to share, some mental health professionals were certain the adversary system used in a criminal trial would distort the scientific information beyond any semblance of objective truth, thereby impairing its usefulness. Other mental health professionals were concerned that some colleagues, when testifying as an expert in a criminal trial, would ignore their general duty as citizens to accept the criteria for criminal responsibility set by the law. Instead, they might pursue personal or professional agendas, giving opinions designed to excuse and obtain treatment for those who had committed crimes.[49] The decision whether to participate as a forensic expert in a criminal trial raised profound ethical dilemmas for many mental health professionals. Nonetheless, most psychiatrists pushed aggressively to expand the influence of psychiatry in criminal trials.

Reform of the Insanity Defense

A favorable climate for reforming the way the criminal justice system treated mentally ill offenders was in now place. The initial focus of this reform movement was the 150-year-old *M'Naghten* test of insanity, which provided that:

> [I]t must be clearly proved that, at the time of the committing of the act, the party accused was labouring under such a defect of reason, from disease of the mind, as not to know the nature and quality of the act he was doing; or, if he did know it, that he did not know he was doing what was wrong.[50]

As we shall soon see, this stringent filter excused very few individuals.

Criticisms of the *M'Naghten* Test

Both before and during the Liberal Era, the *M'Naghten* test had come under heavy attack.[51] But now organized psychiatry provided a powerful impetus for changing it. Increasingly, psychiatrists criticized the *M'Naghten* test, claiming it severely limited their ability to conscientiously present to judges and juries psychiatric information critical to assessing criminal responsibility.[52] Such information included descriptions and analysis of the offender's personality, motivation, mental and emotional processes, and behavioral controls. Noted jurists and legal scholars agreed, arguing that the law must accommodate this new knowledge and that failure to do so was both pragmatically and morally unacceptable.[53]

These groups also faulted the *M'Naghten* test because it arbitrarily selected a single aspect of human mental activity—cognition—as the touchstone of criminal responsibility. Only if a mentally ill person did not know what he or she was doing or that it was wrong could the person be excused under this test. Although psychiatrists had come to the conclusion that mental illness seldom caused complete impairment of any human mental function, *M'Naghten* required a total impairment in cognitive ability. Either a defendant knew or did not know; there were no intermediate states of "knowledge." As a practical matter, very few criminal defendants would be excused, since such extreme dysfunction rarely existed.

Contemporary psychiatric theory taught that mental disease impaired a range of mental functions including volition, emotion, and cognition; however, the *M'Naghten* test accepted cognition as the only type of impairment that would justify a finding of nonresponsibility. Manfred Guttmacher, a noted psychiatrist, criticized the *M'Naghten* test because it put "false emphasis on intellect, reason, and common sense and underemphasizes the emotional pressures that energize behavior."[54] A modern insanity test that incorporated current knowledge about the human psyche would not be so narrow in scope.

The inflexible limits imposed on psychiatric testimony by the *M'Naghten* test also created a serious ethical dilemma for forensic psychiatrists testifying in a criminal trial in which the defendant had raised the insanity defense. They were required to reduce their knowledge of complex psychological problems to the overly simplistic question of whether the defendant knew right from wrong.[55] Experts in the field asserted that in many cases psychiatrists were compelled to commit "professional perjury" when testifying. Bernard L. Diamond was quite blunt about the stark choice a psychiatrist faced when testifying under the *M'Naghten* test. He wrote:

> Whenever a psychiatrist is called upon to testify, under the *M'Naghten* Rule of a knowledge of right and wrong, as to the sanity or insanity of a defendant, the psychiatrist must either renounce his own values with all their medical-humanistic implications, thereby becoming a puppet doctor, used by the law to further the punitive and vengeful goals demanded by society; or he must *commit perjury* if he accepts a literal definition of the *M'Naghten* Rule. [emphasis added][56]

In short, psychiatrists began to subjectively redefine the terms of the *M'Naghten* test, harmonizing their professional opinions with the legal requirements for excusing a defendant as insane.[57] Explicitly redefining the legal test of insanity to permit psychiatrists to present a more comprehensive and psychiatrically relevant opinion would obviate their need to resort to such drastic subterfuge as "professional perjury."[58]

The *Durham* Experiment

In 1954 the Federal Circuit Court of Appeals for the District of Columbia, under the influence of Judge David Bazelon, jettisoned the venerable *M'Naghten* rule of criminal insanity and tried another tack, deliberately creating a new test for insanity, the famous *Durham* rule. This formulation of legal insanity, based on *Durham* v. *United States*, concluded that "an accused is not criminally responsible if his unlawful act was the product of mental disease or mental defect."[59] Initially, this new test was considered truly revolutionary and was greeted quite favorably by both psychiatrists and legal scholars.[60]

Unlike *M'Naghten*, this test did not limit the insanity defense to those mentally ill defendants who did not know what they had done or that it was wrong. Instead of requiring that mental illness cause a specified type of psychological impairment such as a defect in cognition, the *Durham* rule simply asked whether the defendant's mental disease or defect caused the criminal behavior. If it did, the defendant should not be punished. Mental health experts were free to present a thorough psychiatric picture of the defendant, uninhibited by narrow diagnostic categories or restrictive legal concepts.

The *Durham* rule was a judicial invitation to forensic mental health experts to hone their skills by evaluating mentally ill offenders and to make the results of their growing expertise on the puzzling and formidable question of legal insanity available to the legal system.[61] Unfortunately, it would soon become apparent that psychiatrists had no special qualifications or knowledge enabling them to give expert opinions on whether mental illness *caused* criminal behavior. Often, they could not even come to an agreement regarding a definitive diagnosis, which could lead to a "battle of experts" in the courtroom. Nor could they predict the future behavior of the offender with any certainty. Frequently, they were not able to offer specific treatments that were likely to result in cures. In addition, some psychiatric opinions that purported to be expressions of medical facts were suffused with the personal value judgments of the expert witness about the propriety of punishment in general or in a particular case.[62]

Psychiatrists also began to have inordinate influence on juries, because laypersons seldom disagreed with the opinion of "experts." Instead of enhancing the ability of juries as representatives of the community to make the difficult legal, social, and moral judgments embodied in the insanity defense, the *Durham* rule effectively conferred on an elite group of mental health experts the *de facto* power to make these decisions on, what seemed to some, a pseudoscientific basis. Corrective courtroom procedures could not prevent this phenomenon.[63]

The *Durham* rule would generate a tremendous amount of scholarly and judicial discourse on the wisdom of changing the *M'Naghten* test of insanity.[64] Although *Durham* would ultimately prove unable to stand the test of time,[65] it was influential in prodding law reformers and courts to rethink the purposes of the insanity defense and how it should be formulated and litigated.

Mental Illness and Criminal Responsibility in the Liberal Era

Radical changes in social values reshaped American society during the Liberal Era. Basic concepts of individual blame and of social responses to deviant behavior, already being criticized and reshaped, were thoroughly reexamined. As a result, the criminal law underwent a continuing metamorphosis and reflected more clearly America's changing attitudes about the criminal responsibility of mentally ill offenders. Since individual states and the federal government can decide whether mentally ill offenders will be excused from criminal responsibility in its jurisdiction, the opportunities for implementing these shifts in values were plentiful.

The ALI Rule

At about the same time the *Durham* rule came on the scene, other important developments in criminal law were taking place. In 1953 the influential American Law Institute (ALI), a body of noted attorneys, judges, and scholars, undertook a major law reform project to revise the criminal law and to write a Model Penal Code that could be adopted by the states. This project included a reconsideration of the insanity defense to ascertain whether a test other than *M'Naghten* should be proposed. The adoption of the *Durham* rule by the prestigious Federal Circuit Court of Appeals for the District of Columbia gave special impetus to this review. The ALI study became a lightning rod that attracted intense and energetic criticism of the *M'Naghten* test.

Formulating a suitable test for legal insanity was not an easy task.[66] The primary function of an insanity test, the ALI study concluded, was to determine when "a punitive-correctional disposition is appropriate and [when] a medical-custodial disposition is the only kind that the law should allow."[67]

After an intense study period of several years, the American Law Institute adopted a new insanity test, now known as the "ALI test." This test would excuse an offender if mental illness had substantially interfered with his or her ability to comprehend the criminality of his conduct or with his ability to control himself.[68] Adopting this test meant that volitional as well as cognitive impairment would now vitiate criminal responsibility.

This test met many of the objections lodged by the psychiatric profession against *M'Naghten*. It expanded the range of mental functions considered relevant in assessing criminal responsibility and widened the scope of testimony psychiatrists could give.[69] It did not require a total breakdown in an individual's mental functioning—a "substantial" incapacity would suffice. Consequently, a jury should find a defendant legally insane if mental illness significantly interfered with the accused's ability to know what he was doing or that it was wrong or, alternatively, to control himself.

The ALI study concluded that the threat of punishment was unlikely to deter anyone who suffered from serious cognitive or volitional impairment. Punishing such people would not make the community safer. It made more sense to treat and release them when their psychological apparatus had been repaired and they were no longer dangerous. Rehabilitation was the key to this strategy. It was seen both as serving the community's pragmatic self-interest and as a humane response to illness. In addition, since mentally ill offenders did not choose to violate the law, no legitimate retributive value would be served by punishing them.

The new insanity test, formally proposed by the ALI study in 1962, enjoyed an immediate and enthusiastic response. From 1964 through 1980 all but one federal circuit court of appeal adopted the test for use in criminal trials in federal courts in their districts.[70] By 1980 more than half of the states had adopted the test either by judicial or legislative action.[71]

The *M'Naghten* test, formulated in 1843 in Great Britain, had been adopted and used by most states and federal circuit courts of appeal in this country for well over a century without significant change.[72] It is amazing that within sixteen short years so many jurisdictions in the United States abandoned *M'Naghten* and adopted a test which had the clear purpose of increasing the number of defendants who might avoid criminal punishment.

The reviews on the new ALI test, however, were not all favorable. There was some skepticism among both judges and scholars as to its wisdom.[73] In refusing to change the rule of legal insanity in New Jersey from the *M'Naghten* test to either the *Durham* rule[74] or the ALI test, the chief justice of the Supreme Court of New Jersey concluded that there was "an irreconcilable conflict between the present thesis of the criminal law and the thesis ... implicit in the psychiatric view of man."[75] Justice Weintraub was concerned that the criminal law's assumption that humans possess free will and could choose how to act was flatly rejected by an emerging psychological view that all human behavior was causally determined by prior life experiences over which the individual had little or no control. This sort of "determinism," if accepted and implemented by the legal system, would wreak havoc with concepts of deterrence and retribution. If true, deviants could not be punished; they could only be treated or confined.

The "Diminished Capacity" Defense

Although a large number of states and federal circuit courts of appeal had adopted the ALI insanity test within a relatively brief time, other state legislatures did not change their insanity test and continued to use the rather strict *M'Naghten* test. Supreme courts in several of these states, most notably California, became frustrated by the limitations of the *M'Naghten* test and its perceived unfairness to offenders who were seriously mentally ill. To soften the test's harshness, these courts devised a new legal doctrine called the "diminished capacity" defense. (Later, the California Supreme Court would adopt the ALI test for insanity in 1978 for many of the reasons discussed earlier. This would make California's law governing criminal responsibility for mentally ill offenders extremely liberal.[76])

Before adoption of this new defense, psychiatric evidence generally could be introduced only if it tended to establish legal insanity. This new defense, however, permitted defendants to introduce evidence of their mental illness or voluntary intoxication to show they did not act with the particular mental attitude (*mens rea*, literally, "guilty mind" or criminal intent) required to convict them of the specific crime with which they were charged.[77] Psychiatrists could now testify that, in their medical opinion, defendants, though legally sane, nonetheless had suffered from mental illness or defect which rendered them unable to "premeditate" or commit murder with "malice aforethought" or with whatever particular state of mind was required for conviction. If the jury decided the defendant did not act with that specific attitude, it could not convict the accused of that crime. It could find the defendant guilty of a less serious crime or acquit altogether.[78]

The ALI's Model Penal Code also proposed a diminished capacity defense, which would admit psychiatric evidence in a criminal trial if it logically tended to prove or disprove the defendant had acted with the criminal state of mind required for conviction.[79] Ratification by the prestigious ALI of the diminished capacity defense gave this new defense a significant imprimatur, which undoubtedly established its intellectual and moral credentials and thus enhanced its prospects for favorable reception by courts and legislatures throughout the country.

Reaction to the Diminished Capacity Defense

Initially, the "diminished capacity" doctrine was received with enthusiasm by most legal scholars and forensic psychiatrists.[80] The doctrine unshackled the psychiatrist from testifying in the "all or nothing" fashion provided by *M'Naghten*. Psychiatrists were particularly enthusiastic because they were permitted to present to the jury a complete psychiatric assessment of the defendant's mental and emotional processes at the time of the offense. They could also reach back into the defendant's life to provide an antecedent, causal context for his or her mentation and action. Based on this all-encompassing view of the individual, mental health experts could give their professional opinions as to whether the defendant had the capacity to act with the mental state required to commit a crime.

This new legal doctrine mitigated the harshness of the *M'Naghten* rule. In states like California and Washington, which did not adopt the ALI test, juries could use the diminished capacity defense to individualize justice by distinguishing between "normal" criminals and criminals who suffered from serious mental illness but who were not legally insane.[81] Juries were no longer restricted to the confining choice of "not guilty by reason of insanity" or "guilty as charged." This defense provided the criminal law with the doctrinal dexterity needed to discern fine calibrations among criminal defendants and to find seriously ill individuals guilty of less serious crimes or, occasionally, no crime at all. It was also particularly important in capital cases where often some very disturbed defendants faced the death penalty or life imprisonment.[82]

The California Experience

The court decisions of one state in particular, California, gave impetus to adoption of the diminished capacity defense. It came about when several nationally prominent forensic psychiatrists, who were intolerant of the narrow legal limits placed on psychiatric testimony in criminal trials, wanted to gain entry into the processes of shaping and applying criminal law doctrine so that the learning and values of contemporary psychiatry could influence that doctrine and its implementation. Some psychiatrists did not consider the traditional *M'Naghten* insanity test to be the proper beachhead for this assault. Instead, they believed that the traditional concept of *mens rea* was the best available target of opportunity for infusing psychiatric values into criminal law.[83]

And what were those values? Psychiatrist Bernard Diamond described them in this way:

> Psychiatry, like all medicine, is dedicated to the preservation of life and health; it is humanistic and individualistic; its goals are cure and rehabilitation, protection of the individual and protection of society; it is nonjudgmental, amoral (but not unethical) and impious, in that it must treat all alike, friend or enemy, good citizen or criminal, believer or heretic; it is scientific, by which I mean that it is reality-oriented and deals with human beings instead of with abstrac-

tions, fictions, philosophical syllogisms, or theoretical moralities; its method is that of all science—experimentation, statistical analysis, and trial and error within a framework of its own hypotheses; finally it must perpetually put to practical test, and adopt new theories and practices as they become of evident usefulness.[84]

Diamond would later argue that the forensic psychiatrist should abandon the role of detached expert and instead enter the judicial arena as an advocate concerned about actively influencing the jury verdict. The psychiatrist should act as an agent of social change, seeking social justice by promoting changes in the rules of law.[85] Eventually, the opinion of Diamond as well as other well-known psychiatrists would aid and abet the California Supreme Court in adopting the diminished capacity defense.

The initial input of psychiatrists occurred in the 1959 first degree-murder trial of Nicholas Gorshen, in which defense lawyers planned to use psychiatric testimony to disprove premeditation and malice aforethought.[86] The trial court excluded the psychiatric testimony of Dr. Diamond, and Gorshen was found guilty. The case was appealed by the defendant, with the assistance of psychiatric organizations.[87] The California Supreme Court reversed the conviction, ruling that the psychiatric testimony should have been admitted on the issues of premeditation and malice aforethought.

Two years after the *Gorshen* decision, Dr. Diamond wrote an influential article which argued that psychiatric testimony should be admitted in criminal trials on the issue of the defendant's mental state at the time of the crime. It was an unusual call to political action on the part of organized psychiatry to influence how criminal law treats mentally ill offenders.[88] His attitude was less that of a detached scientist and more that of an advocate for a particular normative view of responsibility and punishment.

Partly as a result of Diamond's call to action, the diminished capacity defense became more influential in California. Perhaps the classic example of how this new theory was used to "individualize justice" for a mentally ill offender was the 1964 case of *People* v. *Wolff*.[89] The defendant was a fifteen-year-old boy who carefully planned and deliberately killed his mother so that he would be free to act out his rape fantasies against neighborhood teenage girls. Both defense and government psychiatrists agreed that Wolff was a troubled young man who suffered from serious mental illness but knew it was against the law to kill another human being. According to virtually unanimous expert opinion, it was clear that the defendant, though very ill, was legally sane under the *M'Naghten* test then used in California. The jury found the youth guilty of first-degree murder and the trial judge sentenced him to life imprisonment.[90]

The defendant, with the assistance of a group of forensic psychiatrists, appealed his conviction, claiming the *M'Naghten* test was unconstitutional and that the evidence presented at trial was insufficient to convict him. The California Supreme Court upheld the *M'Naghten* test as constitutional but it reduced Wolff's conviction to second-degree murder. It concluded that the defendant's schizophrenia severely diminished his capacity to act with the "premeditation, willfulness, and deliberation" required for first degree murder.[91] The majority explained that "the true test must include consideration of the somewhat limited extent to which this defendant could *maturely and meaningfully reflect* upon the gravity of his contemplated act."[92] The Court, in effect, decided that justice required sophisticated inquiry into the moral turpitude of each offender. Did the accused have the normal human capacity to undertake a meaningful moral assessment of his or her contemplated conduct? Seemingly, a mentally ill person could know in a formal or literal sense that he would be punished for his action, yet not have the requisite rational and emotional understanding of its true wrongfulness.

In the 1976 case of *People* v. *Poddar*, the California Supreme Court expanded the diminished capacity defense even further. This case involved the first-degree murder trial of a college student who planned over the course of several months to kill a female friend who had spurned his romantic advances.[93] The Court held that a mentally ill defendant could be found not guilty of either first- or second-degree murder, decreeing: "If it is established that an accused, because he suffered a diminished capacity, was unaware of *or unable to act in accordance with the law*, malice could not properly be found and the maximum offense for which he could be convicted would be voluntary manslaughter (emphasis added)."[94] The Court thus permitted *either* cognitive *or* volitional impairment caused by mental illness to negate the element of malice aforethought. As Professor Stephen Morse has cogently demonstrated, the Court's opinion clearly took the operative concepts of the ALI insanity test—cognitive failure to appreciate the wrongfulness of one's conduct and volitional inability to conform to the law's requirements—and packed them into the statutory definition of "malice aforethought" required for first- and second-degree murder.[95]

The *Wolff* and *Poddar* cases involved intentional homicides in which the defendants planned well in advance to kill their victims, had a strong motive to kill, and implemented their plans in a calculated and purposeful manner. Ordinarily, this was strong evidence that they had acted with the "premeditation" and "malice aforethought" required for conviction of murder in the first degree. Nonetheless, the judicially wrought doctrine of diminished capacity effectively redefined what these words, as used in the California homicide law, should mean. This redefinition gave broad license to psychiatric testimony on whether criminal defendants had committed first- or second-degree murder or only voluntary manslaughter, which carried a much shorter maximum sentence.

Once it embarked on the slippery slope of diminished capacity, the California Supreme Court found it difficult to stop. In *People* v. *Wetmore*,[96] the Court held that the defendant could present evidence of his mental illness in order to be acquitted of all charges in a burglary, even though the Court realized Wetmore might be released immediately since he was probably not committable under California's involuntary civil commitment statute. The Court said:

> If the [state civil commitment statute] does not adequately protect the public against crimes committed by persons with diminished mental capacity, the

answer lies either in amendment to that act or in the enactment of legislation
that would provide for commitment of persons acquitted by virtue of a successful diminished capacity defense in the same manner as persons acquitted
by reason of insanity are presently committed.[97]

The diminished capacity defense was an attempt to fine-tune the criminal
justice system by permitting judges and juries to inquire into the defendant's
individual mental and emotional capabilities. If mental illness significantly
hindered a person's ability to comprehend or conform, then the person should
not be punished as severely as one who did not suffer from such a handicap.
The emerging ethos of equal justice obligated the law to treat people who
were fundamentally different in different ways. The diminished capacity defense permitted the law to take into account the growth of new psychiatric
knowledge; to individualize justice, thereby maintaining the moral foundations of the criminal law; and to further the rehabilitative ideal.[98] It also
conferred enormous power on mental health experts to influence trial decisions.

The new concept of diminished capacity met with widespread approval in
the United States. By 1975, approximately twenty-five states had some provision for a diminished capacity defense, and several federal courts of appeal
had also authorized it in some form.[99] This widespread adoption of the diminished capacity defense generally occurred at about the same time that
many states and virtually all federal courts were adopting the ALI insanity
test as the operative rule of law.

Expanding Criminal Excuses Based on Mental Illness

Implicit in the adoption of the ALI test was the notion that psychiatry and
its related fields had developed new knowledge that criminal law must incorporate. In psychiatry, as in any science, one could not expect the known
universe to be static. If psychiatry discovered new forms of mental illness,
then it was only logical that the criminal law consider them.

Even with the guidance of more and more sophisticated and systematic
diagnostic schemes, however, reliable and valid assessment of volitional incapacity is a highly subjective business. And in the event psychiatrists agree
on a specific diagnosis (which they often do not), each is free to give his or
her own interpretation of whether or not a suspect was unable to control his
or her behavior due to mental illness. The ALI test permits a criminal defendant who, in the opinion of a mental health professional, suffered from
such an inability to raise an insanity defense.

The ALI test also had a built-in "time-bomb" logic, that came from the
law's attempt to take into account the growth of psychiatric knowledge. Only
two components were required to excuse a criminal offense: a person must
be suffering from a mental illness and that illness must have weakened the
individual's cognitive or behavioral controls. No other elements beyond
these essential "facts" were required. Therefore, if psychiatry decided in the
future to classify other abnormal behavior as symptomatic of a mental illness

that impaired a person's ability to obey the law, individuals thus afflicted could raise the insanity defense to criminal charges arising out of such behavior.

Volitional Impairment and Shifting Concepts of Responsibility

Toward the end of the Liberal Era, imaginative and skilled defense lawyers sought to extend the rationale of the ALI test to other types of offenders. Armed with new information about human behavior and operating under this more flexible insanity defense, they claimed that their clients suffered everything from "battered wife syndrome" to "Post-Traumatic Stress Disorder."

A plethora of defenses developed. For example, in the case of domestic violence, social scientists asserted that many women who were violently abused by their partners over a long period of time developed a "learned helplessness," which caused them to conclude there was no effective way out of the abusive relationship. In turn, these battered victims lost their ability to control their anger, resulting in a single episode of violence in which they killed or seriously injured their attackers.[100] When presented with such a line of reasoning, juries found some women who stood accused of murdering or seriously injuring their male companions as legally insane.[101]

Some Vietnam veterans successfully used the Post-Traumatic Stress Disorder defense when charged with violent crimes such as homicide and assault.[102] They claimed that stress and other stimuli similar to combat caused "flashbacks" in which they thought they were once again on the battlefield.[103] Some defendants claimed that during these dissociative states they had unknowingly committed violent crimes, thinking they were actually in Vietnam. This defense was used to drop or reduce charges, to enter into favorable plea agreements and obtain reduced sentences, to secure placement in a treatment program, and to obtain verdicts of not guilty by reason of insanity.[104]

Some defendants who successfully raised these defenses had killed their victims in ways which appeared deliberate and planned. Yet the individualization of justice, made easier under the ALI test, created the possibility that many defendants charged with very serious crimes like murder might be acquitted and released.

Attempts were soon made to expand the application of the ALI insanity test to excuse other kinds of criminal behavior. In 1980 the American Psychiatric Association classified pathological gambling as a "Disorder of Impulse Control,"[105] formally conferring disease status on compulsive gambling. Even prior to this action, however, criminal defendants were raising pathological gambling as a defense to criminal charges. In 1979 a criminal defendant in New Jersey successfully pleaded not guilty by reason of insanity to a charge of writing bad checks. The defendant presented expert testimony that he suffered from the mental disease of "compulsive gambling" and, consequently, could not distinguish right from wrong under New Jersey's *M'Naghten* test.[106] In 1980 a defendant in Connecticut was found not guilty of first-degree larceny under the ALI insanity test based on the testimony of a defense psychiatrist who claimed that compulsive gambling was a mental disease.[107] During this period, there were several cases in which defendants invoked this defense to a variety of charges including forgery, embezzlement, and armed bank robbery.[108] Some were successful; others were not.

The success of these criminal defendants in presenting psychiatric evidence about the etiology and impact of pathological gambling and in obtaining jury instructions about its relevance under the ALI insanity defense had enormous implications for future prosecutions of defendants similarly charged. Offenders who gambled extensively or stole significant sums of money to support their gambling compulsion because they could not control themselves might avoid successful prosecution.

Excusing such pathological gamblers created interesting dispositional questions. Where would these individuals be kept and for how long? Were they currently mentally ill and dangerous? Could they be committed under the state's civil commitment laws if they were only considered dangerous to property?[109] What, if any, sort of treatment was available for them?

The potential impact of this new defense was unknown. How many criminal defendants could potentially take advantage of pathological gambling under the insanity defense? Some researchers estimated that there were an estimated 1 to 3 million compulsive gamblers in the United States.[110] The potential social and economic implications of even a relatively small percentage of this group being considered mentally ill and not responsible for criminal acts committed to sustain their gambling was staggering.

Moreover, once criminal behavior such as gambling was excused because it purportedly stemmed from an addiction to gratify impulses labeled for treatment purposes as symptomatic of a mental disease,[111] it might be difficult to prevent other defendants from using the ALI insanity defense. Why shouldn't child molesters, pyromaniacs, and other compulsive criminals be excused as legally insane under this broad excuse since their antisocial behavior could be considered symptomatic of a mental disease?

No Limits?

The possibilities the Liberal Era produced for excusing criminal behavior seemed boundless. A morally sound criminal law that fully considered an individual's characteristics in determining guilt or innocence need not logically be limited to deficiencies caused by mental illness. Indeed, the cause of deviant behavior might be located anywhere in the universe, which would diminish— perhaps even extinguish—any meaningful concept of responsibility for one's actions. During this period, when fundamental assumptions about human behavior and concepts of blameworthiness were being critically examined, the entire legal concept of individual responsibility seemed under attack.

Judge David Bazelon argued that a criminal defendant should not be found guilty "if at the time of his unlawful conduct his mental or emotional processes or behavior controls were impaired to such an extent that he cannot justly be held responsible for his act."[112] Initially, this proposal would at least require some evidence of mental illness before a jury could acquit a criminal defendant. But four years later Judge Bazelon argued in a scholarly article that this test of nonresponsibility should not require that the defendant suffer from mental illness. He wrote:

> The instruction [just described] would freely allow expert and lay testimony on the nature and extent of behavioral impairments and of physiological, psychological, *environmental, cultural, educational, economic*, and *heredity* factors. Its ultimate aim . . . would be to give all of us a deeper understanding of the causes of human behavior in general and criminal behavior in particular (emphasis added).[113]

Under this proposed test of criminal responsibility, virtually any cause that might adversely affect emotional processes or behavioral controls could excuse a criminal from personal responsibility.[114] Defenses such as "black rage," "severe environmental deprivation," and "brain-washing"[115] could be permitted under such a broad rule. In effect, every jury would pass its own judgment on whether any criminal should be held criminally responsible for his harmful acts.[116]

The Shape of Criminal Law at the End of the Liberal Era

On balance, it is fair to conclude that the Liberal Era spawned a criminal law that implemented the intense ideological concerns and empirical assumptions of that period. Substantive criminal law had finally been "modernized," enabling it to use the new advances in knowledge that psychiatry and pharmacology had seemingly made within the previous two decades.[117] Empowered with hopes of cure and the promise of prevention, criminal justice moved away from social control and incapacitation as primary objectives and emphasized the emerging focus on rehabilitation of offenders and their speedy return to the community.

These perceived benefits were not without costs since they included the possibility of more acquittals based on insanity under the ALI test, more frequent acquittals and reduced sentences under the diminished capacity defense, newly categorized mental diseases being favorably presented under the ALI test, and the prospect of acquittals in which defendants did not even have to be mentally ill. The public now began to fear that the floodgates of criminal excuse were about to burst and that the law's message of individual responsibility and protection from violent crime was evaporating.

As fate would have it, developments in the science of human behavior and an awakening of society's sense of responsibility for social conditions were not the only phenomena occurring during the Liberal Era. Crime, particularly violent crime, was increasing at epidemic rates. Not surprisingly, crime control and community safety were being pushed to the foreground of public concern. Inevitably, pressures grew for another cycle of legal reform.

2

Law and Order in the Neoconservative Era

By the close of the seventies, the mood of the country, spurred by dramatic increases in crime, deteriorating economic conditions, and shifting political ideologies, had turned against liberal values. During this period, the rehabilitative ideal came under fierce attack from both the political right and left. And though their objectives and arguments differed sharply, their conclusions were surprisingly congruent: crime and violence were out of control; the social experimentation of the 1960s and early 1970s had gone awry.

In the twilight of the Liberal Era, "law and order" became an important social agenda, influencing significant changes in criminal law. High-profile media cases involving prominent victims and criminal defendants claiming to be mentally ill precipitated fundamental legal reform. Both the insanity defense and diminished capacity defense were abolished or sharply curtailed in many jurisdictions, and new laws were passed to strengthen society's authority to punish, treat, and confine mentally disturbed criminals.

Law and Order as a Social Movement

In the eyes of almost everyone, deinstitutionalization and the restrictive commitment laws of the Liberal Era had generated a new social reality. Large numbers of disturbed citizens haunted the urban landscapes of our major cities. Some committed heinous crimes, including savage multiple murders, attracting extensive media coverage. Others ended up in jails unequipped to cope with their special problems. Many languished in new psychiatric ghettos, living in shabby hotels or boarding houses and eking out a sparse and solitary existence on meager welfare support. Hundreds of thousands of the most disabled had been abandoned to live in abject misery in the name of freedom. Liberalism seemingly wrought new and terrifying consequences, harming the very citizens—the disadvantaged and vulnerable—it purported to protect.[1]

In yet another irony, just as society during the Liberal Era seemed most optimistic about its ability to prevent crime by treating criminals and attacking the external causes of deviant behavior, crime rates surged. The public blamed court decisions and laws enacted during the Liberal Era for both of these phenomena.

To many, the criminal law, abetted by what they considered the soft pseudoscience of psychiatry, had contributed to the breakdown of public safety by coddling dangerous criminals and helping them escape the punishment they so richly deserved. Critics argued that psychiatrists could not even agree among themselves on the specifics of diagnosis nor could they give any assurance of effective treatment. Even worse, some felt that too many insane predators were soon back on the streets, eager to prey on an unsuspecting and unprotected public. The operating assumption of free will and personal responsibility—the mainstay of our criminal law—seemed to be in mortal danger of hopeless dilution. As we saw in Chapter 1, criminal defendants, making some of the more bizarre claims of mental illness, seemed to be getting away with murder! Angered citizens asked: Why should anyone obey the law if no one is responsible? Does this sort of law provide true justice?

In response to public outrage, a broad pattern of legal reform has emerged during the Neoconservative Era that substantially restricts opportunities for mentally ill offenders to avoid criminal responsibility. New legislation has restricted psychiatric testimony in criminal trials, procedures have been adopted to make it more difficult for offenders to successfully assert defenses based on mental illness, and recently enacted criminal commitment reforms ensure that mentally disturbed offenders are confined as long as necessary to protect the public. The Liberal Era policy of releasing mentally ill offenders as soon as possible has taken a back seat in the Neoconservative Era to incarcerating them for as long as necessary to prevent them from committing more crimes against new victims.

This backlash in social attitudes has prodded political candidates seeking offices from the president on down to the city councilman to run on "law and order" platforms. Community safety and the rights of the majority have become the backbone of a social movement. Tolerance for the different and the disadvantaged has given way to demands for tough crime-control measures.

Notwithstanding media sensationalism, public fear of being victimized by violent crime has ample basis. Crime rates against persons and property began to increase significantly in the first five years of the 1960s. As criminologist James Wilson trenchantly put it: "If the figures are to be believed, the increase in crime assumed epidemic proportions in the first few years of the 1960s."[2] During the 1970s crime in general and violent crime in particular continued to increase at alarming rates. According to the Uniform Crime Reports, the rate of violent crime increased almost 50 percent between 1971 and 1980— aggravated assault increased 63 percent, and murder and nonnegligent homicide increased almost 20 percent. Nonviolent crime rose rapidly as well. During that period, the incidence of burglary jumped 43 percent, making people feel they were not safe on the streets or even in their own homes.[3] One study reported that in 1980, 40 percent of all Americans were highly fearful of becoming the victim of a specific violent crime. Another 38 percent

expressed a high level of fear about general safety at home, in the neighborhood, or in the larger community.[4] The harsh social reality was that citizens
feared for their personal safety, the safety of their property, and the safety
of others.

Victims' Backlash

As the crime rate accelerated, more people, of all ages and classes, became
victims of crime. For the first time in our history, many more citizens were
getting a taste of the criminal justice system as witnesses or as victims, often
having been harmed psychologically if not physically. Their exposure to crime
investigation and prosecution led them to believe there was more emphasis
on the rights of the defendant than on their rights. Feelings of powerlessness
on the part of crime victims, fueled by the sluggishness, inefficiency, and
insensitivity of the criminal justice system to their needs, generated passionate
hostility.[5] The late Senator John Heinz of Pennsylvania aptly captured their
frustration: "Victimized first by the offender, too many victims perceive themselves victimized a second time by the system."[6] Often victims were enraged
to learn that, even after the defendant was convicted of a crime, the system
seemed more concerned with helping the defendant than with helping them.
As policy analysts Anderson and Woodard noted:

> In fact, a subtle irony has been at work: while scrupulously defending the
> rights of offenders, the system has ignored the rights of victims and witnesses.
> While emphasizing the rehabilitation of offenders, the system has done little
> to help victims recover from the financial and emotional problems they suffer
> from being victims of crime."[7]

Not unexpectedly, a victims' rights movement began to develop and exert
a powerful influence in the political arena, merging with the general appeal
for law and order. Feminist voices were perhaps the first to be heard. Women
were particularly concerned about how crimes of sexual violence were defined
and prosecuted and how female rape victims were treated by police and
prosecutors.[8] Other groups focused on various categories of crimes and their
victims. For example, beginning in the 1980s, Mothers Against Drunk Driving
(MADD) began increasing the public's attention to the homicides and crip-
pling physical injuries committed by drunk drivers, agitating for harsher punishment of these offenders. Later, politicians would hear from their growing
constituency of senior citizens, who would urge them to propose legislation
to aid elderly crime victims.[9] Around the country, an increasing number of
victims and their families organized. As of 1985, there were at least 2,000
government and privately sponsored victim assistance organizations at local,
state, and national levels.[10] Like a prairie fire, the victims' rights movement
swept the general public into the fray, seeking legal reform and attracting
support from a wide spectrum of Americans.

Their reform agenda had two primary goals. One goal was to repair as
much as possible the damage done to victims. The second was to secure for

victims a legally protected status during the prosecution of those who had hurt them. These reforms were packaged in various proposals as a "victims' bill of rights." Legislatures were lobbied to enact statutes that would provide for financial and psychological assistance to citizens harmed by criminals; these efforts met with remarkable success. As a result of lobbying efforts, by 1985, thirty-nine states, the District of Columbia, and the Virgin Islands had enacted legislation providing compensation to victims of crime.[11]

Much progress was also made on the second goal of reform. Previously, victims had had no legal authority to participate in deciding what the criminal justice system would do to their attackers. The victims' rights movement sought to obtain formal legal status for victims in criminal proceedings,[12] thereby empowering them to demand that the personal interest of the victim be taken into consideration. As a result, many states passed laws that conferred specific rights on victims in the prosecution and sentencing of criminals who harmed them.[13] In 1982 the President's Task Force on Victims of Crime recommended that the Sixth Amendment to the U.S. Constitution be amended to confer constitutional status on the rights of victims.[14]

As public sentiment shifted, politicians found victims' rights to be an issue that cut across party lines, appealing to individuals of diverse backgrounds. Many citizens felt that the criminal justice system had become unacceptably unbalanced in favor of the criminal. Providing victims with their own legal rights was viewed as an effective way to help restore the system to a proper equilibrium.

In the words of law professor and dean Abraham Goldstein, the victims' rights movement also forced society to rethink "some fundamental questions about the objectives of criminal justice and how it should be administered."[15] Indeed, during the Neoconservative Era society turned a suspicious eye toward Liberal Era solutions to those fundamental questions.

Rethinking the Purposes of Punishment

Everyone recognizes that crime harms individual victims most severely—but it also has an insidious impact on society by threatening its inherent capacity to sustain itself and to pursue common goals.[16] As soaring crime rates scarred the public psyche and increased their fears for personal safety, social attitudes about the appropriate goals of the criminal justice system began to undergo noticeable change. In the eyes of many, informal community social controls had collapsed, spawning demands for formal public controls.[17] The influence of families, churches, and neighborhoods seemed to crumble. Americans became more vocal in calling for government protection that the community and social institutions of another era no longer seemed able to provide. These circumstances created a new and powerful mandate for reshaping social institutions—particularly those of the criminal justice system.

Rehabilitation lost its appeal; now retribution, deterrence, and incapacitation were more highly valued. In particular, retribution, dismissed with utter contempt by most scholars and judges during the Liberal Era as a primordial animal instinct unworthy of a civilized society, emerged as a respectable intellectual viewpoint that attracted articulate and persuasive supporters.

The Liberal Critique of the Rehabilitative Ideal

Even groups that might normally be expected to support rehabilitation as the primary goal of the criminal justice system had become disillusioned with the rehabilitative ideal.[18] In 1971, well before the furor that would rise in the eighties, the American Friends Service Committee, a group that works in the area of social change and is part of the American Quaker movement, published *Struggle for Justice: A Report on Crime and Punishment in America.* This monograph offered a scathing indictment of the rehabilitative ideal as the dominant focus of the system. It concluded that "the individualized treatment model, the ideal toward which reformers have been urging us for at least a century, is theoretically faulty, systematically discriminatory in administration, and inconsistent with some of our most basic concepts of justice."[19]

The report went on to argue that, in fact, society knows very little about whether individual or social pathology causes crime. And even if individual pathology does cause crime, it continued, there is no empirically sound basis for concluding that society has the requisite knowledge or expertise (let alone resources) for effectively rehabilitating criminals.[20]

In addition, rehabilitation requires that extraordinary discretionary power be conferred on those who operate the system because treatment, by its very terms, must be individualized. Progress in each person's case will be variable. Consequently, final release back into society may be decided by experts on the basis of criteria likely to be applied inconsistently or even arbitrarily. Such broad discretion, the report found, introduces indeterminacy at an unacceptable level. Nor will the rehabilitative model necessarily ensure community safety or respect individual autonomy. Among other reforms, the committee called for punishment to fit the crime, not the criminal.[21]

Several years later, in 1976, another influential task force examined the practice of punishment during the era of the rehabilitative ideal. In an influential work *Doing Justice: The Choice of Punishments,*[22] an interdisciplinary group formed to study what should be done with convicted criminals concluded: "Crucial practical and moral difficulties are encountered, however, when this ideal [the therapeutic model] is incorporated into the compulsory processes of the criminal law. The simple fact is that the experiment has not worked out."[23] According to the committee, the available evidence simply did not establish that rehabilitation was effective. In addition, the group concluded that the rehabilitative model was—in practice—more punitive, abusive, and discriminatory than an explicitly punitive model would be. Consequently, it rejected a treatment model philosophically grounded in benevolence in favor of a "just deserts" model of punishment.

Under a just deserts model, the severity of punishment would depend on the seriousness of the harm done by the defendant, measured by the crime committed and by the criminal's prior record.[24] In this system, punishment would be a social response to past intentional conduct. Unlike a utilitarian model of crime control that sought to affect society as a whole—most notably by bringing about crime reduction—this model was not aimed primarily at influencing the behavior of others. Nor was its goal to prevent a defendant from committing future crimes either through rehabilitation or confinement. Only what the defendant had in fact done, not who he is or might become, would determine what punishment had been earned. Parole and early release were no longer viable options.[25] The primary purpose of punishment was accomplished at the moment it was imposed. It need not await future unknown and unknowable contingencies to ascertain if it had succeeded in its purpose.

The intellectual left, including Professor Andrew Von Hirsch and his working group, reacted to the harsh reality of a purportedly benign and therapeutic corrections system. The new model Von Hirsch and colleagues proposed would eliminate the inevitable gross disparity in the sentencing of similar defendants so pervasive in a system based on unrestrained discretion.

The model the left embraced was not so much concerned with reducing crime as with redressing an unjust society's penal code. Its goal was to eliminate broad discretion that was too easily abused and to decrease, not increase, the bitter consequences inflicted by the criminal justice system on those who had committed crimes.[26] If the left could secure legislative enactment of a determinate and deflated schedule of punishments, they could severely limit the authority of the state and its custodial agents.

The just deserts model had an irresistible appeal to those who believed society was fundamentally inequitable regardless of social legislation. Since the prospects for a fundamental restructuring of society were quixotic at best, a just deserts model would at least ensure that defendants of different social and economic status would be treated equally under the law. This rough-hewn parity among offenders would diminish—though not eradicate—the unfairness with which impoverished offenders are treated.[27]

The Neoconservative Critique of the Rehabilitative Ideal

There were many different voices in the growing chorus of criticism over the intellectual foundations that supported the Liberal Era's emphasis on reha-bilitation and expanded excuses for offenders.[28] Neoconservatives also wrote scathing critiques of this liberal ideology, attacking its empirical assumptions and normative conclusions. Psychoanalyst and social critic Ernest van den Haag argued that the primary "duty [of governments] is to provide legal order in which citizens can be secure in their lives, their liberties, and their pursuit of happiness."[29] The criminal law is viewed by neoconservatives as an essential means of preserving that order by restricting harmful behavior of individuals for the common good. A credible threat of punishment for lawbreakers is essential if that system of restraint is to be effective. Punishment, therefore, is necessary for social order and individual freedom.[30]

Neoconservatives argued the law could not and should not take into account the various social environments from which offenders came and the incentives for crime those environments created. The very purpose of punishing crime is to restrain all who are tempted to commit it.[31] A strictly environmental theory of crime would excuse virtually anyone and punish no one.

This theory about crime and punishment was not based solely on brute instrumentalism; that is, all lawbreakers must be punished if there is to be social order. Neoconservative critics asserted that there is no basis in fact for concluding social environments cause crime. Indeed, most individuals from different racial groups and from deprived socioeconomic backgrounds were law-abiding citizens. Thus, such environments did not necessarily cause criminal behavior. Nor, the theorists contended, would reducing discrimination and poverty necessarily diminish crime.[32]

Furthermore, there was also provocative evidence that the Liberal Era plan of attacking the socioeconomic causes of crime with ambitious government programs designed to improve social conditions or provide special assistance to needy individuals had actually been counterproductive. Writing in 1975, James Wilson noted:

> Early in the decade of the 1960s, this country began the longest sustained period of prosperity since World War II. . . . A great array of programs aimed at the young, the poor, and the deprived were mounted. Though these efforts were not made primarily out of a desire to reduce crime, they were wholly consistent with—indeed, in the aggregate money levels, wildly exceeded—the policy prescription that a thoughtful citizen worried about crime would have offered at the beginning of the decade. . . . Crime soared. It did not just increase a little; it rose at a faster rate than at any time since the 1930s and, in some categories, to higher levels than any experienced in this century.[33]

The perceived failure of the Liberal Era attempt to cure social ills led others to attack the rehabilitative model. This model radiated a symbolic aura that minimized individual responsibility by suggesting the offender was only partially responsible for his actions. Not only neoconservative intellectuals criticized the model; victims' rights advocates strongly resented the claim that the criminal was simply the victim of a faulty personality in need of repair. As Professor Von Hirsch noted: "Part of the inherent definition of a sick person is a presumption of non-culpability for his disease; when we say 'It's not his fault, he is sick,' we are defining the patient as the victim, not the victimizer."[34] This confusion of the victim's role added gratuitous insult to those who had already suffered physical injury at the hands of a violent criminal.

Not surprisingly, vigorous attacks were made on the prevailing wisdom that most criminal offenders were in some sense sick and simply needed rehabilitation or, in a few cases, incapacitation.[35] Neoconservatives now viewed criminals as individuals who opted to prey upon others for their own gratification. President Reagan encapsulated the emerging public consensus that criminals were evil-meaning individuals who chose their behavior: "It's obvious . . . that deprivation and want don't necessarily increase crime. . . . The truth is that today's criminals, for the most part, are not desperate people seeking bread for their families. Crime is the way they've chosen to live."[36]

The retributive theory of punishment espoused by neoconservatives assumed that human beings were responsible moral agents who had the ability to choose between good and evil. Those who chose to do wrong deserved to be punished. Both for intellectual consistency and maximum effectiveness, criminal law doctrine had to be modified to stress this "legal view" of persons. In particular, mental illness had to be limited in excusing individuals from criminal responsibility. Therefore, neoconservative doctrine viewed reform of the insanity defense as essential in order to expand the class of individuals who would be fit subjects for retributive punishment.

The Emergence of the Neoconservative Era

A broad pattern of law reform across the criminal justice system clearly demonstrated the onset of the Neoconservative Era. Most changes were designed to enhance personal safety and strengthen law and order.

From Indeterminate to Determinate Sentencing

Supported by both the political left and right, the focus of the criminal justice system began to shift from rehabilitation to retribution in the name of even-handed justice and community safety. Its primary manifestation was a pronounced shift in sentencing philosophy. No longer would convicted criminals be given indeterminate sentences during which experts in penology and human behavior would decide when they were successfully rehabilitated and sufficiently docile to be released. Now who they were or might become was less important than what they had done. A fixed sentencing scheme would be the hallmark of a just deserts theory of criminal justice.

Since the emergence of the Neoconservative Era, a number of states and the federal government have enacted determinate sentencing statutes of various kinds. By 1983, forty-nine states had adopted mandatory sentencing laws for serious crimes such as drug offenses.[37] These laws *required* the judge to sentence criminals convicted of selected crimes to serve their prison term without the possibility of parole or furlough. Although quite harsh, these mandatory sentencing laws received widespread public support because

> [they] are usually targeted on especially disturbing behaviors, such as large scale drug sales, or especially unattractive characters, such as repeat violent offenders or people who use guns in violent crimes. . . . [m]andatory sentencing laws command support from politicians and the general public.[38]

At least ten other states—California, Colorado, Connecticut, Illinois, Indiana, Maine, Minnesota, New Mexico, North Carolina, and Washington—adopted some type of determinate sentencing. Most of these states have abolished parole and set forth a specific range of prison terms, usually depending on the offense committed and the offender's prior criminal record.[39] Courts have generally sustained these laws even when they generate harsh results. In 1991 the Supreme Court upheld as constitutional a Michigan law that set a mandatory prison term of life imprisonment without possibility of parole for anyone, including a first-time offender, convicted of possession of more than 650 grams of cocaine.[40]

Congress also felt the pressure to adopt determinate sentencing and passed the Sentencing Reform Act of 1984. Under this law a sentencing commission was established to create guideline ranges for use by federal judges in sentencing convicted criminals. Designed to severely limit the discretion of federal judges, the law bases the severity of sentences on the seriousness of the crime and selected offender characteristics. Factors such as a defendant's race, sex, national origin, creed, religion, socioeconomic status, or physical condition (including drug dependence or alcohol abuse) may not be considered in the sentencing decision.[41] By following these guidelines (now in use in all federal courts), it was estimated in 1989 that federal prison populations would increase approximately ten percent as a result of this new law.[42]

These new laws were designed to eliminate the unpredictable and irrational disparity that so pervaded the American criminal justice system. More important, fixed sentences would also ensure that criminals were incapacitated; if nothing else, society could be confident they would not commit more crimes against the innocent while they were in jail.[43]

Constitutional Validation of the Death Penalty

In 1972 the Supreme Court, by the closest of margins, 5 to 4, struck down the death penalty under the Eighth Amendment's prohibition against "cruel and unusual punishment."[44] Each justice wrote an opinion. Though no clear majority reasoning was adopted, this opinion cast serious doubt on whether it was constitutionally permissible to execute persons convicted of serious crimes in the United States.

In 1976, however, the Supreme Court displayed a change of heart. In *Gregg* v. *Georgia*, the Court, in a 7 to 2 vote, held that capital punishment, if imposed with proper standards and procedures appropriately guiding jury discretion, was constitutional.[45] A clear majority on the Supreme Court concluded that contemporary American society did not reject the death penalty as morally inconsistent with the basic value system of democracy and agreed that both retribution and deterrence can be served by capital punishment. This decision halted what had seemed like an inevitable drift toward an ultimate constitutional abolition of the death penalty.[46] In later decisions, the Court held that juveniles who were 16 years old when they committed crimes[47] and mentally retarded criminals[48] could be executed.

The majority in *Gregg* was clearly influenced by the widespread public support for the death penalty demonstrated after the Court had first questioned its constitutional validity in 1972.[49] After the 1972 *Furman* decision was handed down, thirty-five states had enacted new statutes that provided for the death penalty.[50] Congress had also passed legislation authorizing capital punishment for aircraft piracy that resulted in death.[51] Public opinion polls indicated that support for the death penalty declined from 68 percent in 1953 to 42 percent in 1966. After 1966, however, support began to increase.[52] By 1985, public opinion polls showed that 72 percent of the American public favored retaining the death penalty.[53]

Juvenile Justice: From Therapy to Responsibility

This change of values in public policy and criminal law was mirrored in the juvenile justice system. For decades, the primary goal of the juvenile justice system had been rehabilitation because juveniles were believed to lack the requisite emotional maturity to be held fully responsible for their acts.[54] But serious crimes committed by juveniles soared. Between 1960 and 1971 juvenile violent crimes such as homicide, forcible rape, aggravated assault, and robbery grew by 193 percent. During this same period, violent crimes committed by female juveniles swelled by 341 percent.[55]

Not surprisingly, law reform in a number of states during the 1970s shifted from rehabilitative models of juvenile justice to responsibility models.[56] The new wisdom espoused that juveniles be held responsible for their behavior and be informed in no uncertain terms about the harm their actions had caused. Though the system would do its best to provide opportunities for rehabilitation, it no longer operated on the assumption that juveniles simply needed treatment and other assistance to help them become good adults. Not only was such benign therapy suspect as to its efficacy, but by diminishing the sense of responsibility and personal accountability the law hoped to foster in each individual, it might actually be counterproductive.

The Burger and Rehnquist Courts' Counterattack on Constitutional Rights for Criminals

The previous era's liberal court rulings had contributed to the rising tide of public opinion that the courts were too soft on crime.[57] Beginning in the mid-1970s, the Supreme Court, under Chief Justice Warren Burger and later under Chief Justice William Rehnquist, began to whittle away, restrict, or create exceptions to the broad interpretation of constitutional rights it had previously conferred on criminal suspects and defendants during the Warren Era.[58] For example, police no longer had to read a criminal suspect his *Miranda* rights before asking him questions if they believed it would jeopardize public safety.[59] In another decision, unless an attorney was requested, a suspect was not automatically entitled to the presence of counsel during police interrogation unless criminal charges had been formally made.[60] The Court also upheld as constitutional a New York statute that permitted preventive detention of dangerous juveniles charged with a serious crime[61] and a federal law that permitted denial of bail to dangerous defendants.[62]

More recently, the Court, overturning two of its own recent cases, ruled that prosecutors could introduce evidence of a murder victim's character or the effect of a crime on survivors in seeking the death penalty for a convicted murderer. Justice Rehnquist noted that the prior cases preventing use of "victim impact" evidence by the prosecutor had "unfairly weighted the scales" in a capital trial.[63] The Court also cut back drastically on a criminal's right to seek review of his state conviction in the federal courts.[64]

Frequently, the Burger and Rehnquist Supreme Courts based their decisions on an explicit cost-benefit analysis. They began to emphasize the substantial social "costs" of conferring broadly defined constitutional rights on criminal suspects—namely, the release of clearly guilty and dangerous criminals, with a resulting loss in public safety and community confidence in the legal order. The Court was skeptical that the "benefits" perceived by the earlier Court outweighed these substantial costs.[65] With the recent resignations of Justices William Brennan and Thurgood Marshall—the last bastions from the Liberal Era Warren Court—the conservative domination of the Supreme Court appears complete.

It is fair to conclude that, during the twilight of the Liberal Era, the Supreme Court of the United States was slowly but inexorably moving the norms and procedures of the criminal justice system away from a "due process model" toward a "crime-control model."[66] More recently, this shift has accelerated at a rapid pace. The Court, too, was concerned with the increase in crime and saw effective police investigation, prosecution, and punishment as mainstays of the fight for community safety, perhaps influenced by a growing public perception that too many rights given to criminals made society too vulnerable to criminal attack.[67]

Expanding the Right to Use Deadly Force in Self-Defense

A number of states took steps to expand the right of ordinary citizens to defend themselves in a more violent world. Several enacted "make my day" laws.[68] These statutes relaxed the requirements that governed when citizens could use deadly force to defend themselves from home intruders.[69] Prior law generally permitted an occupant to use deadly force in his home only when he could establish that he honestly and reasonably feared the intruder intended to use deadly force or to inflict serious bodily injury on an occupant; generally the intruder had to actually display or at least threaten use of a deadly weapon.[70] These "make my day" laws made no such requirements; now citizens could defend themselves in their homes if they reasonably thought they were in danger. The new laws acknowledged the increased incidence of burglary as well as other crimes of violence committed in the home by strangers and sought to enhance citizens' rights to defend themselves effectively.

A Changing World, Changing Values, and Changes in the Criminal Law

Despite massive attempts to cure the problem of crime, America has become a more dangerous place. The resulting shifts in institutional and political philosophies reflected the dramatic shift in public opinion that demanded a harsher attitude toward criminal offenders. A fearful public insisted that law enforcement be strengthened to provide greater public safety. Offenders were now perceived as people who had intentionally caused harm and deserved punishment; they were no longer perceived as victims of their upbringing who needed special treatment in a therapeutic environment. This perception also included mentally ill offenders.

3

The Fate of the Insane Offender
in the Neoconservative Era

Striking a Match

A few states had already enacted reforms asserting more control over mentally ill offenders, and the social context for a more pervasive change both in mental health law and policy was in place. All that was needed to ignite significant change were dramatic public events.

Dan White and the Twinkie Defense

The first such event was the trial of Dan White, a former member of the San Francisco Board of Supervisors, who on November 27, 1978, shot and killed Mayor George Moscone, the popular mayor of the city, and Harvey Milk, a member of the Board of Supervisors. In his trial on first-degree murder charges, White claimed his crime was not premeditated or committed with malice aforethought because mental problems, aggravated by erratic junk food binges, had clouded his thought processes. The jury found him guilty of two counts of voluntary manslaughter, a much less serious crime than first-degree murder, and White was sentenced to eight years in prison for deliberately killing two men.

The public was outraged by the jury verdict. Quickly dubbed the "Twinkie defense," White's successful use of the diminished capacity defense sparked rioting in San Francisco. It also provided impetus for change in California's criminal law. Though this trial and the subsequent public disturbance received national media attention, the jury verdict was perceived to be primarily due to the idiosyncratic nature of California's law of diminished capacity. It did not necessarily have national implications for law reform, though it probably exacerbated public disillusionment with forensic psychiatry and the judicial system. What was needed to precipitate significant agitation for national changes in the criminal law was an event of national stature.

John Hinckley and the Shooting of President Reagan

On March 30, 1981, John Hinckley shot President Ronald Reagan and Press Secretary James Brady as they were leaving the Washington Hilton Hotel.

That evening the nation watched in hushed horror as the network news played slow-motion tapes of the assassination attempt. Within days it became evident both that John Hinckley suffered from mental illness and that his attempt to murder the president was premeditated, willful, deliberate. The public was confident that this was one criminal who would not escape his just deserts.

A jury verdict of "not guilty by reason of insanity" sent shock waves throughout the country of such magnitude and duration that they may not yet have come to rest. More than any other single event, the *Hinckley* verdict gave overpowering impetus to the pendulum movement to change the insanity defense.[1] One study noted that in the aftermath of the *Hinckley* verdict: "More than half of the states considered abolishing, reforming, or somehow circumventing [the insanity defense]."[2]

Though there had been earlier proposals to enact a more restrictive insanity defense or to abolish it entirely,[3] the *Hinckley* verdict gave public opinion a powerful push. Immediate attacks were launched against the insanity defense in general, and Congress held hearings to consider abolishing or revising the federal insanity defense in particular.

The Insanity Defense on Trial

Undermining Social Order

Before the Hinckley assassination attempt, many skeptics of the insanity defense criticized it on moral grounds, denying that

> there is any categorical difference between "normal" individuals and the "mentally ill" with regard to ability to control behavior by conscious direction. If the law posits free will for normals ... no empirically verified basis exists for selectively embracing a deterministic premise for those offenders regarded as psychologically abnormal.[4]

Consequently, those who criticize adjusting responsibility on the basis of individual characteristics argued that criminal law should not permit offenders the opportunity to avoid conviction and punishment on account of mental illness. In their view, regard for sound moral principles and realistic understanding of human nature argue in favor of abolishing or severely limiting defenses and excuses based on mental illness.

Other critics asserted that the insanity test, by excusing antisocial behavior, undermined personal accountability and weakened the social order. Criminals, whether mentally ill or not, might view themselves as not responsible for their own behavior. Professor Stephen Morse, in his testimony before a congressional committee considering various proposals to abolish or reform the federal insanity defense in the wake of the *Hinckley* verdict, articulated this position succinctly:

> The criminal justice system sets a standard for society and the criteria promulgated for excuses are an important statement that the system makes to society at large. Therefore, the law should say to the public that it has very high standards and expects its citizens to behave.[5]

Abolishing the insanity defense or limiting it severely would "send a message" to everyone, including potential criminals, that society expects them to obey the law. Even those who suffer from mental illness will not be excused if they knowingly break the law.

The insanity defense and the outcomes it produced in high-profile cases had other negative results. The public lost confidence in the criminal justice system and insanity acquittals in particular undermined public respect for that system.[6] Testifying before Congress in support of abolishing the insanity defense, Attorney General William French Smith summed up the prevailing view that public confidence in public safety had waned.

> The administration's proposal to reform the insanity defense is one part of a larger program of legislation that would restore the balance between the forces of law and the forces of lawlessness. In recent years, through actions by the courts and inaction by the Congress, an imbalance has arisen in the scales of justice. The criminal justice system has tilted too decidedly in favor of the rights of criminals and against the rights of society.[7]

Law and order was seen by many as under fierce attack by criminal forces; abolishing the insanity defense would be an essential step in restoring public security.

Doubts About Psychiatric Expertise and Jury Confusion

The reform proposals also clearly reflected a loss of faith in the new science of human behavior—particularly that proffered by forensic psychiatry. Many critics claimed that psychiatrists and other mental health experts did not have any special expertise enabling them to answer the questions the insanity defense required of them. Some claimed psychiatry simply lacked the precision and accuracy of science or medicine; therefore, it could not provide any special knowledge to either judges or juries on the question of mental illness and its impact on human behavior.[8] Others argued that psychiatric testimony was virtually unintelligible to the average juror.[9] Even Judge Bazelon, who had been a pioneer in opening courtroom doors to psychiatric testimony on insanity, had become disillusioned with how psychiatrists examined criminal defendants, and how they subsequently testified about a defendant's insanity at criminal trials.[10] In short, experts may not be expert after all, and, even if they were, they should not be making the legal, social, and moral decisions juries were supposed to make.

Psychiatrists retorted that the law was asking them to give medical opinions on issues that were essentially normative, involving judgments of community morality and values. Dr. Loren Roth, a noted forensic psychiatrist and scholar, argued in his congressional testimony that

> the question that the jury is being asked is a social and a moral question in light of the medical facts provided. Inevitably, by asking psychiatrists to translate these terms, it is bad for the public, bad for the law, and bad for psychiatry. ... [T]here is no way to translate those medical terms into terms that the law or the jurors would understand.[11]

Too Many Moral Mistakes

There was also a strong sense that too many "moral mistakes" were being made based on dubious expertise.[12] Simply put, the public perceived that too many truly guilty defendants were being acquitted by successfully pleading insanity.[13] Indeed, this may have been why the *Hinckley* verdict struck such a raw nerve in the American psyche. In addition, there was a growing suspicion that psychiatrists infused their own subjective moral values into criminal trials, leading to the displacement of juries by experts.[14] Because of its relatively wide scope, the ALI test afforded maximum latitude for those expert witnesses who chose, consciously or unconsciously, to do so.

Jeopardizing Public Safety

Since it was not clear whether the state could retain custody over a criminal defendant found insane by the courts for a long period of time, a verdict of not guilty by reason of insanity (NGRI) did not necessarily mean the individual received treatment for his mental illness. As we shall see later in this chapter, a number of court cases interpreting the Constitution had strongly intimated that an insanity acquittee might have to be released if the person was no longer mentally ill *or* dangerous. Thus, a defendant who had committed a serious crime could be discharged back into the community in a short time. If not presently dangerous, the defendant might be released still suffering from the mental illness that caused his deviant behavior in the first place. Moreover, since psychiatrists often disagreed on diagnosis and treatment, they might well conclude that, even if still dangerous, an offender found not guilty by reason of insanity was not presently mentally ill. Consequently, he would be released without receiving needed treatment.

Associate Attorney General Rudolph Giuliani, representing the Department of Justice, explained in his congressional testimony that, in some federal cases, criminal defendants who had successfully pleaded the insanity defense had to be released immediately—sometimes even before state civil commitment proceedings could be brought against them.[15] And no one could forget that these frightening people were back on the streets once again.[16]

Psychiatry Rethinks the Insanity Defense

In the aftermath of the *Hinckley* verdict, the American Psychiatric Association (APA) appointed a special work group to reconsider the insanity defense. In 1982 the group issued its report, noting that American attitudes toward the insanity defense had changed precipitously since the early 1970s, when President Nixon first proposed its abolition.[17] Despite mounting pressure to abolish the insanity defense, the APA report concluded that its complete elimination was inappropriate if the criminal law were to maintain its moral integrity.[18] Punishing someone who was not in some meaningful way responsible for choosing his or her action would, in effect, deny responsibility for all human action. Seriously ill criminals need treatment and restraint, the report asserted, not mere custodial punishment.

Nonetheless, the APA realized there were powerful forces pushing to modify or abolish the insanity defense, including the American Medical Association.[19] Some sort of political accommodation was necessary if Congress was to retain the insanity defense in federal criminal cases. Taking this into account, the APA recommended a return to a tough version of the *M'Naghten* test. The insanity defense it proposed would excuse only those mentally ill offenders so seriously ill that they were unable to appreciate the wrongfulness of their behavior.[20] Simply put, only a prior *cognitive* impairment and—unlike the *M'Naghten test*, only a "serious" mental illness—would satisfy this new test and excuse a criminal.

In adopting a purely cognitive test for responsibility, the report may have tacitly admitted that psychiatry lacks the expertise to ascertain whether mental illness interfered with a person's ability to control himself. It observed that psychiatrists were generally more confident in their ability to ascertain whether mentally ill defendants understood the wrongfulness of their acts. The report concluded that the "line between an irresistible impulse and an impulse not resisted is probably no sharper than that between twilight and dusk."[21] It also suggested that more reliable evidence exists to substantiate psychiatric expertise in evaluating cognitive impairment than volitional impairment.

Curiously, the APA report suggested that changes in the legal language describing who is legally insane would probably not have much impact on the sorts of mentally ill persons who are acquitted by reason of insanity. According to the report, "most psychotic persons who fail a volitional test for insanity will also fail a cognitive-type test when such a test is applied to their behavior, thus rendering the volitional test superfluous in judging them."[22]

It is clear that organized psychiatry had executed an adroit and necessary tactical retreat. In urging a return to a tough version of the *M'Naghten* test, the APA accepted more narrow constraints on the admissibility and relevance of psychiatric testimony. If psychiatry had developed new knowledge over the last 150 years, one could conclude from this report that it was not necessarily relevant to assessing criminal responsibility.

The Bar Rethinks Insanity

The American Bar Association (ABA) had been reassessing the insanity defense even before the *Hinckley* trial and verdict. Various mental health standards in the criminal justice system had been under development since 1981 and were scheduled for formal consideration before the ABA House of Delegates in 1984. In light of the furor raised by the *Hinckley* acquittal and the various pieces of insanity defense legislation introduced in its wake, the ABA Task Force expedited its work. It considered three basic proposals: retaining the ALI test; recommending adoption of a *M'Naghten* test; or abolishing an independent insanity test.[23]

Like the APA, the ABA Task Force concluded in its initial report that the moral foundation of the criminal law required an insanity defense for the mentally ill.[24] It endorsed the second alternative, recommending the insanity defense excuse only those individuals who were "unable to appreciate the wrongfulness of [their] conduct."[25] In rejecting calls for abolishing the insanity defense, the report concluded: "To label as criminals those so severely disturbed that they could not appreciate the wrongfulness of their acts offends the moral tenets of the criminal law and the moral intuitions of the community."[26] It agreed with the APA report that psychiatrists could not determine with sufficient accuracy if mentally ill offenders had suffered volitional impairment.[27] Consequently, only cognitive impairment—not volitional impairment—should excuse a mentally ill individual from criminal responsibility. The mental health standards finally adopted by the ABA for the criminal justice system confirmed this position.[28]

The American Medical Association Calls for Abolition of the Insanity Defense

Though other professional groups, including the American Psychological Association[29] and the National Commission on the Insanity Defense,[30] also opposed abolition of the insanity defense, the American Medical Association essentially agreed with the Reagan administration and supported abolition. It concluded:

> The conventional insanity defense has long been subjected to intense and well-deserved criticism. It has outlived its principal utility, it invites continuing expansion and corresponding abuse, it requires juries to decide cases on the basis of criteria that defy intelligent resolution in the adversary forum of the courtroom, and it impedes efforts to provide needed treatment to mentally ill offenders. As a result, it inspires public cynicism and contributes to erosion of confidence in the law's rationality, fairness, and efficiency.[31]

The Legal System Responds

The public demand for changes in the criminal law and the empirical and normative critiques of the insanity defense and related defenses based on mental illness were simply too strong to ignore. Congress and state legislatures acted immediately.

In 1984 the U.S. Congress enacted legislation that took the power to decide which version of the insanity defense to adopt away from federal circuit courts of appeal.[32] Congress now mandated that a uniform insanity test be used in all federal prosecutions. The new test was a very tough version of *M'Naghten* and excused a mentally ill criminal defendant only if "at the time of the offense, the defendant, as a result of a *severe* mental illness or defect, was *unable* to appreciate the nature and quality or the wrongfulness of his acts."[33] Thus the insanity test to be used in all federal courts in the country had been changed virtually overnight from the modern approach favored so strongly by most courts, psychiatrists, and academicians during the Liberal Era to a tough version of the insanity test adopted by the British House of Lords in 1843.

Under the new federal test, in order to be acquitted defendants have to prove that, at the time of the crime, they suffered from a "serious mental illness." This might limit the defense to those suffering from psychoses and who, as a result, were out of touch with reality.[34] Defendants also have to prove that they were incapable of knowing what they were doing or that it was wrong. The test assumes that, once individuals know what they are going to do and that it is wrong, they have enough information to refrain from action. The law no longer inquires into the capacity for choice.[35]

What was even more remarkable about the congressional legislation was that it was widely viewed as an attempt to save the insanity defense from complete abolition. Several of the bills introduced in Congress in the aftermath of the *Hinckley* verdict would have simply done away with the insanity defense altogether and limited evidence of mental illness solely to the issue of the defendant's criminal state of mind at the time of the crime.[36] (Because courts during the Liberal Era had permitted defendants to present psychiatric evidence on their criminal state of mind, most legal observers concluded that criminal defendants now had a constitutional right to present such evidence.)[37] The latter approach was favored by the Reagan administration[38] and would have abolished the insanity defense as a special excuse in all federal criminal trials. At the same time, task forces of both the ABA and APA formulated remarkably similar proposals, endorsed by their respective memberships, which called for retaining the insanity defense, but which called for abandoning the ALI version and replacing it with a tough *M'Naghten* test.[39] In all likelihood, it was only because the ABA and the APA reached similar conclusions that the insanity defense was saved at all in federal prosecutions.

State legislatures were not dormant in the aftermath of the *Hinckley* verdict, either. Since that trial, eight states have changed their insanity defenses by jettisoning the ALI test in favor of some form of *M'Naghten* test.[40] California provided a vivid example of the strength and intensity of public opinion. In June 1982—only 4 years after its Supreme Court had finally adopted the ALI test for insanity[41]—California voters by popular initiative rejected that test and enacted a very narrow insanity defense based on *M'Naghten*.[42]

In 1984 Alaska changed its insanity defense, requiring the defendant to prove that he or she was "unable, as a result of mental disease or defect, to appreciate the nature or quality of that conduct."[43] This test is even more restrictive than the almost century-and-a-half-old *M'Naghten* test, since it does not excuse a mentally disturbed person who knew what he was doing but did not know it was wrong.

The policy objectives of adopting a more restrictive insanity test were seen generally as enhancing community safety and aiding the fight against crime. Fewer criminals could now avoid punishment. Mental health professionals would have less impact in securing insanity acquittals in individual criminal prosecutions, and society would send a clear message that individuals would be held accountable for their harmful acts.

For some state legislatures, however, limiting the insanity test was inadequate—nothing short of abolition would be sufficient. The state legislatures of Idaho, Montana, and Utah abolished the insanity defense altogether.[44] In these states all offenders, even those suffering from serious mental illness, are considered responsible for their actions and, if convicted, can be punished. Only in determining the sentence is mental illness considered. The supreme courts of Montana and Idaho held that abolishing the insanity test is constitutional.[45] And the Supreme Court of the United States has clearly indicated it, too, would not strike down legislation that abolished the insanity defense as unconstitutional.[46]

Guilty but Mentally Ill

The neoconservative revolution in criminal justice values did more than precipitate changes in the criteria of the insanity defense that were less favorable to criminal defendants. Some states passed new laws creating a guilty but mentally ill (GBMI) defense. By 1988, thirteen states had enacted a GBMI defense.[47] Many of the states that adopted the verdict evidently did so in response either to a contentious insanity acquittal or to a violent crime committed by a recently released insanity acquittee.[48]

There are two primary versions of this new defense. The first version permits a jury to find a criminal defendant who has raised the defense of insanity as either "not guilty by reason of insanity" (NGRI) or "guilty but mentally ill" (assuming, of course, that it does not convict or acquit the defendant). A defendant found NGRI cannot be sent to a regular prison for confinement; instead, he must be evaluated to see if he is presently mentally ill and dangerous. For as long as he is determined to be mentally ill and dangerous, he may be confined in a psychiatric institution; otherwise, he must be released.

A finding of GBMI, however, has different consequences for the defendant. He may be sent *either* to a psychiatric facility for treatment *or* to a prison for confinement, whichever the state's prison authorities consider more appropriate. Perhaps more important, he may be kept in custody for the maximum prison term authorized for the crime for which he was convicted, even if he is no longer mentally ill. This sentence permits the state both to treat and to punish a mentally ill offender. Eleven states have passed such laws.[49]

The second version of the GBMI defense is even more harsh on mentally ill defendants. In this version, the verdict simply expresses the jury's collective sense that, although the defendant is guilty of committing a crime, he or she was mentally ill at the time. Once convicted and incarcerated, state penal authorities may, but need not, provide the offender with psychiatric treatment either in a prison or in a hospital.[50] The three states that have abolished the insanity test completely have adopted this form of the GBMI defense.[51]

Critiques of the Guilty but Mentally Ill Defense and the
Judicial Response

Both versions of the GBMI defense have been severely criticized. Some critics
object because it asks the jury to consider a fact that is essentially irrelevant
to the question of guilt or innocence: that is, was the person mentally ill?
Indeed, it may not be relevant to anything that has consequences for the
defendant.[52] Mental illness by itself has never excused a person charged with
a crime from criminal responsibility. Only if mental illness affected specific
behavioral capacities—such as cognition or volition—or prevented the defendant from having a criminal state of mind would he be excused or found
not guilty.[53] In using GBMI as an expedient compromise verdict, the jury
may also be invited to avoid the difficult question of whether the defendant
was legally insane or fully responsible.

The jury may also think the verdict has beneficial consequences for the
defendant and may even think it is individualizing justice when it returns a
GBMI defense. Even the 1981 Attorney General's Task Force on Violent
Crime supported the GBMI defense for this reason, believing it would "enable
a jury to be confident that a defendant who is incarcerated as a result of its
verdict will receive treatment for that illness while confined."[54] Yet defendants
receiving GBMI verdicts have no special right to treatment for their mental
illness. They may still be sent to prisons and receive no psychiatric care.[55]
Indeed, a person found GBMI can even be sentenced to death.[56]

The GBMI verdict authorizes the state to treat a convicted defendant *both*
as a criminal and as a mentally ill person. According to its most severe critics,
the GBMI verdict gives the defendant the *worst* of both worlds—a fixed length
of confinement without hope of early release *and* exposure to involuntary
techniques of behavioral change administered by the state.[57] To its supporters,
however, the GBMI verdict is seen as furthering both the rehabilitative ideal
of the Liberal Era by making treatment available and also ensuring community
security by retaining control over a dangerous person while he serves his
sentence.[58]

Virtually every court has rejected constitutional attacks on the GBMI
defense.[59] They have concluded that a jury finding of GBMI may assist the
judge in sentencing or correctional officials in properly placing the defendant.
Courts have also approved legislatures' enactment of the GBMI defense even
if their purpose was to invite juries to reject insanity defenses, thereby *de-
creasing* the frequency of insanity acquittals and preventing abuse of the
insanity defense.[60] After the initial flurry of state legislatures passing such
statutes, few other states have since adopted the GBMI defense.[61]

The Demise of the Diminished Capacity Defense

Not unexpectedly, the diminished capacity defense also attracted critical commentary shortly after its judicial genesis. Although it had attracted a significant
following during the Liberal Era,[62] the defense remained an extremely controversial body of law. Many scholars and judges applauded the attempt by

courts to individualize justice by taking into account an individual's gross abnormalities, particularly if he was not responsible for them.[63] Others argued that the defense was an open invitation to discrimination and abuse of the judicial process by so-called experts.[64] There was clearly much discontent with the doctrine.

Juries had applied the defense in an extremely unpredictable manner. One jury would convict a mentally ill defendant of a reduced charge; another jury would convict a similar defendant who had committed the same crime of the more serious charge. Equal application of the law based on a person's conduct was virtually impossible. In part, the absence of a clearly articulated doctrine and concise definitional terms contributed to random outcomes.[65] Without clear guidance from the law, juries were increasingly making important decisions about the seriousness of the defendant's crimes based on subjective, arbitrary criteria.[66]

Nor did the psychiatrists who testified in each case always agree that mental illness did in fact interfere with the ability of offenders to think about their actions in a way that made them criminal. The very meaning and consistent application of the criminal law were cast in doubt, as experts seemingly redefined statutory terms in idiosyncratic ways, inviting both jury confusion and public contempt. In some cases, psychiatric experts were giving opinions in court that were based on their personal moral judgments and not on their psychiatric expertise.

As noted earlier, negative reaction to Dan White's successful use of this defense was vehement and swift. In June 1982, California voters passed Proposition 8. Among other things, this public referendum abolished the diminished capacity defense.[67] During the same period, courts in other states more frequently rejected defense requests to use a plea of diminished capacity. While some state courts thought the decision to permit this defense should more properly be left to the legislature,[68] other state courts rejected the defense altogether, because they were reluctant to admit psychiatric evidence that might only confuse the jury.[69] At the federal level, the 1984 Insanity Defense Reform Act passed by Congress abolished the diminished capacity defense, although a defendant can still present evidence of mental illness to prove he or she did not act with a criminal state of mind.[70]

Even More Reform

To make the world safer, critics of the insanity defense wanted to do more than simply change the insanity test. They also wanted to change how psychiatrists conducted their forensic evaluations and how the insanity defense was tried in court. Since diagnosing mental illness and assessing its impact on human behavior are very difficult, proving someone was sane when the crime was committed is a formidable task. According to many reformers, the better approach would be to make the defendant prove he was insane. To improve the quality of the forensic evaluation, the critics charged, psychiatrists needed to thoroughly examine defendants without defense lawyers present.

More important, reformers argued that the government needed more authority to confine successful insanity defendants in psychiatric facilities for as long as they were dangerous. Then in 1985 an unexpected but crucial Supreme Court decision in *Jones* v. *United States* was announced and had a profound impact on how long a state could confine a successful insanity defendant.[71] The decision held that a successful insanity defendant could be kept in a psychiatric facility for the rest of his life, even if he had committed only a minor crime. With all these legislative and judicial reforms in place, defenses based on mental illness became not only harder to win but a potential Pyrrhic victory if won at all.

Shifting the Burden of Proof

The burden of proof in a trial sets the standard of certainty the jury must feel before it can reach a verdict. In a criminal trial, the prosecution must prove "beyond a reasonable doubt" that the defendant engaged in conduct with a criminal state of mind in order to convict him, which means the prosecutor generally has the burden of proof. Although this burden is hard to quantify, some scholars have suggested that a jury must be 90 percent certain of guilt before it should convict.[72] As our criminal law now stands, the prosecution finds it difficult to obtain a conviction because the jury must be told to acquit unless it is satisfied "beyond a reasonable doubt" that the defendant is guilty. This procedural rule is based on the general philosophy of our criminal law that it is better that a guilty defendant go free than an innocent person be convicted.

Along with the question of innocence, the law presumes that every person is sane unless there is some evidence to the contrary.[73] Before the Liberal Era, defendants (and not prosecutors) had to prove they were insane by "a preponderance of the evidence" to successfully establish the insanity defense. This rule required the jury to be more than 50 percent certain the defendant was "insane."[74] But each state was free to make the government prove the defendant was sane in order to convict him.

During the Liberal Era, most jurisdictions shifted the burden of proof to the prosecution, making the government prove the defendant was sane. As of 1978, twenty-seven states and all federal courts[75] demanded that, once the defendant introduced some evidence of insanity, the *prosecution* had to prove the defendant was sane "*beyond a reasonable doubt.*" The sheer difficulty of this task helped ensure that mentally ill defendants who were in fact legally insane would not be convicted. In commenting on this burden of proof, White House Counselor Edwin Meese (subsequently attorney general) was reported to have said: "You couldn't even prove the White House staff sane beyond a reasonable doubt. It's a tremendous burden."[76] Most mistakes would be resolved in favor of acquittal and treatment, and against blame and punishment.

The public, however, perceived this rule as increasing the acquittal prospects of many criminal defendants who should be convicted, including those who were not very sick and those simply faking an insanity defense.[77] These "moral mistakes"—acquitting criminals who could have obeyed the law and should be punished—made people angry. Testifying before Congress, Representative Lawrence Coughlin claimed that

> nothing less than the credibility of our federal judicial system is at stake. The Hinckley verdict has sent out the message that any criminal, no matter how brazen or outrageous his crime, can hope to be exonerated if testimony is presented which creates any doubt as to his sanity.[78]

To avoid such outrageous results, many states have passed laws during the Neoconservative Era that require defendants to prove they are legally insane. By 1985, thirty-five states and the District of Columbia made defendants establish their insanity by a "preponderance of the evidence" or to the jury's satisfaction.[79] One state even insisted defendants prove insanity by "clear and convincing evidence," suggesting the jury be 75 percent certain of insanity.[80] Only eleven states still require the government to prove beyond a reasonable doubt that defendants are sane.[81] In hindsight, the Hinckley trial was indeed influential. At least fourteen states shifted the burden of persuasion from the prosecution to the defendant after Hinckley was found not guilty by reason of insanity.[82] Also in response to the *Hinckley* verdict, Congress passed the Insanity Defense Reform act in 1984. This act required all federal insanity defendants to establish the insanity defense "by clear and convincing evidence"—a standard more burdensome than simply "by a preponderance of the evidence."[83] Federal courts of appeal were no longer free to decide this important question for themselves.

The neoconservative judicial and legislative reforms requiring defendants to prove legal insanity were intended to dramatically change the rate of successful insanity acquittals. In federal courts and most states, juries who were unsure were required to find mentally ill offenders guilty. Only defendants who could persuasively establish their legal insanity would avoid punishment. Mistakes would be ones of inclusion, not exclusion. Personal responsibility for one's actions would be restored as the operating premise of the criminal law.

Evaluating the Defendant: Two Competing Models

The Medical Model of Evaluation

Until the early years of the Liberal Era, a medical model of evaluation was used to examine insanity defendants. The government's mental health experts could question defendants extensively before trial. If they were poor, defendants were usually sent to federal or state psychiatric hospitals for up to three months.[84] Since an insanity evaluation was considered a medical exam, the examining psychiatrist enjoyed extensive private access to the defendant. Because psychiatrists relied so much on the clinical interview to form their opinions, the defendant had to cooperate fully and be candid in answering questions.[85]

Good medical practice dictated that others not be present during this evaluation. Confidence and trust between doctor and patient were essential for an accurate diagnosis and assessment. Consequently, the defendant's lawyer and personal psychiatrist could be excluded because their presence could hamper this sensitive diagnostic search for the truth.[86]

Mental health experts could use the defendant's statements made during the exam to form their professional opinion on the patient's legal insanity. They could also repeat these statements, including those describing the defendant's criminal acts, to the judge and jury to explain how they arrived at their opinion. Juries were told to use the defendant's statements only to evaluate the defendant's insanity defense, not to determine if he or she committed the crime.

The Due Process Model of Evaluation

During the Liberal Era, this clinical model of evaluation was challenged after the Supreme Court handed down several important cases limiting the way police could investigate crime. These cases had implications for insanity defendants, suggesting they might be constitutionally entitled to stronger due process protections during their insanity evaluations. The protections, however, would clearly impair the medical model of evaluation which allowed free and open exchange between doctor and patient. For example, a defendant might be entitled to remain silent and to have a lawyer present while mental health professionals asked questions. This led to a sharp clash between the medical model's quest for accurate psychiatric evaluation and the due process model's concern for restricting government interrogation of criminal suspects. What led to the adoption of this new model?

In 1966 the Supreme Court issued its famous decision in *Miranda* v. *Arizona*.[87] The Court decided police officers must give criminal suspects a standard warning informing them of their Fifth Amendment right to remain silent and to request the assistance of a lawyer. Without the warnings, the prosecution could not use the suspect's answers to police questions to prove guilt. Later Supreme Court decisions gave criminal suspects the right to have a lawyer present during line-ups and during any postcharging interrogation.[88] By and large these cases severely limited how the police could interrogate suspects.

In light of these new constitutional cases, many insanity defendants claimed the Fifth Amendment also entitled them to refuse to be examined by a government psychiatrist. They argued that a psychiatric exam was not unlike police interrogation. Some defendants also argued that the Sixth Amendment entitled them to have their attorney and their own mental health expert present during the examination.

The Due Process Model Gains Support

Even though the Warren Court gave criminal suspects many more constitutional rights, most courts decided that insanity defendants who used their own psychiatric expert could also be examined by a government psychiatrist without an attorney present. This would not violate their constitutional rights.[89]

But during the Liberal Era there was, for the first time, significant judicial and scholarly dissent on these issues. A few courts concluded that an insanity defendant could not be forced to cooperate with a government psychiatrist, even though he might call his own psychiatrist at trial. They held that forced cooperation would "destroy the constitutional safeguards against self-incrimination."[90] Some legal scholars shared this view. They argued that requiring the defendant to be examined by a government expert compromised the underlying values of the Fifth Amendment.[91]

During this same period other courts suggested that insanity defendants had a Sixth Amendment right to have their lawyer present during the exam. In *Thornton* v. *Corcoran*,[92] a defendant argued that he was constitutionally entitled to have both his lawyer and an independent psychiatrist attend the senior staff conference at St. Elizabeth's Hospital in Washington, D.C., when the staff would decide if he was legally insane. Without actually deciding the question, Judge Bazelon—over a scathing dissent by Judge Burger (later chief justice of the U.S. Supreme Court)—intimated that the Sixth Amendment might give a defendant these rights "[i]f his right to cross-examine the [government psychiatric] witnesses against him can be protected in no other way."[93]

For a time it seemed as though the Warren Court revolution in constitutional criminal procedure might spill over into pretrial psychiatric examinations of insanity defendants. As one commentator optimistically wrote: "In short, a criminal proceeding is on the threshold of becoming truly accusatorial, not only during trial, but pre-trial as well."[94]

Such optimism was short-lived. These procedural rights, conferred sporadically by individual courts, might help defense counsel prepare better for trial by becoming more knowledgeable about the psychiatric evaluation of a client; however, most judges felt these procedures could also interfere with the truth-seeking function of a criminal trial by limiting the government's ability to gather essential evidence from the defendant. Consequently, these decisions proved to be sunspots of judicial activism.

The Demise of the Due Process Model of Evaluation

Increasingly, courts in the Neoconservative Era have made it quite clear that the broad due process protections afforded criminal suspects during police investigations do not apply to psychiatric evaluations.[95] Perhaps the strongest articulation of that position is the opinion by Judge—now Supreme Court Justice—Scalia in *United States* v. *Byers*.[96] In this case the court clearly held that the Fifth Amendment did not prevent either a compelled psychiatric evaluation or the use of the defendant's statements to rebut the insanity defense.[97] *Byers* also rejected Judge Bazelon's suggestion in *Thornton* that the Sixth Amendment might require a record of the psychiatric interview or the presence of a lawyer. The *Byers* case once again confirmed that government psychiatrists could have private access to an insanity defendant and could conduct a clinical evaluation; lawyers and outside psychiatrists could be excluded, and no record of the exam had to be made. In sum, no special constitutional "rights" applied.

Judge Scalia was quite blunt in stating the court's reason for its decision. Imposing these restraints on the psychiatric exam would have "unreasonable and debilitating effect[s] . . . upon society's conduct of a fair inquiry into the defendant's culpability."[98] If the defendant is to avoid responsibility and punishment by using the insanity defense, then the community is entitled to know the truth about his mental illness and its impact on his behavior. Only the defendant could provide the essential information. Simple necessity required psychiatric exams and full cooperation.

The *Byers* case foreshadowed the mainstream course of judicial thinking that has increasingly dominated the Neoconservative Era. The Burger and Rehnquist Courts, which limited the rights of criminal suspects, have also required insanity defendants to submit to thorough evaluations by government experts.[99] In addition, other courts have required defendants who raise the defense of diminished capacity to submit to psychiatric evaluations by government experts.[100]

Making the Defendant Take Risks in Securing Psychiatric Witnesses

By the twilight of the Liberal Era, courts had, for the first time, allowed the prosecution to call as witnesses psychiatrists initially hired by the defense to evaluate defendants. Consequently, defendants could no longer "shop around" with impunity until they found an expert witness willing to give testimony favorable to their case. They were now at risk. If a defense psychiatrist examined the defendant and concluded he was legally sane, the prosecutor could subpoena him to testify against the defendant.[101] Although some courts did not permit this stratagem,[102] most did, concluding it did not violate the defendant's Sixth Amendment right to effective assistance of counsel.[103]

Limiting the Opinion of Experts

In the recent neoconservative climate, there have been important legal changes aimed at reducing the influence of mental health experts on juries. In the Liberal Era, mental health experts were usually asked to give their opinions on whether mentally ill defendants were legally insane or acted with diminished responsibility. Frequently, experts were asked the same questions juries had to answer in reaching their verdicts of guilty, not guilty, or not guilty by reason of insanity. Many observers concluded it was very difficult, if not impossible, for juries to give different answers to the same questions as those given by noted experts who had special training and knowledge and had personally examined defendants. Once psychiatrists had expressed their professional opinions, many juries would simply defer to them.

In 1984 Congress changed the federal law to preclude experts from expressing an opinion on whether "the defendant did or did not have the mental state or condition constituting an element of the crime charged or of a defense thereto."[104] Consequently, juries in federal criminal cases would now have to decide for themselves whether defendants were legally insane or acted with a criminal state of mind without benefit of an expert opinion on these same questions. California also passed a law in 1982 that prevented a mental health expert from testifying as to whether a criminal defendant had the "capacity to form any mental state."[105] Lawmakers hoped that limiting the scope of expert testimony would prevent expert opinions from dominating juries.

All of these legal changes have had a significant impact on the insanity defense before and during a criminal trial. On the whole, they have helped the government acquire and present evidence to contest insanity claims, thereby limiting the number of successful insanity pleas. Moreover, unless defendants present persuasive evidence of their insanity, juries are now told to consider them sane.

These reforms have shifted the litigation of excuses based on mental illness away from the adversarial, accusatorial mode of a criminal trial and into a more inquisitorial, administrative search for the truth. This shift is intended to limit the number of persons excused from their crimes due to claims of insanity.

What Happens to Successful Insanity Defendants?

To comprehend the monumental shift in theory and practice governing the fate of a person found NGRI, we turn to several Supreme Court decisions of the Liberal Era that severely limited the government's power to control those adjudged NGRI after trial. These decisions were based on a broad interpretation of the Fourteenth Amendment,[106] with particular emphasis on its equal protection and due process clauses.

Equal Protection

Among those cases the Supreme Court decided during the Liberal Era were several in which the state sought to commit mentally ill offenders to therapeutic institutions. The first important case was *Baxstrom* v. *Herold*, decided in 1966.[107] Johnnie Baxstrom was initially convicted of second-degree assault in New York in 1959 and sentenced to prison. After serving about two years, prison officials decided he was mentally ill and transferred him to a mental hospital run by the state department of corrections for the dangerous mentally ill. Since his prison term was about to expire, the state had no authority to keep him in a psychiatric facility beyond his sentence unless it civilly committed him. In a brief judicial proceeding before a judge—without assistance of counsel—Baxstrom was "civilly committed," though he remained in the same prison hospital.

Patients who were civilly committed under New York State's commitment statute at that time were entitled to a jury review of their initial hospitalization and to judicial review of their placement in a psychiatric hospital for the dangerously mentally ill run by the department of corrections. Baxstrom was afforded neither. This denied him important procedural protections generally given civil patients.

The Supreme Court held unanimously that Johnnie Baxstrom had been denied equal protection of the law under the Fourteenth Amendment and ordered New York State to release him or commit him using the same procedures to civilly commit other mentally ill persons.[108] This case was generally understood to require the state either to civilly commit mentally ill offenders at the expiration of their penal sentence or to release them.

Baxstrom has also been interpreted as establishing that a defendant who committed a harmful act some time in the past could not now be automatically considered mentally ill or dangerous. Thus, a past finding of criminal behavior did not remove the need for a separate determination of whether the person could be civilly committed.[109] Consequently, the general understanding during the Liberal Era was that those found NGRI could be hospitalized for a significant period only if they received the same protections given civilly committed mental patients. *Baxstrom* ushered in an era of liberal reforms for defendants found NGRI.[110]

Due Process

Criminal commitment procedures were also affected by Liberal Era court decisions requiring more due process safeguards for criminals and other dangerous people. In 1967 the Supreme Court had an opportunity in *Specht* v. *Patterson*[111] to consider what procedural protections the Constitution requires before a convicted criminal could be sentenced to a possible life term under a state sexual offender statute. Francis Specht was convicted of a sex offense in Colorado, which carried a maximum sentence of ten years. At a special sentencing proceeding under the Colorado Sex Offenders Act, the judge instead sentenced Specht to an indeterminate sentence of "one day to life." The act allowed for indeterminate sentencing if the trial court believed the convicted sex offender "constitutes a threat of bodily harm to members of the public or is an habitual offender and mentally ill."[112] Without granting Specht a judicial hearing, the right to confront the evidence against him, or to present his own evidence with the assistance of counsel, the trial judge decided Specht was mentally ill and a habitual dangerous sex offender. This meant Specht might spend the rest of his life in prison.

In reviewing his case, the Supreme Court held that Specht had been denied procedural due process under the Fourteenth Amendment, and that the government had to provide him with a meaningful hearing before a magnified sentence could be imposed.[113] The holding in *Specht* implied that no one could be committed to a mental institution without an adequate due process hearing on a person's *present* mental illness and dangerousness. *Specht* was an early example of the extensive civil libertarian reforms that were soon to come.

In 1972 the Supreme Court determined in *Jackson* v. *Indiana*[114] that the state could not indefinitely hospitalize a developmentally disabled person charged with a crime if, realistically, the defendant would never stand trial due to his or her disabilities. The Court said equal protection required the government to hospitalize the accused either under the state's civil commit-ment statute or under its feeble-minded statute. Otherwise, the state had no right to hospitalize a charged but unconvicted offender for the rest of his life. This ruling meant Jackson would receive the same legal protections as others civilly committed under these statutes. In keeping with Liberal Era reforms, *Jackson* also strongly suggested that mentally ill persons, even though they may have committed a crime, could only be hospitalized indefinitely under the general civil commitment statute.

Finally, the Supreme Court held in the 1979 case of *Addington* v. *Texas*[115] that involuntary civil commitment constituted a significant loss of personal liberty. Consequently, constitutional due process required the government attorney to affirmatively establish that a person was currently mentally ill and dangerous by "clear and convincing evidence," not merely by a "prepon-derance of the evidence."[116] In *Addington*, the Court said: "Increasing the burden of proof is one way to impress the fact finder with the importance of the decision and thereby perhaps to reduce the chances that inappropriate commitments will be ordered."[117] The implications of *Addington* were that any mistakes should be on the side of freedom.

Constitutional Theory and the Fate of the Successful Insanity Defendant

These Supreme Court cases had been generally understood by a number of courts to impose significant limits on the state's power to confine a successful insanity acquittee after trial. The cases clearly suggested that a person who was found insane at the time of the crime was not necessarily mentally ill or dangerous after the trial. If the offender was not mentally ill *and* dangerous, then he had to be released from custody or else his constitutional rights would be violated.

In the 1968 case of *Bolton* v. *Harris*,[118] Judge Bazelon held that insanity acquittees could be automatically held after trial in a psychiatric facility for a reasonable period of time, but only to determine if they were *presently* mentally ill and dangerous. If they were not, they had to be released. If the government wanted to confine a person found NGRI beyond that brief period, it had to use the ordinary civil commitment statute.[119]

In 1974 the Michigan Supreme Court held in *People* v. *McQuillan* that both equal protection and due process permitted the state to retain successful insanity defendants after trial for a reasonable time to evaluate their present mental state. After that, however, the court reasoned that the state could only commit them to psychiatric hospitals using standards and procedures substantially equivalent to those used in civil commitment, basing its opinion on the *Baxstrom, Bolton, Specht*, and *Jackson* decisions.[120]

Federal courts were also actively reviewing constitutional challenges to state postacquittal commitment laws. In 1982 the Fifth Circuit Court of Appeals in the *Benham* case struck down a Georgia statute that did not provide those found NGRI with legal protection substantially similar to that afforded persons civilly committed.[121] As of 1981, nineteen states committed successful insanity defendants to psychiatric facilities using the same standards they used in civil commitment.[122]

There seemed to be little doubt that a NGRI verdict extinguished the state's authority to hold the NGRI defendant involuntarily for any significant length of time,[123] although he could be retained for a reasonable time after acquittal to evaluate whether he was presently mentally ill and dangerous. However, if he was to be institutionalized, he had to be civilly committed. Constitutional doctrine effectively transferred the mentally ill offender from the criminal justice system to the civil mental health system. And even if equal protection and due process did not require this move within a reasonable time after the verdict, it was surely required at the end of the maximum term for which the offender could have been sentenced if found guilty.[124]

But it had become increasingly difficult during the Liberal Era to civilly commit mentally ill individuals to state hospitals. In many states the standards severely limited state authority, and commitment procedures were quite rigorous (see Chapter 4). Consequently, the prospects for retaining successful insanity defendants in psychiatric facilities either for public safety or for treatment became much weaker. In many states these offenders could, in theory at least, be out on the streets within months of their acquittal and, in some states, on the same day.[125]

Equal protection had effectively linked the disposition of the insanity acquittee to the civil commitment system. For all practical purposes, most successful NGRI defendants could only be kept under state control if they satisfied the criteria for civil commitment. And even when they were hospitalized, many states permitted the mental health specialists treating them to decide when they were fit to be released.

Public Alarm

By and large, the public did not know what happened to successful insanity defendants after their trial. When the nation learned that John Hinckley could be released from St. Elizabeth's Hospital at virtually any time, public awareness changed dramatically. Many were outraged when St. Elizabeth's announced that Hinckley would be released on a weekend pass for Easter, 1985.[126] As the fear of crime increased, public pressure grew to ensure that dangerous criminals—especially mentally ill offenders—were confined longer. At least criminals could not commit more crimes while in custody. Astute legal scholars have noted:

"Rivers of ink, mountains of printer's lead, forests of paper have been expended . . . " [citation omitted] debating "the volitional prong" and "the cognitive prong" of the defense of insanity, and the relative merits of insanity as an affirmative defense, as contrasted to exclusive reliance on the requirements of *mens rea*. These debates are useful . . . but they do not address directly the crucial political issue of whether a person acquitted by reason of insanity is "getting away with" criminal acts and thus escaping punishment. . . . The public's concern is less with ascertaining whether blame properly can be assigned to a particular defendant than with determining when he will get out. And the delusion of law professors and mental disability professionals to the contrary notwithstanding, it is the public's concern that drives the debate on possible changes in the insanity defense.[127]

Although the Supreme Court had never decided what limits, if any, the Constitution put on the state's power to confine successful insanity defendants, the trend was to have these offenders civilly committed. Yet the public wanted these people held in secure institutions for long periods of time. But the law's hands seemed tied. Only an authoritative pronouncement from the Supreme Court of the United States could untie this Gordian knot. Then, early in the Neoconservative Era and after changes in the composition of the Court, the Justices rendered just such a pronouncement.

The *Jones* Case

In 1983 the Supreme Court decided the case of *Jones* v. *United States*.[128] In 1975 Michael Jones went on trial in the District of Columbia on a charge of shoplifting a jacket. The maximum sentence for this misdemeanor was one year in jail. Jones established his insanity by a preponderance of the evidence, and the jury found him NGRI. He was sent to St. Elizabeth's Hospital in Washington, D.C., for evaluation. Eight years later he was still there.

In 1977 Jones sought a court order requiring the hospital to release or civilly commit him. He argued that the government's authority to hold him had expired at the end of the maximum term for which he could have been imprisoned. To civilly commit him, the government would have to prove to a jury by clear and convincing evidence that he was "mentally ill, and because of that illness likely to injure himself or other persons."[129] This language seemed to require the government to prove that, as a result of mental illness, Jones was dangerous to *people*—not simply property—before it could hospitalize him.

In a 5 to 4 decision the Supreme Court concluded that Jones was legally different from civil committees. The jury's finding—by only a preponderance of the evidence—that Jones was legally insane when he shoplifted the jacket established that Jones was both mentally ill and dangerous when he committed his crime. In an incredible stretch of logic, the majority reasoned that, even though Jones had been found mentally fit to stand trial and some six years had elapsed during which Jones was receiving treatment, the law could continue to presume him mentally ill until he could prove he was not. The Court observed that this presumption "comports with common sense."[130]

In addition, the Court noted that the jury had found that Jones had taken the jacket from the store. This antisocial act conclusively established he was—and continued to be—"dangerous," as that term was used in the civil commitment statute. Although acknowledging the paucity of sound research on whether prior dangerous acts were good predictors of future dangerousness, the Court concluded that, given such uncertainty, courts should give special deference to reasonable legislative judgments.[131]

The Court also decided Jones had been afforded sufficient due process at his release hearing, where a judge had found he was still mentally ill and dangerous. The Court cast aside all claims by Jones that he had been denied equal protection because the state did not civilly commit him.[132] Instead, the only question that remained was whether Jones had been provided adequate due process. Since Jones himself had proved at his criminal trial that he had been mentally ill and since the jury had found he had committed a dangerous act, there was little risk that Jones was committed by mistake to a psychiatric facility. Consequently, the Court decided he had received all the process that was due.[133]

Jones is remarkable for a host of reasons. First, powerful arguments can be made that the decision is inconsistent with *Baxstrom, Specht, Jackson*, and *Addington*. Second, it clearly departed from the holdings of most other court decisions, such as *Bolton, McQuillan*, and *Benham*, discussed previously, which had already examined this very same question. Third, it runs contrary to most academic opinion on the constitutionality of a different commitment system for those found NGRI.[134] Fourth, the Court concluded that a jury's finding of past mental illness under a mere preponderance of evidence—not the "clear and convincing" standard required for civil committees in *Addington*—established a presumption of continuing mental illness even though six years had elapsed during which the defendant was supposedly receiving treatment. Fifth, the Court seemed to accept the commission of any crime, regardless of its triviality, as satisfying the concept of dangerousness required for civil commitment.

Notwithstanding these objections, the Supreme Court informed legislatures and courts across the country that, so long as a judge or jury had actually found a defendant insane, the Constitution no longer required successful insanity acquittees to be treated substantially similar to civil committees.[135] Parallel law reform in civil commitment did not have to be applied to defendants NGRI. Nor did the special authority of the state to retain the mentally ill offender terminate at the expiration of his hypothetical maximum prison term.

The clear message of *Jones* was that legislatures could send NGRI defendants to a psychiatric facility for life without giving them the same protections afforded civil patients. Indeed, a petty criminal could be sent to a psychiatric hospital for a lifetime unless he could persuade a judge or jury he was no longer mentally ill or prone to commit minor crimes.[136] This decision essentially cleaned the slate of the older cases. Lawmakers could now write new statutes providing for postconviction hospitalization of NGRI defendants without having to treat them like civil patients.

This uncoupling of insanity acquittees from civil committees created interesting possibilities and permutations in both the criminal justice and mental health systems. *Jones* signaled that legal reform in civil commitment did not have to be applied to those found NGRI. This had the salutary effect of removing the deadweight of politically unpopular NGRI defendants from the backs of those still seeking liberal reform in civil commitment.[137] In this sense, civil committees were the prime beneficiaries of *Jones*, while mentally ill offenders were the clear losers.

The *Jones* case also authorized states and Congress to balance the availability and wording of the insanity defense with special open-ended confinement of those who used it successfully. This decision explicitly addressed society's fear that the insanity defense posed serious, and perhaps unacceptable, risks to community security.

The Supreme Court had made it clear that, although the state could not punish a NGRI defendant,[138] it could confine those who posed any risk of harm to the community, however slight, for an indefinite period—even a lifetime. Although not specifically discussed by the Court, the opinion also tacitly accepted the argument that more stringent commitment and release provisions may be required to deter criminal defendants from faking or abusing the insanity defense.[139]

This assurance of special lifetime "clutchability" by the criminal justice system was seen by some as necessary to preserve the insanity defense itself.[140] Certainly the harmful political consequences of permitting criminals to avoid criminal conviction and punishment would be minimized. Forced hospitalization would at least further some goals served by punishment, including rehabilitation and incapacitation.

From the perspective of mentally ill offenders, however, the *Jones* case had a potentially devastating effect. Jones himself was a stark example. The case effectively authorized the state to retain *any* mentally ill offender who successfully pleads the insanity defense in a psychiatric hospital for a lifetime unless he can establish he is no longer mentally ill or dangerous. This catastrophic possibility is bound to chill mentally ill defendants' use of the insanity defense. In those states that adopt postacquittal schemes like the one described in *Jones*, it is likely that only defendants charged with serious crimes and facing the death penalty or very long prison terms will be inclined to gamble with their futures.

The Impact of *Jones*

The *Jones* case had significant impact on legal reform in the United States.[141] The Insanity Defense Reform Act of 1984 now provides for automatic, indeterminate commitment of successful insanity defendants charged with serious crimes.[142] This provision has been upheld as constitutional.[143] Prior to this act, only NGRI defendants in the District of Columbia were subject to automatic commitment; all other federal acquittees were released unless the state sought to have them civilly committed.[144]

In addition, numerous states have changed their laws providing for automatic, indeterminate commitment of NGRI defendants, making it more difficult for them to be released.[145] After the verdict in the *Hinckley* trial, nine states revised their statutes to permit mandatory commitment of those found NGRI without an adversarial hearing on present mental illness and dangerousness.[146] Other legal reforms have permitted the state to use the insanity acquittal as evidence of present mental illness and dangerousness,[147] to change the criteria to make it easier to commit NGRI offenders,[148] and to transfer authority over NGRI defendants from the probate court to the criminal court.[149] Four states made it more difficult for acquittees to obtain release.[150]

States made other legal changes as well to ensure greater control over NGRI defendants. Some states required that a court instead of the state psychiatric institution authorize the release of those found NGRI.[151] Others required that victims be notified of any impending release of a NGRI defendant,[152] while a number of states and the federal law permit successful acquittees to be released only with stringent supervision.[153] Some states authorize immediate detention without a hearing of NGRI defendants accused of violating their release conditions.[154]

Even before the *Hinckley* verdict and the *Jones* case, Oregon had revised its law to provide much greater control and supervision of insanity acquittees.[155] In 1978 it established an interdisciplinary Psychiatric Security Review Board (PSRB) which has the authority to place insanity acquittees in psychiatric hospitals for as long as they could have been sentenced to jail for their criminal acts. The board can also authorize community placement of insanity acquittees subject to very stringent conditions. Those found NGRI who are released into the community can be told where to live, what medications they must take, and what substances, such as alcohol, they cannot use. They can also be ordered to report for treatment and for frequent evaluations to see if they are complying with the conditions of their release.

This system permits NGRI defendants to live in the community while also providing intensive monitoring of their behavior. Individuals who fail to comply with their release terms, manifest deterioration in their mental health, or appear to have become dangerous can be quickly returned to a psychiatric hospital. This approach to managing insanity acquittees provides more supervision than the parole system provides for convicted criminals released from prison. This is intentional since the primary purpose of this system is to ensure community protection. As researchers Jeffrey Rogers and Joseph Bloom have noted in describing Oregon's innovative approach: "Whatever the reasons, the public demands . . . security. The PSRB mechanism is a promising approach to providing protection without sacrificing other goals of an insanity system."[156] The PSRB model has been adopted by at least one other state in the belief that the board will exercise greater control over insanity acquittees.[157]

A few states during the Neoconservative Era have made changes in their laws that are more lenient to insanity defendants and acquittees, but these are clearly the exception. As one scholar who has studied the legal changes involving the insanity defense immediately before and after the verdict in the *Hinckley* case wrote:

> In summary, there were approximately 105 reforms made during the post-Hinckley time period [from July 1982 to September 1985]. Approximately 85 of those reforms can be identified as reforms reflecting the concern for public safety in that they work to restrict the use of the insanity defense and to exert more control over acquittees. Only about 20 of the reforms can be identified as supporting the due process trend apparent prior to the Hinckley acquittal and the Supreme Court's decision in *Jones*.[158]

Critics of the insanity defense are pleased by these new rulings and statutes. For them, the insanity defense would no longer be a quick, one-way ticket back onto the streets. Instead, it could be a ticket to a lifetime stay in a psychiatric facility. The public has clearly demanded greater protection from offenders who commit serious crimes and who seek to avoid conviction and punishment by using mental illness as an excuse.

4

Involuntary Commitment
in the Liberal Era

Even when the mentally ill have not committed crimes, they are often viewed as "deranged" or "insane" and regarded as irresponsible or dangerous. Although fear of the mentally ill has remained fairly constant over time, strategies for caring for and controlling them have varied significantly. One such strategy has been involuntary commitment to hospitalize individuals against their will.

Commitment laws in America developed in the late nineteenth century. But rates of hospitalization to cure mental illness reached their high water mark in the years just prior to the Liberal Era. During this period, state hospitals overflowed as Americans used mental institutions to "cure" mental illness and to solve other social problems, such as poverty and homelessness.[1] In the Liberal Era, however, powerful political and social forces compelled states to reform their mental health policy and civil commitment laws and to release patients from public psychiatric hospitals. These forces included the discovery of new treatment technology, intensified concern for the disadvantaged, and the emergence of the welfare state. The Liberal Era was a time of incredible change in how society dealt with the mentally ill. It encompassed deinstitutionalization, the enactment of legal safeguards for civil commitment, and the emergence of community mental health care as the treatment model of choice.

A History of Civil Commitment Laws

Through the first half of the nineteenth century, most mentally ill people were cared for by their families or their communities. Others were simply left to fend for themselves. Not until the second half of the nineteenth century did America develop an extensive system of public hospitals for the mentally ill. As more public hospitals and asylums were built, commitment became easier. Anyone—a relative, physician, neighbor, sheriff, or even a passing traveler—might request an individual be committed for an indefinite period. Housewives were committed by their husbands for neglecting their children and housework. Elderly people were committed because they were feeble or senile and lacked family members willing or able to care for them.

Commitment was so easy to accomplish that in the mid-nineteenth century reformers began to demand legal protection against frivolously motivated detentions.[2] More progressive jurisdictions, such as New York and Massachusetts, established methods to protect the personal rights of patients and to prevent inappropriate commitments. Most states, however, provided no such protection. As a practical matter, it was not difficult to hospitalize the mentally ill, and once committed, staff had almost total control over every aspect of patients' lives.

The High Water Mark of Civil Commitment

During the late nineteenth century, social reformers argued that public institutions could cure a variety of social ills, including crime, mental illness, and poverty. Conveniently, incarceration would also rid the community of troublesome or dangerous elements. Persuaded by these powerful claims of expertise and effectiveness, state legislatures authorized money to build new and bigger hospitals to cope with the social, political, and economic problems caused by rapid industrialization, the massive influx of new immigrant groups, · and the burgeoning number of people who had no place to go and no means to support themselves or their families.

The number of inpatients being treated in state mental institutions increased steadily from the day these institutions first opened their doors until the beginning of the Liberal Era. Increases in patient population were particularly dramatic in these institutions between 1900 and 1940, when the hospitalized population grew from 150,000 to approximately 445,000.[3] A significant proportion of that growth occurred as almshouses and local welfare institutions closed their doors and thousands of their residents were transferred to state mental hospitals.

As the number of mental hospitals grew, they were quickly filled to capacity, and new construction plans were put on the drawing board. By 1955, when the number of inpatients in mental hospitals reached their zenith, there were almost 819,000 inpatient episodes in state and county mental hospitals in the United States. (An inpatient episode is the number of patients in residence at the beginning of a twelve-month reporting period, plus the number of patients admitted during the reporting period.)[4] In fact, the number of residents in mental hospitals far exceeded the number of individuals in prisons during that same year.[5]

The Medical Model of Civil Commitment

The steady growth of involuntary hospitalization that peaked in 1955 was greatly influenced by the medical model of commitment. This model (which was pervasive prior to the early 1970s and has in fact reemerged into prominence today) rests on the assumption that some mentally ill persons are unable to control their dangerous behavior or are too cognitively impaired to recognize their need for treatment. Clinicians, armed with special expertise and acting under authority of law, must assume the role of substitute decision-maker and determine what is in the best interests of society and the impaired individual.

Prior to the Liberal Era, the legal system embraced this paternalistic philosophy and gave doctors broad authority to involuntarily hospitalize citizens they considered mentally ill and either dangerous or in need of treatment. Since hospital superintendents and staff had complete discretion to make virtually all decisions for patients, staff could try almost any procedure—no matter how untested—to treat or punish patients. Superintendents were under no legal obligation to review cases for discharge or to justify a decision to retain a patient.[6] Since there were no maximum limits on how long a person could be confined in a psychiatric hospital, many patients languished in these terrifying places. Some were never heard from again. Once committed, more than one-half of all patients stayed in mental hospitals five years or longer. By 1937, the average length of hospital confinement was 9.7 years.[7]

As recently as the early 1970s, only a few states, such as California and Washington, had eliminated indeterminate hospitalization.[8] Proposals to require periodic judicial review of coercive hospitalization were frequently criticized as impractical because reviews would reduce the time already overworked clinicians could spend on treatment while producing few releases.

The medical model of commitment gave treatment personnel broad decision-making authority over the lives of patients living in mental hospitals. Before the 1970s, this meant that psychiatric patients lost most of their civil rights when they walked through the hospital door. This practice was justified on several grounds. Most mentally disabled people were assumed to be incapable of comprehending or exercising their rights. In addition, severely limiting many personal rights was believed necessary for effective treatment. Finally, orderly hospital administration required the restriction of many patient privileges.[9]

Consequently, strict limitations were placed on patient communication with outsiders—including family, attorneys, and physicians. Staff claimed correspondence with people outside the institution could impede recovery or even harm the patient. In many states, censorship of mail was permitted, ostensibly to save the patient from legal liability or subsequent embarrassment.[10] Since involuntary hospitalization was tantamount to a determination of general legal incompetency,[11] patients were deprived of many legal rights not directly related to their commitment—including their right to contract, make wills, write checks, convey property, vote, and obtain or retain professional or other licenses. These provisions were a holdover from early common law practices which presumed mentally ill people lacked the understanding and reasoning to be responsible for themselves and their property. Among other harsh consequences, these restrictions placed substantial limitations on the ability of patients to retain lawyers to challenge their detention and to secure independent medical evaluations that might enhance their prospects for release.

The inhumane conditions in mental hospitals produced by these paternalistic practices are now legend. The situation was made worse as the Great Depression dealt a heavy blow to social welfare institutions—including psychiatric facilities. Already shabby and hazardous conditions became even worse. Buildings deteriorated and appropriations for staff, food, and maintenance were reduced to a bare minimum. Simply keeping inmates alive often became the norm in many public psychiatric hospitals.[12]

In 1949 Albert Deutsch published a powerful indictment of how the mentally ill were treated in America. Describing his own observations of more than two dozen institutions across the United States in 1945, Deutsch presented compelling evidence of incredible overcrowding, chronic shortages of qualified staff, woefully inadequate facilities, a virtual absence of appropriate medical care, staff abuse of patients, and acts of violence among patients. It was a sickening sight:

> In some of the wards there were scenes that rivaled the horrors of the Nazi concentration camps—hundreds of naked mental patients herded into huge, barnlike, filth-infested wards, in all degrees of deterioration, untended and untreated, stripped of every vestige of human decency, many in stages of semi-starvation.[13]

While not all mental patients resided in such horrible facilities, the pitiful conditions and patient abuse in many public institutions were significant spurs to reform in the 1960s and 1970s.

Scathing attacks were launched against American psychiatrists by lay reformers, neurologists, social workers, and even British psychiatrists, deploring the dismal state of American asylums. Superintendents were criticized for being nothing more than bureaucratic administrators of overcrowded, stagnant facilities who gave little thought to helping their patients get better.

Critics argued that staff in these large asylums could not effectively treat patients confined there. Institutional psychiatry, they claimed, had used medicine as a guise for simply warehousing the mentally ill. Psychiatrists, discontented with their role as mere custodians of the institutionalized insane, lost interest in the "incurables" in public institutions and became more concerned with research and treatment of acute mental illness. Freudian psychoanalysis, which was introduced in the 1920s, had gained more and more influence in the ensuing years. This individualized talk therapy now led many psychiatrists to turn their attention to an entirely different, more desirable patient population which was better educated and more affluent.

This shift in focus is demonstrated by the following statistics. In 1948 approximately one-half of all psychiatrists were employed full time in state mental hospitals. By the mid-1960s, however, only 14 percent of psychiatrists were practicing in public and private mental hospitals, with another 6 percent working full time in psychiatric outpatient clinics. Psychiatrists had left the unglamorous custodial chores of asylums behind and gone into private practice.[14]

The Demise of the Asylum:
Deinstitutionalization and the Emergence
of the Welfare State

Humanitarian Values

By the early 1950s, a move was underway in a few progressive states to break down the walls between the hospital and the community. Those states sought to empty their large mental hospitals of patients and place most of them in the community. Many factors led to this new attitude. Exposés of public mental hospitals portrayed them as "snake pits" teeming with neglected, abused inmates.[15] At this time, hospital rolls were still growing at a steady rate. The physical plants of these institutions—many built before the turn of the century—were crumbling, and states did not want to spend the huge sums necessary to sustain these large institutions. Fiscal conservatives applauded deinstitutionalization because it enabled states to shift significant costs for care of the mentally ill to the federal government,[16] which supported the mentally ill released into the community. Increasingly, large state institutions were seen as pathological—actually causing mental illness and prolonging dependency.[17] Psychiatry had lost much of its credibility. The stage was set for a new cycle of reform.

In 1955 a presidential joint commission claimed that the objective of modern treatment for the seriously mentally ill should be to maintain them in the community in order to avoid the debilitating effects of the institution.[18] With community care, it was felt, patients would be rescued from inhumane warehousing in the back wards of "total institutions"[19] and released into a more natural and therapeutic environment.

Community-based treatment became a "therapeutic panacea."[20] Patient abuse and neglect in hospitals would be eliminated, families would be kept intact, and total dependence on a hospital regimen would be replaced. Reformers believed community-based care would also permit earlier treatment of mental illness, thereby preventing the subsequent onset of more serious symptoms.

In any event, the community mental health programs, launched with much fanfare during the Liberal Era, were to help ensure that most mentally ill citizens retained their freedom to live in the mainstream of American life. Individual rights, including liberty and personal choice, became powerful values in public discourse and policy. Restrictive commitment laws were enacted to protect the mentally ill from unnecessary or mistaken government intrusion into their lives and to keep hospital rolls low. In theory, most citizens seemed prepared to accept any small incremental risk that might be posed by the mentally ill living in their midst.

Psychiatric Doubts Regarding Coercive Commitment

There was more than an undercurrent of doubt among psychiatrists concerning involuntary commitment. Some did not think psychiatry could help patients who were sent to psychiatric institutions against their will. Others held strongly to the notion that, even if beneficial to patients, a doctor-patient relationship required patient consent. Coercion had no place in a healing profession. Radical psychiatrists argued that mental illness was not intrinsic to individuals, but simply a label appended by society to characterize someone who behaves oddly. In this view, psychiatry was simply being used as part of an abusive system to repress those who had problems in living.[21] Other critics, consistent with the contemporaneous focus on individual civil rights, claimed that legal regulation of coercive psychiatric care was essential if mistakes and abuses were to be held to a tolerable level.

New Medicine

Another major precursor to the Liberal Era concept of community-based treatment was the introduction in America of antipsychotic drugs for the treatment of psychiatric disorders. Drugs such as chlorpromazine and thorazine became commercially available in the 1950s, at about the same time the number of patients in state mental health facilities reached its peak. Shortly afterward, the patient population began to decline sharply. The correspondence in the timing of the introduction of these drugs and the resulting precipitous decline in hospitalization led the Joint Commission on Mental Illness and Health to conclude that "drugs have revolutionized the management of psychotic patients in American mental hospitals, and probably deserve primary credit for reversal of the upward spiral of the state hospital inpatient load."[22] The widespread use of psychoactive drugs may have been the most significant development in the history of institutional psychiatry.[23]

Drugs appealed to psychiatrists and hospital staff because they were simple to use and paralleled the advances being made in the field of medicine, which the field of psychiatry had so long sought to emulate. Prescribing and administering medication gave psychiatrists and other hospital personnel a clearer identification with medical practice and new confidence in their clinical management skills.

Drugs provided a treatment alternative for the thousands of mentally ill people who had languished in institutions without much promise of discharge, and they were less expensive and more versatile than other treatments. For example, the cost of personnel and machinery for electroconvulsive shock therapy (ECT) far exceeded the cost of drug treatment, which was estimated at the time to cost only pennies a day. Drugs were also portable and therefore available for use in nursing homes, board-and-care facilities, general hospital wards, and for people living at home. The drug revolution created the expectation that even patients with the most intractable mental illnesses would be cured and able to live normal lives.

With the most visible effects of mental illness blunted by drugs, relatives felt a greater sense of confidence that family members could eventually return home. Psychiatrists also felt confident that more patients could return to their homes, as patients would receive needed treatment through a growing number of outpatient facilities. Consequently, many patients were discharged from psychiatric institutions.

Public awareness of and concern for the cruel conditions in mental hospitals as well as the availability of new drugs were certainly influential factors affecting the decline in the hospital census. However, these factors alone were not a sufficient catalyst for the dramatic changes in mental health policy during the late 1960s and 1970s. State hospital populations had begun to decline slowly after 1955. But by the mid-1960s, the decline had quickened noticeably, due to a coalescence of significant social and economic factors.[24]

Emergence of the Welfare State

Federal Responsibility for the Needy

During the Depression and the years following World War II, Americans increasingly believed the federal government should assume some measure of responsibility for citizens who were "down and out" or disabled, if local and state governments would not provide for them. One reason for this was that the tax structure had changed during the postwar period, giving greater income to the federal government and relatively less to state and local governments. Thus the federal government was in a stronger financial position to assist the needy.

Severely mentally ill people who do not have supportive families have always faced formidable difficulties in obtaining the basic necessities of life. Many of these citizens, confined to mental hospitals, could live in the community if they were provided with an economic boost to be self-supporting outside. But not until the rapid expansion of welfare programs in the 1960s did such a financial support system become widely available. Once income supplements and disability payments were in place, many mentally ill persons were financially able to leave the hospital and survive in the community.

Community-based care received immediate bipartisan political support. Not only was it viewed as a progressive social reform, it also provided states with a golden opportunity to shift the ever heavier financial burden of hospital care to the federal government. Both the costs of inpatient care and the demand for hospital beds had accelerated well into the 1950s, severely straining state budgets. Even after the number of lengthy inpatient stays decreased, the Joint Commission on Accreditation of Hospitals and federal inspectors required hospitals to upgrade the quality and conditions of psychiatric inpatient care.[25]

Other developments in hospital care, such as the unionization of hospital labor, contributed to escalating costs of institutionalization. Eight-hour workdays and forty-hour workweeks doubled the unit cost of state hospital care. States had to cope with the demands of inflation, yet at the same time upgrade deteriorating facilities and add staff. Caught in this financial vise, states were only too happy to cancel plans for expensive new hospital construction and thereby realize some of the largest savings from deinstitutionalization.[26]

The financial reports from this period clearly portray the economic choices faced by the states. In 1974 the annual average cost of care for a patient in a public mental hospital was $11,250.[27] By comparison, the cost to the New York State mental health department for a year of outpatient care for one person in 1974 was $531.[28] In 1968 dollars, the state of New York saved an estimated $585 million per year by discharging patients from hospitals and shifting them to other sources of income support.[29]

The fiscal goal for states was clear: Use new federal funding opportunities to reduce the resident population of state mental institutions. States that lagged behind in developing a comprehensive plan to accomplish this would be responsible for paying the ever- accelerating costs of hospital-based care.[30] Although states moved at differing speeds to capture federal dollars, virtually all began to look to federal funding sources to cover the costs of care for the mentally ill.

By 1966, states had an array of funding possibilities to secure federal aid for the mentally ill: Old Age Assistance, Aid to Permanently and Totally Disabled, Old Age and Survivor Insurance, Medicare, and Medicaid. Although virtually none of these programs were designed with the specific intent of supporting the mentally ill, their general value as social welfare programs made them important sources of money for this special group.

The federal Social Security Act of 1935 established the first federal income support program for the elderly, who constituted a large proportion of public mental hospital residents in 1955. In 1960 amendments to this act gave states an opportunity to provide nursing home services and home health care through the subsidies of Medical Assistance to the Aged. Other programs enacted in the 1960s were used as income-maintenance mechanisms, preventing many unnecessary hospital admissions and reducing the number of residents in public institutions.[31] Furthering the trend toward deinstitutionalization was the fact that federal law prevented residents of state institutions and mental hospitals from receiving benefits during their inpatient tenure. Nursing homes, public and private general hospitals, and other health-care providers, however, were eligible for governmental reimbursements. This policy created strong incentives to remove patients from public hospitals and encouraged the significant growth of these alternative providers.

In 1965 the Social Security Act was amended to provide medical care for individuals over age sixty-five who receive income support under other assistance programs and for the poor and medically indigent. Although the target population was much broader than the mentally ill, this new program provided payment for physical and mental health care services for many mentally disabled people.[32]

The federal government was clearly determined to reduce the inpatient census of public mental hospitals. Regulations prohibited payment of Social Security benefits to people residing in them. The 1966 amendments to the Comprehensive Health Planning and Public Health Services Act mandated that 15 percent of state grant allotments for public health services be directed toward community-based mental health services. By 1967, this proportion was increased to 70 percent. The Social Security amendments of 1972 included financial penalties for states that did not control unnecessary use of mental hospitals. Placement in skilled and intermediate-level nursing facilities was thereby encouraged. States could shift to the federal government the significant costs of providing care for the mentally ill in exchange for providing community mental health services and hospital care for those who needed it. Not surprisingly, the discharge of patients from public mental hospitals began to accelerate in the mid-1960s and continued into the 1970s when federal financing was at its zenith.

A Bold New Approach and the Constitutional Sword

The Mental Retardation Facilities and Community Mental Health Center Construction Act of 1963 established, in President John F. Kennedy's words, a "bold new approach" to transfer the treatment and management of the mentally ill to the community. The act formally shifted federal policy away from hospitals and other forms of institutional care toward an extensive system of community-based centers, adapted to the needs of citizens living in the local neighborhoods.

This legislation for community mental health centers created a mechanism for states to build and staff new facilities in the community. The new centers would take the place of large custodial institutions for the chronically, severely mentally ill by developing a local support and treatment system. They would provide inpatient services, outpatient care, emergency treatment, partial hospitalization, and consultation and education, regardless of the patient's ability to pay. In enacting this legislation Congress assumed that, in many cases, mental illness could be prevented by early treatment in the community and that even chronic patterns of severely disturbed behavior could be improved.

Factors other than federal legislation spurred deinstitutionalization. The judicial activism so pronounced in criminal law reform also had sweeping impact on mental institutions, and certain decisions were major victories for civil libertarians. In the late 1960s and early 1970s, activist lawyers representing the mentally ill filed lawsuits in federal courts throughout the country, claiming that a number of state commitment statutes were unconstitutional. These legal challenges were grounded in a fundamental reconceptualization of coercive hospitalization. Attorneys argued that involuntary commitment should not be perceived as a government activity that benefits a distressed person in need. Instead, it should be understood as state action that takes away the fundamental right of liberty protected by the Constitution. Attorneys argued that involuntary commitment also harms the mentally ill in other ways, including stigmatizing them by labeling them as "crazy" and subjecting them to intrusive biotechnology. Courts were particularly willing to rely on new psychiatric learning and to look at how institutions actually worked when resolving major public policy clashes.

Advocates for the mentally ill contended that the U.S. Constitution imposed strict limits on the state's authority to deprive a mentally ill citizen of freedom. The only state interest sufficiently compelling to permit preventive detention was the prevention of harm. Thus, only those mentally disturbed individuals who were dangerous to themselves or others could be hospitalized against their will. Hospital confinement of mentally ill individuals who were not dangerous was simply impermissible under the Constitution.

In addition, these lawyers argued that safeguards had to be built into the system to provide fairness and to prevent mistakes in commitment decisions. Moreover, according to them, the Constitution guaranteed a number of important rights to the mentally ill who were placed in psychiatric institutions against their will. From a lawyer's point of view, only a legal model of commitment, which spelled out more precisely who could be committed and which used many of the individual protections embraced in the criminal justice system, could satisfy constitutional requirements.

These legal challenges met with amazing success. In the 1972 landmark case of *Lessard* v. *Schmidt*,[33] described by psychiatrist Loren Roth as the "bellwether for the decade,"[34] a federal district court struck down Wisconsin's commitment statute as unconstitutional. It held that the statutory authority to commit was impermissibly broad because it permitted the forced hospitalization of mentally ill citizens who were not dangerous. The court also concluded that the state's procedures for commitment and detention were constitutionally inadequate because they failed to require effective and timely notice of why detention was being sought. They also failed to require adequate notice of rights, including the right to a jury trial, and permitted detention longer than forty-eight hours without a judicial hearing. Assistance of counsel was not guaranteed, hearsay evidence was permitted, and so was self-incrimination. The procedures did not require proof beyond a reasonable doubt that a patient was both "mentally ill" and "dangerous," and failed to require those seeking to commit someone to consider less restrictive alternatives than hospitalization.

Other courts, particularly federal district courts, followed suit, striking down state commitment statutes as unconstitutional. These opinions generally concluded that therapeutic commitments violated substantive due process or were unconstitutionally vague.[35] For example, one court declared unconstitutional a state statute that permitted commitment of a mentally ill person "in need of . . . treatment in a mental health facility . . . [who] lacks sufficient insight to make a responsible [treatment] decision." The judge concluded that a person who was not dangerous and who was capable of making a rational treatment decision could not be hospitalized against his or her will. A person was rational, in the judge's view, if he or she could "weigh the costs and benefits of commitment or treatment."[36] The committing authority should review the process of the individual's decision to refuse treatment but not its wisdom.

Many other courts limited involuntary civil commitment to the mentally ill who posed a threat of harm to themselves or others. A few courts went even further, requiring the government to establish dangerousness by evidence of recent overt acts manifesting the individual's imminent dangerousness.[37] Thus, compulsory hospitalization to provide treatment for those mentally ill who needed but refused to seek or accept it was generally considered unconstitutional.

Lessard forced Wisconsin to make sweeping revisions in its commitment law. More important, it raised the distinct possibility that other state statutes might soon be struck down as unconstitutional, based on the substantive and procedural challenges successfully made in this case. State legislatures across the country, spurred by lawsuits and a cascade of decisions similar to *Lessard*, were forced to reevaluate their commitment laws.[38]

As courts prodded legislatures and state agencies into action, laws were passed protecting the civil liberties of the mentally ill. Intricate legal and administrative review procedures were put into place throughout the mental health systems to ensure that even the most disadvantaged clients could assert their newly minted rights. Even the terminology of social control changed so that "patients" became "clients" of the welfare state.

This reevaluation also led to a decided preference for community-based care,[39] and it soon became apparent that deinstitutionalization and the development of short-term community alternatives were not well served by existing laws that made long-term hospitalization too easy.

In 1969 California jettisoned its old civil commitment law because it was vague in defining who might be detained, allowed indeterminate commitment, and failed to provide those about to be committed with adequate legal protection. California's new law was designed to keep hospital populations down by limiting commitments and ensuring that patients stayed out of hospitals after their release. This civil libertarian commitment law would enhance the emerging treatment strategy of choice—community treatment—while also keeping the lid on state expenditures for large psychiatric institutions. Soon after, other states enacted similar commitment laws, including Massachusetts in 1972, Washington in 1973, Virginia in 1974, and New York in 1975.

Commitment laws of the Liberal Era were designed to achieve two broad, constitutionally based objectives. First, they were crafted to minimize the risk of inappropriate deprivation of liberty by defining clearly and narrowly who may and may not be committed against their will. These reforms assumed that far too many people had been committed under prior statutes. Many of these involuntary patients were, in fact, not dangerous and could provide for their basic human needs in the community, with some support. Thus, the substantive criteria for commitment were significantly tightened, thereby limiting the population targeted for involuntary detention. Second, procedural safeguards, patterned after the criminal justice system, were provided to minimize arbitrariness and abuse. These revised commitment laws also gave patients a number of important rights and set forth more precisely how committed patients were to be treated in hospitals.

Substantive Criteria

Many of the reform statutes authorized involuntary commitment of mentally ill persons only if they were considered dangerous to themselves or others.[40]

Hospitalization solely for the benefit of treating the mentally ill was no longer an acceptable goal. Since most mentally ill people are not "dangerous," these statutes reduced coercive hospitalization dramatically. States were assured their hospital populations would decline and that only nondangerous patients would be discharged. For example, California narrowed the substantive criteria for commitment by requiring a showing of probable cause that an individual is mentally ill *and* either a "danger to self, others or gravely disabled." Danger to others was defined as the "imminent" infliction or attempt to inflict substantial bodily harm, including, for example, assault or murder. Danger to self was defined as violence purposefully directed at one's own body, such as suicide or mutilation. "Grave disability" covered persons who, because of mental disorder, were unable to provide food, clothing, and shelter essential for their survival. Only if there was serious risk of loss of life would involuntary commitment be permitted.

These commitment criteria were based solely on behavior. Mental illness by itself did not justify coercive placement in a psychiatric facility; it also had to cause specific types of pronounced irrational and harmful behavior to require coercive government intervention. The criteria focused the decision-maker's attention on conduct that was readily observable and could be easily established in a judicial hearing.

It was thought that by making the criteria for commitment so clearly definable, many errors in clinical judgment would be prevented. Research had shown that psychiatric diagnosis was inaccurate and unreliable and that psychiatrists had no special ability to predict dangerous behavior.[41] The evidence indicated that supposed experts might confine many people who were not actually mentally disturbed or dangerous. But policymakers were willing to permit involuntary commitment based on expert psychiatric testimony only if it was based on observable behavior manifesting those conditions. This would significantly reduce the number of false positives; that is, persons mistakenly committed to psychiatric hospitals as disturbed and dangerous who, in fact, were not. Any risk of uncertainty or error would—in theory at least—be resolved in favor of the individual liberty of the mentally ill patient.[42]

Procedural Safeguards

Under the legal model, new procedures were imposed on the civil commitment system. The commitment process was now seen as an adversarial contest between the state and the individual. Since government action could result in the loss of liberty, the final decision-maker should be neutral and, preferably, a judge. Families and mental health professionals might have useful information to present, but they would no longer make the commitment decision. In many states all requests for involuntary commitment had to be initially evaluated by qualified mental health professionals working for the state. Medical administrators—not families or physicians—would then decide whether or not to seek commitment.

Many state statutes provided prospective patients with extensive procedural protections during the admissions process. In Washington state, for example, a mental health professional could unilaterally detain someone for a maximum of seventy-two hours.[43] A judicial hearing with the assistance of counsel was required if continued detention was to occur. The court could authorize commitment for only fourteen additional days, at which time the patient was eligible to be released or entitled to a jury trial if the state sought to commit him for another ninety days. A patient automatically received a judicial review of his hospitalization every six months. Automatic judicial review, typical in many state statutes, marked the rejection of indeterminate hospital confinement at the discretion of the medical staff. A patient now was much less likely to disappear forever once the door to the mental hospital shut behind him.

Reform statutes also placed limits on the treatment authority of the medical staff. Psychosurgery, such as lobotomies (which destroyed portions of the brain) and electroshock (which induced convulsions), were virtually prohibited in public psychiatric facilities. Legal reforms prevented these intrusive modes of biotechnology from being used on humans against their will.

In sum, civil commitment laws were changed to emphasize the capacity of the mentally ill to make their own choices about their own best interests. New standards and procedures were adopted to limit who could be put into psychiatric institutions against their will. Revolutionary state statutes, like those of California and Washington, clearly indicated a new era of civil commitment had arrived. Individual liberty and civil rights were paramount values. Only the most compelling state interests would justify coercive psychiatric hospitalization. Moreover, the government had to prove its case in an adversary hearing, replete with procedural protections for the citizen-patient.

Minimizing Coercion and Maximizing Liberty

During the Liberal Era a number of courts concluded that a citizen's loss of liberty should be kept to the minimum necessary to accomplish the state's treatment objectives. These courts held that patients must be treated in the least restrictive environment possible. In the 1966 case of *Lake* v. *Cameron*, Judge Bazelon, over a bitter dissent by then Judge Warren Burger, concluded that federal law— and perhaps even the Constitution—required that a patient in the District of Columbia should not be confined to a psychiatric facility if she could live with assistance in the community. Although the state has a legitimate and substantial purpose in involuntary commitment, the court held, the circumstances of confinement must be calculated to avoid unnecessary infringement of the patient's liberty. This principle became known as the "least restrictive alternative" (LRA) and was later extended to require consideration of less restrictive placement within a hospital.[44] This constitutionally based doctrine was incorporated into a number of state commitment statutes.[45]

Least restrictive alternative was used strategically by mental health activists to promote deinstitutionalization in several ways. First, they argued that those mentally ill individuals who could be cared for in the community could not be put into institutions. Second, advocates pushed the doctrine to its logical limits, arguing that the LRA concept also required governments to provide community-based care to ensure that patients were not confined in institutions unnecessarily.[46]

Judicial Activism on Behalf of Institutionalized Mental Patients

In the years before the Liberal Era, courts had virtually ignored what happened to mental patients in public psychiatric hospitals. Most federal judges had refused to hear complaints raised by mental patients about conditions in these facilities. Beginning in the 1970s, however, judges, particularly federal judges, abandoned their traditional "hands-off" policy that had allowed state administrators and psychiatrists virtually unlimited discretion in running state mental health facilities. Courts became much more willing to conclude that mental patients hospitalized against their will had constitutional rights. Judges were now willing to assess whether rights were being violated in these facilities.[47] Bruce Ennis, a well-known civil libertarian lawyer and advocate for the rights of mental patients, noted in 1978 that the rapid pace and extent of

> change in judicial attitudes are astonishing, and to my knowledge, unprecedented. In no other area of the law of which I am aware has so much changed, so fast. In 1973, there were perhaps 30 test cases on the rights of patients pending in the state and federal courts. Today [1978], the number is probably closer to 300, and is growing every day. In 1971, there were perhaps ten lawyers in the entire United States with substantial training or experience in representing mental patients in test-case litigation. Today, there are more than a thousand.[48]

As we saw in the Introduction, the Liberal Era was a time in which courts became involved in major institutional reform through cases brought by activist lawyers on behalf of prisoners, schoolchildren, juveniles, mental patients, and other powerless and disadvantaged groups. Advocates for mental health reform turned to the courts because most legislatures were unwilling or unable to devote a sufficient share of scarce resources to provide minimally adequate conditions in state psychiatric hospitals. Reformers set out to expose these institutions as custodial warehouses with no realistic prospect of affording humane care and treatment. Mental health activists frequently found federal judges willing to take an assertive role in changing institutions and the behavior of state bureaucrats.[49]

Some courts determined that the intolerable and inhumane conditions in state mental hospitals were a denial of patients' constitutional right to treatment.[50] To remedy this unacceptable situation, they issued orders specifying how these hospitals were to be run. Some judicial orders set specific staff-to-patient ratios. They also set limits on how many patients could be confined in certain facilities and required each patient be provided with a modicum of privacy and comfort.[51] Other courts ordered state hospitals to take steps necessary to provide humane and therapeutic environments, to hire adequate numbers of qualified mental health professionals, and to prepare a treatment plan for each individual patient.[52]

"Hands-on" judicial activism was seen by some as essential if state hospitals were to be decent places to treat patients.[53] State mental health administrators were continually looking over their shoulders, wondering if they would be the next defendant in a lawsuit seeking a dramatic infusion of public funds or a wholesale release of patients from their institutions.

One of the earliest and most publicized examples of judicial involvement in the daily operation of mental hospitals was the federal district court's ruling in *Wyatt* v. *Stickney*.[54] The case, filed in 1970 on behalf of involuntarily confined patients seeking to upgrade conditions at a state psychiatric hospital in Alabama, marked what some observers refer to as the beginning of a "revolution" in recognizing the rights of mentally disabled persons.[55]

Wyatt was a prime example of the federal court's willingness to play a hands-on role in the administration of the state hospitals (and eventually the state prisons) in Alabama. After state officials there failed to correct miserable hospital conditions, federal Judge Frank Johnson issued extraordinarily detailed orders specifying constitutional requirements for the hospital's physical plant, its staffing levels, and individualized patient treatment plans.[56] Judge Johnson also considered appointing a special master to be involved in the day-to-day operation of the institution. In declaring and implementing constitutional rights for the incarcerated, courts forced legislatures either to appropriate additional funding to improve conditions in state psychiatric institutions or to release many of their patients.

Initially, the American Psychiatric Association (APA) resisted judicial pronouncements enforcing a right to treatment for the mentally ill. In the association's view, "the definition of treatment and the appraisal of its adequacy are matters for medical determination."[57] In 1977, however, the APA reconsidered its position and concluded that it "now joins and endorses those efforts toward this goal by stating its explicit support of this right."[58] The realization that the judicially crafted right to treatment meant that more resources would be made available to psychiatric facilities may well have influenced this change of heart.

Courts were not satisfied with simply seeing to it that public mental hospitals were no longer custodial warehouses. Increasingly, they also decided to ensure that committed patients did not lose all their rights even though hospitalized. Judges determined that patients put into hospitals retained the right to form their own thoughts and to make their own decisions. Moreover, hospitalization by itself did not establish a patient's incompetency. Thus, except in emergencies, mentally ill individuals could still make their own treatment decisions based on informed consent, unless they were judged to be incompetent.

Many courts held that civilly committed patients have a right to refuse treatment, including the right not to take psychotropic medication.[59] Emerging evidence that drugs are intrusive and can have serious irreversible and even fatal side effects[60] made courts more receptive to arguments that patients had a constitutional right to refuse prescribed drugs. There was still a question of what to do with those patients judged incompetent to make treatment decisions. In light of evidence that staff members in many public hospitals prescribed large doses of drugs either to punish patients or to make them easier to handle, a number of courts held that a judge, not the medical staff, should decide for an incompetent patient, using the jurist's own "substituted judgment" as to what he or she thought the patient might decide if competent.[61]

Courts actively enunciated and protected other patient rights, including the right to receive minimum wages for work; to have visitors; to receive and send uncensored mail; to have access to books, TV, radio, and telephone; and to practice their religion.[62]

The Supreme Court and Civil Commitment

Given the flurry of lawsuits in lower federal courts, it was only a question of time before the Supreme Court would review some of them. The first non-criminal civil commitment case to reach the high court was the 1974 *O'Connor v. Donaldson* case.[63]

Kenneth Donaldson, initially diagnosed as a paranoid schizophrenic, was civilly committed to the Florida State Hospital in Chattahootchee, Florida, in 1957 at the request of his parents. No one ever alleged Donaldson was dangerous; he was committed solely for treatment. During his entire time in confinement, Donaldson was kept in wards with dangerous criminal patients and given virtually no treatment of any kind. Dr. O'Connor, the hospital superintendent, arbitrarily prevented Donaldson from being released either to the custody of a reputable community group in Minneapolis, which ran halfway houses for mental patients, or to a college friend. As a result, Donaldson, who could readily have been placed in the community, was capriciously confined in a crowded mental hospital where he languished for almost fifteen years, receiving virtually no treatment.[64]

Donaldson launched a successful civil rights lawsuit and recovered damages totaling $48,500 from Dr. O'Connor. In deciding the case, the Court explored the constitutional limits on state authority to hospitalize the mentally ill. The majority concluded that a finding of "mental illness" alone does not justify confining people against their will and keeping them there indefinitely.[65] The Court found that "a State cannot constitutionally confine . . . a nondangerous individual who is capable of surviving safely in freedom by himself or with the help of willing and responsible family and friends."[66]

In addition, the Court indicated that

> the mere presence of mental illness does not disqualify a person from preferring his home to the comforts of an institution. Moreover, while the State may arguably confine a person to save him from harm, incarceration is rarely if

ever a necessary condition for raising the living standards of those capable of surviving safely in freedom, on their own or with the help of family or friends.[67]

The majority also made it clear what it was *not* deciding:

Specifically, there is no reason now to decide whether mentally ill persons dangerous to themselves or to others have a right to treatment upon compulsory confinement by the State, or whether the State may compulsorily confine a nondangerous, mentally ill person for the purpose of treatment.[68]

Despite this disclaimer, the Court's general and wide-ranging discussion on the limits of state commitment power was very influential in the subsequent development of civil commitment law. Lawyers and psychiatrists generally agreed that *Donaldson* precluded committing a mentally ill person capable of living in the community simply to make him more comfortable. Although much less certain, many thought the decision strongly implied that the mentally ill could only be committed to prevent them from harming themselves or others. If this reading proved correct, the case would effectively prevent involuntary hospitalization solely for treatment. Due to its broad but imprecise language, *Donaldson* reinforced the Liberal Era trend toward severely limiting the government's authority to hospitalize only those mentally ill who are dangerous.

In summary, courts, including the Supreme Court, pushed states to reform outdated civil commitment laws and to enact statutory provisions that would prevent mental health authorities from slipping back into the commitment patterns of the past. Here the judiciary played a pivotal role in establishing commitment criteria and procedures that would limit who might be detained in institutions, and in dramatically changing the physical and social environment within these institutions.

The Pendulum Reaches Its Apex

During the Liberal Era, social policy posed a fundamental challenge to the prevailing wisdom that psychiatrists should be allowed unfettered discretion to coerce mentally ill citizens into psychiatric hospitals for their own good. State action was now seen as a deprivation of constitutionally protected liberty that could only be undertaken for limited purposes and with strict procedural safeguards. Pervasive legal regulation of both commitment and treatment was essential if civil liberties were to be protected and unacceptable mistakes and abuse eliminated.

By the end of the Liberal Era, approximately twenty-five states had limited involuntary civil commitment to those mentally ill persons considered dangerous.[69] Coercive hospitalization was not permitted for the sole purpose of treatment. This narrowing of state commitment authority, together with the stringent procedural protections adopted by most states, resulted in a precipitous decline in state hospital inpatient populations.

To a few skeptics, however, the civil commitment reforms enacted during the Liberal Era were seen as both antitherapeutic and antipsychiatry.[70] In any event, government paternalism was significantly diminished for the mentally ill.

Most psychiatrists, however, were confident that active treatment in a community made more sense than long-term confinement in a hospital. These psychiatrists implicitly promised great benefits to patients and to society if only society would provide sufficient resources to treat the mentally ill voluntarily in the community. But this view of community care as a therapeutic panacea that also safeguarded a patient's civil liberties was not universally shared. Some psychiatrists and lawyers argued that many mentally ill patients simply lacked the capacity to recognize and pursue their own best interests. Coercion was essential if true freedom, psychic as well as physical, was to be achieved. Others warned that poor planning and inadequate funding for community care made it a recipe for disaster.[71]

During this period of deinstitutionalization and enactment of legal safeguards, a changing economic picture in the United States was also taking shape. By the late 1970s, programs for the mentally ill were heavily dependent on disappearing federal dollars and on shrinking revenues from states whose economies were falling on hard times. What was to become of the hundreds of thousands of mentally ill citizens who could no longer be put forcibly into public psychiatric facilities or cared for in the community? In short, a new social reality was emerging that would generate intense pressure to solve this second generation of problems.

5

Involuntary Commitment in the Neoconservative Era

David Rothman has warned that the "reforms of one generation become the scandals of the next."[1] History shows that society applauds those who design reforms and then applauds later reformers who expose the emerging failures of the reformed system. This cycle then repeats itself. For example, critics who exposed the state hospital system in the 1950s were heroes. By the end of the 1970s, when the failures of deinstitutionalization had become all too apparent, then critics from all corners blamed those erstwhile reformers and their reforms for an astounding array of contemporary social problems.

Deinstitutionalization and libertarian commitment laws had achieved their primary goals of dramatically reducing the number of patients in state hospitals and maximizing individual freedom. Indeed, the number of inpatient episodes in state mental hospitals had plummeted and the number of outpatient visits had mushroomed.[2]

But deinstitutionalization was not a therapeutic miracle. It spawned new problems. Many chronically and severely mentally ill people were abandoned to "psychiatric ghettos" in inner cities where they lived chaotic lives of poverty and abuse.[3] Others ended up in jails or living on the streets. Deinstitutionalization became synonymous with criminalization, homelessness, and public fear. For the vast majority of the seriously mentally ill, treatment and support were unavailable.

By the late 1970s, a growing chorus of voices urged a new generation of legal reforms to ease the restrictions on involuntary hospitalization in order to provide essential treatment. Frustrated by their inability to hospitalize persons they believed would benefit from inpatient care, a new cast of reformers sought to make civil commitment easier. Families joined forces with organized psychiatry to lobby for expanded civil commitment laws. These groups also sought to increase the woefully inadequate levels of public funding for mental health.

A Litany of Disappointments

Throughout the course of social change, the initial optimism that accompanies major mental health reforms soon gives way to pessimism and therapeutic nihilism because of the increasing number of chronic patients whose condition only gets worse. Although many innovations have proven successful with mildly acute mental health problems, virtually none have fulfilled their initial promise of improving care for the chronically mentally ill or preventing mental illness altogether.[4]

Deinstitutionalization is now being described by family members, professionals, and the media as a policy that has failed both the mentally ill and society at large.[5] The primary evidence of this failure is based on the criminalization of the mentally ill, the creation of psychiatric ghettos, the alarming rise of homelessness in America, the disappearance of a "safe haven" for the seriously ill, and the fear their presence generates in communities. There may also be hidden agendas that are at the heart of efforts to relax strict criteria for involuntary commitment, including removing social misfits from the streets, providing respite for families that have exhausted emotional and financial resources caring for disturbed loved ones, and putting psychiatrists back in control of the commitment process.

Criminalization of the Mentally Ill

Vocal critics blamed deinstitutionalization and restrictive civil commitment laws for channeling the mentally ill into the jails and prisons of America. As early as 1972, Professor Jacob Abramson claimed that, in the year following implementation of California's restrictive civil commitment law (Lanterman-Petris-Short Act), the number of arrests in California increased significantly and the number of people pleading incompetent to stand trial doubled.[6] His report was followed by further research and speculation that civil libertarian commitment laws resulted in more mentally ill persons being arrested for and convicted of crimes.[7] The extent of this "criminalization" is still hotly debated in the research literature.[8] But by the end of the Liberal Era, there is no doubt that the mentally ill were increasingly coming into contact with the criminal justice system.

This is not surprising. Police have always served as a frequent resource for mentally ill people.[9] When a disturbance involved a mentally ill person, police officers would usually try to find a solution to the problem without making an arrest or a trip to a hospital emergency room.[10] Restrictive commitment laws, however, limited police authority, making it difficult, if not impossible, for them to hospitalize people with bizarre behavior. Police could arrest these people, take them to jails, and press charges if necessary, but could not forcibly place them in mental health facilities. To use one observer's words, "jails and prisons [became] the new long-term repository for mentally ill individuals who, in a previous era, would have been institutionalized within a psychiatric facility."[11]

But even restrictive commitment laws permitted detention of dangerous individuals. Why, then, did deinstitutionalization increase the number of mentally ill the criminal justice system had to deal with? First, as the population grew, the sheer number of mentally ill people living in communities rose;

police contact with them was bound to increase. Second, as hospital placement became less available to families and doctors, police were called in to settle more disputes. Because of its responsibility to respond to community complaints and to keep the peace, the criminal justice system became, in effect, the "poor man's psychiatrist."[12]

Third, the substantive criteria of most Liberal Era commitment laws limited involuntary hospitalization to individuals who were dangerous to themselves or others—not those merely exhibiting aggressive or frightening behavior. Therefore, communities had to cope with more borderline individuals who, in the past, would have been committed but now were—in theory—to receive treatment in the community. Many private clinicians and community mental health centers, however, refused to take patients who were hard to manage or who had no money or insurance to pay their bills. Some hospitals would not take persons who had criminal charges pending.[13] Once again, the criminal justice system found itself the system that "couldn't say no."[14]

The absence of mental health resources within jails and prisons meant that many mentally ill individuals, now confined with criminals, would be punished instead of treated. The traumatizing effects of punishment and moral blame were heaped on this unfortunate population. Many became labeled as both mad *and* bad.

Psychiatric Ghettos and Uncaring Nursing Homes

Because detention in public hospitals was harder to accomplish, many mentally ill people resided in dilapidated welfare hotels, boarding houses, and adult homes, where social and psychological decay was rampant.[15] Without financial or social resources to improve their lot, many previous residents of state mental hospitals (or those who might have been confined in earlier years) drifted to urban settings that were, in many cases, as squalid as asylums of the past. Professors U. Aviram and Steven Segal coined the term "psychiatric ghettos" to describe the situation.[16]

In addition, mentally ill people were increasingly being admitted on a voluntary basis to general hospitals, private psychiatric hospitals, nursing homes, and other facilities. Since these patients were not involuntarily committed to these institutions, there was minimal legal protection for their special needs and virtually no monitoring of rights or the conditions in which these patients lived. (Ironically, many of these placements were not truly voluntary. Patients were often threatened with involuntary hospitalization if they refused; others simply did not or could not object to placement in these alternative institutions.)[17]

Although the total number of inpatient episodes in county and state mental hospitals had declined significantly between 1965 and 1981, the total number of inpatient episodes with psychiatric diagnoses in all other health facilities had increased dramatically.[18] Some critics charged unscrupulous nursing home operators maximized their profits by providing inadequate services to residents or, even worse, by abusing them or drugging them into passivity. In short, the pathway for a significant number of chronically ill people led from the state hospital to squalid housing or uncaring nursing homes.

The Homeless Mentally Ill

The growing problem of the homeless became one of the most tragic and compelling social dramas of the 1980s. Estimates of the number of homeless ranged from 250,000 to two million on any given day.[19] The 1990 census reported that about 230,000 people were homeless in America; 180,000 of these were counted in shelters for the homeless and 50,000 were counted at selected street sites. Most thoughtful observers, including even the Census Bureau, consider these figures to be too low. Even conservative estimates put the number of homeless between 500,000 and 600,000.[20]

Although the exact numbers are in dispute, by the mid-1980s, the number of homeless had increased, their average age was dropping, the proportion who were mentally ill was increasing, and the percentage who were women had skyrocketed.[21] By 1985, the United States had a larger and more diverse group of citizens needing food, shelter and clothing than at any time since the Great Depression.[22] The growing visibility of alcoholics, drug addicts, runaways, the seriously mentally ill, unemployed families, and single people "down on their luck" fostered a full-blown public image of a psychiatric ghetto in the inner city.

People looked for causes and one readily presented itself. Deinstitutionalization was described in most reports as *the* major culprit in creating homelessness.[23] The media and some professional groups charged that restrictive commitment statutes were also a major cause.[24] Such attitudes were bolstered by some early, poorly calculated estimates of the proportion of homeless who were mentally ill, which put the figure as high as ninety percent.[25] These inaccurate estimates reinforced a natural inclination to assume that a situation so frightening and unfortunate as homelessness must be caused by mental illness rather than by socioeconomic factors over which people had little control. This belief gained further credence when, in 1988, presidential candidate George Bush made a campaign statement claiming that virtually all people who are homeless are mentally ill. A few commentators even claimed that, because homelessness put people at such high risk for psychiatric problems, there was little reason to distinguish between the homeless mentally ill and the homeless population at large.[26] Thus, the assumption that mental illness could cause homelessness seemed to make sense.

But this answer was far too simple. As more accurate information became available, it became apparent that increased homelessness in America was due primarily to economic and political factors, including loss of jobs and resulting unemployment, the decline in real wages, problems paying rent, the accelerated formation of single parent households, family conflict, rapid increases in divorce, sharp declines in the affordability of housing, and regional population shifts.[27] Of course, the higher number of people experiencing mental illness and engaging in substance abuse also made the problem worse.

Although credible information on the characteristics of the homeless is very hard to acquire, the most methodologically sound estimates fix the proportion of homeless who are mentally ill at about one-third.[28]

The disappearance of single room occupancy hotels dealt a particularly heavy blow to impoverished, mentally ill residents who needed a bed and an address where benefit checks could be mailed.[29] The dilapidated buildings where poor, mentally ill people had been able to find shelter and a modicum of life support were reclaimed by the more affluent who wished to take advantage of low-cost investments. The gentrification of inner cities dried up the supply of hotel rooms that could be rented from the small Social Security Insurance checks that came to the mentally disabled. When these low-rent "flophouses" gave way to the wrecking ball, the last fragile grip of their residents on stable living arrangements was demolished.[30] As the stock of low-income housing in American cities shrunk, the mentally ill were at greater risk for homelessness because they were poor competitors in an increasingly competitive housing market.[31]

Although millions of Americans were living chaotic lives of poverty and abuse on the streets, fewer social services were available to provide them with assistance. Great Society programs either vanished or were severely eviscerated. The number of shelters, food banks, and community treatment facilities still in existence were no match for the growing number of clients who needed them.

Not all critics blamed the policy of deinstitutionalization for the phenomenon of homelessness. An American Psychiatric Association Task Force concluded that homelessness among the mentally ill was not caused by deinstitutionalization per se but by failure in the way the policy was carried out.[32] While community treatment was a laudable ideal, community resources never replaced the functions of hospitals—especially for chronically ill patients.

The APA report on the homeless concluded that most chronically mentally ill people had become homeless because they were poor at coping with life on their own. Many drifted away from sheltered homes because they wanted more freedom to engage in restricted behaviors such as drinking or taking drugs. Once on their own, they stopped taking prescribed medications, lost touch with public welfare systems, and went without medical and psychiatric care.

As policymakers struggle with the problems of the homeless, the sheer number of seriously mentally ill citizens visible in communities continues to increase. Professor David Mechanic attributes the growth in the number of chronic mentally ill in the country to demographic changes in the population. The extent of most serious mental illness depends both on the incidence of the disorder and the size of the population at risk. As the number of young adults (who are at higher risk for schizophrenia, depression, and other disorders) increases, one should expect a greater number of seriously mentally ill citizens.[33] Many of the problems evident now were predicted years ago by Professor Morton Kramer, based on projecting demographic trends.[34] As

Mechanic has noted: "Unless the society was prepared to maintain a massive public hospital system, or alternative institutions, for new occurrences of mental illness, the problem would have been evident in communities regardless of what we did."[35]

Today many young schizophrenics and other seriously impaired individuals live on the streets or mingle with those who do. They are aware of their civil liberties and have no intention of seeking or receiving treatment from psychiatrists. Although they might benefit from treatment in the community, existing programs have little chance of attracting and holding these individuals. Mechanic argues that

> blaming deinstitutionalization for these problems is wrongheaded since most of these patients are not appropriate clients for long- term institutional care. ... [T]he vast majority of seriously mentally ill prefer deprivations in the community to coercion, however well-intentioned.[36]

The Benefits of Asylum

Many mentally ill people who were released into the community needed housing, work, therapy, medication management, rehabilitation, social services, and, especially, case management. Not surprisingly, many former patients failed to obtain these services or to provide themselves with the essential food, clothing, and shelter hospitals had routinely provided. To some observers, deinstitutionalization failed because there were simply too many opportunities for the mentally ill to "fall through the cracks." It was a short step for critics to conclude that the social costs of deinstitutionalization were too high and that involuntary hospitalization had to be more readily available for patients needing refuge from the pressures of ordinary life.[37]

For all its failures, the mental hospital had supplied mentally ill patients with shelter, food, clothing, and asylum—all coordinated under one roof.[38] Patients received medical care, monitoring, a social network, needed support and structure, and—perhaps—advocacy to get goods and services.[39] Institutions thereby provided an indispensable function missing in all community-based programs: *total responsibility* for continued patient care. With the hindsight of thirty years' experience of deinstitutionalization, it is now obvious that institutions have the *opportunity* built in for supplying this highly prized clinical commodity. To ensure continuity of care outside hospitals, the community has to become their functional equivalent by making available these same essential services. But without the coercive structure of the hospital, there is no way to assure that basic human services will be provided, through either formal or informal means.

Since many mentally ill people have serious psychiatric problems that are likely to disable them throughout their entire lifetime, the APA Task Force concluded there must be a place for seriously ill people to receive sanctuary and asylum. For some patients, a hospital would serve this purpose. The APA report implied that most committed patients only need crisis intervention on a short-term basis; however, a small number would need long-term asylum either in a hospital or in a locked ward.[40] The Task Force on the homeless mentally ill recommended that involuntary civil commitment laws should be changed to allow hospitalization for those in need of either short-term or long-term treatment.[41] In sum, the APA concluded that more coercion was needed to compel the mentally ill to enter and stay in psychiatric facilities.[42]

Hidden Agendas? The Disturbed and the Disturbing

The criminal justice system was unable to control the behavior of all those mentally ill individuals who no longer met the Liberal Era's statutory commitment requirements. And, not surprisingly, the disruptive, bizarre, and aggressive behavior of these individuals did not go away. Many mentally ill people were homeless but could not be committed. Although hesitant to admit it, most people were upset by seeing individuals on their streets who appeared to be helpless and yet demonstrated frightening behavior. By the end of the Liberal Era, both the public's toleration for disturbing behavior and the resources available to cope with these troublesome individuals had diminished.

Many families had made endless, vain attempts to obtain mental health services for their disturbed loved ones. Virtually all had experienced the crushing frustration of coming up empty-handed. Even families with unlimited financial resources realized that "cure" is, at best, disappointing or, at worst, illusory. Because of both psychological "burn-out" and diminishing financial resources, many families sought involuntary hospitalization as a means of transferring to the state both fiscal and therapeutic responsibility for their mentally disabled family member.[43] Families had quickly become disillusioned with the Liberal Era's commitment reforms and the false promise of community treatment, since these "reforms" only seemed to make matters worse.

Although many family members would disagree, there is an inherent conflict between the wishes of an uncooperative mentally ill person and his or her family. Few people want to be confined in mental hospitals, coerced into treatment programs, or pressured to take powerful medications. Although it may be a heartbreaking step for families to take, commitment removes the troublesome and sometimes frightening member from the family home, thereby providing at least a temporary respite from stress, responsibility, and fear. Yet many families have not acknowledged that this need is served by easy commitment. Given both their concern that loved ones are being denied decent care and treatment and their own self-interest in having some respite, it is little wonder family groups have been the most vocal advocates of policies that would make involuntary hospitalization more accessible.

The minority of those psychiatrists who treat severely mentally ill people also want to make involuntary therapeutic hospitalization easier to provide vital treatment to those who need it but refuse it because they are sick. During the Liberal Era, psychiatrists claimed that laws limiting coercive hospitalization only to the dangerous mentally ill had turned them into jailers instead of healers. Consequently, they were unable to help those most likely to benefit from treatment.

The battle that ensued between psychiatrists and lawyers was often couched in terms of professional status and control. Psychiatrist Loren Roth claimed that "a large number of patients have been kidnapped by a small number of lawyers in order to make a philosophical point on their own behalf."[44] On the other side of the ramparts, lawyer Leonard Rubenstein suspected that psychiatrists, in seeking more control over commitment, were out to protect their own guild interests.[45] Thus, debates over the scope and shape of involuntary commitment have been animated by powerful professional groups seeking authority and status.

The visibility and increasing number of severely symptomatic deviants in their midst pushed community members to their limits of tolerance during the Liberal Era. Fear of the mentally ill increased, and social preferences shifted away from individual liberty and toward state coercion. Because the public perceives protection from the mentally ill as the primary role of the hospital,[46] increased use of involuntary hospitalization seemed the safest course for regaining control over out-of-control people.

Most communities do not understand, sympathize with, or want seriously disturbed mental patients in their midst. Society will go to elaborate lengths to exclude persons whose behavior deviates from prevailing norms.[47] The social protectionism of the Neoconservative Era has had a predictable course in the mental health system. Critics declared that deinstitutionalization had failed and that restrictive civil commitment policies created a mental health system out of control. The obvious solution was to change restrictive hospitalization laws and to reinvigorate the treatment and asylum—as well as the social control—functions that hospitals previously provided for patients and the community.

The political payoffs for more inclusive commitment policies were obvious: Civil commitment is a relatively quick and effective method for ridding the streets of unsightly, troublesome people. Although the method is likely to err on the side of committing many people who are not dangerous or are able to make their own treatment decisions, expansive detention is less likely to overlook those who are. Many believed involuntary hospitalization could help those in need of treatment while also controlling the number of deviant individuals on the streets. Altruism could co-exist with self-interest. Both were important political motives, and which was stronger was impossible to ascertain.

Great Expectations

Behind the disappointments with Liberal Era policies and accusations about its sequelae were several key forces that set the stage for a new cycle of reform. Many mentally ill did not live productive lives in their communities, and the promise of new treatments proved overly optimistic. A comprehensive system of lower-cost, high-quality care was never developed as a viable alternative to hospitals. And states were not easily able to shift the cost of care for the mentally ill to the federal government. Each of these developments played an important role in diminishing the promise of freedom and activating a new campaign for easier commitment.

Furthermore, over time, America's perceptions of psychiatric expertise have gone through a number of cycles, with each spurred by great expectations for the prevention and cure of mental illness.[48] In the late nineteenth century, the asylum was expected to create an environment in which the insane would be restored to health. At the turn of the twentieth century, the preeminent mental health philosophy, known as the mental hygiene movement, stressed disease prevention and anticipated the ultimate eradication of mental illness. In turn, drugs developed in the 1950s and later created heady expectations that the mentally ill could be fully reintegrated into society as functioning citizens. As each of these reforms failed to deliver on their promises, new approaches were sought to deal with chronically impaired people who failed to respond to the current concept of innovative treatment.

The public perceives that psychiatry has the necessary clinical armamentarium to heal the sick, and this perception leads to expectations of "cure." Buoyed by enthusiasm for the next cycle of reform, mental health professionals have often made promises they could not keep. Sweeping claims were made at the outset of the Liberal Era about the marvelous results of drug therapy. Medication could control psychotic symptoms of the most disturbed patients, enabling them to take advantage of community treatment programs. The public, in turn, had an exaggerated sense of how effective mental health treatment could be. Like other illnesses, they assumed mental illness could be cured if clinicians are allowed to use their expertise. In short, a new technology and treatment context created infectious optimism that the mentally ill could become productive citizens again.

But technology has limits. It is now clear that as many as fifty percent of all schizophrenics may not benefit from neuroleptic drugs. Many patients do not display a clinical response to them. Of those who do respond, twenty-five to thirty percent relapse within one year and fifty percent relapse within two years.[49]

More recent discoveries promise greater cures and give psychiatrists a more bountiful pharmacopeia. In addition, there have been amazing discoveries in neurobiology. And increased precision of the APA's Diagnostic and Statistical Manual[50] for diagnosis and research have spawned optimism that a therapeutic panacea is once again around the corner. The publication of an updated version of the Diagnostic and Statistical Manual by the APA has created far greater consensus regarding the scope, content, and nomenclature of psychiatric diagnosis. This development, in itself, has increased the likelihood that clinicians speak the same language and offer more reliable diagnoses than in the past.

In the present cycle of reform, expectations of "cure" have taken two distinct turns. One promises impressive successes for certain types of psychiatric disorders, such as depression, bipolar affective disorders, and even schizophrenia. The second uncharacteristically and bluntly acknowledges that there is little that can be done to "cure"—or even treat—other severely and chronically ill people. The current "return to the asylum" strategy is directed primarily toward these treatment failures.

Because of the failed expectations left from the Liberal Era, psychiatrists in the Neoconservative Era have concluded that many chronically ill people need ongoing hospitalization, both for long- term asylum as well as for short-term "tune-ups." Hospitalization is viewed by psychiatrists and the public as a better alternative for the patients who are so-called treatment failures than life in the community.

Ironically, it is not clear that mere custodial care would pass constitutional scrutiny. In the *Donaldson* case, the Supreme Court strongly intimated that involuntary hospitalization for "pure asylum"—that is, simply improving one's quality of life—is not constitutionally permitted. Indeed, many cases subsequent to *Donaldson* strongly suggest the state cannot commit a mentally ill person able to live in the community unless the individual is dangerous.[51]

A Fractionalized System

Both civil libertarians and advocates of expanded commitment laws now agree that deinstitutionalization resulted in highly fractionalized care at best, or, at worst, no treatment at all. This was caused primarily by the gross inadequacies of the fledgling community-based care system that was supposed to replace institutional care. With deinstitutionalization, the central authority of the hospital was replaced by unconnected private and public agencies that did not cooperate or communicate with one another. Shortcomings in the community-based systems were evident everywhere: The definition of the eligible client population was unclear, treatment focused on short-term problems, and there was little or no follow-up care. Some critics blamed the inadequacy of resources on right-to-treatment litigation that had forced states to upgrade hospitals at the expense of community services.[52] Other observers blamed the fractionalized care on the lack of planning before and during deinstitutionalization. In any event, the result was a disorganized "non-system" with no consensus about what to do with the chronically mentally ill.[53]

Community mental health centers provided services designed to help individuals who had acute treatable mental health problems, including the "worried well," such as patients who desired family or marital counseling, stress management, or increased life satisfaction. While this model proved successful for patients who respond to brief, intermittent therapy, these programs did not prove successful with chronic patients whose disabilities require management over an entire lifetime.[54] Many clinicians were simply not interested in providing aftercare, even though it is an essential service for chronically impaired patients. With few incentives for anyone to assume daily responsibility for the severely impaired, many patients began a linear path downward, becoming sicker and more resistant to help with each passing day. They were referred to increasingly less desirable care facilities. They might be sent from a neighborhood clinic to a public hospital outpatient clinic or, more likely, just dropped from the active caseload of the mental health center.[55] In sum, community mental health centers provided very little service to chronically ill people.

Another factor contributing to the disarray of community mental health services was the lack of a consistent, comprehensive plan for the role hospitals would play in the mental health delivery system. While some reformers envisioned the complete disappearance of public mental hospitals, most were content to see only a small number of inpatient beds maintained for the detention and care of the relatively few patients too dangerous for release. They pointed out that downsizing some hospitals and closing others would save money, which could then be spent on community care. Administrators of scaled-back hospital programs would still have more money to spend on each patient, since there would be fewer patients. Community care was promoted as cheaper than institutionally based care that allowed savings to be spent on better, less restrictive programs. Everyone could win.

Unfortunately, hospital costs did not go down. Bringing aging facilities into compliance with standards imposed both by regulatory bodies such as the Joint Commission on the Accreditation of Hospitals and by the courts[56] proved to be expensive. In addition, plans to close hospitals were met with staunch resistance from labor unions and residents of rural communities whose economies often depended on the hospital. Politicians were loath to close even underutilized hospitals. Caught in heavy crossfire, politicians almost always yielded to their constituents and to powerful labor groups.[57]

Economic Forces

Although substantial financial investment was made in community mental health centers from their inception in the 1960s ($1.5 billion in 1980), serious financial shortfalls hampered adequate development of community treatment and support programs. Even when capital construction funds became available to build outpatient facilities in the mid-1960s, money for staffing and operations was scarce. Because centers were expected to become self-sufficient over time, money to operate them became increasingly difficult to obtain. Many centers lived hand-to-mouth, searching for alternative funding sources, federal distress grants, or other means simply to stay afloat. The vast majority of community mental health centers still eke out a marginal financial existence, living on shoestring budgets.

To add to this dismal financial picture, mental hospitalization costs did not decrease. In constant dollars, annual hospital expenditures increased steadily until they leveled off in 1975. Although the length of stay per patient decreased, the cost per day almost tripled.[58] Thus, there was no "hospital dividend"; the expected savings in hospital care could not be shifted to community care as had been promised.

As we saw in the Introduction, general economic conditions in the United States deteriorated during the 1970s, moving the country away from economic expansion toward fiscal austerity. Toward the end of the Liberal Era, federal and state-supported welfare programs were eliminated or substantially curtailed. Benefits to dependent citizens (Aid to Families with Dependent Children, Medicaid, Supplemental Security Income) were early targets for budget cutters as the "Great Society" became a slogan for a failed social experiment. In its wake, the Reagan administration adopted policies that cut back the welfare state tremendously, transferring even more fiscal responsibility to the states. While battles over Medicare cuts occupied the media and the public, politicians were removing reimbursement for mental health services from state and federal budgets.

Federal block grants reduced the total amount of money available to states for public expenditures. States themselves limited Medicaid eligibility by restricting mental health benefits. Federal expenditures on Social Security Disability coverage—a program that included a large number of mentally disabled persons—had grown so much during the 1970s that Congress amended the act in 1980 to require states to review all awards at least every three years. These administrative reviews resulted in a loss of benefits to large numbers of severely mentally ill people. Many mentally ill recipients lost their apartments and faced a significant reduction in their standard of living. For some, it meant life on the streets.

By the onset of the Neoconservative Era, no one was even marginally satisfied with the public mental health system in the United States. Although many different political and social forces had led to the dismal state of affairs, a growing number of Americans specifically blamed deinstitutionalization policies and restrictive civil commitment laws. In 1985, Alan Stone, former president of the American Psychiatric Association, stated:

> I believe that a growing majority of informed Americans now question the libertarian model and recognize its human costs, which are increasingly visible on the streets of every American city. Families with mentally ill members have learned that state laws patterned on this radical model prevent them from getting needed help at critical times. They know that these laws in practice have often become a rationalization for an unresponsive, underfunded mental health bureaucracy, which only adds legal barriers to their mounting woes.[59]

The Counterrevolutionaries

Early in the Neoconservative Era, family members of the mentally ill and mental health professionals presented an agenda for action that reflected public concern over the homeless and the mentally disabled. A coalition of influential interest groups combined for the avowed purpose of reversing the policies and reforms of the Liberal Era.

Families as the New Advocates

Unlike other groups in need, such as developmentally disabled children and the nation's elderly, the mentally ill have always lacked effective political advocacy. The mentally ill, especially those with chronic disabilities, tend to be adults with long-standing behavioral problems, and their disabilities have often led to family disruptions and isolation from relatives and friends. Thus many natural allies of the mentally ill were reluctant to speak out on their behalf. Although they have sporadically formed patient advocacy groups in major American cities, the mentally ill have not established their own effective national advocacy organizations.[60]

However, families of chronic patients, even when distanced geographically or emotionally from their disabled member, had occasionally spoken out on mental health policy, with varying effectiveness. In the 1950s and 1960s, family groups were loosely organized, voluntary organizations. Since they represented so many diverse subgroups of the mentally ill, they did not form a cohesive organization with a broadly supported political agenda.[61] Instead, they served primarily as local support groups for members, occasionally lobbying state legislatures to increase public spending on mental health.

It was not until the 1970s that loosely organized family groups set aside their disparate agendas and formed political action associations with active chapters in virtually every state. Organizations such as the National Advocates for the Mentally Ill (NAMI) developed chapters in a growing number of states and made coordinated political activism their top priority. At the center of their political agenda was legal reform to make involuntary commitment easier and the application of political pressure to obtain increased public funding and services for the mentally ill.

Families thus became "advocates" for the mentally ill, effectively masking the conflict of interest between those mentally ill citizens who wanted to stay out of psychiatric facilities and family members who wanted them hospitalized. Legislatures increasingly accepted these family advocacy groups both as experts on mental illness and as spokespeople for the best interests of the mentally ill.

Organized Psychiatry Joins the Fray

Psychiatrists welcomed the emerging family movement because it provided significant political strength to their own law reform efforts. Moreover, once hostile families, who previously had been blamed by some schools of psychiatry for their family members' afflictions, now became staunch allies of psychiatrists' reform efforts.[62]

Although the vast majority of clinicians eschewed practicing in public hospitals, those who did had been the first to criticize deinstitutionalization. Many had been skeptical from the outset about the wholesale discharge of mental patients. They had raised concerns about the quality and availability of care outside hospitals for those patients who needed confinement. Professionals would also have less control in a decentralized community mental health system. Caring for a seriously ill patient in a hospital was much easier than making complicated arrangements for community care or arranging for care after discharge. In hospitals, patients could be forced to take medications, behavior could be strictly controlled, and appointments with therapists would be kept. Psychiatrists had also objected to nonphysicians making medical decisions, as when a judge determined whether a patient had to take medication. They had other concerns as well. Where in a community health care system would patients receive treatment and monitoring? How could severely and chronically disabled people survive the hazards of freedom inherent in community-based living?

The legal restrictions imposed on the commitment process posed other threats to psychiatrists. The new restrictions were time-consuming, placing hurdles in the path of clinicians who wanted to involuntarily hospitalize a patient. Also, time spent in court was time not spent seeing patients, harmful both professionally and financially. Adversarial hearings could mean that a psychiatrist's clinical judgment would be challenged by nonmedical professionals, such as lawyers—although judges usually deferred to the clinician's judgment.[63] The entire legal process delayed and complicated treatment.

Motivated by these drawbacks to restrictive commitment, organized psychiatry has become politically active. The American Psychiatric Association has retained high-powered attorneys and intervened in numerous court cases. The APA has pressed for reform of state commitment laws, arguing that they should be changed to make it easier to hospitalize the mentally ill who desperately need treatment. Judicial and political activism on such a scale by psychiatric organizations has been unprecedented in the twentieth century. Once again, psychiatry has promised that they could help if only legal controls are loosened and more money is spent on providing treatment for patients hospitalized involuntarily.

In this domain, psychiatric expertise and influence appear once again ascendant. Instead of viewing the decision of whether to hospitalize a patient involuntarily as a legal, social, and moral issue, legislatures and courts are increasingly seeing the debate as medical. Currently, restrictive regulation of commitment is deemed excessive, expensive, and counterproductive—harming the mentally ill, not helping them. Society has renewed confidence in the ability of mental health professionals to provide appropriate care and social control in hospitals for those too disturbed to seek help on their own.

The Metamorphosis of "Rights"

The opponents of restrictive civil commitment attacked, and then captured, the rhetoric of "rights" that had been so instrumental during the Liberal Era in eliciting both court decisions and legislation that made commitment more difficult. Foes ridiculed the meaninglessness of conferring rights while describing how mentally ill patients were harmed by restrictive commitment statutes. Although Liberal Era law reform provided civil liberties for the mentally disabled, as one pundit commented, the mentally ill were "dying with their rights on."[64] Thus, giving patients rights was viewed by opponents as antithetical to long-term patient interests.

But a strange metamorphosis occurred in this rights debate. Over time, opponents of restricted commitment willingly conceded patients had rights; however, these primary rights included the right *to* treatment in humane institutions that would cure debilitating illnesses.[65] In short, patients had a right to decent living conditions and to mental health care. This new rhetoric has been highly effective in persuading policymakers, particularly legislators and judges, to rethink the mental health law and policy spawned by the Liberal Era, and to embrace the renewed emphasis on expanded coercive hospitalization that emerged in the Neoconservative Era.

The Political Pressures Mount

As the public became anxious about community safety and about helping people they believed had been abandoned, politicians were expected to "do something" to remove the mentally ill from the community. Fear of crime and the resulting emphasis on victims' rights provided a favorable context for change. Public concern over threats as diverse as AIDS, homelessness, and criminality reinforced the pressure on lawmakers to clean up the streets and make communities safe once again. Extending the state's coercive power to the mentally ill was a logical step.

High-visibility media cases in which a mentally ill person killed innocent victims often exacerbated public apprehension and resulted in legislative activity to review and revise state statutes. The murder of a wealthy Seattle couple in 1978 by their mentally disturbed neighbor, Angus McFarlane, just hours after he had been refused voluntary treatment in a state mental hospital galvanized the Washington State legislature into action. A new statute, making it easier to commit the mentally ill, went into effect there on September 1, 1979. A multiple killing in a Pennsylvania shopping mall by a troubled woman with a history of mental illness and hospitalization sparked extensive public hearings on whether it should be easier to commit the dangerous mentally ill. When Juan Gonzalez used a samurai sword to kill two passengers and wound nine others on the Staten Island Ferry in 1986, there was a surge in involuntary commitments based on dangerousness in New York City, resulting in extreme overcrowding of city hospitals.[66]

For politicians, coercive hospitalization was a pragmatic response to public demands for safety. Pressure mounted on elected officials to remove the legal obstacles to detention posed by restrictive commitment laws. Hospitalization was seen as a fail-safe method for getting sick and frightening people off the streets—pragmatic as well as altruistic. Adopting strategies such as the famous cold-weather policy of former New York City Mayor Ed Koch (which involuntarily hospitalized homeless people who refused to go to a shelter in freezing weather) or broadening civil commitment laws after a brutal murder by a released mental patient demonstrated positive political response to pervasive public threats. In some instances, legislators passed commitment legislation that made involuntary hospitalization much easier without realistically assessing the financial, social, and patient care consequences of these changes. The unintended—but readily foreseeable—result was an incredible overload on the state mental health systems.[67]

Self-Interest versus Altruism

As American political and social attitudes push in new directions, perceptions of the state's responsibility to protect the community and modify the behavior of disturbed and disturbing people have led families, politicians, and the citizen-on-the-street to question civil libertarian commitment laws and practices. In the eyes of the majority, the safety and well-being of the community have been jeopardized by liberal policies that favor deinstitutionalization. Protecting individual liberties at the expense of the majority's rights has also victimized the very people those policies had professed to serve—the mentally ill.

A return to the asylum is the logical outcome of this trend. Americans are less willing to tolerate the mentally ill within their communities, but this intolerance is mixed with genuine pity for such common urban phenomena as impoverished bag ladies sleeping on city grates. With a mixture of self-interest and altruism, policymakers and mental health professionals are now advocating another round of reforms that fit neatly into the emerging neoconservative ideology. These reforms stress the rights of the majority over the rights of individuals and place responsibility for deviant behavior squarely on the shoulders of the perpetrator. No longer is it acceptable for deviants to "do their own thing" on the streets of American cities.[68]

While some critics scoff at the likelihood of a serious move toward reinstitutionalization, that movement has already begun. At least eight states have broadened their criteria for involuntary hospitalization.[69] Several states are experiencing large increases in their inpatient census after years of watching those hospital populations plummet.[70] The number of patients in private and public hospitals with psychiatric diagnoses is growing at an unprecedented rate.[71]

This admissions phenomenon includes—but is not limited to—a growing number of juveniles whose commitment has recently caught the attention of the news media.[72] According to Dr. Jerry M. Wiener, president of the American Academy of Child and Adolescent Psychiatry, "private psychiatric beds for teenagers is the fastest growing segment of the hospital industry."[73] Another indication of reinstitutionalization is National Institute of Mental Health data, which reveal that in 1980 there were only 184 private, free-standing psychiatric hospitals; in 1988, there were 450. In addition to psychiatric specialty centers, there are nearly 2,000 general hospitals that offer inpatient psychiatric services. Business again seems to be booming.[74]

As we shall see in the next chapter, the courts—traditional mainstay of individual rights—have by and large ratified formal and informal legal reforms permitting expanded involuntary detention. They have also indicated greater willingness to defer both to legislative and executive initiatives and to psychiatric expertise. As a result, more and more citizens considered mentally ill will likely be confined to psychiatric institutions in the years to come.

6

The Road Back

The forces for change have proved powerful. Persuaded by the special pleading of influential coalitions, shocked by highly publicized murder cases, and pressured by constituents whose cities have been overrun by legions of homeless squatters, state legislators have moved to make involuntary hospitalization of the mentally ill easier. Mayors and city councils have used executive action to get mentally ill people off the streets. Policymakers, law enforcement officials, and citizens' action groups have insisted that government coercion be extended through new and creative means such as outpatient commitment.

From every quarter critics have loudly proclaimed that the pendulum of individual freedom swung too far during the Liberal Era. They argue that the legal rights and protections offered to mentally ill people who resist treatment created tragedy in their lives and chaos in the community. In response, courts have become increasingly reluctant to nullify legislative and executive initiatives aimed at coercive treatment of the mentally ill. Moreover, the Supreme Court has clearly signaled that judges should generally defer to the opinions of professionals in lawsuits challenging the way institutions deal with the mentally ill. Faced with little chance for success in the courts, civil liberties advocates are more reluctant to bring lawsuits seeking to improve conditions in state psychiatric hospitals. Many court decisions are also limiting the right of patients to refuse drugs and other therapies, reasoning that the law should not impede hospital staff who are trying to bring about the very aim of coercive hospitalization—treatment of people who need it. Measures to increase patient autonomy are increasingly taking a back seat to more pragmatic concerns.

Psychiatric status and power are once again ascendant in the ever-expanding use of civil commitment. The expertise of mental health professionals who felt the mentally ill needed more control is increasingly trusted and given wide play in pursuing both therapeutic and preventive–detention goals for society. The rights of the mentally ill have yielded to the rights of the majority. Liberalism and legalism have been overwhelmed by demands for protection and paternalism.

117

Enlarging the Therapeutic State

By the mid-1970s, legal reforms restricting civil commitment and protecting the civil liberties of the mentally ill had reached a crest.[1] Virtually every state had changed its civil commitment laws so that only the most dangerous or severely impaired patients were hospitalized involuntarily. Only those considered dangerous to themselves or others were generally committed to psychiatric hospitals.[2] The inpatient census of public mental hospitals plummeted. Most mentally disturbed citizens were treated voluntarily or not at all.[3]

Toward the end of the 1970s, however, a modest but discernible trend toward broadened civil commitment laws gained momentum. A number of state laws expanded the authority of public mental health officials to confine the mentally ill for treatment. Washington was the first to chart this new path in commitment, but other states—including Alaska, Hawaii, Arizona, Kansas, North Carolina, Oregon, and Texas—soon followed.[4] Some states enacted statutes that went beyond narrow definitions of dangerousness and "grave disability" and permitted involuntary hospitalization of individuals whose everyday functioning was deteriorating.[5] These "need for treatment" provisions represented a clear departure from the narrow commitment criteria of the Liberal Era which required dangerousness to self or others. Other states, including New Jersey, New York, Illinois, Pennsylvania, California, and the District of Columbia, considered expanding the state's therapeutic commitment power but decided against it, primarily because of the enormous costs involved.

Washington State provides an excellent example of how commitment laws were expanded. In 1979 the state legislature revised the civil libertarian commitment law it had passed only six years earlier and enacted a broader statute intended to cast a wider net.[6] Family advocacy groups such as Family Action for the Seriously Emotionally Disturbed (FASED) and Washington Advocates for the Mentally Ill (WAMI) had actively lobbied to revise the state's restrictive 1973 Involuntary Treatment Act. Publicity following a 1978 multiple murder by a troubled young man denied voluntary admission to the state's largest psychiatric hospital portrayed the state mental health system as an inefficient, inaccessible bureaucracy handcuffed by a stringent civil commitment law.[7] Ironically, the legislative reforms were not intended to make it easier to commit dangerous individuals[8] or provide more beds for voluntary patients. Instead, the changes in the law made involuntary therapeutic commitment easier.

Families had complained to their legislators that mentally ill members experiencing deteriorating mental health could not be recommitted under the 1973 Involuntary Treatment Act (ITA) so long as the family provided them with essential food, clothing, and shelter. Even though mentally ill persons might be seriously disturbed, they were not considered "gravely disabled" under the 1973 ITA if they had the bare necessities for survival. Only by abandoning a sick loved one—usually to the streets—could families secure hospitalization.

The Washington 1979 ITA expanded the commitment authority of the state based on *parens patriae* power by broadening the definition of "grave disability." Under the 1979 ITA, "grave disability" was designed to permit involuntary hospitalization of mentally ill patients who started to "decompensate"—that is, began experiencing serious symptoms of mental illness after being released from a psychiatric hospital.[9] This new law permitted "preemptive" action—hospitalizing the mentally ill caught in a downward spiral before they hit bottom. Now, families could seek involuntary commitment as soon as a patient began to get noticeably worse.

Washington State thus addressed one of the most troubling aspects of caring for the chronically mentally ill. The condition of many patients was stabilized in the hospital, but deteriorated after discharge because they often stopped taking their medications. Others abused alcohol or drugs after their release. Although not dangerous to others or in immediate danger of serious harm, mental health professionals and family groups argued that these individuals needed treatment to restabilize and improve their deteriorating condition. The released mental patients often refused help and could not be forced into hospitals because of restrictive civil commitment laws. The Washington statute authorized coercive institutionalization (or reinstitutionalization) when, in the opinion of mental health professionals, a mentally ill person was failing in the community and needed treatment. The Washington statute has since proved useful in committing the homeless mentally ill.[10]

Courts were also less willing in the Neoconservative Era to strike down as unconstitutional state statutes that conferred wide commitment discretion on mental health professionals. For example, in 1982 the New York branch of the American Civil Liberties Union, representing committed patients, filed suit in federal court seeking to have New York's commitment statute declared unconstitutional.[11] New York law permitted involuntary hospitalization of a mentally ill individual "for which care and treatment in a hospital is essential to such person's welfare and whose judgement is so impaired that he is unable to understand the need for such treatment."[12] The ACLU argued that this provision was constitutionally "overbroad" because it permitted forced hospitalization of nondangerous individuals. The ACLU also claimed it was impermissibly "vague," as it conferred too much discretion on public mental health professionals to decide who might be involuntarily hospitalized. In 1983 the U.S. Court of Appeals disagreed and upheld the statute against these constitutional assaults.[13] The appellate court concluded that, as interpreted by New York courts, the commitment criteria prevented the commitment of nondangerous citizens who can survive in the community, and thus the statute was constitutional.

The American Psychiatric Association, which had opposed the restrictive civil libertarian commitment laws of the Liberal Era, proposed the most comprehensive version of a need-for-treatment approach to involuntary commitment when it published its Model Law on Civil Commitment of the Mentally Ill in 1983. The Model Law allows commitment of seriously ill persons who are "likely to suffer substantial mental or physical deterioration" as well as commitment of those dangerous to themselves or unable to care for their needs.[14]

The essential goal of the Model Law was to allow involuntary confinement and treatment of those mentally ill who show signs of psychotic deterioration but are not necessarily dangerous. To reach this group, the Model Law recommended limiting commitment to persons who are: (1) seriously mentally ill, (2) suffering, (3) incompetent to make medical decisions, and (4) treatable. This law assumes that involuntary confinement in a mental hospital can be justified only on the basis of paternalism.[15] If enacted, the statute "would permit commitment of many of those severely mentally ill people who, ignored by current commitment laws and abandoned by the mental health system, now roam the streets aimlessly and without hope."[16] (Interestingly, a mentally ill individual who was dangerous but not treatable could not be committed under the APA Model Law; they would be left to the criminal justice system.)

Arizona has recently taken neoconservative commitment reforms a step farther by adopting a civil commitment law in 1990 that is based on the APA's Model Law but is far more expansive. The Arizona law still permits commitment of persons dangerous to themselves or others, as it had before, but the provisions of the new law authorize commitment of patients who meet the APA Model commitment criteria[17] or whose condition are deteriorating.[18]

Legislatures across the country have been influenced by the need-for-treatment rationale proposed by the APA because of the growing number of homeless mentally ill and because of mounting pressure from family groups and the public. California lawmakers, who considered the adoption of a need-for-treatment law in 1987, offered three reasons in favor of expanding involuntary commitment. They believed restrictive commitment statutes contribute significantly to a "revolving door" syndrome for young, chronically ill schizophrenics; cause homelessness; and discourage treatment of someone who is "deteriorating and will soon be in crisis."[19]

In a joint task force report prepared for the California legislature, these concerns were made clear:

> There has been a dramatic increase in the number of homeless individuals who are mentally ill and unable to adequately care for themselves. . . . The cumbersome legal process of involuntary treatment is a significant contributing factor. The policy of "deinstitutionalization" has moved many formerly hospitalized clients into the streets. This policy has also prevented many who need acute and/or long-term treatment from being hospitalized.[20]

Only the prohibitive cost of expanding the state's therapeutic commitment authority persuaded California not to enact such a law. The legislature looked at what had happened to the State of Washington. Washington State's mental health budget had incurred runaway cost increases after enactment of the 1979 Involuntary Treatment Act, and other adverse effects, including acute overcrowding in state hospitals, had been observed.[21] This frightened the California legislature[22] as well as a number of other states.

Not all jurisdictions felt compelled to make statutory changes in civil commitment laws in order to expand their commitment authority. Instead, they made wide-ranging, ad hoc reinterpretations of existing law to give police and mental health professionals broadened commitment power. New York City, at the direction of then-mayor Ed Koch, implemented two plans to detain and evaluate the homeless mentally ill. The "cold weather emergency" plan assumed that refusing shelter in freezing weather was evidence of an inability to ensure survival. In October 1986, he decided that once a cold weather emergency (defined as temperatures below 32 degrees between 4 P.M. and 8 A.M.) was declared, New York City police were authorized to transport homeless people who refused to go to a public shelter voluntarily either to a shelter without their consent or to a psychiatric hospital. In October 1987, the mayor also authorized "Project Help" teams, composed of psychiatrists, nurses, and social workers, to forcibly move those homeless considered seriously mentally ill from the streets to city hospitals.[23] Both plans assumed that living on the streets creates a danger to self that justifies coercive state intervention under the *parens patriae* power.

The detention of homeless Joyce Brown was given wide media play in 1987 when she was involuntarily committed during one of Koch's cold weather emergencies. The incident provoked a flood of sentiment in favor of sheltering and treating people like Brown—whether or not the hapless person agreed to the plan. Although public sentiment favored Koch's position, some critics argued that the government was interfering with her right to live as she chose and Big Brother should leave her alone.

Outpatient Commitment

Another method, which has been used to extend the state's coercive power over those mentally ill living in the community, is involuntary outpatient commitment.[24] This is a system in which an outpatient can be ordered to comply with certain treatment requirements, such as taking medication or reporting periodically to mental health facilities to attend counseling sessions.[25] The police can take a patient who fails to comply to a hospital for counseling or automatically recommit that person to a hospital.

As of 1985 twenty-six states had explicitly created provisions for outpatient commitment.[26] North Carolina (1983), Hawaii (1984), and Georgia (1986) in particular have enacted outpatient commitment laws that are drawing considerable attention from lawmakers in other states. These states permit outpatient commitment of persons who are not dangerous but who are expected, without the compulsory treatment, to deteriorate and become dangerous. Because a person treated on an outpatient basis does not suffer the drastic loss of liberty that hospitalization would cause, some states provide less procedural protection for patients receiving compulsory outpatient treatment.

North Carolina, for example, does not automatically provide the patient with an attorney. Cross-examination of the psychiatrist is also not permitted at the commitment hearing.[27] Outpatient commitment thus allows the patient a fair amount of freedom, and at the same time permits the state to use some coercion in providing treatment. This approach strikes a compromise between those who support therapeutic hospitalization for those mentally ill who are dysfunctional in society and those who support commitment only of the dangerous.[28]

But there are critics of this system.[29] While laws authorizing coercive outpatient treatment to prevent a patient from becoming dangerous or from decompensating and being hospitalized again arguably avoid unnecessary hospitalization, they also introduce compelled treatment into what had previously been a purely voluntary program.[30] Some observers have argued that outpatient commitment is a more comprehensive and pervasive form of social control than hospitalization because it tracks every aspect of the patient's private life in the community. It also increases the number of persons subject to government control.[31]

Diminishing Procedural Due Process

In addition to changes in commitment standards and the proliferation of outpatient commitment statutes, changes have also been implemented in the procedures used to commit, treat, and release the mentally ill. On balance, these recent adjustments have been aimed at expediting the commitment process by providing less legal protection to the mentally ill than they had previously enjoyed.

As we saw in Chapter 4, the procedural changes in civil commitment implemented during the Liberal Era usually placed final commitment authority with the courts and provided patients with substantial protection against inappropriate hospitalization. Patients were entitled to written notice of a hearing, the assistance of an attorney, the right to cross-examine mental health experts, and other important opportunities to contest their coercive hospitalization. Courts would also review confinement periodically to ensure patients were released when their condition no longer justified continued detention in a hospital.

The Liberal Era's procedural protections had met with immediate criticism from many mental health professionals who felt commitment should be based solely on a patient's need for treatment. In their view, this was essentially a medical question that should be answered by clinicians with the necessary expertise, not uninformed judges. In addition, these critics believed that the complicated steps that had to be taken to commit a seriously ill patient only delayed or denied needed treatment.[32] Admittedly, this criticism was mainly one of degree. Although many people bemoaned the "legalization" of the commitment process, even its most vocal critics agreed that it had simply been too easy to hospitalize patients in the years before the Liberal Era and that some procedural protection for patients was necessary.[33]

Skeptics of restrictive civil commitment also argued that observing all the protocols of due process was too costly. For example, virtually all states provide judicial review of initial commitment decisions at predefined intervals, ranging from seventy-two hours after admission to six months. This review requires paying the cost of judges and lawyers, and, in rare circumstances, seating a jury. It is also costly to transport patients back and forth from the hospital to the courtroom. During the review process, mental health professionals spend countless hours preparing and giving testimony instead of treating patients. These expenses have proved extremely burdensome to state mental health systems, diverting limited resources away from treatment. As the federal appellate court said in *Rennie* v. *Klein* in 1981: "Diversion of these funds to finance non-essential administrative procedures [to consider patients' treatment refusals], however beneficial and desirable, will not provide help for the patient's most critical needs."[34]

Critics have further asserted that most committed patients are "passive, stuporous, or uncommunicative, or in perfect agreement with the physician's recommendation. Others [patients] protest initially, but after a few days of hospitalization have had a change of mind."[35] From this perspective, the due process commitment model is an overly protective and unnecessary system that harms those very individuals most in need of treatment. Complex restrictive procedures are seen as unnecessary, wasteful, and empty rituals.[36]

Family members and clinicians have complained bitterly about the procedural hurdles placed in the path of involuntary commitment. Clinicians claim the adversary nature of commitment hearings damages the therapeutic relationship they are trying to establish with patients. They allege the courtroom-like atmosphere of a formal hearing confuses and frightens patients and appears to put psychiatrists in league with the court. Moreover, some mental health professionals assert that, too often, lawyers act against the best interests of their clients by blocking the commitment of an obviously needy person.[37]

Ironically, many procedural protections do operate quite poorly. Available research indicates that in many cases the right to an attorney is of negligible value due to poor attorney performance, staggering caseloads, or judicial deference to experts.[38]

In response to these concerns, the APA Model Commitment Law includes a number of important changes that would diminish the procedural protection afforded patients in initial commitment hearings. The framers concluded that not all rules of evidence and procedure used in a criminal trial should be used in commitment hearings. They argued that "except for constitutionally required due process safeguards, the evidentiary and procedural rules used in criminal cases should be evaluated with an open mind as to their propriety in civil commitment hearings."[39]

The procedural protections and rules of evidence introduced to commitment hearings during the Liberal Era were not instituted to hamstring authorities but were designed to ensure that commitment decisions be based on reliable evidence and accurate fact-finding. In direct contrast to Liberal Era objectives, neoconservatives favor procedures that get to the facts efficiently and do not tie the experts' hands. For example, the 1983 APA Model Law would allow hearsay evidence to be introduced at commitment hearings.[40] This would permit government lawyers to use information provided by individuals who would not testify in person, such as treating staff and family members, to secure a patient's commitment. If this were permitted, the attorney for a patient could not cross-examine these witnesses.

In keeping with the need-for-treatment model, commitment hearings would also be informal. Unlike defendants in a criminal trial, patients would have no right to subpoena or cross-examine witnesses and no right to remain silent. Spouses would be allowed to testify against their mates. Exceptions would be granted to the psychotherapist–patient privilege of confidentiality, permitting a mental health professional to disclose to the court confidential statements made to the professional by the patient. The APA law would also delay when the patient has a right to have the assistance of a lawyer. At the probable cause hearing (held within five days of the emergency detention), the patient would have no right to appointed counsel, although counsel would be provided to indigent patients at hearings where detention is sought for thirty days or longer.

Although the evidence is still quite modest, a trend toward limiting the procedural protections for patients has begun. Mental health officials applaud most of the procedural changes in the detention or hearing phase of commitment because of their potential for significant savings of time and money. For example, abolishing the right to direct confrontation of adversary witnesses minimizes the amount of time psychiatrists and other hospital staff spend in court. Making detention periods lengthier (e.g., thirty days instead of fourteen days) reduces the number of commitment hearings that judges, clinicians, and lawyers must attend.[41]

Paul Appelbaum, a noted scholar of commitment of mental patients, has said that current signs of change are "fragile omens [that] hold out the hope that society is beginning to recognize the cost of legalizing civil commitment and the need to balance protections against unwarranted commitment with assurances that needed treatment will take place."[42] He believes procedural changes may ultimately exert more influence on civil commitment than changes in commitment criteria.

The Supreme Court and Due Process

At the close of the Liberal Era, the Supreme Court handed down two cases which clearly indicate that procedural due process in commitment hearings need not be as extensive as that provided criminal defendants. Instead, it is adjustable, depending on the state and individual interests involved.

In the 1979 case of *Addington* v. *Texas*,[43] the Court held that the Constitution only required the state to establish the facts necessary to secure commitment of a mentally ill person by "clear and convincing evidence" instead of by "proof beyond a reasonable doubt," as required to convict a defendant in a criminal trial. The "clear and convincing" standard required less certainty and confidence by the judge or jury in their verdicts than the criminal standard did.[44] Although acknowledging commitment is a significant deprivation of liberty, the Court concluded that the state has an important interest in protecting the public from dangerous individuals and in caring for mentally ill citizens who cannot care for themselves. Imposing too high a standard of proof might prevent the state from accomplishing its protective and therapeutic goals.

The reemergence of this more paternalistic rationale fit neatly into the emerging neoconservative agenda. The Court also observed that since hospitalization is not intended to punish patients but rather to help them, mistakes are of less concern. Chief Justice Warren Burger noted that:

> the layers of professional review and observations of the patient's condition, and the concern of family and friends generally will provide continuous opportunities for an erroneous commitment to be corrected. Moreover, it is not true that the release of a genuinely mentally ill person is no worse for the individual than the failure to convict the guilty. One who is suffering from a debilitating mental illness and in need of treatment is neither wholly at liberty nor free of stigma.[45]

Thus, the Court seemed to conclude that most citizens entering the commitment system were mentally ill and would benefit from hospitalization even if they fell outside narrowly defined commitment criteria. Besides, any mistakes would be caught in due course.

Justice Burger also observed that "given the lack of certainty and the fallibility of psychiatric diagnosis, there is a serious question as to whether a state could ever prove beyond a reasonable doubt that an individual is both mentally ill and likely to be dangerous."[46] Since psychiatry is so imprecise an art, the majority on the Court was willing to require less confidence on the part of jurors when resolving these admittedly difficult questions by permitting a lower standard of proof. The vast majority of states have now adopted the "clear and convincing" standard for establishing the grounds for commitment.[47]

A short time later, the Supreme Court virtually did away with extensive legal scrutiny when parents sought to commit their children to state psychiatric hospitals. In *Parham* v. *J.R.*,[48] Justice Burger, once again writing the majority opinion, concluded that a minor was entitled to due process to protect against erroneous hospitalization; however, the process "due" a child was quite modest. The decision to commit had to be made by a "neutral decision-maker" who had to "carefully probe the child's background."[49] Finally, the commitment had to be reviewed periodically by professional staff.

Translated into concrete terms, according to the Court, minors were only entitled to have a mental health professional—not a judge—decide on whether to admit them to the state hospital because physicians were more competent to make these medical decisions.[50] *Parham* can best be understood as abruptly shifting some commitment decisions away from the legal model and back to one based on the medical model. In this case, children are not entitled to a hearing before a judge, representation by a lawyer, and the right to confront and present evidence. In contrast to reforms of the Liberal Era, *Parham* concluded that neutrality, expertise, and the genuine concern of parents are as effective in preventing mistakes and abuse as a judicial hearing.

Both *Addington* and *Parham* signal a retreat from a legal model of rigorous procedural due process and a return to a more flexible system of commitment in which the clinical judgment of mental health professionals is given strong deference. Both Court decisions assumed that most mentally ill patients committed to hospitals were better off there than in the community or in their homes. These cases may also portend a growing acceptance by our highest court in the land of involuntary hospitalization of nondangerous citizens solely for treatment.[51]

Courts Take a Laissez-Faire Approach to Hospitals

The Right to Treatment

As we saw in Chapter 4, Liberal Era courts, particularly federal courts, had been willing—almost eager—to monitor conditions in state psychiatric institutions to ensure that they were safe and humane and provided some reasonable promise of improving a patient's condition.[52] As early as 1966 a federal court, again under the leadership of Judge David Bazelon, concluded that a committed mental patient had a statutory right to "treatment which is adequate in light of present knowledge."[53] Judge Bazelon strongly suggested that the Constitution forbade the government from confining a mentally ill person to a hospital unless it provided treatment.

The 1972 landmark case of *Wyatt* v. *Stickney*[54] made an even stronger statement in support of patients' rights to treatment when it announced that all mentally ill patients confined against their will in mental hospitals in Alabama did have a constitutional right to treatment. Finally, in 1974 the Supreme Court concluded in the *Donaldson* case[55] that a mentally ill person confined to a state psychiatric hospital *for treatment* was constitutionally entitled to some minimal level of treatment.[56]

By the beginning of the Neoconservative Era, however, federal courts had become reluctant to interfere in the internal administration of public institutions. A vivid example of this judicial retreat involving a public mental hospital was the Supreme Court's 1979 decision in *Youngberg* v. *Romeo*.[57]

Nicholas Romeo, a mentally retarded thirty-three-year-old adult with the mental capacity of an eighteen-month-old child, sued to enforce a constitutional right to safe conditions and freedom from unnecessary physical restraint. In his suit Romeo also sought court-ordered training and activity programs designed to reduce his aggressive behavior and to maintain and develop his self-care skills. While at a state institution for the developmentally disabled, Romeo was injured several times, and thus the Court determined that the defendant was entitled to protection from other patients and from self-inflicted harm, and that he could not be put in restraints without a legitimate purpose. But the majority also concluded that the state was under no constitutional obligation to furnish Romeo with the best training currently available. Instead, the state must provide reasonable training, which might help keep Romeo safe from injury, and avoid unnecessary use of physical restraints.

One of the most provocative aspects of this 1979 case is the clear signal by the Supreme Court that judges should not second-guess professionals when they make judgments in good faith about what is best for their patients. As Justice Harry Blackmun explained:

> Moreover, there certainly is no reason to think judges or juries are better qualified than appropriate professionals in making such decisions. . . . For these reasons, the decision, if made by a professional, is presumptively valid; liability may be imposed only when the decision by the professional is such a substantial departure from accepted professional judgment that the person responsible actually did not base his decision on such a judgment.[58]

The *Youngberg* opinion also made it clear that employees could not be successfully sued for failing to exercise reasonable professional judgment if inadequate state funding made that impossible. The Court said:

> In an action for damages against a professional in his individual capacity, however, the professional will not be liable if he was unable to satisfy his normal professional standards because of budgetary constraints; in such a situation, good-faith immunity would bar liability.[59]

Both *Parham* and *Youngberg* clearly indicate that the Burger Court sought to reverse the activism manifested by federal courts during the Liberal Era. These later decisions cautioned judges against intervening in the daily operation of state institutions and to withdraw from creating and enforcing "rights." The Burger Court signaled that there is nothing special about legal training or being a judge that qualifies the judiciary to make the difficult decisions trained mental health professionals must make on a daily basis.

Clinicians wholeheartedly agree that they should be left alone to provide professional care, without judges and lawyers constantly looking over their shoulders. And they will have a greater chance to do that during the Neoconservative Era.

In *Pennhurst* v. *Halderman*, the Supreme Court further tethered activist federal courts.[60] It held that developmentally disabled citizens could not sue state officials in federal courts to force them to provide the training and services these citizens claimed were guaranteed them by state law.

The number of lawsuits seeking enforcement of a right to treatment on behalf of mental patients confined in state hospitals has declined noticeably during the 1980s. Less fearful of being hauled into federal court, states can now commit more citizens to psychiatric hospitals without paying the full price of an expansive commitment policy—an upgrading of staff, treatment, and facilities. The conservative Supreme Court clearly wishes to defer to the power granted the states by the Constitution in the federal system.

Diminishing the Right to Refuse Treatment

The discovery of psychotropic drugs during the 1950s was undoubtedly the most significant technological development in modern times affecting the way society cares for the mentally ill.[61] Psychoactive drugs eliminated many of the symptoms of mental illness and shortened hospital stays.[62] Many psychiatrists considered these drugs essential to treatment, especially for schizophrenics, and regarded it as malpractice not to give them to acutely psychotic patients.[63]

The availability of drug treatment persuaded mental health professionals that many mentally ill citizens previously confined in state psychiatric hospitals could live independently in the community. These drugs were expected to make the former patients more normal in appearance and behavior, which would also alleviate many community fears about accepting released patients.

Not until the 1960s and 1970s did the dark side of the continued use of these wonder drugs emerge.[64] Researchers and clinicians began to notice that continued administration of drugs sometimes caused serious and harmful side effects, which impaired the psychological and physical well-being of their patients. For example, some suffered from uncontrollable physical restlessness and agitation, while others suffered from general passivity, dryness of the mouth, and loss of sexual function. In the most extreme cases, the side effects were fatal.[65]

When knowledge of these serious side effects became widespread in the 1970s, lawyers for patients confined in public hospitals brought lawsuits, claiming their clients had a constitutional right to refuse psychoactive drugs. Popularly known as the right-to-refuse-treatment cases, attorneys argued that, just like any other legally competent person, patients committed to a psychiatric facility for treatment had a right to decide whether the benefits of medication outweighed the potential harm.[66] They also claimed that forced drugging interfered with their clients' constitutionally protected thought processes.

Toward the end of the Liberal Era, two federal district courts issued decisions which held that, except in emergencies, involuntarily detained patients had a constitutional right to refuse drugs.[67] These courts, however, took two fundamentally different approaches to implementing this right. One used a "medical second-opinion" approach, while the other used a strictly legal model of judicial review.

In the first approach, the appeals court in the 1978 *Rennie* v. *Klein*[68] case ruled that a physician had to meet with a patient who resisted medication and explain the risks and benefits of drug treatment and its alternatives. Then the medical team and the medical director, after reviewing the case, could, if they all agreed, medicate the refusing patient. As the majority phrased it: "Due process procedure must therefore provide an opportunity for the exercise of professional judgment."[69]

Using this "medical second-opinion" model, courts can view the decision to administer drugs as a medical decision for which judges have no special competence. Making a treatment decision through an adversarial legal process wastes scarce judicial and medical resources.

The legal model took an entirely different approach to the question of refusing drug treatment. In 1979 a federal court in Massachusetts held in *Rogers* v. *Okin*[70] that an involuntarily committed patient could be medicated forcibly only in an emergency. Otherwise, the patient had an absolute First Amendment right to refuse drugs as long as he was competent.[71] In the absence of an emergency, the patient could be medicated only after a separate judicial adjudication of incompetency and with the approval of an appointed guardian. The First Circuit Court of Appeals, in reviewing the *Rogers* case, cut back somewhat on the constitutional protection afforded patients by the trial court. Nonetheless, it agreed that in most cases judges—not doctors— would decide whether drugs would be given to nonconsenting patients.

By the time the Liberal Era was drawing to a close, some other state and federal courts had granted to competent involuntary patients the right to refuse drugs in nonemergency situations. Involuntary patients were also entitled to due process before they could be medicated without their consent. Some federal courts were on record as requiring staff to consider using the least restrictive means of treating the patient.

However, when the U.S. Supreme Court finally confronted the medical second-opinion model of *Rennie* v. *Klein* and the legal model of *Rogers* v. *Okin*, it did not decide which method was required by the Constitution. Instead, both cases were sent back to the lower courts.

The justices chose to send the *Rennie* case back to the Third Circuit Court of Appeals for reconsideration in light of the Court's decision in *Youngberg* v. *Romeo*.[72] *Youngberg*, as we saw earlier, indicated in no uncertain terms that judges should defer to the professional judgment of medical specialists. Only if the treating professional did not comply with reasonable professional standards of care should a court overrule the decision of a psychiatrist. This action suggested that a majority of the Supreme Court favored a medical model of due process in which the treatment decisions of physicians were presumptively correct and only required peer review.

The Court also sent *Rogers* back to the Massachusetts Supreme Judicial Court requesting that the state court decide what, if any, rights an involuntary patient had under Massachusetts law to refuse medication.[73]

The Third Circuit essentially reaffirmed its earlier decision upholding a medical model of due process.[74] Massachusetts' highest court, however, held that a competent patient has a right under state law to refuse psychoactive drugs unless he is dangerous. If a judge determines the patient is competent, his refusal is to be respected unless the government could demonstrate that, without medication, the patient would suffer very serious harm.[75] If determined incompetent, the judge should step into the patient's shoes and determine what the patient would choose if he were competent. This approach became known as the "substituted judgment" doctrine.[76] Some courts have followed the medical second-opinion approach,[77] while others have basically used a legal model of substituted judgment.

A more clear-cut demonstration of the Supreme Court's support for the medical model was to come. In March 1990, the U.S. Supreme Court overturned a Washington State Supreme Court decision which held that both convicted prisoners and involuntarily committed patients had a constitutional right to a judicial hearing before they could be forced to take drugs against their will. The U.S. Supreme Court decided in *Washington* v. *Harper*[78] that state psychiatrists could forcibly give a competent but mentally ill prisoner psychoactive drugs over his objection. Providing an independent administrative review of the decision to medicate was all the Constitution required. Although Harper was a prisoner and not a civilly committed patient, this case intimates that the current Supreme Court would only require a second medical opinion before a civil patient could be medicated without his or her consent.

Not surprisingly, the American Psychiatric Association comes down squarely on the side of medical decision-making on all treatment issues. The APA's 1983 Model Law would effectively eliminate the right of an involuntary patient to refuse treatment once committed.[79] This would be accomplished by requiring a judge to find that a patient is incompetent to make his or her own treatment decision as part of the initial commitment determination,[80] a tactic essentially eliminating the right-to-refuse-treatment question altogether. Since a patient must be found incompetent to make a treatment decision before he can be hospitalized under the Model Law, psychiatrists would have virtually complete treatment authority over all involuntary patients.[81]

Mental health professionals think it is absurd for the law to permit coercive hospitalization of a mentally ill person who is in desperate need of treatment and then, once committed, to prevent the very treatment that is essential if the patient is ever to be released from the hospital.[82] Without the use of these drugs, many patients will simply be "warehoused," thus violating their right to treatment. In the view of treatment professionals, a right to refuse treatment defeats the whole purpose of involuntarily hospitalizing a person.

Least Restrictive Alternative Treatment

Since the very early years of the Liberal Era, the Supreme Court has required that government action that limits important individual rights should be no more intrusive than necessary to accomplish its purpose.[83] During the 1960s and 1970s, some courts concluded this constitutional principle may require state agencies to deprive the mentally ill of only as much freedom as is essential to accomplish this goal.[84] At least thirty-six states require that involuntary commitment be the least restrictive placement feasible, and twenty-six states require that institutionalized patients be treated in the least restrictive alternative possible.[85] This requirement is based on the commonsense notion that a patient should lose no more liberty than is necessary to treat him.

During the Liberal Era, a number of lawsuits resulted in decisions requiring that committed patients be placed in treatment settings that provided more freedom than hospitals.[86] Other courts applied the doctrine to postcommitment hospital placement, in effect dictating the assignment of patients to specific facilities or wards.[87] Some courts even ordered states to create less restrictive community treatment settings for the mentally ill.[88] Least restrictive alternative treatment was applied by judges to suggest that psychotropic drugs cannot be given to a refusing patient if less intrusive alternatives—tranquilizers, sedatives, isolation, or even no treatment at all—are effective.[89]

More recently, however, the trend toward the least restrictive alternative has been reversed. Several courts have concluded that mentally ill patients do not have a constitutional right to be placed in the least restrictive setting. Moreover, states are not required to construct community placement alternatives to facilitate the release of the mentally disabled from public institutions.[90] The Reagan administration supported these opinions; in one case the Justice Department filed a brief arguing that citizens had no right either under the Constitution or federal law to be placed in the least restrictive community setting.[91] In the 1979 case of *Youngberg* v. *Romeo*,[92] the Supreme Court clearly signaled that neither the developmentally disabled nor the mentally ill have a constitutional right to be placed in the least restrictive setting.

Some observers believe that the wave of successful lawsuits based on the least restrictive alternative has crested.[93] This is not surprising as it is quite apparent the current Supreme Court would conclude that the Constitution does not require that care and treatment take place in the least restrictive setting. In turn, lower courts are increasingly unwilling to require state governments to spend significant state funds from their limited budgets to create these placement alternatives.[94] Nor are trial judges inclined to second-guess mental health professionals' judgments about the most appropriate treatment setting for their patients.

A Confluence of Interests

The confluence of these dominating streams of judicial thought is a clear indication that judicial protection of the rights of the mentally ill is on the wane. Some state legislatures are expanding the power of the government to commit the mentally ill to state psychiatric facilities for a therapeutic purpose. Courts are less likely to order that those patients who can be treated with less restrictive alternatives—such as halfway houses or outpatient treatment—be placed in these settings. Nor are they willing to monitor the conditions in state hospitals to ensure that patients' constitutional and statutory rights to treatment are being protected.[95] Legislatures, free from credible threats of successful lawsuits, can satisfy public demands for more coercive approaches to controlling the mentally ill. Psychiatrists are now likely to have much more free reign to treat patients as they see fit.

The insanity and civil commitment reforms of the Neoconservative Era have been in place for almost a decade. It is time to consider the available evidence regarding the impact of these reforms on crime control, treatment of mental patients, community security, and other pressing social goals.

7

Does Legal Reform
Make a Difference?

Obviously, legislators, bureaucrats, and the public expect the new laws regarding involuntary commitment and mentally ill criminals to change individual behavior and to improve public safety. But do the new laws actually work? Frequently, lawmakers enact statutes without any evidence that the new laws will bring about the desired changes. This may be because they are unaware of existing information that might help them make decisions or because no informative research exists. Sometimes policymakers simply ignore useful information if it does not fit neatly into their agenda. Consequently, legal initiatives may not work in the manner intended or they may have unexpected side effects.

Clearly, many laws are enacted for purely political purposes. Legal changes may be the result of a hasty reaction to public anger and demands for solving a perceived crisis. Other laws may be passed even though public officials know enacting legislation can do little more than appease the public's demand for action. Sometimes laws are grudgingly passed because of pressure from the courts or the federal government.

Have mental health law reforms had the impact intended by their architects? What unintended consequences have resulted in their wake? Has mental health law reform over the last three decades been based on sound empirical information or has it relied solely on contemporary social values? Did legislation merely express the public's deeply held values without serious consideration of the changes the reforms might actually bring? Although we know less than we should about the effect of reforms in the law, we can learn some important lessons by examining what we do know about these changes.

The Insanity Defense

Most citizens distrust the insanity defense because they believe too many dangerous offenders use it to "beat the rap" for serious criminal offenses. The public is also reluctant to acquit a person who has clearly committed a harmful act because they believe a successful insanity defense results in releasing a dangerous person who will once again prey on innocent victims, and this fear has fueled much of the heated debate over this defense.

Despite the intensity of public feeling about the use and abuse of the insanity defense, defendants use this defense in less than 1 or 2 percent of all American criminal cases. And of those who plead insanity, only about one-third successfully convince a judge or jury they are legally insane. Although 3 million criminal charges are filed each year in the United States, only a few hundred people are actually acquitted by reason of insanity.[1]

Nevertheless, studies have shown that the general public, legislators, and even defense lawyers far overestimate the number of people who are acquitted by reason of insanity. In an interesting series of studies conducted in Wyoming, college students, state legislators, local mental health authorities, and community residents grossly overestimated the number and success rate of NGRI pleas. During the study period, insanity pleas were actually entered in Wyoming in less than one-half of 1 percent of all felony cases, and of those entered only 1 percent were successful. In sharp contrast, estimates of the frequency of the plea ranged from 13 percent by state mental hospital professionals to 43 percent by community residents. Even state legislators believed 21 percent of all criminal defendants plead insanity. Similarly, estimates of the success rate of the insanity defense were extremely inaccurate, ranging from a low of 19 percent by state mental health professionals to a high of 44 percent by college students. State legislators were close behind the latter group, with their guess that 40 percent of insanity pleas were successful. Despite clear evidence to the contrary, it appears very likely that the extensive publicity given to insanity cases leads people to believe the plea is used widely to avoid punishment.[2]

Many Americans think insanity acquittees are usually those who have committed heinous crimes such as assassination, rape, or mass murder. Many offenders, however, found not guilty by reason of insanity are charged with less serious crimes, such as assault, writing bad checks, drug use, and shoplifting. Minor property offenses are common among those found NGRI, and in some jurisdictions minor crimes constitute the majority of crimes committed by insanity acquittees. There is a wide range among states in the number of serious crimes committed by insanity defendants. About one-quarter of the acquittees in Connecticut and New Jersey had been charged with murder (compared with Michigan and New York, where half of all acquittees were charged with murder or attempted murder), and only 5 percent in Missouri and Oregon had murdered their victims.[3]

Many insanity acquittees do not have long histories of severe mental disorder and frequent psychiatric hospitalizations. Less than half—approximately 40 percent—of insanity acquittees have had at least one prior hospitalization for mental illness, and about half of the insanity acquittees are diagnosed as psychotic at the time of the crime. While we know that about two-thirds of hospitalized insanity acquittees are psychotic, very little is known about what clinical characteristics (e.g., depression, anxiety, involvement with drugs and alcohol) are significant to the judge or jury in assessing a defendant's mental status at the time of the crime. It is important to remember, however, that nearly one-third of hospitalized insanity acquittees are *not* diagnosed as psychotic and, conversely, many defendants diagnosed as psychotic are *not* found legally insane.[4] Therefore, many insanity acquittees are not out of touch with reality, and many seriously mentally ill defendants are not legally insane.

A common perception persists that NGRI defendants are especially dangerous to strangers—killing at random on the streets and schoolyards of American cities. Since no one knows who their victims will be, everyone is at risk. Furthermore, Americans tend to believe only an insane offender could commit such reprehensible acts as a mass slaying or serial murders. These images of suspects are often generated by media characterizations of them as "former mental patients" or a person "with a long history of mental illness." In fact, the offender-victim relationship of NGRI offenses parallels that of non-NGRI criminal acts. In crimes such as homicide and assault, the victim and the offender are usually acquainted; for property offenses, the victim is generally a stranger. Thus, the high-profile media events of random violence committed by an "insane" person overshadow the fact that most insanity defendants behave like most criminals in selecting their victims.[5]

In another common misperception, the public fears that a defendant runs no risk by pleading insanity and that the insanity "loophole" jeopardizes community safety. If the NGRI tactic is successful, they think the defendant will escape confinement either through quick release or by spending much less time in custody than a defendant convicted of a similar offense. If the plea fails, nothing was lost from the attempt.[6]

Research has shown that defendants who successfully assert the insanity defense spend *significantly longer* time in confinement for serious offenses than defendants convicted of similar crimes who did not raise the defense.[7] Length of detention appears to be "calibrated by the seriousness of the crime for which the defendant was found not culpable." Steadman goes on to conclude that

> [u]nless one accepts the proposition that the more serious the psychopathology and the longer the course of treatment, there should be no necessary relationship between the NGRI offense and the length of hospitalization. What seems to be operative here is a public policy that demands retribution in the form of hospitalization.[8]

There is also no support for the assumption that a defendant has nothing to lose from pleading insanity. A recent study showed that individuals who unsuccessfully pleaded NGRI were confined 22 percent longer than those who had not raised the insanity defense,[9] probably because defendants who actually go to trial with an insanity defense did not plea bargain for a lesser punishment before the verdict came in. Many convicted criminals eliminate or reduce the time they might otherwise serve by plea bargaining. Since an insanity plea is usually an admission that the defendant committed the charged offense, there is no room to bargain for a reduced charge once the jury has rejected the NGRI plea. Thus, defendants who plead insanity but are found guilty are more likely to find themselves behind bars longer because they did not plea bargain.

The public also fears "insane" criminals will prey on communities again after their release. Are insanity acquittees likely to repeat their crimes once they are released? Defendants found NGRI do have substantial rates of rearrest, ranging from 13 percent in Oregon to 61 percent in Connecticut. But their recidivism rates are almost the same as those for convicted felons who committed similar crimes. Although successful insanity defendants are rearrested for offenses ranging from shoplifting to murder, the most frequent charges are assault, burglary, theft, and robbery. While the rearrest rate for NGRIs is similar to that of other felons, NGRIs are arrested two to three times more frequently than patients released from mental hospitals. Thus, the pattern of rearrest among insanity acquittees resembles that of any convicted felon.[10]

Do criminal defendants "fake" the insanity defense under current law? Unfortunately, no one knows. We do know, however, that the mental health professional's diagnosis of serious mental illness at the time of the crime is a controlling factor in a successful insanity defense.[11] It seems fair to conclude then that insanity defendants must be able to fool the expert before they can fool the jury.

Regrettably, legislators, prosecuting attorneys, mental health professionals, and the public have a grossly inaccurate understanding of the true scope and actual consequences of the insanity defense. Despite the many myths, very few people escape a criminal sentence because of mental status. Furthermore, the defense is not reserved for heinous crimes such as mass murder, assassination, or random violence. There is also some indication that mentally ill offenders have *more* to lose from pleading insanity than if they had not. Thus, these misconceptions provide slippery footing for the design and implementation of meaningful insanity defense reforms.

Different Insanity Tests, Different Outcomes?

Throughout the twentieth century, legal scholars and psychiatrists have debated the relative pluses and minuses of various formulations of the insanity defense. Much of the debate has been over the theoretical implications of specific insanity tests used by judges and juries in criminal trials, while avoiding the question of whether the different tests make any actual difference in the real world. Although an enormous amount of energy has been expended on choosing the exact wording for the insanity defense, the American Psychiatric Association doubts that the precise formulation determines whether or not a defendant is acquitted by reason of insanity. Many observers believe the impact of different formulations depends almost entirely on how they are applied in the courtroom.[12]

As Professor Keilitz aptly notes, "declarations that changes in wording will have little or no effect . . . are just as conjectural as the opposite position."[13] It is difficult to ascertain if choice of language has subtle yet significant effects on the opinions of expert witnesses, the arguments made by counsel, decisions by the lawyers and trial judge, or, perhaps most important, on jury deliberations.[14] Whether reformers can achieve their intended results by changing the wording of the insanity test is yet to be determined with confidence, although there have been a number of studies that sought to answer that question.

The Insanity Defense During the Liberal Era

Most jurisdictions adopted the American Law Institute's version of the insanity test or the *Durham* rule with the expectation that more mentally ill offenders would be acquitted and thereby treated instead of punished. Very little empirical evidence, however, has been systematically examined to explore whether this hoped-for result came to pass. Only four studies—each with considerable methodological limitations—have investigated what actually happened when a jurisdiction switched from a strict test like *M'Naghten* to a more liberal version of the insanity defense.

Even with their flaws, however, the four studies provide evidence that adopting a more expansive test did increase the frequency of successful insanity defenses. For example, in the seven years after the District of Columbia replaced the *M'Naghten* test with the *Durham* rule, the number of successful insanity cases increased from less than one-half of 1 percent to over 14 percent. Although most of the increase occurred more than five years after the *Durham* decision, it appears likely that *Durham* did have a significant effect on acquittals.[15]

There is also weak but provocative support for the conclusion that switching from the *M'Naghten* test to the ALI test also resulted in more successful insanity pleas. Between 1966 and 1972, Oregon had only 44 successful insanity pleas using the *M'Naghten* test; between 1972 and 1982, a total of 734 insanity acquittals occurred using the ALI standard. Maryland experienced an increase of 143 percent in the proportion of defendants found not guilty by reason of insanity in the years after that state changed from *M'Naghten* to ALI.[16]

On the other hand, Wyoming's change from a combination of *M'Naghten* and the "irresistible impulse" test to the ALI revealed no significant changes, but this result may have been due to the extremely small number of cases available for study. In fact, the quality of the data from the four studies of insanity defense reforms during the Liberal Era is so poor that they provide nothing more than informed speculation that changing the insanity test criteria makes a difference in actual practice.[17] It is apparent though that the number of successful insanity defenses did increase in the District of Columbia, Oregon, and Maryland in the years following revision of their insanity test. While this increase cannot be attributed unequivocally to the reforms themselves, it does indicate that adoption of a more lenient insanity test may result in more insanity acquittals.

There are other factors that have nothing to do with the precise wording of the insanity test that may explain some of these changes. For example, mere population growth means a larger number of criminals and an increase in the number of mentally ill people.[18] Thus, one would expect there would be more criminal defendants, and more of them would plead insanity successfully. Yet, while population growth may explain the increase in volume, it does not explain the growth in the proportion of mentally ill offenders.

Changes in related areas of law may also have a direct impact on the insanity defense. For instance, revisions in New York's criminal procedures controlling the disposition of NGRI acquittees appear to have resulted in an increase in the number of persons adjudicated NGRI. Prior to 1971, when acquittees were automatically committed to a department of corrections facility, only a handful of persons were found insane. After 1971, when acquittees began to be transferred to the department of mental hygiene, there was a sizable jump in the number of acquittals. It appears lawyers, judges, and juries thought changes in the place of confinement increased the likelihood insanity acquittees would receive psychiatric treatment.[19] This, in turn, may have encouraged more insanity pleas and verdicts.

Court decisions can also increase the number of insanity acquittals. In *State* v. *Krol*, the New Jersey Supreme Court held that there must be a hearing to determine whether NGRI defendants are presently mentally ill and dangerous before they can be confined in a mental hospital. Before this decision, NGRI acquittees in New Jersey were hospitalized for an average of 26.3 months. Following *Krol*, average hospitalization periods were reduced to 6.4 months.[20] Thus, more defendants may have been willing to plead insanity because of the reduced time spent in hospitals, and more of those may have been successful.

Although the impact of insanity defense reforms in the Liberal Era has been poorly charted, it is likely that a small increase occurred in the actual number of people excused from their crimes because of insanity. This outcome may have been due either to changes in the insanity test or to other factors that occurred during this time. Given the small number of offenders successfully using the insanity defense, the cause of the public uproar at the dawn of the Neoconservative Era must be found elsewhere.

The Insanity Defense During the Neoconservative Era

Although some people assume it was the attempted presidential assassination by John Hinckley that led to the rash of insanity defense reforms in the 1980s, the legislative reforms actually began several years before Hinckley's 1982 insanity acquittal. While Hinckley's acquittal galvanized public anger, antagonism toward excusing criminal behavior because of mental illness was consistent with the general mood of Americans in the 1980s. In an era obsessed by law and order, excuses based on mental illness are bound to have a tenuous hold.[21]

Scholarly and public debate during this era focused on either modifying or abolishing the insanity defense, or altering the consequences of an insanity acquittal. Negative public reaction to events like the release of 150 insanity acquittees and the violent crimes two of them committed following the Michigan Supreme Court's 1974 decision in *People* v. *McQuillan* fed the flames of public displeasure over the legal system's failure to protect the public. When unpopular decisions like the Hinckley insanity acquittal or the Dan White "Twinkie defense" became front-page headlines, law-and-order initiatives such as Proposition 8 in California forced legislators to make sweeping legal changes to limit the insanity defense and the diminished capacity defense. Major insanity defense reforms of the Neoconservative Era, perhaps presaged by that of Michigan in 1975, spread to other states and Congress throughout the early 1980s.[22]

Although the reforms varied in their precise content, they shared three common themes. First, they reflected the belief that fewer people should escape their just deserts through the loophole of insanity. In some states, this meant eliminating the defense altogether; in other jurisdictions, it meant a tougher test. Where total abolition was not a politically viable alternative, legislators would at least modify the insanity test to lessen the chance a criminal might escape punishment.

The second theme was to increase the criminal justice system's control over mentally disordered offenders. This was the major purpose underlying the guilty but mentally ill (GBMI) defense. Successful insanity defendants are *acquitted* of their crimes and switched into the mental health system; in contrast, GBMI defendants are *convicted* and can receive the same prison sentence as other defendants found guilty, including prison terms and the death penalty. By providing this full range of dispositions, the GBMI alternative offers greater control over the mentally ill offender than was possible after a NGRI acquittal. Third, some of the reforms—especially in the case of the GBMI defense—were intended to enhance the likelihood of treatment for this special group of severely mentally impaired inmates.[23]

Legislatures and the public hoped insanity defense reform would change the criminal justice system. When the GBMI verdict was established in Georgia, Illinois, and Michigan, nearly half of the legislators, attorneys, judges, mental health personnel, and corrections officials surveyed expected a decrease in the use of the insanity defense. One-fourth of them believed legal change would also increase the prospects of treatment for mentally disordered offenders. Nearly one-quarter believed the GBMI alternative would increase the criminal justice system's control over offenders.[24]

Research is now becoming available that illuminates how these expectations fared in the years following insanity defense reform. Most of the research focuses on the implementation of various GBMI statutes and examines three fundamental questions:

1. *Does the GBMI defense curtail use of the insanity defense?* Proponents of the GBMI defense claimed it would decrease the number of successful insanity defenses. If the availability of the GBMI verdict has had

any such impact, it has been very slight. In Michigan the frequency of NGRI verdicts appears undisturbed by the arrival of GBMI as an alternative verdict. In Illinois the number of NGRI acquittals actually increased following enactment of the GBMI legislation. In the first year after Georgia enacted the GBMI defense, eighty-eight defendants were found GBMI and forty-two were acquitted by reason of insanity—two more insanity acquittals than in the previous year. Thus, providing GBMI as an alternative to the insanity defense apparently has had little, if any, impact on the number of insanity acquittals.[25]

When California's Proposition 8 limited the use of the insanity defense and the diminished capacity defense in 1982, the rate of insanity pleas or acquittals, the characteristics of those using the insanity defense, or the length of confinement did not change.[26]

2. *Has the GBMI defense increased control over mentally disordered offenders?* Although enhanced control over mentally disordered offenders was one of the primary motivations for enacting the GBMI defense, evidence demonstrating this result is very weak. GBMI offenders are sometimes given longer sentences than non-GBMI offenders. For example, in Georgia the average sentence for a GBMI offender is about twelve years, compared with just over nine years for all other offenders committed to the Georgia Department of Rehabilitation. In Michigan, 21 percent of GBMI offenders received sentences of sixteen or more years compared with only 12 percent of non-GBMI prison inmates. The average length of confinement for GBMI offenders in Michigan has been longer than for defendants acquitted by reason of insanity. GBMI confinement lasted just under four years as compared with a year-and-a-half for NGRI acquittees.

Although GBMI defendants as a group tended to receive longer sentences, these differences are small and may be due to other factors. A more definitive answer to whether the GBMI alternative increases control over mentally disordered offenders depends on whether the longer sentences for GBMI offenders have been imposed for the same crime or whether the stiffer sentence is the result of more serious crimes.[27] The results of an ongoing study by Steadman and his colleagues should provide more answers to these questions in the near future.

3. *Does the GBMI defense encourage treatment of mentally disordered offenders?* Contrary to the expectation that accompanied GBMI legislation, GBMI offenders are no more likely to receive treatment than mentally disordered offenders not found GBMI. GBMI offenders are eligible for treatment in most states only if a postconviction mental health evaluation indicates this need and if resources are available to provide it. While at least 90 percent of GBMI offenders actually receive postconviction evaluations, in those states which have been studied, examiners recommend treatment for them in only 64 to 72 percent of the cases. Not all of those for whom treatment is advised ever receive treatment or care. Hence, this goal of insanity defense reform has not been met.[28]

Early neoconservative reforms of the insanity defense used "front-end" trial procedures and insanity test wording—designed to influence jury verdicts—to decrease the number of insanity acquittals. To limit the number of successful NGRI verdicts, these reforms usually concentrated on outright abolition of the defense, revisions in wording, enactment of the GBMI defense, or shifting the burden of proof. After Montana abolished the insanity defense in 1979, dismissals based on incompetency to stand trial increased substantially. This phenomenon led Steadman and his colleagues to conclude that "dismissal based on incompetency to stand trial became a substitute for acquittal based on the insanity plea."[29] Increased use of an alternative disposition for mentally ill offenders provides further support that front-end reforms have generally had little or no impact on the number of pleas or the number of people "excused" for their crimes.

It appears that, if insanity defense reform is to work as intended, it must focus on "back-end" reforms that determine what happens to a successful NGRI defendant after the trial. Back-end reforms ensure greater control by requiring insanity defendants to spend more time in psychiatric facilities, thus making their release more difficult. Such measures would help prevent the release of offenders who are still mentally ill and dangerous.

Other back-end reforms require more aggressive community supervision on release. For example, Oregon's Psychiatric Security Review Board extends the surveillance and control of mentally disordered offenders after their release. In short, later neoconservative law reform is now concentrating on making the release of successful insanity defendants more difficult and strengthening community monitoring after release.[30]

The only goal of insanity defense reform that appears realistic is keeping the mentally ill offender within reach of the criminal justice system by automatic commitment after trial, more stringent release standards and procedures, and outpatient commitment. With the approval of the Supreme Court in the *Jones* decision, states will probably become more aggressive in their attempts to confine and control mentally ill offenders who successfully use the insanity defense.

Involuntary Civil Commitment

A strange irony appears when considering the insanity defense and involuntary civil commitment. Despite the fact that relatively few people ever plead insanity and even fewer are successful, the insanity defense is one of the most hotly debated and controversial issues in law.[31] On the other hand, involuntary civil commitment of the mentally ill—a legal system that affects approximately 1.2 million persons every year—is virtually unknown to most Americans.[32]

Studies of the prevalence of mental disorders clearly establish that serious mental illness is found in all segments of society and in all social classes. Yet, people who are involuntarily committed tend to be social outcasts even before they walk through the hospital door. Overwhelmingly, they are poor and unemployed or working in poorly paid jobs. They rarely have more than a high school education, and most lack skills or experience for anything but the lowest-paying jobs.[33]

Those civilly committed have few personal and social resources for maintaining control over their lives. They tend to be young, white males who are single, divorced, or separated from their spouse. Most civil committees are not married at the time of their commitment, and a surprisingly large proportion have never been married. Those who are single may never have been able to form stable relationships; those who are divorced or separated may suffer from disintegrated social networks, loss of housing, and heightened emotional difficulties.[34]

Although only a minority of civil committees are married, most have ties to their families and have turned to them at one time or another for help. In fact, family members are most likely to initiate contact with commitment authorities, either by bringing the mentally ill person directly to a mental hospital or enlisting the assistance of police. Once a mentally ill person creates a disturbance in the community, the willingness of a family member to be responsible for that person is an important factor in whether he or she is committed.[35]

When civil commitment candidates arrive at an emergency room, they are likely to be diagnosed as having a serious mental disorder. Candidates with prior hospitalizations demonstrate even more serious and long-standing problems and are more likely to be committed. At least half of all persons who are committed have diagnoses of major mental disorders such as schizophrenia, depression, manic-depressive illness, or other psychosis. The majority have been hospitalized at least once before, thus contributing to a high proportion of chronic patients in public mental hospitals.[36]

But if serious mental illness is found in all sectors of society, why are only poor people committed to state mental hospitals? As noted by Professor Virginia Hiday, "The more privileged have their own alternatives." This includes care at home, private hospitals, or treatment and control before behavior becomes unmanageable. The middle class turns to civil commitment only when one of its members is extremely dangerous or after their resources or patience have run out.[37]

What do we expect to accomplish by sending the mentally ill to hospitals? Most expect hospitalization will protect the public and the patient. If there is one consistent stereotype of hospitalized mental patients, it is that they are violent and uncontrollable. When Liberal Era commitment laws made "dangerousness" a criteria for detention, critics predicted hospitals would become battlegrounds full of untreatable, dangerous patients. It is now clear, however, this did not happen, and civilly committed patients are not particularly dangerous, either before, during, or after they are taken into custody by commitment authorities.

Dangerousness is a confusing, inconsistently applied concept meaning many things to many people. Even though dangerous behavior has been the centerpiece of virtually all Liberal Era commitment law, the concept has been poorly defined or unspecified altogether.[38] Consequently, virtually any behavior can be called "dangerous." Under the law, people may be detained against their will because they threaten or attack another person, themselves, or property.[39] The behavior itself may range from very serious acts such as an attempt to kill someone to very trivial acts such as yelling at passersby. Some commitment statutes consider neglect of one's own bodily needs (e.g., inability to provide food, shelter, and clothing) as dangerous behavior.

Even when sweeping, normative definitions of dangerousness are used, researchers have found that the behavior of a large proportion of hospitalized patients does not meet the statutory definition of dangerousness, and that even fewer patients have actually committed violent acts. Designations of dangerousness are most often based on conclusions about a candidate's general level of functioning instead of on the objective facts of the behavior itself. For example, Professor Carol Warren found that the medical records of only 40 percent of candidates for hospitalization in one California jurisdiction contained reference to assaultive, violent, or threatening behavior. Other researchers found no relationship between the dangerousness of hospitalized patients and their certification as dangerous to themselves or others, or as gravely disabled.[40]

On the contrary, a variety of studies have shown the vast majority of committees are hospitalized because of annoying or bizarre behavior. They are not hospitalized because they are threatening someone's safety. Often family members use civil commitment to get some relief from intolerable or objectionable behavior. In a study of Florida committees, the average candidate for civil commitment showed "poor judgment and occasional neglect of basic needs, indicated by limited insight or vague threats of self-harm or suicide."[41]

Hiday's work has also confirmed that the vast majority of civil commitment candidates are not dangerous, much less violent, following their court hearings. She traced the behavior of over 700 commitment candidates for six months after their hearings, regardless of whether they were hospitalized. Using hospital records, community mental health records, and arrest records, she found that almost three- fourths of the subjects did not commit violent acts, make threats, or cause unintentional harm. The small proportion who behaved dangerously rarely inflicted actual injury on themselves or others.[42]

Even the small proportion of patients who in fact exhibit physically assaultive behavior cease their aggression quickly after admission. Most dangerous behavior occurs the first day after admission and does not recur during the patient's hospital stay. Aggressive patients are usually administered psychoactive drugs immediately on their arrival. These medications calm most patients and subdue their most florid symptoms. Admission into a hospital removes them from the aggravating environment of the community and places them in a ward designed to control aggressive behavior.[43]

Almost all involuntary patients spend only brief periods of time in public mental hospitals. Most are released after a few days or weeks in the hospital and return to where they came from. Only a few studies have followed patients released from hospitals back into the community to monitor their behavior. Those studies have found that patients released from state mental hospitals have an arrest rate from about one to twenty-eight times higher than the rate of the general population for assault or homicide and approximately three times higher than the general population for all other offenses. Most arrests are for nonviolent property offenses or use of illegal substances.[44] One study of discharged patients found a high rate of suicide and a surprisingly high number of deaths from medical causes, indicating higher rates of morbidity and mortality in this group.[45]

It is not evident that dangerousness, even though it was the foundation of most Liberal Era commitment laws, became the most important criterion for involuntary hospitalization. It may be that mental health professionals labeled clients whom they thought needed treatment as dangerous in order to secure their hospitalization.[46] Contrary to expectations, Liberal Era commitment reforms did not result in the commitment of primarily dangerous people. The reforms also discouraged commitment of the nondangerous chronically mentally ill who needed treatment. What effect, then, did Liberal Era reforms have on the commitment process?

Assessing the Impact of Civil Commitment Reforms

Despite their relative obscurity, civil commitment laws have always mirrored public attitudes about mental illness, individual responsibility, and community safety. For the past quarter-century, these laws have been viewed as an important instrument for articulating the rights of the mentally ill and controlling hospitalization practices. When Liberal Era reformers set out to close mental hospitals and promote community treatment, they overhauled involuntary commitment laws to enforce deinstitutionalization policies. Liberal Era reformers wanted the vast majority of mentally ill people returned to their communities to live as they chose, free from state coercion. In the eyes of many, the mentally ill had more to fear from incarceration in hospitals than from living on their own.

When strict limitations on forced hospitalization were blamed for creating homelessness and contributing to the alarming rise in the number of mentally ill people in our cities and towns, expansion of commitment authority was moved to the top of the neoconservative agenda.

Researchers have measured the impact of Liberal Era reforms and more recent Neoconservative Era reforms to ascertain whether statutory revisions in commitment laws accomplished what reformers intended. Despite a variety of methodological limitations, the studies do shed light on whether legal reforms brought about changes in commitment practices. The largest group of studies is from states that sought during the Liberal Era to decrease the number of commitments through more restrictive substantive criteria, more stringent procedural rules, or—in most cases—both. Empirical analysis of the more recent neoconservative change is also available, but the number of studies is far more limited due to the recency of this law reform.[47]

Civil Commitment During the Liberal Era

Studies clearly demonstrate that when legislative reforms have been enacted to limit the use of involuntary commitment, there has been an immediate decrease in the number of commitments for at least two years. But the decline in admission rates is short-lived. A recent synthesis of seventeen such studies indicates that admission rates eventually reach or exceed prereform levels.[48] Thus, restrictive commitment laws appear unable to reduce the rate of involuntary hospitalizations for more than a brief period.

Several hypotheses have been suggested to account for this finding. First, some observers suggest that restrictive commitment laws create a "revolving-door" phenomenon, in which length of treatment is inappropriately shortened. The resulting inability to provide necessary treatment for an extended time almost ensures that the patient will be recommitted soon after release. According to this claim, the same patients return to hospitals again and again, thereby creating accelerating commitment rates. There is no sound evidence for this conclusion, however. In fact, studies indicate that postreform increases are due to accelerating rates of first-time commitments as well as rising readmission rates.[49]

A second hypothesis suggests that commitment standards based on dangerousness may bring only the most difficult patients into public psychiatric hospitals, thus increasing the chances that patients who meet these restrictive criteria are likely to be committed again and again. But no empirical information is available to support or refute this assumption.[50]

Third, a number of researchers have suggested that the subsequent increases in admissions following Liberal Era reforms reflected an adjustment period for mental health professionals. Initially, commitment authorities felt compelled to use a narrow interpretation of the legal reforms. But because mental health workers believed the new laws were too restrictive and denigrated their expertise, they eventually ignored them or found ways around them and began to commit those they believed should be committed. While this explanation is quite plausible, clear empirical support for it is lacking. We do know, however, that throughout the Liberal Era there was extensive judicial deference to mental health professionals. Judges most frequently followed professionals' recommendations to hospitalize patients even in the absence of adequate evidence that the criteria for civil commitment were met.[51]

But if admission rates returned to their original levels a few years after civil libertarian laws were enacted, how did public mental hospitals empty their beds, close wards, and reduce their inpatient censuses? Contrary to public opinion, hospitals did not close as a result of Liberal Era reforms. The total number of state mental hospitals has not changed much over the past thirty-five years. What did change was the average length of hospital stay. Institutions emptied because increases in the number of admissions did not keep pace with declines in the average length of a hospital stay. The result was a decrease in the average daily census of almost 80 percent, with the sharpest decline occurring between 1965 and 1975.[52]

There is no question that the average length of stay in public mental hospitals decreased dramatically during the Liberal Era. State mental hospitals and Veterans Administration psychiatric hospitals experienced sharp reductions in the length of time patients were confined. Even private hospitals decreased their patients' length of stay during this period, although fluctuations in length of stay were more likely to reflect the availability of beds than compliance with restrictive civil commitment laws.[53]

Who Remained in Hospitals?

Once hospitals began to empty, who was left behind? A number of studies reported that, except for a decrease in the average age of committed patients, the demographic profile of involuntary patients did not change much after civil libertarian reforms. The drop in the average age probably reflected the growing practice of caring for many older patients in nursing homes, board-and-care homes, or other nontraditional alternatives instead of in the geriatric wards of public mental hospitals.[54]

In fact, state hospitals are still populated by poor patients who look much the same as they did before the legal changes of the 1960s and 1970s. The difference in the years following legal reform was that many more patients were admitted to hospitals on a voluntary basis. Prior to the Liberal Era reforms, significant differences had existed between involuntary and voluntary patients. Older, poor men with little education were more likely to be committed than young, female, better-educated patients who came to hospitals voluntarily. Following Liberal Era reforms, the characteristics of voluntary and involuntary patients became more alike, leading some to conclude that candidates who once would have been forcibly committed were now willingly accepting hospitalization. A more cynical interpretation of this finding is that patients formerly committed against their will were now given an ultimatum of accepting "voluntary" admission or facing involuntary commitment.[55]

Only a few studies attempted to report changes in diagnostic patterns before and after legal reform. Most found that diagnostic patterns were not altered by Liberal Era reforms. The range of bizarre as well as trivial behavior associated with involuntary detention probably remained unchanged following the narrowing of civil commitment criteria.[56]

There is strong evidence that Liberal Era commitment reforms increased the number of hospitalized patients who had arrest records. The precise reason for this development is unclear. It may be due to the implementation of dangerousness as the dominant criterion for commitment or, alternatively, to the increased use of civil commitment by the criminal justice system. But it should be noted that arrests are not a valid measure of dangerousness. Most arrests are for property crimes or for felonies that do not threaten or attempt serious physical harm to others.[57]

Paternalism in the Courtroom

Virtually all states included enhanced procedural protections for patients when they enacted Liberal Era reforms. These procedures were intended to make commitment hearings more like criminal trials and much less like informal inquiries so that the patients' interest in liberty and in making their own treatment decisions would be adequately protected. Confronted with court decisions such as *Lessard* v. *Schmidt*, state legislatures passed laws that provided detainees with the right to counsel, to hearings before judges, and the right to call their own witnesses and to cross-examine government witnesses.

It is virtually impossible to measure the impact of these procedural reforms alone because we cannot untangle their effects from the effects of changes in the statutory commitment criteria that occurred at the same time.[58] Yet, the vast majority of studies found significant changes in the commitment process following implementation of procedural protections. In a host of research studies, improvements were observed in the quality of initial commitment hearings and in every step of the commitment and release process. Legal counsel was usually available, hearings lasted longer, and evidence for commitment was examined more carefully by the court. Attorneys were more likely to challenge psychiatric opinion aggressively and to seek alternatives to inpatient treatment. As a result, patients were more likely to be released— even when psychiatrists recommended hospitalization.[59]

On the other hand, some of the same studies present evidence that procedural protections did not always enhance the accuracy or fairness of commitment hearings. In many instances, evidence was not always examined thoroughly, counsel was often passive or nonadversarial, and mental illness was assumed rather than proved objectively. In an extensive series of studies on the role of counsel in commitment, Hiday found that attorneys are still more likely to accept the role of "participant" instead of adversary in commitment proceedings. While a few attorneys do adopt an adversarial role, according to Hiday, most do not feel comfortable in that position even when they are explicitly encouraged by the presiding judge. Most lawyers assume their clients do not know what is best for them. Consequently, many lawyers, instead of seeking what their clients want, work with families and doctors to achieve what they collectively think is the best outcome for the client—even when that means hospitalization.[60]

The existing research indicates wide variations across jurisdictions and among key participants in the effective use of procedural protections. It is clear that even rigorous procedural protections will be ineffective if judges feel most patients belong in hospitals and most defense lawyers do not represent their clients vigorously and competently. While Liberal Era commitment statutes provided more formal procedural protections for those facing civil commitment, civil libertarians are far from satisfied with the actual results of these reforms.[61]

Civil Commitment During the Neoconservative Era

By the beginning of the Neoconservative Era, there was widespread antipathy for the civil libertarian reforms of the 1960s and 1970s. When counterreforms were launched to broaden involuntary commitment criteria, the impact was swift and certain. When Washington State (where the legal reforms have been studied most thoroughly) changed its law in 1979 to permit commitment of mentally ill individuals in need of treatment as well as those who were dangerous, there was a 180 percent increase in total admissions to the largest state mental hospital over the two years following the legal change. Involuntary admissions increased by 91 percent in the first year after the legal change. Involuntary admissions actually began to rise nine months *before* the effective date of the revised statute, the result of an anticipation effect in which mental health professionals and judges simply operated as though the new statute was actually in effect.[62]

Other researchers have also observed increases in commitment following legislative attempts to broaden commitment criteria. Their findings are less persuasive, however, because their research addressed either a slightly different issue or the legal change they studied was a mixture of broadened and narrowed criteria.[63]

Do Neoconservative Reforms Accomplish Their Mission?

There is little doubt that legal reforms broadening commitment authority will accomplish their goal: Many more people will be involuntarily hospitalized. Although it is impossible to generalize from the experience of one state, it is nevertheless useful to examine what happened in Washington. Commitment rates rose so rapidly that new admissions overwhelmed the largest state mental hospital, leading to a "cap" on admissions at 90 percent of bed capacity. To make matters worse, the Washington State Supreme Court ordered the hospital to accept all incoming involuntary patients, even if there were no beds for them.[64]

It is not surprising voluntary patients virtually disappeared from Washington's public mental health system. When Washington provided more expansive authority to commit gravely disabled patients, detention shifted away from dangerousness toward *parens patriae* commitments. By 1981, three out of every four commitments relied on the grave disability standard, while dangerousness to self or others accounted for only one-quarter of involuntary detentions.[65]

The increase in gravely disabled patients should not be interpreted as a change in the clientele of the state hospital system, however. In fact, the clinical and demographic profile of patients who were committed to state mental hospitals did not change at all. Following the 1979 revision of the law, more and more of the same types of patients were admitted and readmitted to state custody. Only the particular legal authority used to detain the incoming patients was altered. Under the revised law, people who had engaged in violent behavior were more likely to be detained under the state's *parens patriae* authority as gravely disabled than under its police power as dangerous. Therefore, the measurable changes were primarily in the extraordinary increase in the number of patients hospitalized involuntarily and in the legal authority invoked to detain them. The behavior that brought them to the attention of commitment authorities did not change.[66]

The Gap Between Perception and Reality

Legal reform appears to have had varying effects on the insanity defense and civil commitment practices. Despite the clear intentions of reformers, changes in the insanity defense have had little, if any, impact on the number of persons excused from their crimes due to mental illness. Nor have changes been particularly helpful in ensuring that mentally ill offenders are confined in secure facilities for a longer period of time. Although the public may believe these changes made their world safer, neoconservative insanity reforms were mostly symbolic. They reflected society's adamant demand for restoring law and order in a world perceived to be on the brink of lawlessness.

The impact of neoconservative change in civil commitment law is more complex. Broadening civil commitment authority may be more successful than the reforms that restricted involuntary confinement. Although a legislative mandate to reduce the number of patients in mental hospitals is likely to cause an immediate short-term decline in the number of involuntary commitments, patterns of detention return to their prereform levels after a relatively brief time. Reductions in hospital censuses during the Liberal Era appear to have been achieved through reductions in the average length of stay rather than by limiting admissions to hospitals.

New laws authorizing *broadened* commitment authority can be powerful forces for change—even if the consequences are unintended. Mental health authorities, families, and law enforcement officials appear eager to commit patients they think need treatment—even before the effective date of a new law. If hospitals are full, voluntary patients will be discharged to make room for involuntary patients. Commitment rates may not slow down even after hospitals run out of beds for new patients, although there may be pressure to develop an informal system of rationing scarce beds. Decision-makers in the commitment process will use their expanded authority to hospitalize people who cannot be cared for anywhere else.

It is interesting to surmise why legal reform has had such a varying impact on the operations of these complex systems of social control. The criminal justice system has remained virtually unchanged in the way it processes mentally disordered offenders. The mental health system, on the other hand, changed significantly by expanding social control over thousands of America's citizens. Why the difference?

One obvious explanation why changing the operative insanity test or abolishing it altogether did not make much difference is that it affects so few criminal defendants. Yet given the public's intense antagonism toward mentally disordered offenders, this explanation may be too simplistic. Another explanation may be that jurors who make case-by-case insanity determinations have the opportunity to dispel the myths of the insanity defense in the courtroom. Jurors are free to excuse a single person unburdened by stereotypical visions of the insane offender. Insanity verdicts, therefore, make sense for this tiny subgroup of offenders. Although the insanity defense is still not trusted by the public, the jury can do justice to the individual in the single case. Jurors may feel confident the offender will receive treatment and will also be confined as long as the defendant is still a threat. Thus, both fairness and community safety are well served.

But the mental health system of commitment did undergo real change as a result of the reform. The expert opinions of mental health professionals are now more influential in civil commitment hearings. Liberal Era commitment laws had constrained professional authority by requiring the court instead of psychiatrists to make the final detention decisions and by limiting commitment primarily to the dangerous mentally ill. Initially, mental health professionals only activated commitment when they had a reasonable chance of securing court-ordered confinement. It is not surprising that legislation that sought to curtail the power of professionals was strongly opposed by them and, eventually, circumvented. After an adjustment period of a few years, mental health professionals apparently learned how to manipulate their recommendations to fit the law and commit those they believed needed hospital treatment.[67]

The conclusion that the insanity defense and involuntary civil commitment are *perceived* as important forms of social control has been strengthened by these recent developments in mental health law. From one cycle of reform to another, the insanity defense and civil commitment law have been poignant expressions of societal theories of responsibility and autonomy as well as a mirror of how we value punishment and treatment.

Despite the shortcomings of research, it is actually possible to observe the impact of legislative change on the way mentally disordered people are processed by the criminal justice and mental health systems. The consistency of the data is impressive, even though replication and elaboration of available findings are sorely needed.[68] What light does this research shed on the future of mental health law and policy in the United States? In the last chapter, we address this important question.

8

Out of Sight, Out of Mind:
The Future of Mental Health
Law and Policy

Law and policy reforms are products of their time and of times gone by. Reform is shaped both by dominant social values and by the legacies of successes and failures inherited from prior reforms.[1] While major shifts and minor adjustments in our social values keep the pendulum of reform in constant motion, we can say with some certainty that we are no longer at the threshold of the Neoconservative Era. We are in its midst. Disillusionment with Liberal Era policies has brought us face to face with contemporary demands to restore law and order and to reestablish the rights of the majority. And in this whirlwind of social change, the mentally ill have been swept along.

A wealth of evidence confirms the onset of an era in which the rights of the community are protected at the expense of individual freedom. The political processes that support reform have shifted, the uses of psychiatric expertise have been modified, and mental health law itself has been reshaped.

Why Did the Liberal Era Fail?

To understand why the neoconservative reforms have been instituted, we need to understand what went wrong with the idealism of the Liberal Era. The Great Society had tried mightily to understand how mental illness influenced criminal behavior. Countless efforts had been made to help, not blame, this special class of offender. The Great Society had also tried to enable most other mentally ill citizens to live on their own in the community. But by the twilight of the Liberal Era, virtually everyone agreed something was seriously wrong with the criminal law's apparent coddling of mentally disordered offenders and with social programs for the care and control of the noncriminal mentally ill.

Psychiatry had proffered new insight into how mental illness impaired a person's ability to obey the law. During the Liberal Era, many judges and psychiatrists readily accepted this new knowledge and enthusiastically set

150

about reshaping the criminal law. But public support for this modern view of criminal behavior quickly faded toward the end of the Liberal Era and during the onset of the Neoconservative Era. Why?

This is a complex question and probably can never be answered with complete authority. It appears very likely, however, that one major reason for the loss of public confidence and support was the skyrocketing crime rates of the 1960s and early 1970s. As noted in Chapter 2, therapeutic approaches designed to reduce crime, and social welfare programs designed to alleviate poverty and discrimination seemed only to have exacerbated the crime problem. Unexpectedly, crime exploded in America.

Fear is a powerful agent for social change. And as numerous polls showed, many Americans lived in fear for their own safety and for their loved ones. As a result, implacable public pressure to fight a vigorous war on crime surfaced. It is likely that most citizens saw mentally ill offenders as a significant threat to public safety. Although their actual numbers belied this fear, mentally disordered offenders tended to receive more than their fair share of media coverage. Prominent media cases undoubtedly generated public clamor for changes in the law. Politicians were, for the most part, eager to respond. Here was a clear opportunity to "do something" to fight crime.

As we saw in Chapter 7, the Liberal Era insanity reforms could not have appreciably increased crime rates in America. But the sequence of events, in which Liberal Era insanity reforms were followed by soaring crime rates, may well have persuaded most citizens that the two were closely associated. If crime rates soared *after* the enactment of the these reforms, then these reforms must have *contributed to* the increase in crime. Insanity reforms were seen as the most important example of the Liberal Era being soft on crime.

It is likely that the insanity reforms of the Liberal Era were not necessarily doomed to failure at the outset. But their foundation was simply too tentative to withstand the shock of cascading crime rates. In all likelihood, these reforms were simply overtaken by extraneous events.

It is also possible that liberal reforms might have shown more staying power if "back-end" reforms that regulated the release of criminals back into communities had not also deprived society of its ability to control for any appreciable period mentally ill offenders acquitted of criminal responsibility. Had the laws ensured that these offenders would be confined as long as they were dangerous, the neoconservative "front-end" insanity reforms might not have been so urgent and so extensive. But because the liberal back-end reforms could make no such guarantees, the community lived in fear of the mentally ill offenders who resided in their midst.

The Failure of Deinstitutionalization: Was It Just Money?

In the mid-1960s deinstitutionalization and community treatment appealed to virtually everyone involved in redesigning the Liberal Era's mental health system—the courts, including the Supreme Court, psychiatrists and other mental health providers, law enforcement, lawyers, and the public. Yet by the outset of the Neoconservative Era, these reforms were under severe attack by almost all the same people. Why did such universally supported strategies fail so miserably?

While deinstitutionalization resulted in the discharge of hundreds of thousands of hospitalized mental patients, most agree that community-based treatment was simply not available for the majority of them. Thus, vital support services did not pick up where hospitals left off for many of these patients. Most observers also agree that community care never had a chance to succeed because not enough money was spent to build the system.

But that conclusion raises other, more serious questions: Were Liberal Era reformers poised on the verge of a bona fide breakthrough in the treatment and care of the chronically mentally ill? Did their reforms fail only because vital funding was not provided at the crucial moment? The answer to these questions, in our view, is a resounding "no." Even if enough money had been spent to build the community care network that Liberal Era reformers contemplated, that network would still have had fatal flaws.

There are a number of factors that doomed Liberal Era reforms. First, they promised more than could be delivered to an ever-expanding target population. Second, reformers insisted they were acting only for altruistic motives; they never acknowledged powerful self- interests or the full costs of reform. Third, and perhaps most important, the fundamental mismatch between the nature of chronic mental illness and the system devised to treat it was ignored. In short, we designed the wrong system.

Too Many Promises to Too Many People

The Liberal Era's emphasis on rehabilitation and community treatment lowered society's resistance to expanding social control.[2] Because the state's purpose was to *help* rather than punish, the public was more comfortable stretching the therapeutic net and forcing therapy on a wider population of deviants.[3] The criminal law was more willing to consider spouse batterers, alcoholics, and child abusers, just to name a few, as suffering from "diseases" and to permit them to be diverted from jails into treatment programs. A "diagnosis" qualified a person for entry into the mental health system, spreading shrinking mental health dollars over more and more people.[4] In addition, a metamorphosis of the mentally ill offender took place: The wrongdoer was now a "victim" who deserved treatment rather than punishment.

Too many people were swept into the mental health system under the assumptions that they suffered from illnesses they could not control and that treatments were available to cure them. In fact, available technology did not have ready cures, and many mentally ill patients and offenders were quickly released from treatment and returned unsupervised to the community. Offenders' rights to privacy—as well as the freedom to reoffend—seemed to have priority over community safety. The public felt deceived by the empty promises of rehabilitation made by the mental health system.

But this expansive view of who should be "treated" has been carried forward into the Neoconservative Era. The mental health system seems willing—even anxious—to still "treat" a wide range of mentally ill citizens even though they may have very little to offer them.

Altruism and Convenience

Reforms are always a blend of altruism and self-interest or, as David Rothman might say, conscience and convenience.[5] And Liberal Era reforms were no exception. They failed partly because good intentions were blended with a large dose of self-interest. The reforms were also overwhelmed by the harsh realities of implementation.

Liberal Era reformers saw deinstitutionalization and treatment as ways to hasten the healing process. Therapeutic alternatives to prisons and less restrictive alternatives to hospitals would reduce the stigma and disability of mental illness and give "victims" a greater chance for recovery. Community mental health centers, halfway houses, and other community placement alternatives were expected to treat the mentally ill while also preparing them for a normal life. Virtually everyone agreed that successful care and treatment in the community was preferable to the abuse that often occurred behind the closed doors of custodial institutions.

But, as in other eras of reform, many political agendas needed to be satisfied. Deinstitutionalization was seen by public officials as a way to significantly reduce state mental health budgets. As noted in Chapter 4, some of the most significant savings of deinstitutionalization came from cancellation of plans to build new, or update aging, state mental hospitals. The federal government offered to help pay the cost of community-based care, alleviating the inpatient hospital care traditionally paid by the states. Closing state hospitals would result in significant savings that could be diverted to less expensive community care or to other pressing needs. Even with the best of intentions, however, state and local governments were unable or unwilling to pay the full cost of implementing these new strategies. Unfortunately, the federal government also fell far short of providing the necessary financial support for community treatment. As a result, hospitals were not closed, and community mental health centers were not made available to poor, seriously ill people.

Consequently, the mentally ill continued to be treated intensively in hospitals and then discharged, only to return—unsupported—to communities. Once they left the hospital, many patients on psychoactive medications stopped taking those drugs. Civil libertarian commitment laws kept many of these deteriorating patients from being returned to hospitals—the only place where treatment was available. Thus, practical matters of cost and convenience overtook the altruistic motives that had spurred the original reforms.

A Classic Mismatch: Community Care and the
Chronically Mentally Ill

Perhaps the most fatal mistake of the Liberal Era was designing a community mental health system that focused primarily on the needs of the acutely mentally ill—individuals who suffer from mental health problems which are amenable to short-term, intensive counseling—while virtually ignoring the needs of the chronically mentally ill. Community mental health centers, the mainstays of the Liberal Era mental health system, adopted an acute care treatment model that encouraged brief therapy, and provided excellent treatment to some acute patients. By making these services available in the community, it was assumed that adequate care would also be provided to chronic patients. This was a situation ripe for disaster.

Chronic patients, especially those on the public dole, were less than welcome at these clinics. Clinicians at community mental health centers preferred to work with people who would respond to brief, focal therapy, and who therefore had a reasonable chance of improvement. In the end, many community mental health centers simply did not provide services to match the needs of the chronically mentally ill patient who had previously been hospitalized or who might have been sent to hospitals before the Liberal Era. Consequently, the chronically mentally ill were left to their own devices without much help from anyone.

New Roles and Rules in the Neoconservative Era

To counter these failures, both real and perceived, a new round of legal reforms has been enacted and the role of psychiatry has once again shifted.

Courts Retreat While Legislatures Advance

The Neoconservative Era has been marked by a shift in institutional dominance. During the Liberal Era, legislatures, which traditionally represent the will of the majority, had taken a back seat to courts in shaping mental health law and policy. Today legislatures have returned to center stage in formulating policy. Congress and state legislatures have enacted a wide range of new laws designed to protect the community by controlling the mentally ill more firmly.

In virtually every state in which the ALI insanity test was abandoned in favor of a more conservative test, it was the legislature that made the change. Legislatures in many states created and refined the GBMI defense. Other state legislatures simply abolished the insanity defense altogether, a tactic that effectively took the question of criminal responsibility of mentally ill offenders out of judicial hands completely. Constitutional challenges to these preemptive legislative strategies were unsuccessful.[6]

Courts, the mainstay of civil liberties in the United States, have backed away from the judicial activism of the Liberal Era. Today judges almost never strike down legislation imposing responsibility or control on the mentally ill. Nor do courts intervene in the day-to-day operation of psychiatric institutions. Judges have also withdrawn from the "moral forum" of the criminal law.[7] Individual rights for the mentally ill are now more than ever dependent on the sufferance of the majority.

Psychiatry as a Dominant Instrument of Social Control

The forensic role of mental health professionals has changed dramatically in the Neoconservative Era. Liberal Era reforms gave psychiatrists expansive authority to testify in criminal trials while placing strict limits on their role in involuntary hospitalization. During the Neoconservative Era, legislation has sharply limited their expert testimony in criminal trials, while restoring more authority to them in civil commitment.

Why? To establish greater control over lawbreakers, the criminal law has become more forceful in its view that human beings are morally responsible agents who should be praised for their good actions and punished for their bad actions. As the Neoconservative Era unfolds, the social norms of individual responsibility are undergoing a remarkable metamorphosis. Individualizing justice and providing rehabilitation are no longer paramount policy goals of the criminal justice system. Instead, making criminals pay for their crimes and enhancing community safety appear to be the guiding values of this period. In theory, mental illness is much less important to the recurring problem of crime and punishment. Fairness to the individual has been subordinated to the security needs of the community. Even those offenders believed to be mentally ill and unable to control their actions are to be held responsible. This "legal view of persons" assumes human beings are endowed with free will and have the rational capacity to choose their behavior.[8] Reinforcing this perspective has permitted the criminal law to insist on personal accountability. Consequently, criminal responsibility and release have become moral, social, and legal questions; they are no longer medical ones. And society's values—not scientific knowledge—have become the key to answering these questions. As a result, decision-making authority in criminal trials is now considered better left to juries or judges as representatives of the community, thereby minimizing the need for the opinions of mental health professionals.

In sharp contrast to insanity defense reforms, civil commitment is once again being characterized as a medical question and not a moral, social, and legal one. Thus, concepts of free will and responsibility have less relevance to this scientific model of human behavior. This view provides intellectual support for coercively intervening in the lives of the mentally ill to reassert social control over irrational people.

Consistent with this view, the Supreme Court has conferred greater authority on mental health professionals to make decisions regarding involuntary hospitalization and to override patient refusals of treatment. Although acknowledging that mentally ill individuals have constitutional rights, the Court is comfortable relying on medical professionals to protect them.

At first glance, neoconservative attitudes toward psychiatric experts reflect a strange ambivalence toward psychiatric expertise. Criminal law rejects it; civil commitment embraces it with open arms.

How can one reconcile this seemingly contradictory attitude of the law toward psychiatry? One possible answer is to deny there is a contradiction at all. It may simply be a straightforward judgment by legislators that psychiatric expertise is limited to diagnosing and treating mental illness and predicting future harm (even though the available research shows that psychiatrists are very poor predictors of dangerous behavior). In their view, mental health professionals have no special competence to determine whether mental illness should excuse an individual from criminal responsibility for past behavior.[9] This is certainly a plausible view.

But we think there is a more compelling explanation. Neoconservative insanity defense and civil commitment reforms value psychiatric expertise when it contributes to the social control function of law and disparage it when it does not. In the criminal justice system, psychiatrists are now viewed skeptically as accomplices of defense lawyers who get criminals "off the hook" of responsibility. In the commitment system, however, they are more confidently seen as therapeutic helpers who get patients "on the hook" of treatment and control. The result will be increased institutionalization of the mentally ill and greater use of psychiatrists and other mental health professionals as powerful agents of social control.

Mental Illness and Personal Responsibility: Inconsistency in the Law

Viewed broadly, neoconservative law reforms in both criminal and civil law are inconsistent in how they impose responsibility on the mentally ill. Commitment reforms expand the state's authority to intervene early to prevent the mentally ill from harming themselves or others or from becoming psychiatrically more disturbed and disturbing. They provide a legal mechanism to anticipate and prevent harm on the theory that the mentally ill are *not* capable of responsible and rational choice. Thus, psychiatric prophylaxis is required.

The insanity reforms, however, assume most mentally ill offenders *are* capable of rational and responsible choice. Consequently, any intentional harm they commit renders them fit objects of blame and punishment. Ironically, as a result of these reforms, our contemporary legal system increasingly denigrates individual responsibility of the mentally ill *before* they cause harm but imposes it *after* they do.

Although these approaches to personal responsibility vary dramatically between criminal and civil law, they dovetail nicely to maximize community safety. Moreover, both the insanity and commitment reforms use institutionalization as the primary strategy for coping with those mentally ill who disturb the community or commit harmful acts. As a result, more mentally ill individuals will be sent either to prisons or hospitals for longer periods of time. The public has demanded this greater measure of safety.

Evaluating Neoconservative Reforms

In adjusting to a new social reality, neoconservative ideology rejects the progressive tradition that guided the Liberal Era. Will this new value system provide a sufficient foundation for a wise and effective mental health policy, or is it also doomed to failure? In our view, future policy must incorporate many of the major premises of the Neoconservative Era. If unconstrained, however, these premises have disturbing implications for the mentally ill and for society as a whole. Indeed, we believe America is perilously close to losing touch with its core values and doing irreversible damage to the mentally ill. Let us explain.

The Need for Community Safety

The community is entitled to security, and the majority has rights that must be respected and protected. No policy that creates unacceptable and unnecessary risks for ordinary citizens can hope to maintain the political support essential to survive, let alone flourish. Laws that do not protect the majority's right to reasonable collective and personal safety will not be morally just and will breed anger and resentment. The pressure to circumvent these laws will be irresistible.

The neoconservative emphasis on personal responsibility for intentional harmful acts is salutary. The normative message of this new era should strengthen the law's operating assumption that most people are capable of choosing their behavior. This emphasis should marginally enhance the law's ability to shape human conduct to protect innocent persons from harm. More important, the law's insistence on personal responsibility will symbolically reassure the community that the law is in step with their basic values, perhaps assisting society to act more cohesively in its quest for both justice and security.

Many recent insanity reforms accomplish this goal. Adopting the *M'Naghten* test instead of the ALI test, although primarily a matter of community preference, is compatible with this objective. While this reform may slightly decrease the number of successful insanity defenses, it will help ensure that the criminal law is based on a sounder empirical foundation. Mental health experts find it difficult to ascertain whether mentally disordered offenders can control their behavior. Permitting juries to excuse offenders on such an unprovable claim leaves too much room for moral mistakes, with the resulting loss of public confidence.

In addition, mental health law must take into account the need to identify accurately and excuse only those seriously ill offenders who truly cannot be blamed for their crimes. Thus, a thorough evaluation of insanity defendants by government psychiatrists, unimpeded by defense psychiatrists and lawyers, is essential. A defendant who raises the insanity defense is, in effect, admitting he committed a criminal act but asking to be excused because of his mental condition. The law can and should insist that these defendants fully disclose their mental and psychological processes both to government experts and to the jury to enable the jury to render a just decision based on accurate information. Making defendants prove their insanity will also ensure that the truly responsible are not acquitted by reason of insanity.

More important, the law must permit the confinement and treatment of those found NGRI who are still mentally ill and dangerous. Decisions like the *Jones* case[10] (discussed in Chapter 3)—though rightly criticized on different grounds—permit society to treat NGRI offenders differently from civil patients. This will assure the community sufficient control over them after they have been excused of their crime. Oregon's Psychiatric Security Review Board (PSRB) provides a model of community surveillance that addresses the public's demand for safety while allowing patients who appear ready to return to the community.[11] These reforms should also function as confidence-builders, creating more willingness in the public to accept the insanity defense. There is no need to manufacture highly artificial, irrelevant, and confusing defenses like the GBMI defense. This new verdict does not diminish the frequency of insanity verdicts, nor does it ensure that mentally ill offenders are confined as long as necessary or are provided with treatment.

Destroying the Moral Foundation of the Criminal Law

Nonetheless, there is every reason to believe society may push some of the neoconservative premises regarding the insanity defense too far. Abolishing the insanity defense completely and making mental illness totally irrelevant to criminal responsibility will jeopardize the moral foundation of criminal law. In some cases, serious mental illness can effectively destroy the basic human capacities necessary for law-abiding behavior. Punishment in those cases is not only pointless; it is cruel.

Society should not punish when it cannot blame. Stressing community safety without regard to individual responsibility and rehabilitation may seriously erode the humanistic values that give America its special vision of merciful justice. It will also ensure that justice is not served in individual cases when clearly mad offenders who should be considered beyond the reach of the criminal law are convicted and punished. Imposing lifetime hospitalization on petty criminals like Michael Jones is a callous and calculated ploy designed to discourage the insanity defense instead of protecting the community against truly dangerous offenders. Such draconian threats should not be used to dampen inquiry into moral fault.

Control over offenders found NGRI who are still mentally ill and dangerous is clearly appropriate and necessary. Everyone will be better off if severely disordered and dangerous offenders are sent to a mental health facility for treatment and control. But society should not effectively abolish the insanity defense by threatening all successful insanity defendants with a fate far worse than would befall them if they were convicted. And it is important to remember that no one can make the world perfectly safe; justice requires the release of those found NGRI when they do not pose substantial risks to community safety. To do otherwise may seriously damage the moral integrity of criminal law and the fundamental humanitarian instincts of society.

Perhaps most important, it must be realized that "insane" offenders are an insignificant component of America's crime problem. The insanity defense is seldom used and usually unsuccessful. Most successful insanity defendants spend *more* time confined than if they had been convicted. Once released, statistics show they are no more dangerous than other convicts released from prison. The mentally ill are at serious risk of being singled out and treated especially harshly because of the anxiety over crime in general.

The Misuse of the Therapeutic State

A more chilling result of the backlash to failed liberal reforms looms on the horizon. Already during the Neoconservative Era there has been serious abuse of the rehabilitative ideal. Some neoconservative strategies have exploited the original vision of the therapeutic state to serve purely social control functions. In the name of treatment, the government has been empowered to both punish and treat the mentally ill at the same time. Other reforms have authorized the state to obtain lifetime control over criminals by labeling them "mentally abnormal."

The GBMI defense allows the state to treat mentally ill offenders both as "bad" and "mad." They can be punished for their full prison term and also given drugs or subjected to other intrusive technologies to bring about a change in their behavior. This dual power can easily be abused.[12]

Treatment has also been used as a subterfuge to ensure lifetime incarceration of offenders who have served their full prison terms and, after having fully paid their debt to society, are entitled to release. For example, sexual psychopath statutes enacted during the Liberal Era permitted many sex offenders to be sent to a psychiatric hospital for treatment instead of to a prison for punishment. In many states, a sex offender could be hospitalized as long as he was mentally disordered, dangerous, and in need of treatment. During the twilight of the Liberal Era, however, most states repealed these statutes because sex offenders were no longer considered mentally ill or treatable on an involuntary basis. Most states now sentence sex offenders to prison terms and provide treatment to those sex offenders who voluntarily request it.

In 1990 Washington State enacted a law authorizing lifetime civil commitment of "sexually violent predators" due to be released from prison or living lawfully in the community.[13] The Washington law requires the government first to punish sex offenders as fully responsible offenders by sending them to jail for very long terms. It then recognizes the miraculous onset of "mental abnormality" just as they are about to walk out the prison gate, thereby permitting lifetime commitment for "treatment." This law also permits the state to hospitalize for life any convicted sex offender who has already been released from prison even though he is now law abiding, if the authorities think he is likely to reoffend.[14]

In effect, Washington State borrowed an indeterminate treatment model for sex offenders from the Liberal Era—the sexual psychopath law—and converted it into a system of lifetime preventive detention. In an attempt to avoid this stratagem from being struck down as unconstitutional, the Washington legislature conveniently labeled these offenders as "mentally abnormal," dangerous, and in need of treatment—to be provided in prison.[15] In short, lawmakers deliberately abused the therapeutic state, using it to maximize community safety but at the cost of denying fundamental human rights.

These misuses of the therapeutic state were spawned by current demands for law and order. The public is too willing to accept forced treatment when it is used to shackle criminals, but not when it is perceived as a maneuver to escape punishment and detention.

Caring for the Seriously Mentally Ill

First Premises

We accept that mental illness can significantly impair an individual's behavioral controls, endangering the individual or others. Thus, the state will have to use coercion and institutionalization to care for and control some seriously disordered citizens. Nonetheless, since coercion deprives citizens of their constitutionally protected right to freedom, it is an objectionable means that must be justified and limited.[16] We think there are two major limitations that must be placed on the use of state coercion on the mentally ill.

First, state compulsion must lead to acceptable ends. Only if society is willing to actually provide therapeutic and supportive placement and services for the mentally ill should legal compulsion be used. Second, coercion must be subjected to the least restrictive alternative principle. Compulsion should be used only to the extent necessary and only if the mentally ill retain the maximum freedom of action and choice possible. With these two limiting principles in mind, let us examine how the state should care for the seriously mentally ill.

The Primacy of Voluntary Community Care

America desperately needs a mental health system that provides support and care for the chronically mentally ill in the community on a voluntary basis. Most mentally ill citizens are not dangerous and, with assistance, can live on their own. To be effective, this system must avoid the mistakes of the Liberal Era. In our view, major reforms are needed.

The community mental health system must serve the clinical and social needs of the chronically mentally ill. But adding these individuals to this system is not enough; programs must be reoriented to address this major public priority. Although the problems of the chronically mentally ill are difficult and unattractive, inattention to their needs is a major failure of the current treatment system. This means we must refocus exclusive attention away from care for the acutely ill and the worried well toward those who have suffered from serious mental illness over a long period of time. A community network must provide easier access, including aggressive outreach, to this group of difficult patients.

In addition, we should not make promises we cannot keep. Treatment resources should be concentrated on methods that have demonstrated success. For example, affective disorders such as depression can be treated quite effectively and should receive treatment emphasis. Community-based programs that have proven efficacy should be promoted, including those that provide long-term community support and treatment for people who need supervision for their entire lives.

We also need to have realistic aspirations for this system. It is unlikely that significant long-term improvement can be attained in many cases. Maintaining many chronic patients on medications, assisting them in obtaining adequate shelter, and continuing them on government assistance programs may be the best we can hope for. We must also accept the fact that many of the mentally ill will live in extremely modest housing, including single-room-occupancy residences and psychiatric shelters. These are certainly better than cardboard boxes, jail cells, and in many cases, as we shall argue shortly, hospitals.

We should also adopt aggressive incentives for encouraging psychiatrists and other mental health providers to practice in the public health system. America heavily subsidizes the training of thousands of psychiatric residents each year. We deserve a modicum of public service from them in return.[17]

Coercion and institutionalization should not be the cornerstone of our mental health policy. It is a sad commentary that, by and large, only the poor are committed to state mental hospitals. This fact suggests that whether a mentally ill citizen is forcibly hospitalized depends primarily on wealth and status, and not on the illness. Whenever possible, we should assist the mentally ill to maintain independent lives in the community.

The Limits of Involuntary Hospitalization

The mental health system will need to use coercion to provide services, care, and treatment for some seriously mentally ill people. A number of them are so out of touch with reality that they cannot make rational choices. They threaten to harm others or themselves. Or they are simply unable to provide themselves with the basic food, shelter, and clothing necessary to survive. Only a tiny fraction of patients are so disturbed and dangerous that they will be hospitalized for a long time.

Short-term emergency hospitalization is justified to protect some people when serious harm is imminent. It is also acceptable to restore the ability of the seriously impaired to survive.[18] Without involuntary hospitalization, some may literally die, and death inevitably moots philosophic debates about autonomy, freedom, and rights. But the number of such individuals is very small and does not include most street people, even though these homeless individuals live rather stark lives. (Other mentally disturbed citizens who are not imminently dangerous to themselves or others but disturb the community by committing crimes should be controlled through the criminal justice system. As discussed in earlier chapters, most of these individuals can and should obey the law. This approach, however, will require jails to provide much better psychiatric services than they currently do.)

The public mental health system must also provide follow-up treatment and supportive services for these seriously ill patients once they are released from hospitals. It is unconscionable to simply open the hospital door and expect most of them to successfully find their way back to the community. Many will need assistance finding housing, obtaining government benefits, and integrating into the community mental health system. For too many mentally ill Americans, our mental health system has degenerated into an either/or disaster: Either you are committed to hospitals primarily for short-term therapy or you are released back into the streets without any help at all.

The Unacceptability of Involuntary Therapeutic Hospitalization

There is a serious risk that the public will demand new, overly inclusive civil commitment laws authorizing mental health professionals to commit mentally disturbed citizens to hospitals simply for treatment or to improve their living conditions. We oppose such laws. If enacted, we fear mental health professionals will use coercion and institutionalization as "therapeutic" instruments of first rather than last resort. Involuntarily committing the mentally ill to hospitals for treatment can be a quick solution to removing the disturbed and the disturbing from public view. Mental health professionals do not have to spend time finding a suitable placement in the community—assuming it is even available—and persuading the individual to accept it. Moreover, hospitalization usually means the immediate administration of fast-acting drugs to subdue and control the patient. But the chronically mentally ill need more than periodic doses of powerful drugs and sporadic sojourns in overcrowded state hospitals. Conscience can too easily yield to the convenience of a hasty but ineffectual solution for a serious, long-term problem.

When expanded therapeutic commitment laws give mental health professionals renewed opportunity to work wonders on a newly "enfranchised" group of patients, the public expects miracles. Tragically, however, the promise of cures for the seriously mentally ill are not well founded. At best, drugs control the symptoms of mental illness, thereby helping restore a patient to more normal functioning, but they do not cure the underlying illness. And the serious irreversible side effects from drugs harm many patients.[19] Not infrequently, staff use drugs to manage patients for their own convenience rather than prescribe them for the patient's benefit.[20]

Any benefits that accrue from receiving a "tune-up" in the hospital must be balanced against the debilitating effects brought on by prolonged institutionalization. Hospitalization may diminish patients' capacity to make decisions on their own and to live outside institutions, because most important decisions are made for them while they are institutionalized.[21] Even short-term involuntary hospitalization can also severely disrupt patients' basic social arrangements. They may lose their apartment, their jobs, social contacts, and sense of routine. In addition, essential financial benefits such as Social Security disability payments terminate when a patient is hospitalized. Reapplication is risky because many claims are denied and many marginally functioning individuals are simply unable to reapply successfully. Delays in restarting these benefits are inevitable.

The Washington State experience with changing its involuntary treatment statute, discussed in Chapter 7, poignantly raised the question of whether involuntary hospitalization helped or harmed the mentally ill.[22] In 1979 Washington State expanded the statutory authority to hospitalize a mentally ill person for treatment. Many patients committed to state hospitals under the new law had never been in hospitals before. When committed, these new patients stayed in hospitals longer than other patients and returned with greater frequency, thereby consuming more and more scarce resources. On the one hand, these individuals may have been in desperate need of the assistance a hospital (among other agencies) can provide—including food, clothing, shelter, and medical care. Thus, the 1979 statute may have given them the aid they required.

On the other hand, once they were committed to a hospital, they were likely to return again and again to the hospital for these services. We believe that expanding therapeutic commitment simply sets up a cycle of dependency in which the mentally ill spin in and out of revolving hospital doors. Washington, like other states, had very little to offer them in the community. With the state using an all-or-nothing mentality, the mentally ill received episodic treatment (that could have been provided elsewhere) from the most intensive, expensive resource any mental health system has to offer—the hospital.

We think the Washington study suggests that involuntary hospitalization for treatment may make people *less able* to live in the community. Thus, we are extremely skeptical that forcing even the most seriously ill individuals into hospitals for treatment actually helps them in the long run. Providing them with continuing social services and health care on a voluntary basis or involuntarily in a less expensive, less restrictive environment is far preferable.[23]

Moreover, Washington abandoned patients who sought hospital treatment on a voluntary basis.[24] The 1979 Washington law increased the number of *involuntary* patients so dramatically that *voluntary* patients were pushed out of hospitals. They were left to fend for themselves in the community as best they could.

Intrigued by the results of our Washington study, we did further research to see if there was any persuasive evidence substantiating the claim that involuntary hospital treatment actually helps the mentally ill live independently in the community after their release. To our amazement we could find *no* scientifically sound research supporting this claim. In fact, this major premise of reformers who would expand the therapeutic, coercive power of the state has never been studied rigorously. Thus, there is no reliable evidence establishing that involuntary hospital treatment helps the mentally ill to adjust to living on their own after they are discharged.[25]

In light of our empirical research, we have concluded that coercive hospitalization must be reserved for the dangerous mentally ill and those whose lives are at risk because they cannot provide themselves with the necessities of life. The dominance of the medical model and America's renewed confidence in claims of psychiatric expertise and technological solutions have made society quite willing to hospitalize the mentally ill for their own good even when confronted with powerful contrary evidence that coercive hospitalization might inflict serious, unnecessary harm on many of the patients society is trying to help. Forced hospitalization also encourages the public to continuously short-change the community mental health system.

Thus, we do not support legal changes that would authorize coercive hospitalization on a broadly defined "need-for-treatment" basis. Nor do we think hospitals are the appropriate place for most seriously mentally ill people, although we certainly believe that voluntary hospitalization should be available to those who need and seek it. If our mental health law ignores the evidence provided by objective empirical research, it will do more harm than good.

The Hospital as Asylum

Some experts now claim that many mentally ill people should be involuntarily hospitalized to provide a lifetime of shelter and protection from the harsh vicissitudes of contemporary life. Put simply, the mentally ill do not need treatment, they need asylum.[26] This new justification for coercive hospitalization echoes the nineteenth-century ideology of providing lifetime compassionate care and custody for the disabled in state asylums. But it raises more provocative questions at the close of the twentieth century. Is it in their best interest to provide mentally ill citizens with a caring and humane environment—albeit one they did not choose—to raise their standard of living or to provide them with asylum?

Despite the seductive appeal of this humanitarian plea, the Supreme Court in the *Donaldson* case clearly indicated the government cannot constitutionally take away a person's liberty for "pure asylum." As Justice Potter Stewart said:

> May the state confine the mentally ill merely to ensure them a living standard superior to that they enjoy in the private community? That the State has a proper interest in providing care and assistance to the unfortunate goes without saying. But the mere presence of mental illness does not disqualify a person from preferring his home to the comforts of an institution. Moreover, while the State may arguably confine a person to save him from harm, incarceration is rarely if ever a necessary condition for raising the living standards of those capable of surviving safely in freedom on their own or with the help of family or friends.[27]

Nonetheless, our long-standing commitment to individual responsibility does not require us to desert those who genuinely need public assistance. Abandoning people who are down and out in America is nothing short of social Darwinism. Many mentally ill citizens require temporary safe havens. But, as mentioned earlier, for all but a few persons, that should only consist of *voluntary* placement in facilities which alleviate stress and provide a supportive and caring environment. Neither coercion nor institutionalization is required to provide a safe haven for most mentally ill citizens.

The Homeless Mentally Ill

Homelessness is a provocative contemporary issue that some reformers would exploit so as to use coercive hospitalization to provide asylum for the mentally ill. The impulse to help the homeless has been a powerful force to expand the net of therapeutic commitment. In our view, the therapeutic state is being distorted to solve the problem of homelessness. To understand why this strategy for coping with homelessness is a catastrophe in the making, we must be more forthright about why people are homeless in America.

Most homeless people are not mentally ill individuals living on the streets because restrictive commitment laws prevent them from receiving desperately needed hospital treatment. The most rigorous research shows that no more than one-third of all homeless Americans can be considered mentally ill.[28] While the fact that many homeless people are mentally ill demonstrates the tragic deficiencies of the mental health system, it does not establish that mental illness causes homelessness.

Most people are homeless as a result of socioeconomic factors.[29] Rising rates of mental illness have contributed to homelessness but cannot explain its rapid proliferation. Many mentally ill individuals are homeless because they, too, have exhausted government benefits, cannot obtain employment, have no family or social support, and are generally poor competitors for the increasingly limited resource of low-income housing.[30] Although most homeless mentally ill could benefit from help with their mental disabilities, coercive hospitalization is unwarranted for all but a very few. Most homeless mentally ill need access to low-income housing or financial and social services to help them obtain shelter, as well as other social, economic, and medical assistance.

By involuntarily hospitalizing the mentally ill because they are homeless, we are choosing to medicalize what is primarily a social and economic problem. Blaming homelessness on mental illness is appealing because it locates the fault in the individual rather than in society's social and economic structure. The better solution is to provide realistic assistance to the homeless and to the homeless mentally ill to obtain the essential services for keeping them off the streets. This would, of course, include mental health care for the homeless mentally ill. And it would also require more social services to meet a broad spectrum of needs.

Even for those few mentally ill who cannot secure life-sustaining shelter as a result of their illness, involuntary hospitalization is a fleeting and ultimately unsatisfying solution. Hospitalization may briefly stabilize their condition but provides only temporary respite from the calamity of their social situation. If we do not help these seriously ill people obtain shelter in the community before and after they are hospitalized, coercive hospitalization will, at best, provide an intermittent Band-Aid that will not solve their homelessness or prevent their inevitable recommitment. It will only temporarily reclaim public buildings, parks, and sidewalks for the more privileged.

Outpatient Commitment

Some mentally ill citizens will need to be controlled while living in the community. Coercion through outpatient commitment will be necessary to make certain that they receive the social, economic, and medical support essential to maintain themselves outside of hospitals. This commitment helps ensure that patients' needs are met by the most appropriate service. A match of needs and solutions is both good medicine and good law.

In addition, outpatient commitment appears to be reasonably effective in keeping patients on necessary medication, thus enabling them to live in the community. This control should also help prevent patients from deteriorating, since they frequently stop taking their medication after they are discharged from a hospital. It also minimizes governmental restraint on the patient's liberty, thereby conforming to the least restrictive alternative principle.

The use of outpatient commitment also passes our litmus test for limiting coercive interventions to those that appear to work. Preliminary studies indicate outpatient commitment can be an effective alternative to hospitalization when structured like programs currently in operation in North Carolina, Hawaii, and Wisconsin.[31] Finally, outpatient commitment may avoid making many mentally ill patients worse off through involuntary hospitalization.

A cautionary note is necessary. The American public has always overestimated the power of the law to control human behavior. Significant resource constraints and limited sanctions for violating the terms of outpatient commitment require that this strategy be used sparingly.[32]

A Compelling Cost-Benefit Analysis

Neoconservatives correctly point to the need to set clear priorities for public spending. Total expenditures for state mental hospitals in 1988 alone were just over $8 billion.[33] That reflects a staggering investment in public mental health services.

The available funding for mental health care in the United States will surely be even more limited in the decades to come. We must stop simply calling for more money to make mental health care work. Instead, we must formulate our policies in light of the economic realities and the resource constraints that actually exist.

The neoconservative emphasis on reinstitutionalization is a particularly risky strategy in view of present-day economics. Hospitals are voracious "black holes" that consume an inordinate proportion of finite funding. The primacy of the medical model, which is the cornerstone of this new strategy, requires expensive bricks and mortar and highly trained staff.

Accessible community facilities, such as drop-in centers, halfway houses, and specialized shelters for the mentally ill, are far less expensive than hospitals and provide the respite many mentally ill need from time to time. Residential alternatives available on a continuous basis make sense financially and clinically for the vast majority of chronically mentally ill people who need a caring and less stressful environment.

Diminished Judicial Involvement in Mental Institutions

Judicial involvement in the public mental health system should be decreased. Courts should neither run mental health institutions nor dictate precisely how mental health professionals must carry out the difficult task of caring for the mentally ill. Money spent on the micromanagement of institutions is money not spent on providing care and services for patients.

As a corollary, we need to accept that government and its mental health professionals are not inevitable threats either to the constitutional rights or well-being of the mentally ill. Instead, mental health policy should encourage government to provide a wide range of social and medical services for the mentally ill. Mental health care and treatment must be an important component of those services. We should not disparage psychiatrists and other mental health professionals as mere government bureaucrats or members of self-serving guilds. Rather, we need to facilitate their willingness and ability to serve the mentally ill.

On the other hand, courts cannot abandon the mentally ill. They must stand by in case they are needed. One perceptive judge has captured the contradictory logic in the Supreme Court's recent decisions, which conclude that patients have rights but then defer to professional judgment to protect those rights.

> The *Youngberg* proposition that there is no reason to think judges or juries are better qualified than appropriate professionals in making [treatment] decisions may not be reasonably disputed. Conversely, however, I do not believe that there can be any quarrel with the proposition that those professionals are not better qualified than judges or juries in balancing delicate constitutional rights and duties.[34]

It is crucial that judges exercise independent judgment in commitment hearings and not defer to the opinion of experts. Careful judicial gatekeepers to the involuntary commitment system can help ensure that only those who truly need involuntary hospitalization are placed there. By refusing to order inappropriate commitment, independent judges can channel many mentally ill individuals into community placement alternatives that should enhance their long-term prospects for living decent lives outside institutions. In this way, judges can save many patients from the harm hospitalization can cause.

Courts must also remain ready to correct clear cases of overcrowding or abuse in public hospitals and to provide constitutional guidance to protect patients' rights. It is not acceptable to jam more patients into hopelessly overcrowded hospitals, as the Washington State Supreme Court did when, despite a state law guaranteeing every patient the "right to adequate care and individualized treatment,"[35] it ordered the major state hospital to take all patients even if there were no beds for them. Sadly, the court concluded, "Treatment delayed and inadequate must surely be better than no treatment at all."[36] Such judicial timidity is simply unacceptable. If public facilities do not meet professional standards for adequate care, courts should consider ordering the state to stop admitting new patients and, if necessary, to release more patients until acceptable levels of staffing have been met. This necessary and appropriate exercise of judicial power will not involve courts in daily hands-on management of state psychiatric facilities. But it will keep the mentally ill from being sent to overcrowded, understaffed hospitals that may do more harm than good, while also creating political pressure on the state to bring its facilities into constitutional compliance. Most important, this limited judicial activism will ensure that commitment is for the patient's benefit and not for society's convenience.

Courts must also stand ready to review cases in which patients are given psychoactive medication over their objection after medical review. Without the prospect of judicial recourse, there will be insufficient pressure on mental health professionals to practice good medicine. Administrative review simply works better when decision-makers are aware that courts may review their decisions. Judicial review is especially required if more and more mental patients are to be committed to hospitals. Harried staff will then be under intense pressure to use drugs to manage patients instead of to help them.

The Medical Model and Expertise: Deference and Disappointment

The reemergence of preventive detention and paternalism as dominant strategies in the Neoconservative Era enhances the allure of expertise. Mental health professionals are once again asserting their ability to predict and prevent, to help and heal. Their claims are seductive.

The American public appears increasingly willing to accept the professionals' assertions of expertise and to give them more legal authority to confine and treat the mentally ill. Commitment laws have been explicitly rephrased to facilitate this expanded mandate for mental health professionals.[37] In too many instances judges in commitment hearings believe claims that cure is available, even though little help is actually on hand to provide lasting improvement for the long-term psychiatric, social, and economic condition of many seriously mentally ill individuals. The Supreme Court clearly thinks judges should defer to professional judgment and stay out of mental hospitals.

Everyone expects psychiatrists to deliver on the promise that broadened commitment authority together with more resources can finally solve the problems of the mentally ill. Recent widely publicized advances in biological psychiatry seem to promise that a "silver bullet" to cure mental illness is just around the corner.

It is important to remember that in mental health treatment factors other than science and technology are involved. The recent discovery of the drug clozapine, which appears to effectively control some cases of schizophrenia,[38] emphasizes the disappointing limits of America's resources to administer this powerful treatment to indigent patients who desperately need it: The cost of the drug and its administration exceeds the capacity of public coffers to pay for it.[39] Thus, those who can pay for the drug will reap its benefits while legions of poor mentally ill will continue to live with the demons of their disease. Hence, while biomedical discoveries for the mentally ill are promising, they have yet to offer much assistance to patients in public mental hospitals, where health service rather than biochemistry is still the preeminent need.

Pronouncements of scientific breakthroughs that will cure the minds of the mentally ill are still, at present, promises that cannot be kept. Once again, the mental health professions are setting themselves up for a bitter public disappointment when expectations of cure are not met. So a new cycle of recrimination is bound to occur. Mental health professionals now must be more candid with the public about what they can and cannot do for the seriously mentally ill who rely on public mental health services. Psychiatrists should also be more candid with themselves about their reemergent role as coercive agents of social control.

The Limits of Our Wisdom

Some of our readers may be disappointed that we have not offered a detailed blueprint for mental health policymakers to follow in constructing a new system of care and control for seriously mentally ill offenders and patients. They may feel that such a prescription must accompany any critique of America's mental health law and policy. While that expectation is understandable, providing a precise formula for reform has never been our aim. We have resisted the powerful temptation to suggest another panacea that would simply drive mental health policy and law around yet another blind curve. Like many others, we have been disappointed with what the Progressives gave us as their panacea and with how Liberal Era reformers carried out their comprehensive vision of the future. Similarly, we have strong reservations about the wisdom and efficacy of the neoconservative agenda.

What we hope to have provided instead is a careful analysis that places these complex issues into the context of historical successes and failures. Until people understand why these choices for reform were made and where they have led us, the prospects for lasting improvements in mental health law and policy remain dim.

Fears for the Future

Converting kindness into convenience is a simple and short step. Neoconservative commitment reforms were initially sponsored by psychiatrists and families with mentally ill members who sought to secure desperately needed treatment for the mentally ill. But these agitators for reform did not receive much support for law reform until the public became weary of the hordes of severely ill people roaming the streets of America or until a mentally deranged individual committed a heinous crime given wide media play.[40]

Many of the mentally ill in U.S. cities are being forcibly removed from the streets to overcrowded, shabby, and unsafe shelters. Others are being coercively dumped into crowded and understaffed state hospitals. This action strongly suggests that coercive institutionalization is less for the benefit of the mentally ill and more for the public's convenience. Again, legal reform ostensibly undertaken for humane reasons can quickly be transformed into a powerful instrument of social repression. It is imperative that mental health policy be vigilant to guard against this destructive metamorphosis.

America is at risk of losing touch with its fundamental values. The quest for complete safety in a more threatening world is understandable. Society, however, should not scapegoat the mentally ill in its search for community security. Currently civil liberties do not enjoy the cachet they did in the Liberal Era. But individual rights are more than passing fancies. They are the soul of America. When revising mental health law and policy to ensure adequate protection of the community, we must be careful to be fair to disabled citizens. It is too easy to rearrange fundamental social policy out of fear and anger.

In shaping future mental health policy, we must pay closer attention to sound empirical information than we have in the past. A clear look at the available research throws surprising light on neoconservative mental health reforms. Legislative tinkering with specific formulations of the insanity test may be an important expression of public values, but it does not change real-life practice very much. The formulation of commitment criteria makes a real difference only when laws empower mental health authorities to assert their authority and use their expertise to hospitalize patients against their will. Societal and professional *values*, not the language of a law, largely determine whether the civil commitment system will exert greater control over the mentally ill. Law itself is limited in its ability to control the behavior of government officials.

Liberal and Neoconservative era reforms have not changed the composition of the client population in either the criminal justice or the mental health systems. The target group for these special interventions never seems to change. For millions of poor, mentally ill Americans, jails and psychiatric wards remain the "court of last resort" because we consistently fail to rehabilitate these people or find another place where they do not threaten other members of society. Neoconservative reforms make it clear that the public doesn't want that place to be in our midst.

Sadly, policymakers tend to ignore what we do know about mental health law reform either because they are unaware of such knowledge or because they just don't care. At present, it seems research (too much of which, admittedly, is of poor quality) is used more often to support the arguments of advocates or opponents of legal change rather than to provide dispassionate direction. Apparently, Americans do not want to be confused by facts. They want quick solutions to perceived problems which are congruent with their values and (mis)perceptions.

Currently we are relying on excessive coercion and institutionalization to provide community security and to help the mentally ill. Momentum for expanding control over the mentally ill is growing at a rapid rate. Increasingly, psychiatrists and other mental health professionals will no longer serve as illuminators of moral fault and therapeutic helpers of those in need. Instead, they will serve as agents of social control, whether or not they are comfortable with that assignment. The trend back to the asylum in the name of security and treatment is ominous. The stage is set for another round of bitter disappointment accompanied by acrimonious accusations that psychiatry has failed once again.

We believe that most Americans are not being candid about whose interests are being served. Our nation now appears more interested in punishing, confining, preventing, and controlling than it is in caring, helping, treating, and restoring. Compassion is a powerful rhetorical device for securing social change. But it can too easily disguise self-interest. At the very least, we should be honest about our hopes and aspirations. If social control is the primary object of today's reforms—and we think it is—we should say so bluntly. This acknowledgment will at least permit thoughtful analysis and critique of mental health law reform. It will also permit our system of governmental checks and balances, particularly the judiciary, to operate more effectively.

Keeping the mentally ill out of sight will surely keep them out of mind. But this strategy is pernicious. Liberal Era reforms took place in the courts and on the streets of American cities in full view of their champions and critics. We have *all* been able to measure the shortcomings of those well-intended but short-sighted reforms. The real-life consequences of neoconservative reforms will be less visible and therefore more prone to abuse. Simply put, as this cycle of reform is played out behind closed doors, we will be less likely to detect and correct problems in prisons and psychiatric institutions as they inevitably materialize. The prospects for a new round of media exposés of "snake pits" within our institutions will increase, but those who are victims of our modern-day largesse will have already suffered from our good intentions.

There is still time to slow the pendulum of law reform. Caution in pursuit of reform is no vice. America can preserve and blend much of what is good from both the Liberal and Neoconservative Eras to construct a wise, compassionate, and efficient mental health policy. It is not too late.

NOTES

Introduction

1. As quoted in Frank J. Ayd, Jr., *Medical, Moral and Legal Issues in Mental Health Care* (Baltimore: Williams & Wilkins, 1974), 146.

2. Leona L. Bachrach, *Asylum and Chronically Ill Patients*, Am. J. Psychiatry 141(8) (August 1984): 976–78.

3. Gerald Grob, *The Forging of Mental Health Policy in America: World War II to New Frontier*, J. Hist. Med. & Allied Sci. 42 (October 1987): 410–46, 411.

4. Excellent accounts of the mentally ill in America have been written. A few of the best include Albert Deutsch, *The Mentally Ill in America: A History of Their Care and Treatment from Colonial Times*, 2d ed., rev. and enl. (New York: Columbia University Press, 1949); D. J. Rothman, *The Discovery of the Asylum: Social Order and Disorder in the New Republic*, 1st ed. (Boston: Little, Brown & Co., 1971); D. J. Rothman, *Conscience and Convenience: The Asylum and Its Alternatives in Progressive America* (Boston: Little, Brown & Co., 1980); G. Grob, *Mental Illness and American Society, 1875–1940* (Princeton, N.J.: Princeton University Press, 1983); Michel Foucault, *Madness and Civilization: A History of Insanity in the Age of Reason* (New York: Pantheon Books, 1965).

5. For a discussion of the early deinstitutionalization movement, see P. Lerman, *Deinstitutionalization and the Welfare State* (New Brunswick, N.J.: Rutgers University Press, 1982).

6. Progressivism refers to specific ideological assumptions about the nature of punishment and treatment. According to David Rothman, the Progressive Era was a period when reformers zealously rejected punitive, standardized forms of treatment and punishment in favor of more therapeutic and individualized alternatives for each offender or patient. For a full discussion of the Progressive Era and its impact on mental health practices, see Rothman, *Conscience and Convenience*; and Rothman, *The Discovery of the Asylum*.

7. D. J. Rothman, *The Courts and Social Reform: A Postprogressive Outlook*, Law & Hum. Behav. 6 (1982): 113–19.

8. Rothman, *Conscience and Convenience*.

9. Rothman, *The Discovery of the Asylum*.

10. Ibid.

11. See, for example, William H. Chafe, *The Unfinished Journey: America Since World War II* (New York: Oxford University Press, 1986); Todd Gitlin, *The Sixties: Years of Hope, Days of Rage* (New York: Bantam, 1987); Taylor Branch, *Parting the*

Waters: America in the King Years, 1954–63 (New York: Simon and Schuster, 1988); Hugh Davis Graham, *The Civil Rights Era: Origins and Development of National Policy, 1960–1972* (New York: Oxford University Press, 1990).

12. The roots of mental health law reform in the United States reach back to the earliest attempts of American settlers to control the behavior of the dangerous "insane." For excellent discussions of the early attempts to confine the mentally ill, see Deutsch, *The Mentally Ill in America*; Rothman, *The Discovery of the Asylum*; A. Dershowitz, *The Origins of Preventive Confinement in Anglo-Saxon American Law— Part I: The English Experience*, U. Cin. L. Rev. 43 (1974): 1–60; A. Dershowitz, *The Origins of Preventive Confinement in Anglo-Saxon American Law—Part II: The American Experience*, U. Cin. L. Rev. 43 (1974): 781–846; G. Grob, *Mental Illness and American Society, 1875–1940* (Princeton, N.J.: Princeton University Press, 1983).

13. Gitlin, *The Sixties*, 12.

14. John Kenneth Galbraith, *The Affluent Society* (Boston: Houghton-Mifflin, 1958).

15. Chafe, *The Unfinished Journey*.

16. Council of Economic Affairs, cited in Chafe, *The Unfinished Journey*, 239.

17. Chafe, *The Unfinished Journey*, 233.

18. R. A. Cloward and L. E. Ohlin, *Delinquency and Opportunity: A Theory of Delinquent Gangs* (New York: Free Press, 1960).

19. Graham, *The Civil Rights Era*, 3.

20. Ibid.

21. Rothman, *The Courts and Social Reform*.

22. Ibid.

23. S. A. Scheingold, *The Politics of Rights: Lawyers, Public Policy and Political Change* (New Haven: Yale University Press, 1974).

24. For an interesting discussion of how the courts escaped the suspicions directed toward bureaucracies in the 1960s and 1970s, see Richard Gaskins, *Second Thoughts on "Law as an Instrument of Social Change,"* Law & Hum. Behav. 6 (1982): 153–68.

25. Lawrence H. Tribe, *American Constitutional Law*, 2d ed. (Mineola, N.Y.: Foundation Press, 1988).

26. Owen Fiss, *The Social and Political Foundations of Adjudication*, Law & Hum. Behav. 6 (1982): 121–28.

27. Abraham Chayes, *The Role of the Judge in Public Law Litigation*, Harv. L. Rev. 89 (May 1976): 1281–316; David L. Horowitz, *The Courts and Social Policy* (Washington: Brookings, 1977); H. Friendly, *The Courts and Social Policy: Substance and Procedure*, U. Miami L. Rev. 33 (1978): 21–42; Owen Fiss, *Foreword: The Forms of Justice*, 93 Harv. L. Rev. (1979): 1–58; Fiss, *Social and Political Foundations of Adjudication*.

28. Fiss, *Social and Political Foundations of Adjudication*, 121.

29. *Brown* v. *Board of Education*, 347 U.S. 483 (1954), 349 U.S. 294, 75 S. Ct. 753, 99 L. Ed. 1083 (1955).

30. This is not to suggest that state and local governments acted swiftly to implement the social changes ordered in *Brown*. For a description of the events which followed *Brown*, including decades of delays in implementation, see Branch, *Parting the Waters*.

31. For prisoners: *Palmigiano* v. *Garraphy*, 443 F. Supp. 956 (D.R.I. 1977) [federal court found it had a clear "duty" to require state prison officials to remedy constitutional violations; the Court appointed a master to review, monitor, and report on programs designed to ensure state prison officials remedied constitutional violations

existing at the Rhode Island Correctional Facility]. For handicapped children: *Mills v. Board of Education*, 348 F. Supp. 866 (D.D.C. 1972) [the court held that the state must provide each child with free, suitable, and publicly supported education regardless of the degree of the child's impairment or the state's lack of sufficient funding]. For the poor: *Goldberg v. Kelly*, 397 U.S. 254, 90 S. Ct. 1011, 25 L. Ed. 2d 287 (1970) [the Supreme Court held that due process guarantees welfare recipients an evidentiary hearing before termination of benefits; recipients' interest in uninterrupted assistance, coupled with the state's interest in not terminating payments erroneously, outweighed the state's interest in conserving fiscal and administrative resources]. For women: *Reed v. Reed*, 404 U.S. 71, 92 S. Ct. 251, 30 L. Ed. 2d 225 (1971) [see note 39]. For the mentally ill: *Wyatt v. Aderholt*, 503 F.2d 1305 (5th Cir. 1974) [the court held that the state could not confine mentally ill persons to state mental hospitals without providing care and treatment; since patients have a constitutional right to treatment, the federal court was not intruding on the province of the legislature]. For a collection of related cases, see G. Frug, *The Judicial Power of the Purse*, U. Pa. L. Rev. 126 (1978): 715–94.

32. *Gideon v. Wainwright*, 372 U.S. 335, 83 S. Ct. 792, 9 L. Ed. 2d 799 (1963); *Miranda v. Arizona*, 384 U.S. 436, 86 S. Ct. 1602, 16 L. Ed. 694 (1966).

33. *Roe v. Wade*, 410 U.S. 113, 93 S. Ct. 705, 35 L. Ed. 2d 147 (1973).

34. *United States v. Guest*, 383 U.S. 745, 86 S. Ct. 1170, 16 L. Ed. 239 (1966) [federal civil rights statute used to overturn interference with an individual's "fundamental" right to travel]; *Roe v. Wade*, 410 U.S. 113, 93 S. Ct. 705, 35 L. Ed. 2d 147 (1973) [Texas statutes making abortion a criminal offense struck down as interfering with the right of privacy encompassing a woman's decision to terminate her pregnancy]; *Loving v. Virginia*, 388 U.S. 1, 87 S. Ct. 1817, 18 L. Ed. 2d 1010 (1967) [Virginia laws prohibiting interracial marriage found to be an unconstitutional violation of an individual's "fundamental freedom" to marry]; *Malloy v. Hogan*, 378 U.S. 1, 84 S. Ct. 1489, 12 L. Ed. 2d 653 (1964) [Fifth Amendment privilege against self-incrimination held to apply to persons charged with state crimes]; *Stanley v. Georgia*, 394 U.S. 557, 89 S. Ct. 1243, 22 L. Ed. 2d 542 (1969) [Georgia statute making the private possession of obscene material a crime violates the First Amendment right to receive information].

35. *Griswold v. Connecticut*, 381 U.S. 479, 85 S. Ct. 1678, 14 L. Ed. 2d 510 (1965) [Connecticut law making the use of contraceptives a criminal offense struck down as an unconstitutional invasion of a married person's right of privacy].

36.

> We recognize the legitimate and indeed exigent interest of States and localities throughout the Nation in preventing the dissemination of material deemed harmful to children. But the interest does not justify a total suppression of such material, the effect of which would be to "reduce the adult population . . . to reading only what is fit for children."

Jacobellis v. Ohio, 378 U.S. 184, 195, 84 S. Ct. 1676, 12 L. Ed. 2d 793 (1964), quoting *Butler v. Michigan*, 352 U.S. 380, 383 (1957).

37. *New York Times Co. v. United States*, 403 U.S. 713, 91 S. Ct. 2140, 29 L. Ed. 2d 822 (1971) [government request for an injunction against the publication of a classified study regarding U.S. involvement in Vietnam denied by the U.S. Supreme Court; the Court said that any system of prior restraint of expression comes to the Court "bearing a heavy presumption against its constitutional validity"].

38. *Papachristou v. Jacksonville*, 405 U.S. 156, 92 S. Ct. 839, 31 L. Ed. 2d 110 (1972) [Florida vagrancy ordinance found unconstitutionally vague because it failed

to give fair notice that certain conduct was forbidden by the ordinance and because it encouraged arbitrary arrest and convictions].

39. *Loving* v. *Virginia*, (1967) [Virginia statute forbidding interracial marriage found unconstitutional because it restricted the freedom to marry solely on the basis of racial classifications, thereby violating the "central meaning of the Equal Protection Clause"], *Griffin* v. *County School Board of Prince Edward County*, 377 U.S. 218, 84 S. Ct. 1226, 12 L. Ed. 2d 256 (1964) [Prince Edward County, Virginia, public schools ordered reopened after U.S. Supreme Court decides that the "public schools were closed and private schools operated in their place with state and county assistance," unconstitutionally ensuring that black and white children not go to the same school]; *Graham* v. *Richardson*, 403 U.S. 365, 91 S. Ct. 1848, 29 L. Ed. 2d 534 (1971) [state laws restricting or denying welfare benefits to aliens found unconstitutional by the U.S. Supreme Court, which held that the state's valid interest in fiscal integrity may not be accomplished by invidious distinctions between classes of citizens]; *Reed* v. *Reed*, 404 U.S. 71, 92 S. Ct. 251, 30 L. Ed. 2d 255 (1971) [Idaho statute giving preference to males over females as estate administrators found invalid by U.S. Supreme Court; giving mandatory preference to either sex to reduce judicial workload was an arbitrary legislative choice forbidden by the equal rights protection clause of the Fourteenth Amendment]; *Weber* v. *Aetna Casualty & Surety Co.*, 406 U.S. 164, 92 S. Ct. 1400, 31 L. Ed. 2d 768 (1972) [Louisiana workmen's compensation law favoring legitimate children over unacknowledged illegitimate children for purposes of receiving benefits found unconstitutional as not justified by any legitimate state interest].

40. *United Steelworkers of America, AFL-CIO- CLC* v. *Weber*, 443 U.S. 193, 99 S. Ct. 2721, 61 L. Ed. 2d 480 (1979) [company affirmative action plan that set hiring goals of blacks at each plant equal to the percentage of blacks in the local labor force and that reserved for blacks 50 percent of the openings in craft training programs upheld as constitutionally permissible vehicle for eliminating traditional patterns of racial discrimination].

41. *Fullilove* v. *Klutznick*, 448 U.S. 448, 100 S. Ct. 2758, 65 L. Ed. 2d 902 (1980) [federal law earmarking for minority businesses 10 percent of the federal funds going to local public works projects held to be a valid use of racial and ethnic criteria to accomplish constitutional objectives]. Comment, *The Nonperpetuation of Discrimination in Public Contracting: A Justification for State and Local Minority Business Set-Asides After Wygant*, Harv. L. Rev. 101 (1988): 1979–83.

42. Richard Gaskins, *Second Thoughts on "Law as an Instrument of Social Change."*

43. N. N. Kittrie, *The Right to Be Different: Deviance and Enforcement Therapy* (Baltimore: Johns Hopkins University Press, 1973), 38.

44. *In re Gault*, 387 U.S. 1, 25–26, 87 S. Ct. 1428, 18 L. Ed. 2d 527 (1967).

> The early conception of the Juvenile Court proceeding was one in which a fatherly judge touched the heart and conscience of the erring youth by talking over his problems, by paternal advice and admonition, and which, in extreme situations, benevolent and wise institutions of the state provided guidance and help to save him from a downward career. . . . But recent studies have, with surprising unanimity, entered sharp dissent as to the validity of this gentle conception. . . . For example [one study indicates] that when the procedural laxness of the "parens patriae" attitude is followed by stern disciplining, the contrast may have an adverse effect upon the child, who feels that he has been deceived or enticed.

45. *Goldberg* v. *Kelly*, 397 U.S. 254, 90 S. Ct. 1011, 25 L. Ed. 2d 287 (1970); *Morrissey* v. *Brewer*, 408 U.S. 471, 92 S. Ct. 2593, 33 L. Ed. 2d 484 (1972).

46. C. S. Diver, *The Judge as Political Powerbroker: Superintending Structural Change in Public Institutions*, Va. L. Rev. 65 (1979): 43–106.

47. The previous reluctance of courts to become involved in major government institutions had been popularly known as the "hands off" judicial philosophy. Note, *Decency and Fairness: An Emerging Judicial Role in Prison Reform*, Va. L. Rev. 57 (1971): 841–84, 842–44, as cited in *Procunier* v. *Martinez*, 416 U.S. 396, 404–5, 94 S. Ct. 1800, 1807, 40 L. Ed. 2d 224 (1974). The Court in *Procunier* rejected the "hands off" doctrine.

48. Archibald Cox, *Federalism and Individual Rights Under the Burger Court*, Nw. U.L. Rev. 73 (1978): 1–25.

49. Scheingold, *The Politics of Rights*.

50. Horowitz, *The Courts and Social Policy*; C. S. Diver, *The Judge as Political Powerbroker*; R. F. Nagel, *Separation of Powers and the Scope of Federal Equitable Remedies*, Stan. L. Rev. 30 (1978): 661–724; Note, *Judicial Intervention and Organization Theory: Changing Bureaucratic Behavior and Policy*, Yale L.J. 89 (1980): 513–37.

51. Minimum cell size: *Pugh* v. *Locke*, 406 F. Supp. 318, 334 (M.D. Ala. 1976), *aff'd* and *remanded sub nom* [court required minimum living space for each prisoner]. Discharge plans for patients leaving hospitals: See, for example, *Wyatt* v. *Stickney*, 344 F. Supp. 373 (M.D. Ala. 1972). High school under judicial control: *Hart* v. *Community School Board*, 383 F. Supp 699 (E.D.N.Y.) *supplemented*, 383 F. Supp. 769 (E.D.N.Y. 1974), *aff'd* 512 F.2d 37 (2d Cir. 1975) [federal district court restructured junior high school to achieve racial integration]. See Note, *Judicial Intervention and Organization Theory*. Reorganization of city government: See *Hawkins* v. *Town of Shaw, Mississippi*, 461 F.2d 1171 (5th Cir. 1972) [court directed defendant town officials to submit plan to eliminate disparities in municipal services to inhabitants who were poor and black].

52. Episodes of mental hospitalization reached their peak in 1955, with approximately 818,832 inpatient episodes occurring in that year. However, large-scale decreases in that number did not occur until the 1960s, with the sharpest decline in the period 1965 to 1975. For example, inpatient episodes declined from their high of 818,832 in 1955 to 804,926 in 1965. By 1975, that number had plummeted to 598,993. For a complete discussion of this phenomenon, see C. A. Kiesler and A. Sibulkin, *Mental Hospitalization: Myths and Facts About a National Crisis* (Beverly Hills: Sage, 1987).

53. Peter Steinfels, *The Neoconservatives: The Men Who Are Changing America's Politics* (New York: Simon and Schuster, 1979); Robert B. Reich, *The Next American Frontier* (New York: Times Books, 1983); Chafe, *The Unfinished Journey*.

54. Katherine S. Newman, *Falling from Grace: The Experience of Downward Mobility in the American Middle Class* (New York: Free Press, 1988), 25.

55. Daniel Patrick Moynihan, *Maximum Feasible Misunderstanding: Community Action in the War on Poverty* (New York: Free Press, 1969), 170.

56. Daniel Patrick Moynihan, *The Politics of Guaranteed Income: The Nixon Administration and the Family Assistance Plan*, 1st ed. (New York: Random House, 1973); Lewis A. Coser and Irving Howe, eds., *The New Conservatives: A Critique From the Left* (New York: Quadrangle, 1974); Irving Kristol, "What Is a Neoconservative?" *Newsweek*, January 19, 1976, p. 87; Daniel Bell, *The Cultural Contradictions of Capitalism* (New York: Basic Books, 1976).

57. Jonathan Brant, *The Hostility of the Burger Court to Mental Health Law Reform Litigation*, Bull. Am. Acad. L. & Psychiatry 11 (1983): 77–90; J. Resnik, *Failing Faith: Adjudicatory Procedure in Decline*, U. Chi. L. Rev. 53 (1986): 494–560.

58. D. J. Rothman and S. Rothman, *The Willowbrook Wars* (New York: Harper & Row, 1984).

59. Jack B. Weinstein, *The Effect of Austerity on Institutional Litigation*, Law & Hum. Behav. 6 (1982): 145–51.

60. Peter Collier and David Horowitz, *Destructive Generation: Second Thoughts About the '60s* (New York: Summit Books, 1989).

61. This is not to suggest that the "pendulum" actually stops moving during any given period; in fact, reform is always under way. See Thomas Kuhn, *The Structure of Scientific Revolutions*, 2d ed. (Chicago: University of Chicago Press, 1970).

62. Kristol, "What Is a Neoconservative?", p. 17. Peter Steinfels in *The Neoconservatives* has been careful to point out that neoconservatism is a movement that is reluctant to identify itself—or at least reluctant to identify itself as conservative. This is because many adherents of the emerging neoconservative philosophy are people who at one time considered themselves to be staunch liberals. It is also due to the fact that, as with other political philosophies, there are many crosscurrents, inner differences, and variations in beliefs that make any one "center of gravity" hard to identify. For further discussion of the concept of neoconservatism and its basic tenets, see also Kristol, "What Is a Neoconservative?" and Coser and Howe, *The New Conservatives*. Other prominent representatives of neoconservative thinking are Daniel Bell, *The Coming of Post-Industrial Society: A Venture in Social Forecasting* (New York: Basic Books, 1973); Bell, *The End of Ideology: On Exhaustion of Political Ideas in the Fifties* (Glencoe, Ill.: Free Press, 1976); Bell, *The Cultural Contradictions of Capitalism*; Moynihan, *The Politics of Guaranteed Income*; and Nathan Glazer, *Affirmative Discrimination: Ethnic Inequality and Public Policy* (New York: Basic Books, 1975).

63. Bell, *The Coming of Post-Industrial Society*.

64. S. Levitan and C. M. Johnson, *Beyond the Safety Net: Reviving the Promise of Opportunity in America* (Cambridge, Mass.: Ballinger, 1984).

65. Glazer, *Affirmative Discrimination*.

66. Ibid., 201.

67. Ibid.; Steinfels, *The Neoconservatives*.

68. George Gilder, *Wealth and Poverty* (New York: Basic Books, 1981); George Gilder, "Why I Am Not a Neo-Conservative," *National Review*, March 5, 1982: 218–22.

69. Ronald Reagan, *The Creative Society* (New York: Devin-Adair, 1968), 4.

70. Collier and Horowitz, *Destructive Generation*, 16.

71. James Q. Wilson, *Thinking About Crime* (New York: Basic Books, 1975).

72. J. Trombetta, "Criminals Beware: The Screen Avengers Are Coming!" *L.A. Times*, July 12, 1981, "Calendar" section, p. 1; George P. Fletcher, *A Crime of Self Defense: Bernhard Goetz and the Law on Trial* (New York: Free Press, 1988).

73. In *United States* v. *Leon*, Justice Byron White noted:

> The substantial costs exacted by the exclusionary rule [which prevented prosecutors from using illegally obtained evidence to convict criminals] for the vindication of Fourth Amendment rights have long been a source of concern. . . . Indiscriminate application of the exclusionary rule, therefore, may well generat[e] disrespect for the law and the administration of justice.

468 U.S. 897, 907, 104 S. Ct. 3405, 82 L. Ed. 2d 677 (1984).

74. *Illinois* v. *Gates*, 462 U.S. 213, 103 S. Ct. 2317, 76 L. Ed. 2d 527 (1983) [rigid standard for issuance of a search warrant, based on an informant's reliability and basis of knowledge, rejected in favor of a more flexible "totality of the circumstances"

inquiry]; *New York* v. *Quarles*, 467 U.S. 649, 104 S. Ct. 262, 81 L. Ed. 2d 550 (1984)[Court found a public safety exception to the *Miranda* rule that a suspect be told his constitutional rights before the police may ask questions].

75. The Bail Reform Act of 1984, § 3142(e) (1983 Ed. Supp. III).

76. *United States* v. *Salerno*, 481 U.S. 739 (1987) [upholding the Bail Reform Act of 1984, which allows a federal court to detain an arrestee if the government demonstrates by clear and convincing evidence at an adversary hearing that no release conditions "will reasonably assure" the safety of any other person and the community].

77. B. Weinraub, "President Unveils $1.2 Billion Plan to Battle Crime," *New York Times*, May 16, 1989, p. A1, col. 1.

78. NAACP Defense Fund, Jason DeParle, "Abstract Death Penalty Meets Real Execution," *New York Times*, June 30, 1991, p. E2, cols. 1–3.

79. 492 U.S. 490, 109 S. Ct. 3040, 106 L. Ed. 2d 410 (1989).

80. *Roe* v. *Wade* (1973). The Court also granted review to three more cases challenging abortion laws in Illinois, Minnesota, and Ohio. The Illinois case was settled before the Supreme Court heard it.

81. *Rust* v. *Sullivan*, 111 S. Ct. 1759, 114 L. Ed. 2d 233, 59 U.S.L.W. 4451 (1991).

82. *Harris* v. *McCrae*, 448 U.S. 297, 100 S. Ct. 2671, 65 L. Ed. 2d 784 (1980). The Hyde Amendment, which severely limits the use of federal Medicaid funds for abortion, was held to be constitutional. *Planned Parenthood Ass'n of Kansas City, Mo., Inc.* v. *Ashcroft*, 462 U.S. 476, 103 S. Ct. 2517, 76 L. Ed. 2d 733 (1983) [parental consent may be required in order for minors to obtain an abortion].

83. David L. Horowitz, *The Judiciary: Umpire or Empire?* Law & Hum. Behav. 6 (1982): 129–143; Scheingold, *The Politics of Rights*; Nagel, *Separation of Powers and the Scope of Federal Equitable Remedies*; R. Morgan, *Disabling America: The "Rights Industry" in Our Time* (New York: Basic Books, 1984); Paul S. Appelbaum, *The Supreme Court Looks at Psychiatry*, Am. J. Psychiatry 141(7) (1984): 827–35.

84. 438 U.S. 265, 98 S. Ct. 2733, 57 L. Ed. 2d 750 (1978).

85. *Pasadena City Board of Education* v. *Spangler*, 427 U.S. 424, 96 S. Ct. 2697, 49 L. Ed. 2d 599 (1976) [finding that, although a district court properly ordered an initial school desegregation plan, the court exceeded its authority by requiring yearly readjustments to maintain a desired racial mix in perpetuity]; *Crawford* v. *Los Angeles Board of Education*, 458 U.S. 527, 102 S. Ct. 3211, 73 L. Ed. 2d 948 (1982) [upholding a state constitutional amendment that precluded court-ordered busing unless federal equal protection clause violated]; *Riddick* v. *School Board of City of Norfolk*, 784 F.2d 521 (1986) [upholding termination of a school district's mandatory busing plan following a finding that the school had been sufficiently desegregated].

86. Steinfels, *The Neoconservatives*.

87. 57 U.S.L.W. 4132 (U.S. Jan. 23, 1989) (No. 87–998) [holding that legislative declarations of past and present discrimination in the construction industry were insufficient without detailed factual proof to justify rigid racial quotas for awarding government contracts to minorities].

88. 490 U.S. 642, 109 S. Ct. 2115, 104 L. Ed. 2d 733 (1989). The tension among members of the Court was evidenced by Justice Harry Blackmun's comment that "[o]ne wonders whether the majority still believes that race discrimination—or, more accurately, race discrimination against nonwhites—is a problem in our society, or even remembers that it ever was." 490 U.S. 642, 662 (1989) (Blackmun dissenting).

89. 490 U.S. 642, 651 (1989). The Court also held that statistical evidence relied on to establish disparate impact discrimination must be shown to result from specific employment practices. Although the employer bears the burden of providing evidence

of a legitimate business justification for employment practices that the employee has shown to be discriminatory, the burden of persuading the trier of fact remains with the employee. The proper comparison is between the racial composition of persons holding the jobs at issue and that of the qualified job market.

90. 490 U.S. 755, 109 S. Ct. 2180, 104 L. Ed. 2d 835 (1989) [holding that white fire fighters in Birmingham, Alabama, could challenge consent decrees resulting from lawsuits filed against local government by a group of black individuals and the NAACP, which set up a detailed plan to correct the city's discriminatory hiring and promotion practices. The Court said the white fire fighters could challenge the plan in court despite the fact they had chosen not to participate in the initial proceedings which led to the decrees].

91. Glazer, *Affirmative Discrimination*.

92. Tribe, *American Constitutional Law*; Cox, *Federalism and Individual Rights Under the Burger Court*; Appelbaum, *The Supreme Court Looks at Psychiatry*.

93. Neal Milner, "The Denigration and Diminishing of Rights" (Paper presented at the 14th International Congress on Law and Mental Health, Montreal, Canada, June 1988).

94. S. Goldman, *Reagan's Judicial Legacy: Completing the Puzzle and Summing Up*, Judicature 72 (1989): 318–30.

95. "Reagan Is Moving to End Program that Pays for Legal Aid to the Poor," *New York Times*, March 6, 1981, p. A1, col. 2; "U.S. Issues Rules to Tighten Legal Aid to Poor and Elderly," *New York Times*, Sept. 4, 1983, p. 1, col. 5. See generally, Legal Services Corporation, Eligibility Regulations, 45 C.F.R. §§ 1611.1-.9 (1986).

96. R. E. Gould and R. Levy, "Psychiatrists as Puppets of Koch's Roundup Policy," *New York Times*, Nov. 27, 1988, p. A3, col. 4.

97. R. D. McFadden, "Florida Judge Orders Hospital Quarantine for Youth in AIDS Case," *New York Times*, June 12, 1987, p. B4, col. 3; "Quarantine Lifted in AIDS Case, But Boy Involved Is Confined," *New York Times*, June 17, 1987, p. B9, col. 4.

98. See Anthony M. Platt, *The Child Savers: The Invention of Delinquency*, 2nd ed. (Chicago: University of Chicago Press, 1977).

99. For an analysis of the criminal justice and mental health systems, see Rothman, *Conscience and Convenience*.

Chapter 1

1. David Abrahamsen, *Confessions of Son of Sam* (New York: Columbia University Press, 1985), viii, 2–5.

2. H. M. Hart, *The Aims of the Criminal Law*, Law & Contemp. Probs. 23 (1958): 401–41.

3. H. L. Packer, *The Limits of the Criminal Sanction* (Stanford, Calif.: Stanford Press, 1968). See also, Judge David Bazelon's concurring opinion in *U.S. v. Barker*, 514 F.2d 208, 227 (1975).

4. H. L. A. Hart, *Punishment and Responsibility* (New York: Oxford University Press, 1968).

5. J. Feinberg, *Doing and Deserving* (Princeton, N.J.: Princeton, 1970). Legal insanity should be distinguished from incompetency to stand trial. Insanity focuses on the defendant's mental health at the time the crime was committed; incompetency

focuses on the defendant's condition at the time of trial. A mentally ill defendant cannot be prosecuted if he or she is unable, because of mental illness, to understand the charges against him or her, the nature of the proceedings, or to assist the defense attorney. Such an individual is considered "incompetent" to stand trial.

6. *Durham* v. *United States*, 214 F.2d 862 (D.C. Cir. 1954). See also, R. Bonnie, *The Moral Basis of the Insanity Defense*, A.B.A.J. 69 (1983): 194–97.

7. Hart, *The Aims of the Criminal Law*.

8. H. Gross, *A Theory of Criminal Justice* (New York: Oxford University Press, 1979). The commentary to the Model Penal Code asserted that the primary function of an insanity test is to determine when "a punitive-correctional approach is appropriate and [when] a medical-custodial disposition is the only kind that the law should allow." *Model Penal Code and Commentaries*, § 4.01, commentary at 164–65.

9. But see critics who disagree with this premise, for example, T. Szasz, *The Myth of Mental Illness* (New York: Hoeber-Harper, 1961); J. H. Hardisty, *Mental Illness: A Legal Fiction*, Wash. L. Rev. 48 (1973): 735–62.

10. Daniel M'Naghten was found "totally insane" in 1843 after he shot and killed Edward Drummond, the secretary to the British prime minister, thinking his victim was the prime minister Sir Robert Peel. M'Naghten believed that Peel and the pope were conspiring against him. See Rita J. Simon and David E. Aaronson, *The Insanity Defense: A Critical Assessment of Law and Policy in the Post-Hinckley Era* (New York: Praeger, 1988).

11. J. Goldstein and J. Katz, *Abolish the Insanity Defense—Why not?* Yale L.J. 72 (1963): 853–76. For a discussion of the empirical data regarding this point, see Chapter 7.

12. S. J. Brakel and R. Rock, *The Mentally Disabled and the Law*, 2d ed. (Chicago: American Bar Foundation, 1971).

13. *Jacobson* v. *Massachusetts*, 197 U.S. 11, 25 S. Ct. 358, 49 L. Ed. 643 (1905); *Williamson* v. *Lee Optical*, 348 U.S. 483, 75 S. Ct. 461, 99 L. Ed. 563 (1955).

14. *Bunting* v. *Oregon*, 243 U.S. 426, 37 S. Ct. 435, 61 L. Ed. 830 (1917) [upholding as a proper exercise of state police power a state law limiting the number of hours worked each day]; *West Coast Hotel Company* v. *Parrish*, 300 U.S. 379, 57 S. Ct. 578, 81 L. Ed. 703 (1937) [upholding a Washington law establishing minimum wages and working conditions for women and children as a proper exercise of the state police power to protect health and morals]. Christopher Gustavus Tiedeman, *A Treatise on the Limitations of Police Power in the United States* (1886), § 89, Regulation of Sale of Certain Articles of Merchandise. *Jacobson* v. *Massachusetts*, (1905) [upholding a state compulsory vaccination law, saying that "upon the principle of self-defense, or paramount necessity, a community has the right to protect itself against an epidemic of disease which threatens the safety of its members"]. *Zucht* v. *King*, 260 U.S. 174, 43 S. Ct. 24, 64 L. Ed. 194 (1922) [refusing to invalidate a Texas law excluding unvaccinated children from school].

15. Brakel and Rock, *The Mentally Disabled and the Law*; *Developments in the Law: Civil Commitment of the Mentally Ill*, Harv. L. Rev. 87 (1974): 1190–406.

16. A. Dershowitz, *Preventive Confinement: A Suggested Framework for Constitutional Analysis*, Tex. L. Rev. 51 (1973): 1277–324, 1277; A. Dershowitz, *The Origins of Preventive Confinement in Anglo-American Law*, U. Cin. L. Rev. 43 (1974): 781–846. See also, D. Hermann, *Preventive Detention: A Scientific View of Man and State Power*, U. Ill. L.R. 1973 (1973): 673–99; 1990 Wash. Laws, Chapter 3, §§ 1001–13 [authorizing lifetime confinement of selected sex offenders only *after* they have served their full prison terms if they are considered likely to reoffend].

17. A. Dershowitz, *The Law of Dangerousness: Some Fictions About Predictions*, J. Legal Educ. 23 (1970): 24–47.

18. B. Ennis and T. Litwack, *Flipping Coins in the Courtroom: Psychiatry and the Presumption of Expertise*, Calif. L. Rev. 62 (1974): 693–752, 693; see also J. Monahan, *Risk Assessment of Violence Among the Mentally Disordered: Generating Useful Knowledge*, Int'l J.L. & Psychiatry 11 (1989): 249–57.

19. Psychiatrists are poor predictors of dangerousness. Generally speaking, they are accurate in predicting violence in no more than one out of three cases. See Chapter 4 for a thorough discussion of psychiatrists' ability to predict dangerousness.

20. *Parens patriae*, literally "parent of the country," refers traditionally to the role of the state as sovereign and guardian of persons under a legal disability to act for themselves such as juveniles, the insane, or the unknown. *State of West Virginia v. Chas. Pfizer & Co.*, 440 F.2d 1079, 1089 (1971).

21. S. J. Brakel, J. Parry, and B. A. Weiner, *The Mentally Disabled and the Law*, 3d ed. (Chicago: American Bar Foundation, 1985).

22. Mentally ill defendants were determined incompetent to stand trial if they were unable to assist their attorneys at trial and to understand the nature of the proceedings against them. As the Supreme Court said in *Pusky* v. *United States*, 362 U.S. 403, 404 (1960): "It is not enough for the judge . . . to find that the defendant [is] oriented to time and place and [has] some recollection of events . . . the test must be whether he has a rational as well as a factual understanding of the proceedings against him."

23. Goldstein and Katz, *Abolish the Insanity Defense—Why Not?*

24. Of course, some, though not many, were acquitted by reason of insanity.

25. Their views are well stated in the classic article, *A Rationale of the Law of Homicide*, Colum. L. Rev. 37 (1937): 701–61. Professor Wechsler later became the reporter for the Model Penal Code and was extremely influential in determining how this major law reform project would structure the insanity defense. See also Packer, *The Limits of the Criminal Sanction*, p. 16; Hart, *The Aims of the Criminal Law*; and A. Goldstein, *The Insanity Defense* (New Haven: Yale University Press, 1967), 12.

26. Packer, *The Limits of the Criminal Sanction*, 9.

27. Jerome Hall, *Justice in the 20th Century*, Calif. L. Rev. 59 (1971): 752–68. See also, H. Weihofen, *The Urge to Punish; New Approaches to the Problem of Mental Irresponsibility for Crime* (New York: Farrar, Strauss and Cudahy, 1956).

28. As noted by numerous commentators, any social system of punishment serves multiple goals. See Hart, *The Aims of the Criminal Law*; Packer, *The Limits of the Criminal Sanction*; George P. Fletcher, *Rethinking Criminal Law* (Boston: Little, Brown, 1978).

29. David J. Rothman, *Conscience and Convenience: The Asylum and Its Alternatives in Progressive America* (Boston: Little, Brown, 1980), 5. These views came to the foreground during the Liberal Era. See, for example, President's Commission on Law Enforcement and Administration of Justice, *The Challenge of Crime in a Free Society* (Washington, D.C.: U.S. Government Printing Office, 1968); D. Bazelon, *The Concept of Responsibility*, Geo. L.J. 53 (1964): 5–18; Ramsey Clark, *Crime in America* (New York: Simon & Schuster, 1970).

30. Rothman, *Conscience and Convenience*.

31. Ibid., 132–35. This was really a form of "preventive detention." These particular offenders were to be confined because it was predicted that they would commit other crimes if released, and the only way to prevent this was to keep them in prison.

32. Rothman, *Conscience and Convenience*.

33. Ibid., 6.

34. Ibid., 55.

35. Ibid.

36. Ibid.

37. F. A. Allen, *Criminal Justice, Legal Values, and the Rehabilitative Ideal*, J. Crim. L., Criminology & Police Sci. 50 (1959): 226–36, 226. Indeed, in 1959 Professor Allen concluded that

> [I]n no other period has the rehabilitative ideal so completely dominated theoretical and scholarly inquiry, to such an extent that in some quarters it is almost assumed that matters of treatment and reform of the offender are the only questions worthy of serious attention in the whole field of criminal justice and corrections.

Ibid., 227.

38. Karl Menninger gave popular voice to the emergence of rehabilitation as the primary, perhaps even the exclusive, goal of the criminal justice system. Karl Menninger, *The Crime of Punishment* (New York: Penguin Books, 1968), 215. See also, B. L. Diamond, *From M'Naghten to Currens, and Beyond*, Calif. L. Rev. 50 (1962): 189–205.

39. *Sas* v. *Maryland*, 334 F.2d 506 (4th Cir. 1964).

40. Brakel, Parry, and Weiner, *The Mentally Disabled and the Law*, 739–40.

41. N. N. Kittrie, *The Right to Be Different: Deviance and Enforced Therapy* (Baltimore: Johns Hopkins University Press, 1971), 1–4.

42. Jerome Hall remarked:

> The common assumption underlying the shift in current attitudes [toward rehabilitation], aided by congenital American optimism, is that if only we spend enough millions and train many more psychiatrists, vocational guidance experts and others, we will acquire the necessary knowledge and know-how to reform all, or nearly all criminals.

J. Hall, *Justice in the 20th Century*, Calif. L. Rev. 59 (1971): 752–68, 756–57.

43. Peter Conrad and J. W. Schneider, *Deviance and Medicalization: From Badness to Sickness* (St. Louis: Mosby, 1980).

44. Kittrie, *The Right to be Different*.

45. Goldstein, *The Insanity Defense*, 14–15.

46. Judge Bazelon opined:

> [The 1950s] was a time of ascendancy for our faith in science and technology. In the wake of the discovery of atomic energy, the prestige of scientific experts was at a new high. It rose even higher after the soviets in 1957 launched Sputnik, the first satellite, and the Space Age began. The new drugs enabled psychiatrists to claim membership in this scientific community.

D. Bazelon, *Questioning Authority* (New York: Knopf, 1987), 40.

47. R. Brancale, *Diagnostic Techniques in Aid of Sentencing*, Law & Contemp. Probs. 23 (1958): 442–60, 445.

48. Menninger, *The Crime of Punishment*.

49. A. A. Stone, *Law, Psychiatry, and Morality* (Washington, D.C.: American Psychiatric Press, 1984).

50. 101 Cl. & F. 200, 8 Eng. Rep. 718 (H.L. 1843).

51. Criticisms have been well detailed in numerous writings and judicial opinions, including Edward De Grazia, *The Distinction of Being Mad*, U. Chi. L. Rev. 22 (1955): 339–55; Manfred S. Guttmacher, *The Psychiatrist as an Expert Witness*, U. Chi. L. Rev. 22 (1955): 325–30; Richard H. Kuh, *The Insanity Defense—An Effort*

to *Confine Law and Reason*, U. Pa. L. Rev. 110 (1962): 771–815; S. E. Sobeloff, *Insanity and the Criminal Law: From M'Naghten to Durham and Beyond*, A.B.A.J. 41 (1955): 793–96, 877–79; H. Weihofen, *The M'Naghten Rule in Its Present-Day Setting*, Fed. Probation 17(3) (1953): 8–14; *United States* v. *Freeman*, 357 F.2d 606 (2d Cir. 1966); *United States* v. *Currens*, 290 F.2d 751 (3d Cir. 1961); *State* v. *White*, 93 Idaho 153, 456 P.2d 797 (1969).

52. Guttmacher, *The Psychiatrist as an Expert Witness*. He noted that the *M'Naghten* test, by limiting psychiatric testimony solely to cognitive ability, in turn limited what the psychiatrist could testify to at a trial. In addition, many psychiatrists had concluded that psychiatry had no special diagnostic techniques for ascertaining whether a mentally ill person in fact knew the difference between right and wrong. And yet another scholar of the insanity defense later refuted the claim that the *M'Naghten* test limited the ability of psychiatrists to present their diagnoses and conclusions to juries. Professor Goldstein is one of those who maintains that the *M'Naghten* rule did not prevent psychiatrists from presenting all of their observations and conclusions to juries. Goldstein, *The Insanity Defense*.

53. R. Waelder, *Psychiatry and The Problem of Criminal Responsibility*, U. Pa. L. Rev. 101 (1952): 378–90; Bazelon, *The Concept of Responsibility*. See also note 57.

54. Guttmacher, *The Psychiatrist as an Expert Witness*, 326.

55. De Grazia, *The Distinction of Being Mad*, 342; M. S. Guttmacher and H. Weihofen, *Psychiatry and the Law* (New York: Norton, 1952), 406.

56. B. L. Diamond, *Criminal Responsibility of the Mentally Ill*, Stan. L. Rev. 14, (1961): 59–86, 60–61.

57. B. L. Diamond, in discussing a case in which he had testified, argued that

This perjury can be justified and explained away by all sorts of rationalizations: the defendant really didn't know what she was doing; her act was so totally deviant from any normal maternal behavior and the evidence of mental disease so conclusive, that she just couldn't have known the "nature and quality" of her act; or the word "know" in the *M'Naghten* formula doesn't mean what it says, but rather means "to appreciate," or "to comprehend," or "to realize in its full meaning." Professor Jerome Hall [citation omitted] and Dr. Gregory Zilborg [citation omitted] both endorse this widening of the scope of the word "know." I endorse this too, but I don't like having to take refuge in such semantic devices.

Diamond, *Criminal Responsibility of the Mentally Ill*, 62.

58. Of course, it could be argued that what really angered psychiatrists was the law's dictating to them what information would be considered legally relevant in determining guilt and not that the information they could present to the jury was restricted. Some psychiatrists seemed to assume that all psychiatric insight should be considered legally germane to assessments of criminal responsibility. Ibid.

59. *Durham* v. *United States*, 214 F.2d, 862, 874–875 (D.C. Cir. 1954). This rule was patterned on the insanity test used by New Hampshire for over a century; *State* v. *Jones*, 50 N.H. 369 (1871); *State* v. *Pike*, 49 N.H. 399 (1870).

60. Harry Kalven, *Insanity and the Criminal Law*, U. Chi. L. Rev. 22 (1955) 317–404.

61. Bazelon, *Questioning Authority*, 39–70.

62. R. Arens, *Insanity Defense* (New York: Philosophical Library, 1974).

63. *Carter* v. *United States*, 252 F.2d. 608 (D.C. Cir. 1957) [defining the term "product"]; *McDonald* v. *United States*, 312 F. 2d 847 (D.C. Cir. 1962) [defining the

terms "mental disease or defect"]; *Washington* v. *United States*, 390 F.2d 444 (D.C. Cir. 1967) [defining the proper role of the forensic psychiatrist as an expert witness].

64. See, for example, Kalven, *Insanity and the Criminal Law*; A. Krash, *The Durham Rule and Judicial Administration of the Insanity Defense in the District of Columbia*, Yale L.J. 70 (1961): 905–52; Charles W. Halleck, *The Insanity Defense in the District of Columbia—A Legal Lorelei*, Geo. L.J. 49 (1960): 294–320.

65. In *United States* v. *Brawner*, 471 F.2d 969 (D.C. Cir. 1972), the Federal Court of Appeals for the District of Columbia abandoned the *Durham* rule in favor of the ALI test.

66. *Model Penal Code and Commentaries* § 4.01, commentary at 164–65 (1962). The ALI commentary makes this clear:

> No problem in the drafting of a penal code presents larger intrinsic difficulty than that of determining when individuals whose conduct otherwise would be criminal ought to be exculpated on the ground that they were suffering from mental disease or defect when they acted as they did.

67. Ibid., 156–60.

68. Section 4.01, *Mental Disease or Defect Excluding Responsibility*,

> (1) a person is not responsible for criminal conduct if at the time of such conduct as a result of mental disease or defect he lacks substantial capacity either to appreciate the criminality [wrongfulness] of his conduct or to conform his conduct to the requirements of law, (2) as used in this Article, the terms "mental disease or defect" do not include an abnormality manifested only by repeated criminal or otherwise anti-social conduct.

The test was first proposed in 1954 and it was finally adopted in 1962.

69. Goldstein, *The Insanity Defense*, 57. See also, J. M. Livermore and P. E. Meehl, *The Virtues of M'Naghten*, Minn. L. Rev. 51 (1967): 789–856, 800–808.

70. Federal Circuits: *United States* v. *Freeman*, 357 F.2d 606 (2d. Cir. 1966); *United States* v. *Currens*, 290 F.2d 751 (3d. Cir. 1961); *United States* v. *Chandler*, 393 F.2d 920 (4th Cir. 1968); *Blake* v. *United States*, 407 F.2d 908 (5th Cir. 1969); *United States* v. *Smith*, 404 F.2d 720 (6th Cir. 1968); *United States* v. *Shapiro*, 383 F.2d 680 (7th Cir. 1967); *Pope* v. *United States*, 372 F.2d 710 (8th Cir. 1967); *Wade* v. *United States*, 426 F.2d 64 (9th Cir. 1970); *Wion* v. *United States*, 325 F.2d 420 (10th Cir. 1963); *United States* v. *Brawner*, 471 F.2d 969 (D.C. Cir. 1972).

71. Simon and Aaronson, *The Insanity Defense*, 44–45.

72. This is not to say that all states used the *M'Naghten* test. Some, like Vermont, did not. Nor is it to say that courts had not experimented with radically different tests. In fact, the Circuit Court of Appeals for the District of Columbia under the intellectual leadership of Judge Bazelon had earlier adopted a new and radically different type of insanity test in 1954 when it adopted the *Durham* test.

73. *State* v. *Lucas*, 30 N.J. 37, 152 A.2d 50 (1959) (Judge Weintraub); Livermore and Meehl, *The Virtues of M'Naghten*, 789–856.

74. 214 F.2d 862 (D.C. Cir. 1954).

75. *State* v. *Lucas* (1959).

76. *People* v. *Drew*, 149 Cal. Rptr. 275, 583 P.2d 1318 (1978).

77. During this time the United Kingdom adopted its own version of this doctrine, termed "diminished responsibility," which was quite different conceptually from the diminished capacity defense. The Homicide Act of 1957 provides:

> 2.-(1) Where a person kills or is a party to the killing of another, he shall not be convicted of murder if he was suffering from such abnormality of mind (whether arising from a

condition of arrested or retarded development of the mind or any inherent causes or induced by disease or injury) as substantially impaired his mental responsibility for his acts and omissions in doing or being a party to the killing.

2.-(3) A person who, but for this section, would be liable, whether a principal or as accessory, to be convicted of murder shall be liable instead to be convicted of manslaughter.

Homicide Act, 1957, 5 & 6 Eliz. 2, Ch. 11, Sec. 2(1), 2(3), Sched. 6.

78. In *People* v. *Wetmore*, 22 Cal. 3d 318, 583 P.2d 1308, 149 Cal. Rptr. 265 (1978), the California Supreme Court held that evidence of mental illness was admissible in the guilt or innocence phase of California's bifurcated trial procedure to negate the *mens rea* of burglary—breaking and entering with the intent to commit a theft—even if it would result in an acquittal. The Court acknowledged that the rationale of the diminished capacity defense required that the defendant must be permitted to introduce all evidence that was logically relevant to the presence or absence of state of mind elements. It said:

> The prosecution must prove all elements of the crime beyond a reasonable doubt; we do not perceive how a defendant who has in his possession evidence which rebuts an element of the crime can logically be denied the right to present that evidence merely because it will result in his acquittal.

Id., 328, 583 P.2d 1308 at 1315.

79. In 1961 it formally adopted Section 4.02 of the Model Penal Code, which would make admissible in a criminal trial evidence of mental disease or defect when it is relevant to the state of mind required as an element of the charged offense. This section provides:

> Section 4.02. Evidence of Mental Disease or Defect Admissible When Relevant to Element of the Offense [Mental Disease or Defect Impairing Capacity as Ground for Mitigation of Punishment in Capital Cases].
>
> (1) Evidence that the defendant suffered from a mental disease or defect is admissible whenever it is relevant to prove the defendant did or did not have a state of mind which is an element of the offense.
>
> [(2) Whenever the jury or the Court is authorized to determine or to recommend whether or not the defendant shall be sentenced to death or imprisonment upon conviction, evidence that the capacity of the defendant to appreciate the criminality [wrongfulness] of his conduct or to conform his conduct to the requirements of law was impaired as a result of mental disease or defect is admissible in favor of sentence of imprisonment.]

80. G. E. Dix, *Psychological Abnormality as a Factor in Grading Criminal Liability: Diminished Capacity, Diminished Responsibility, and the Like*, J. Crim. L., Criminology & Police Sci. 62 (1971): 313–34; Diamond, *Criminal Responsibility of the Mentally Ill.*

81. In *People* v. *Henderson*, the California Supreme Court expressly acknowledged that "[i]ts [the diminished capacity defense] purpose and effect are to ameliorate the law governing criminal responsibility prescribed by the *M'Naghten* rule." 60 Cal. 2d. 482, 490, 386 P.2d 677, 682, 35 Cal. Rptr. 77 (1963). The judicial creation and expansion of a doctrine that circumvented legislatively enacted law regulating the relevance of mental illness to criminal responsibility could well be considered violation of the separation of powers required under the Constitution. This is particularly true in the area of criminal law where the legislative branch is recognized as the primary source of substantive criminal law. The California Supreme Court itself has acknowl-

edged that there is no longer a common law of crime in that state. *Keeler* v. *Superior Court of Amador County*, 2 Cal. 3d 619, 470 P.2d 617, 87 Cal. Rptr. 481 (1970).

82. One of the seminal court decisions in California that created the diminished capacity defense was *People* v. *Wells*, 33 Cal. 2d 330, 202 P.2d 53, *cert. denied*, 338 U.S. 836, 221 P.2d 947 (1949). The defendant was a mentally ill convict who faced mandatory capital punishment if found guilty of assaulting a prison guard. The pressure to avoid executing such an individual was immense.

83.

> I believe there is, and that the key to the development of a state of rapport between psychiatry and the law exists within the ancient doctrine of *mens rea*. I am convinced that within the jurisprudence of the criminal law there is a nuclear concept—*mens rea*—which is capable of an evolutionary development which will provide an effective bridge of communication between psychiatry and the law and which will provide ample room within the judicial process for the psychiatrist to move about freely without offense to the values and goals inherent in medical psychology.

Diamond, *Criminal Responsibility of the Mentally Ill*, 66.

84. Ibid., 60.

85. B. L. Diamond, *The Fallacy of the Impartial Expert*, Arch. Crim. Psychodynamics 3(2) (1959): 221; B. L. Diamond, *The Psychiatrist as Advocate*, J. Psychiatry & L. 1 (1973): 5–21; B. L. Diamond, *From Durham to Brawner, A Futile Journey*, Wash. L. Q. (1973): 109–25.

86. Diamond, *Criminal Responsibility of the Mentally Ill*, 75–83.

87. A fairly large number of psychiatrists from across the United States filed an amicus curiae brief arguing that psychiatric evidence should be admitted to prove or disprove a mental element of a crime.   ⁓

88. Diamond, *Criminal Responsibility of the Mentally Ill*, 82. Diamond wrote candidly:

> I concede that this whole business of lack of mental capacity to premeditate, to have malice or to entertain intent, is a kind of sophistry which must not be allowed to remain an end in itself. Right now we must utilize these legal technicalities to permit the psychiatrists to gain entrance into the trial court and to allow the judge and jury to give full consideration to the deeper and more complex mental and emotional factors of the defendant.

89. 61 Cal. 2d 795, 394 P.2d 959, 40 Cal. Rptr. 271 (1964).

90. Interestingly, the jury recommended that the adolescent be sent to a hospital for the criminally insane, even though it found that he was not insane under the *M'Naghten* test. If convicted of first-degree murder, the adolescent faced possible life imprisonment. 61 Cal. 2d 795, 394 P.2d 959, 961, 40 Cal. Rptr. 271 (1964).

91. 61 Cal. 2d 795, 821, 394 P.2d 959, 975 (1964).

92. Ibid., 821; 394 P.2d at 975 (1964).

93. The defendant was a psychiatric patient who killed a female friend who rejected his amorous advances, a case which spawned tort liability for the psychiatrists who negligently failed to warn the intended and identifiable victim, Tatiana Tarasoff. *Tarasoff* v. *The Regents of the University of California*, 17 Cal. 3d 425, 551 P.2d 334, 131 Cal. Rptr. 14 (1976).

94. *People* v. *Poddar*, 10 Cal. 3d 750, 758, 518 P.2d 342, 348, 111 Cal. Reptr. 916 (1974).

95. Under the rubric of the "diminished capacity" defense, California's Supreme Court arguably had in effect created its own mini-version of the ALI insanity test.

See S. J. Morse, *Diminished Capacity: A Moral and Legal Conundrum*, Int'l J.L. & Psychiatry 2(3) (1979): 271–98.

96. 22 Cal. 3d 318, 583 P.2d 1308, 149 Cal. Rptr. 265 (1978).

97. Id.; 22 Cal. 3d, 583 P.2d 1316, 149 Cal. Rptr. 273.

98. In addition to giving juries less extreme choices than the stark ones of guilty as charged or innocent by reason of insanity, some commentators thought that the defense plea of diminished capacity would also enhance the treatment prospects of offenders who successfully used it. Prison officials would now know which prisoners were seriously ill and required treatment. Diamond, *Criminal Responsibility of the Mentally Ill.*

99. See T. H. D. Lewin, *Psychiatric Evidence in Criminal Cases for Purposes Other than the Defense of Insanity*, Syracuse L. Rev. 26 (1975): 1051–115. Some of these states include: Alabama, Alaska, Arkansas, California, Colorado, Connecticut, Hawaii, Idaho, Iowa, Kentucky, Missouri, Montana, Nebraska, Nevada, New Mexico, New York, Ohio, Oregon, Rhode Island, Texas, Utah, Virginia, District of Columbia. In addition, some form of the diminished capacity defense has been authorized in the following federal cases: *U.S.* v. *Brawner*, 471 F.2d 969 (D.C. Cir. 1972); *Rhodes* v. *U.S.*, 282 F.2d 59 (4th Cir.), *cert. denied*, 364 U.S. 912 (1960); *U.S.* v. *Dunnahoe*, 6 U.S.C.M.A. 745, 21 C.M.R. 67 (1956). Other states may also have adopted the defense. R. P. Bryant and C. B. Hume, *Recent Developments, Diminished Capacity—Recent Decisions and an Analytic Approach*, Vand. L. Rev. 30 (1977): 213–257. Some jurisdictions permit the defendant to present evidence of mental illness to disprove all statutory mental elements. Others limit the admissibility of such evidence either to specific intent crimes or to homicide charges.

100. Lenore E. Walker, *The Battered Woman* (New York: Harper & Row, 1979); L. E. Walker, R. K. Thyfault, and A. Browne, *Beyond the Juror's Ken: Battered Women*, Vt. L. Rev. 7 (1982): 1–14; *Ibn-Tamas* v. *United States*, 407 A.2d 626 (1979).

101. Faith McNulty, *The Burning Bed* (New York: Harcourt Brace Jovanovich, 1980).

102. E. S. Milstein, S. Elliott, and K. D. Snyder, *PTSD: The War Is Over, The Battle Goes On*, Trial 19(1) (1983): 86–89, 87; *State* v. *Heads*, 106, 126 (First Jud. Dist. Ct. Caddo Parish (Oct. 10, 1981)).

103. One aspect of PTSD (post-traumatic stress syndrome) that is particularly prevalent among combat veterans is its association with criminal behavior. Some veterans experience flashbacks, which occur as dissociative states lasting from a few minutes to several hours or even days, during which components of the event are relived and the individual behaves as though experiencing the event at that moment. American Psychiatric Association, *Diagnostic and Statistical Manual of Mental Disorders: DSM-III-R*, 3d ed. rev. (Washington, D.C.: APA, 1980), 247.

104. Milstein, Elliott, and Snyder, *PTSD: The War Is Over, The Battle Goes On*, and cases cited therein.

105.

Diagnostic criteria for pathological gambling:
A. The individual is chronically and progressively unable to resist impulses to gamble.
B. Gambling compromises, disrupts, or damages family, personal, and vocational pursuits, as indicated by at least three of the following:
   (1) arrest for forgery, fraud, embezzlement, or income tax evasion due to attempt to obtain money for gambling
   (2) default on debts or other financial responsibilities
   (3) disrupted family or spouse relationship due to gambling

    (4) borrowing of money from illegal source (loan shark)

    (5) inability to account for loss of money or to produce evidence or winning money, if this is claimed

    (6) loss of work due to absenteeism in order to pursue gambling activity

    (7) necessity for another person to provide money to relieve a desperate financial situation

  C. The gambling is not due to antisocial personality disorder.

American Psychiatric Association, *Diagnostic and Statistical Manual of Mental Disorders*, 247.

The enumerated essential features of this disease do not represent discrete clinical entities. Instead, they consist either of criminal acts or the behavioral consequences of gambling. One commentator severely criticized the logic of this diagnosis:

> Diagnostically, much of the behavior required of the individual to qualify for the diagnosis of Pathological Gambling is of a criminal or quasi-criminal nature. I suggest that the logic of requiring such behavior in order to make the diagnosis in order then to be exculpated for the same behavior is circular.

A. L. McGarry, *Pathological Gambling: A New Insanity Defense*, Bull. Am. Acad. Psychiatry & L. 11(4) (1983): 301–8; American Psychiatric Association, *Diagnostic and Statistical Manual of Mental Disorders*, 291–93.

  106. *State* v. *Campanaro*, Nos. 632–79, 1309–79, 1317–79, 514–80, & 707–80 (Superior Court of New Jersey Crim. Div., Union County, 1980). The expert witness in this case was Robert L. Custer, M.D. Dr. Custer was active on the committee that formulated the compulsive gambling defense, at the same time he was medical adviser to Gamblers Anonymous. McGarry, *Pathological Gambling*. Dr. Custer testified on behalf of criminal defendants in several cases in which the defense of pathological gambling was raised.

  107. The prosecutor did not even contest the defense claim that compulsive gambling was a mental disease. *State* v. *Lafferty*, No. 44359 (Connecticut Superior Court, June 5, 1981). But see, *U.S.* v. *Lyons*, 731 F.2d 243, 245 (5th Cir. 1984) [court rejected defendant's claim that pathological gambling should support an insanity defense under the ALI test].

  108. See McGarry, *Pathological Gambling*, and cases cited therein.

  109. See Ann H. Rubin, *Beating the Odds: Compulsive Gambling as an Insanity Defense—State v. Lafferty*, Conn. L. Rev. 14 (1982): 341–67.

  110. H. R. Greenberg, "Psychology of Gambling," in *Comprehensive Textbook of Psychiatry, III*, ed. H. I. Kaplan, A. M. Freeman, and B. J. Sadock (Baltimore, Md.: Williams and Wilkins, 1980), 3274–83.

  111. It should be noted that DSM-III-R expressly cautions: "The use of this manual for non-clinical purposes, such as determination of legal responsibility . . . must be critically examined in each instance within the appropriate institutional context," p. 12.

  112. Judge David Bazelon in a dissenting opinion in *United States* v. *Brawner*, took this position. 471 F.2d 969, 1032 (D.C. Cir. 1972).

  113. D. Bazelon, *The Morality of the Criminal Law*, S. Cal. L. Rev. 49 (1975): 385–405, 396. See also, *United States* v. *Alexander*, 471 F.2d 923 (D.C. Cir. 1973) [court rejects defense of "rotten social background" and "black rage" in charge of murder]; R. Delgado, *"Rotten Social Background": Should the Criminal Law Recognize a Defense of Severe Environmental Deprivation?* Law & Inequality 3 (1985): 9–90.

114. For a powerful critique of Judge Bazelon's views, see S. J. Morse, *The Twilight of Welfare Criminology: A Reply to Judge Bazelon*, S. Cal. L. Rev. 49 (1976): 1247–68.

115. Black rage: *United States* v. *Alexander*, 471 F.2d 923 (1973); *Fisher* v. *United States*, 149 F.2d 28 (1945). Severe environmental deprivation: *United States* v. *Alexander*, 471 F.2d 923 (1973) (Bazelon, C.J., dissenting). Brainwashing: *United States* v. *Hearst*, 563 F.2d 1331 (9th Cir. 1977), *cert. denied*, 435 U.S. 1000 (1978).

116. See M. R. Gardner, *The Renaissance of Retribution—an Examination of Doing Justice*, Wis. L. Rev. 1976 (1976) 781–815, 808–11.

117. Goldstein, *The Insanity Defense*, 46.

Chapter 2

1. J. Abramson, *The Criminalization of Mentally Disordered Behavior: Possible Side Effect of a New Mental Health Law*, Hosp. & Commun. Psychiatry 23(4) (1972): 101–5; J. C. Bonovitz and J. S. Bonovitz, *Diversion of the Mentally Ill into the Criminal Justice System: The Police Intervention Perspective*, Am. J. Psychiatry 138(7) (1981): 973–76; J. C. Bonovitz and E. B. Guy, *Impact of Restrictive Civil Commitment Procedures on a Prison Psychiatric Service*, Am. J. Psychiatry 136(8) (1979): 1045–48; U. Aviram and S. P. Segal, *Exclusion of the Mentally Ill*, Arch. Gen. Psychiatry 29 (1973): 126–31; F. L. Ball and B. E. Havassy, *A Survey of the Problems and Needs of Homeless Consumers of Acute Psychiatric Services*, Hosp. & Commun. Psychiatry 35(9) (1984): 917–21; E. L. Bassuk, *The Homelessness Problem*, Sci. Am. 241 (1984): 40–45; E. L. Bassuk, L. Rubin, and A. Lauriat, *Is Homelessness a Mental Health Problem?* Am. J. Psychiatry 141(12) (1984): 1546–50; H. H. Goldman and J. P. Morrissey, *The Alchemy of Mental Health Policy: Homelessness and the Fourth Cycle of Reform*, Am. J. Pub. Health 75(7) (1985): 727–31.

2. James Q. Wilson, *Thinking About Crime* (New York: Basic Books, 1975), 7.

3. In 1970, the number of aggravated assaults was 331,190. That number increased to 614,210 in 1979. In 1970, the number of murders and nonnegligent homicides was 15,860. By 1979, the number had increased to 21,460. Federal Bureau of Investigation, *Crime in the U.S.: Uniform Crime Reports for the United States* (Washington, D.C.: U.S. Dept. of Justice, Federal Bureau of Investigation, 1971, 1980, 1988). Only in 1981 did the number of serious crimes reported to law enforcement authorities level off and then decrease very slightly. See also, *New York Times*, August 27, 1982, p. A8, col. 1.

4. See Research & Forecasts, Inc., *The Figgie Report on Fear of Crime: America Afraid, Parts I, II and III* (Willoughby, Ohio: A-T-O, Inc., 1980). Although the level of fear apparently held by the average community does not correspond to the incidence of crime itself, the rate at which all crime increased during the decade cited suggests that the public's fear is well founded.

5. R. L. Aynes, *Constitutional Considerations: Government Responsibility and the Right Not to Be a Victim*, Symposium Issue, Pepperdine L. Rev. 11 (1984); S. Abrahamson, *Redefining Roles: The Victim's Rights Movement*, Utah L. Rev. (1985): 517–67, 523.

6. According to 128 Cong. Rec. § 13,063 (daily ed., Oct. 1, 1982) (Statement of Sen. Heinz), many victims did not even report their crimes to the police. Richard T. Sparks, "Research on Victims of Crime: Accomplishments, Issues, and New Directions," in *Crime and Delinquency Issues: A Monograph Series* (Rockville, Md.: U.S.

Dept. of Health and Human Services, 1982), 15; W. G. Skogan, *Measurement Problems in Official and Survey Crime Rates*, J. Crim. Just. 3 (1975): 17–31, 20–23.

7. J. R. Anderson and P. L. Woodard, *Victim and Witness Assistance: New State Laws and the System's Response*, Judicature 68(2) (1985): 221–44, 221.

8. Susan Brownmiller, *Against Our Will: Men, Women, and Rape* (New York: Simon and Schuster, 1975); V. Berger, *Man's Trial, Woman's Tribulation: Rape Cases in the Courtroom*, Colum. L. Rev. 77 (1977): 1–103; J. Gittler, *Expanding the Role of the Victim in a Criminal Action: An Overview of Issues and Problems*, Symposium Issue, Pepperdine L. Rev. 11 (1984): 117–82. For a general discussion of rape shield laws and defendant's constitutional rights, see Note, *Rape Victim Confrontation*, Utah L. Rev. (1985): 687–722.

9. Faris, "Foreword" to *Aging* (March–April 1978); Ford, "Crime Message Notes Aging Among Violence Victims, Recommends New Statutes," *Aging* (August 1975).

10. These include NOVA, the National Organization for Victim Assistance, founded in California in 1976 as an umbrella organization to coordinate efforts of victim advocacy groups, and VALOR, the Victims Assistance Legal Organization, founded in 1979 to provide a wide range of assistance to victims of crime. National Organization for Victim Assistance, *Victim's Rights and Services: A Legislative Directory* (Washington, D.C.: 1984).

11. Anderson and Woodard, *Victim and Witness Assistance*, 222. These authors have compiled a comprehensive listing of which states provide compensation for crime victims together with useful information on the scope of these programs. See Table 1, at 224–25. Victim compensation programs may have a perverse implication for society's fight against crime. Dean Goldstein has observed that the compensation programs "are based on the assumption that crime is so pervasive a condition and civil remedies against offenders so illusory that the burden of crime must be shared by the entire society." A. Goldstein, *Defining the Role of the Victim in Criminal Prosecution*, Miss. L.J. 52 (1982): 515–61, 523.

12. Justice Shirley S. Abrahamson of the Wisconsin Supreme Court has observed: "Although the victims' rights movement is not a single force speaking with a single voice or united in the reforms it seeks, the movement's basic theme can be summarized as a privatization of the concept of criminal justice." Abrahamson, *Redefining Roles: The Victims' Rights Movement*, 519.

13. For example, Indiana and Nebraska permit certain victims to comment on the plea bargains that the prosecutor intends to offer criminal suspects. Ind. Code Ann. § 35–35–3–5; Neb. Rev. Code Ann. §§ 29–120, 23–1201(1). Other states require that the views of the victim be explicitly considered by sentencing courts. Illinois, Maryland, and New York require that "victim impact statements" be included in the presentence report prepared for the judge prior to sentencing. Ill. Ann. Stat. Ch. 38, par. 1005- 3–2(3); Md. Code Ann. Art. 41, § 124(c)(1)(2); N.Y. Crim. Proc. Law § 390.30(3). Some states, including Minnesota, New Jersey, Tennessee, and Vermont, actually allow the victim to prepare some or all of the impact statement. Minn. Stat. Ann. § 609.115(1b)(c); N.J. Stat. Ann. Tit. 2C, § 44–6(b); Tenn. Code Ann. § 40–35–207(8); Vt. Stat. Ann. Tit. 28, § 204(e). Other states require that notice be given to victims when their attacker is released from custody or escapes. These states include California, Minnesota, Rhode Island, and Vermont. Cal. Penal Code § 11155(a); Cal. Penal Code § 11155(b); Minn. Stat. Ann. § 611A.06; R.I. Gen. Laws § 12–28–4(13), 13–8–9.1; Vt. Stat. Ann. Tit. 13 § 5304(2) (Supp. 1990). Many states now require that prosecuting attorneys notify victims of the final disposition of their cases. Vt. Stat. Ann. Tit. 13 § 5304(2) (Supp. 1990). See also, Lauren Bowerman, *Victim's Rights:*

Vermont's New Law, Vt. L. Rev. 11 (1986): 695–704. Other states provide that protection be afforded witnesses from harm or threats from criminals or their friends arising out of their cases. Many states have taken steps to protect witnesses from intimidation and harassment from criminals or the families and friends of criminals. Alabama, Arizona, and Colorado punish threats directed at anyone whom the offender "believes" will be called as a witness. Ala. Code Ann. § 13A–10–123(a); Ariz. Rev. Stat. Ann. § 13–2802(A); Colo. Rev. Stat. § 18–8–604, repealed, L. 84 p. 503, 7, effective July 1, 1984. In 1982 Congress passed the Victim and Witness Protection Act, which provided greater protection to victims and witnesses. 102 P.L. 33, 18 U.S.C. § 1512 et seq. A few states provide witness advocates or ombudspersons, whose role is to advise and counsel victims and witnesses about their rights. Anderson and Woodard, *Victim and Witness Assistance.*

14. It proposed that the following language be added to the Sixth Amendment: "Likewise, the victim, in every criminal prosecution shall have the right to be present and to be heard at all critical stages of judicial proceedings." *United States President's Task Force on Victims of Crime: Final Report* (Washington, D.C.: The Task Force, 1982), 114.

15. A. Goldstein, *Defining the Role of the Victim in Criminal Prosecution*, 518.

16. James Wilson has put the point nicely:

Predatory crime does not merely victimize individuals, it impedes and, in the extreme case, even prevents the formation and maintenance of community. By disrupting the delicate nexus of ties, formal and informal, by which we are linked to our neighbors, crime atomizes society and makes of its members mere individual calculators estimating their own advantage, especially their own chances of survival amidst their fellows. Common undertakings become difficult or impossible, except for those motivated by a shared desire for protection.

Wilson, *Thinking About Crime*, 21.

17. Ibid., 35.

18. Initial skepticism concerning the rehabilitative ideal began to emerge in the mid-1960s. Alan Dershowitz, "Background Papers," in Andrew Von Hirsch, *Doing Justice: The Choice of Punishments, Report of the Committee for the Study of Incarceration* (New York: Hill and Wang, 1976).

19. American Friends Service Committee, *Struggle for Justice: A Report on Crime and Punishment in America* (New York: Hill and Wang, 1971), 12.

20. Ibid., 40–47.

21. Ibid., 83–99; 147–48.

22. Von Hirsch, *Doing Justice.*

23. Ibid., xxxviii.

24. Ibid., 66–76.

25. Ibid., 102.

26. Ibid., xviii–xix. The committee recommended that penalties be set in accordance with the principles of *"parsimony*, that less intervention is preferred unless a strong case for more intervention can be made . . . [and] *diminishing returns* (once penalties reach modest levels of severity, further increase are unlikely to have much added deterrent usefulness) (136). It also recommended a penalty scheme that would deflate the punishment scale substantially from current levels. Sentences for most crimes would not exceed three years, and only the most serious offenses would be punished by sentences over five years. Ibid., 132–40. Other penalties, such as warnings, loss of leisure time, or fines instead of imprisonment, would be given for minor crimes. Ibid., 119–23.

27. Ibid., 143–49.

28. In fact both the Johnson and Nixon administrations had urged that crime control be considered a high priority domestic issue during their administrations. Donald F. Newman, *In Defense of Prisons*, Psychiatric Annals 4(3) (1974): 6–17. Thus, crime control measures clearly predated the Neoconservative Era.

29. Ernest van den Haag, *Punishing Criminals, Concerning a Very Old and Painful Question* (New York: Basic Books, 1975), 1.

30. Ibid., 8–50.

31. Van den Haag wrote:

> For, if the law is to restrain anyone at all, those who are tempted to do what it prohibits must be restrained as much as those who are not. They must be restrained even if the conditions in which they are constrained to live tempt them to break the law. . . . Else, the forbidden act would be prohibited only to those not inclined or tempted to commit it.

Ibid., 44–45

32.

> Many people, black and white, living in the conditions ordinarily associated with high crime rates—such as poverty or inequality—do not commit crimes, whereas many people not living in these conditions do. It follows that these conditions are neither necessary nor sufficient to cause crime. Crime rates have risen as poverty and inequality have declined. It follows that high crime rates need not depend on more poverty or inequality, and are not remedied by less.

Ibid., 102.

33. Wilson, *Thinking About Crime*, 4.

34. Von Hirsch, *Doing Justice*, xxxvii.

35. Citing Gwynne Nettler, van den Haag placed much of the blame for this general view of criminals held during the Liberal Era on the social sciences:

> The behavioral sciences have helped shift the load of responsibility from individuals to environments. Their message allocates responsibility for conduct to causes beyond the control of the actor. He is seen as a product . . . Modern morality . . . converts sin to sickness and erases fault. Its working hypothesis is that if behavior is caused its agent is not culpable.

G. Nettler, *Shifting the Load*, Am. Behav. Sci., (January/February 1972), as quoted in van den Haag, *Punishing Criminals*, 117–18.

36. Address by President Ronald Reagan to the International Association of Chiefs of Police, in New Orleans, Louisiana, Sept. 28, 1981, *quoted in* D. Bazelon, *Questioning Authority* (New York: Knopf, 1988), 93.

37. Michael H. Tonry, *Sentencing Reform Impacts* (Washington, D.C.: National Institute of Justice, 1987), 77–85.

38. Ibid., 25. In 1973, for example, New York State enacted the "Rockefeller Drug Law," which required harsh mandatory prison terms for narcotics offenses and limited plea bargaining.

39. Tonry, *Sentencing Reform Impacts*.

40. *Hamlin* v. *Michigan*, 111 S. Ct. 2680, 115 L. Ed. 2d 836 (1991).

41. The Sentencing Reform Act of 1984 (Title II of the Comprehensive Crime Control Act of 1984, 18 USCA 3551).

42. United States Sentencing Commission, *Federal Sentencing Guidelines Manual, 1990 Edition* (St. Paul, Minn.: West Publishing, 1989), 10.

43. As James Wilson succinctly wrote: "The purpose of isolating—or, more accurately, closely supervising—offenders is obvious: Whatever they may do when they are released, they cannot harm society while confined or closely supervised." Wilson, *Thinking About Crime*, 173. Sending convicted criminals to jail might also be a very effective measure to reduce crime. Wilson contends: "The gains from merely incapacitating convicted criminals may be very large. . . . There is strong evidence that repeaters commit a great deal of the serious crimes." Ibid.

44. *Furman* v. *Georgia*, 408 U.S. 238, 305, 97 S. Ct. 2726, 33 L. Ed. 2d 346 (1972) (Brennan, J., concurring); *Furman* v. *Georgia*, 408 U.S. 238, 369, 92 S. Ct. 2726, 33 L. Ed. 2d 346 (1972) (Marshall, J., concurring).

45. *Gregg* v. *Georgia*, 428 U.S. 153, 96 S. Ct. 2909, 49 L. Ed. 2d 859, *reh. den.*, 429 U.S. 875, 97 S. Ct. 197, 50 L. Ed. 2d 158 (1976).

46. The plurality opinion of Justice Stewart rejected the claim that "standards of decency had evolved to the point where capital punishment no longer could be tolerated." Ibid., at 428 U.S. 179. In so doing, the Court limited the significance of *Furman* v. *Georgia*, 408 U.S. 238 (1972), which had cast doubt on the substantive authority of the state under the Eighth Amendment to the U.S. Constitution to impose the death penalty, either for retributive or deterrent purposes. See the opinions of Justice Brennan and Justice Marshall for a full explication of this view.

47. *Stanford* v. *Kentucky*, 492 U.S. 361, 109 S. Ct. 2969, 106 L. Ed. 2d 306 (1989).

48. *Penry* v. *Lynaugh*, 492 U.S. 302, 109 S. Ct. 2934, 106 L. Ed. 2d 256 (1989).

49. *Furman* v. *Georgia*, 408 U.S. 238, 97 S. Ct. 2726, 33 L. Ed. 2d 346 (1972); *Stanford* v. *Kentucky*, 492 U.S. 361, 109 S. Ct. 2969, 106 L. Ed. 2d 306 (1989).

50. *Gregg* v. *Georgia*, 428 U.S. 153, 180, 96 S. Ct. 2909, 49 L. Ed. 2d 859 (1976).

51. Ibid., 428 U.S. 153 at 180.

52. Wilson, *Thinking About Crime*, 195– 96.

53. In 1972 a Gallup poll had indicated that 57 percent of the American people favored the death penalty. In his opinion in the *Furman* case, Justice Marshall discounted the value of public opinion polls as a means of ascertaining public morality. He wrote:

> While a public opinion poll obviously is of some assistance in indicating public acceptance or rejection of a specific penalty [citation omitted], its utility cannot be very great. This is because whether or not a punishment is cruel and unusual depends, not on whether its mere mention "shocks the conscience and sense of justice of the people," but whether people *fully informed as to the purpose of the penalty and its liabilities would find the penalty shocking, unjust, and unacceptable.* (emphasis added)

Furman v. *Georgia*, 408 U.S. 238, 361 (1972). Evidently Justice Marshall was willing to assess a hypothetical public morality instead of relying on the public to do it, since in his judgment the public was not as fully informed as himself. Of course, there could be no methodological constraints on how the moral pulse of this hypothetical public should be measured nor could there be any empirical counterevidence, since such a task was nothing more than mere fiction. H. Zeisel and A. Gallup, *Death Penalty Sentiment in the United States*, J. Quantitative Criminology 5, (1989): 285–96.

54. S. J. Fox, *Juvenile Justice Reform: An Historical Perspective*, Stan. L. Rev. 22 (1970): 1187–239. See, generally, M. R. Gardner, *Punitive Juvenile Justice: Some Observations on a Recent Trend*, Int'l J.L. & Psychiatry 10 (1987): 129–51; A. Walkover, *The Infancy Defense in the New Juvenile Court*, UCLA L. Rev. 31 (1984): 503–62.

55. Department of Health, Education, and Welfare, *Juvenile Court Statistics*

(DHEW pub. no. SRS73–03452, 1971), as cited in Alan Stone, *Mental Health and the Law: A System in Transition* (Washington, D.C.: National Institute of Mental Health, 1975), 145.

56. *In re Gault*, 383 U.S. 1, 87 S. Ct. 1428, 18 L. Ed. 2d 527 (1967); J. W. Mack, *The Juvenile Court*, Harv. L. Rev. 23 (1909): 104–22; Fox, *Juvenile Justice Reform*. See, generally, Gardner, *Punitive Juvenile Justice*; Walkover, *The Infancy Defense in the New Juvenile Court*.

57. See, for example, "63% in Gallup Poll Think Courts Are Too Lenient On Criminals," *New York Times*, March 3, 1968, p. 40, col. 3 (66 percent in poll disagreed with the Warren Court decision restricting police tactics in obtaining confessions).

58. Leonard W. Levy, *Against the Law: The Nixon Court and Criminal Justice* (New York: Harper & Row, 1974); S. A. Salzburg, *Foreword: The Flow and Ebb of Constitutional Criminal Procedure in the Warren and Burger Courts*, Geo. L.J. 69 (1980): 151–209.

59. *Miranda* v. *Arizona*, 384 U.S. 436, 86 S. Ct. 1602, 16 L. Ed. 694 (1966), held that the state could not use incriminating statements obtained from a criminal suspect during custodial interrogation to establish his guilt at trial unless the police had read the suspect what came to be called the *Miranda* warnings. The warnings advised a suspect of his rights to remain silent and to obtain the assistance of a lawyer. *New York* v. *Quarles*, 467 U.S. 649, 104 S. Ct. 2626, 81 L. Ed. 2d 550 (1984), held that the police did not have to give a criminal suspect his *Miranda* rights before questioning him if doing so would jeopardize public safety.

60. *Moran* v. *Burbine*, 475 U.S. 412, 106 S. Ct. 1135, 89 L. Ed. 2d 410 (1986). The Court held that the confession given by a criminal suspect in custody after *Miranda* warnings have been given, but without his lawyer present, was admissible even though, in this case, the suspect's sister had retained a lawyer who had asked police not to interrogate the suspect in the lawyer's absence.

61. *Schall* v. *Martin*, 467 U.S. 253, 104 S. Ct. 2403, 81 L. Ed. 2d 207 (1984).

62. *United States* v. *Salerno*, 481 U.S. 739, 107 S. Ct. 2095, 95 L. Ed. 2d (1987).

63. *Payne* v. *Tennessee*, 111 S. Ct. 1386, 113 L. Ed. 2d 443, 59 U.S.L.W. 3652 (1991).

64. *Coleman* v. *Thompson*, 111 S. Ct. 2546, 59 U.S.L.W. 4789 (1991); *McClesky* v. *Zant*, 111 S. Ct. 1454, 59 U.S.L.W. 4288 (1991).

65. Typical of such analysis was the Court's opinion in *United States* v. *Leon*, 468 U.S. 897, 104 S. Ct. 3405, 82 L. Ed. 2d 677, *reh. den.*, 468 U.S. 1250, 105 S. Ct. 52, 82 L. Ed. 2d 942 (1984). In the *Leon* case, a majority of the Supreme Court held that, under a new "good faith" exception to the exclusionary rule, evidence seized by the police pursuant to a warrant not supported by probable cause could be used by the government to convict the suspect. This case is important because it marks one of the first instances in which the Burger Court actually reversed constitutional doctrine articulated by the Warren Court. There is little doubt that the Warren Court would have excluded this evidence. In the jargon of labor negotiations, the *Leon* case was clearly a "give-back" to the community of some of the rights previously granted criminal defendants. In applying cost-benefit analysis the majority concluded:

> Whether the exclusionary sanction [excluding illegally seized evidence from a criminal trial] is appropriately imposed in a particular case . . . must be resolved by weighing the costs and benefits of preventing the use. . . . The substantial social costs exacted by the exclusionary rule for the vindication of Fourth Amendment rights have long been a source of concern. . . . An objectionable collateral consequence of this interference with the criminal justice system's truth finding function is that some guilty defendants may

go free or receive reduced sentences as a result of favorable plea bargains (citation omitted).... Indiscriminate application of the exclusionary rule, therefore, may well "generate disrespect for the law and administration of justice."

United States v. *Leon*, 468 U.S. 897, 906–8 (1984).

66. H. L. Packer, *The Limits of the Criminal Sanction* (Stanford, Calif.: Stanford University Press, 1968).

67. In 1982 the President's Task Force on Crime Victims proposed the abolition of the exclusionary rule. Among its reasons for this proposal, the report argued that "the rule punishes the innocent victim and all law-abiding citizens by preventing effective prosecution." *United States President's Task Force on Victims of Crime*, 25.

68. For example, in 1985 the Colorado legislature passed a law that permits an occupant of a dwelling to use deadly force against an intruder if the occupant has a "reasonable belief" that a crime has been or will be committed and that the intruder "might use any physical force, no matter how slight." Colo. Rev. Stat. § 18–1–704.5 (1986). See W. Wilbanks, *The Make My Day Law: Colorado's Experiment in Home Protection* (Lanham, Md.: University Press of America, 1990). See also, Del. Code Ann. § 76–2–405 (1985) (authorizing use of deadly force against an intruder when an occupant of a dwelling "reasonably believes" the intruder would inflict "personal injury" upon the occupant or others); Utah Code Ann. § 76–2–405 (1985) (a person using deadly force against an intruder is "presumed" to have acted reasonably and to have had a reasonable fear of death or serious bodily injury if the unlawful entry or attempted entry was made by "force," "surreptitiously," or by "stealth").

69. See, generally, J. Q. La Fond, *The Case for Liberalizing the Use of Deadly Force in Self-Defense*, U. Puget Sound L. Rev. 6 (1983): 237–84.

70. Some state statutes permitted an individual to use deadly force to resist the commission of a felony in his residence. Nonetheless, courts often limited the right to use deadly force by requiring that the victim fear for his life or safety. See, for example, *State* v. *Griffith*, 91 Wash. 2d 572, 589 P.2d 799 (1979). See, generally, W. LaFave and A. Scott, *Criminal Law*, § 5.7 (2d ed. 1986); La Fond, *The Case for Liberalizing the Use of Deadly Force in Self-Defense*, 239–40.

Chapter 3

1. I. R. Kaufman, "The Insanity Plea On Trial," *New York Times Magazine*, August 8, 1963. In a New York Times newspaper opinion poll conducted after the Hinckley acquittal, 75 percent of the respondents said they did not favor excusing people for their criminal acts on account of insanity. *New York Times*, June 13, 1982, p. B6, col 1.

2. I. Keilitz and J. P. Fulton, *The Insanity Defense and its Alternatives: A Guide for Policymakers* (Williamsburg, Va.: National Center for State Courts, 1984), 13.

3. In 1973 the Nixon administration proposed a bill to abolish the federal insanity defense. Criminal Code Reform Act of 1973, §1400, § 501, 93d Cong., 1st Sess. (March 17, 1973). Montana had abolished the insanity defense in 1979. The legislature believed abolishing this defense would reinforce the accountability of criminal defendants, avoid the difficult and complex legal issues engendered by this defense, and would allow courts to consider mental illness at sentencing. Keilitz and Fulton, *The Insanity Defense and Its Alternatives*, 13.

4. R. J. Bonnie and C. Slobogin, *The Role of Mental Health Professionals in the*

Criminal Process: The Case for Informed Speculation, Va. L. Rev. 66 (1980): 427–522, 432.

5. *Insanity Defense in Federal Courts: Hearings Before the Subcomm. on Criminal Justice, House Judiciary Comm.*, 97th Cong., 2d Sess. 211 (1982).

6. Testimony of Senator Orrin Hatch of Utah, *Insanity Defense: Hearings Before the Senate Judiciary Comm.*, 97th Cong., 2d Sess. 14 (1982).

7. *Insanity Defense: Hearings Before the Senate Judiciary Comm.*, 97th Cong., 2d Sess. 26–27 (1982).

8. Testimony of Abraham L. Halpern, M.D., *Insanity Defense: Hearings Before the Senate Judiciary Comm.*, 97th Congress, 2d Sess. 283 (1982). Testimony of Loren Roth, M.D., *Insanity Defense in Federal Courts: Hearings Before the Subcomm. on Criminal Justice, House Judiciary Comm.*, 97th Cong., 2d Sess. 58–62 (1982). The critics of the insanity defense include those skeptical of psychiatry's methodology who

> argue that even if psychological abnormality can in fact compromise a person's ability to direct his behavior, the available tools for measuring volitional impairment are too primitive for the law's purposes. Absent a proven organic etiology, method skeptics feel that hypothesized clinical functional disorders have not been demonstrated with sufficient clarity to provide a scientific basis for the important legal and moral distinctions drawn by the criminal law or for reliable decisions in individual cases. The method skeptics tend to be especially troubled by the inadequacies and abuses of psychiatric participation in adjudications of insanity.

Bonnie and Slobogin, *The Role of Mental Health Professionals in the Criminal Process*, 433. See also B. J. Ennis and T. R. Litwack, *Flipping Coins in the Courtroom: Psychiatry and the Presumption of Expertise*, Calif. L. Rev. 62 (1974): 693–752, 693; Daniel N. Robinson, *Psychology and the Law: Can Justice Survive the Social Sciences?* (New York: Oxford University Press, 1980), 24–25.

9. Attorney General William French Smith told a congressional committee considering reform of the federal insanity defense that "since experts disagree about both the meaning of the terms used to discuss the defendant's mental state and the effect of particular mental states on actions . . . trials . . . are arduous, expensive and . . . thoroughly confusing to the jury." *Insanity Defense: Hearings Before the Senate Judiciary Comm.*, 97th Cong., 2d Sess. 29 (1982).

10. D. Bazelon, *The Morality of the Criminal Law*, So. Cal. L. Rev. 49 (1976): 385–405; D. Bazelon, *Psychiatrists and the Adversary Process*, Sci. Am. 230(6) (1974): 18–23.

11. *Limiting the Insanity Defense: Hearings Before the Subcomm. on Criminal Law, Senate Judiciary Comm.*, 97th Cong., 2d Sess. 258–59 (1982). Even in the early 1950s many psychiatrists had taken the position stated more recently by Dr. Roth. For example, Manfred Guttmacher had asserted early on that the *M'Naghten* test itself was deficient because psychiatry had no special skill in assessing whether a mentally ill person knew that what he was doing was wrong. In a presentation to the ALI drafting group, he criticized the *M'Naghten* test saying:

> What we [psychiatrists] are asked is whether the defendant had sufficient intellect or a sufficiently clear mind at the time of the crime to know what these generally accepted standards [of morality] were. We are balking at this, it seems to me, primarily because of our inability to measure this with any degree of accuracy.

This criticism has also been made by other psychiatrists, including Karl Menninger, *The Crime of Punishment* (New York: Viking Press, 1968). See also, *The Insanity*

Defense in New York: A Report to Governor Hugh L. Carey (New York State Department of Mental Hygiene, 1978).

12. Richard J. Bonnie, *The Moral Basis of the Insanity Defense*, A.B.A.J. 69 (Feb. 1983): 194–97.

13. In 1976 a popular best-seller chronicled the bizarre career of Garrett Trapnell, who claimed to have successfully fabricated the insanity defense several times. See E. Asinof, *The Fox Is Crazy Too: The True Story of Garrett Trapnell, Adventurer, Skyjacker, Bankrobber, Con-Man, Lover* (New York: Morrow, 1976). See R. G. Singer, *Essay—Abolition of the Insanity Defense: Madness and the Criminal Law*, Cardozo L. Rev. 4 (1983): 683–707, 692; S. J. Morse, *Excusing the Crazy: The Insanity Defense Reconsidered*, So. Cal. L. Rev. 58 (1985): 777–836, 797.

14. Bazelon, *Psychiatrists and the Adversary Process*, 18.

15. *Insanity Defense: Hearings Before the Senate Judiciary Comm.*, 97th Cong., 2d Sess. 38 (1982).

16. Law professor Richard Bonnie asserted that "[p]resent dissatisfaction with the insanity defense is largely rooted in public concern about premature release of dangerous persons acquitted by reason of insanity." *Insanity Defense: Hearings Before the Senate Judiciary Comm.*, 97th Cong., 2d Sess. 256 (1982).

17. In 1973 President Nixon had called without success for its abolition. S. 1, 94th Cong., 1st Sess. (Jan. 15, 1975). In 1981 an Attorney General's Task Force on Violent Crime submitted legislation that would have abolished the insanity defense and limited the relevance of psychiatric testimony to whether or not the defendant acted with the state of mind required by law for commission of the crime. Over the years some scholars have urged abolition of the insanity defense, arguing that mental illness is relevant only to disposition and not to determination of guilt. See, for example, B. Wooton, *Crime and the Criminal Law: Reflections of a Magistrate and Social Scientist* (London: Stevens, 1963); H. L. A. Hart, *The Morality of the Criminal Law* (Jerusalem: Magnes Press, 1964); Seymour Halleck, *Psychiatry and the Dilemmas of Crime: A Study of Causes, Punishment, and Treatment* (New York: Harper, 1967), 341–42; J. Goldstein and J. Katz, *Abolish the Insanity Defense— Why Not?* Yale L.J. 72 (1963): 853–76.

18. *American Psychiatric Association Statement on the Insanity Defense* (Washington, D.C.: American Psychiatric Association, 1982), 9.

19. *The Insanity Defense in Criminal Trials and Limitations of Psychiatric Testimony* (Report of the Board of Trustees, American Medical Association, 1983).

20. This additional limitation would significantly increase the probability that persons with antisocial personalities would be held accountable for their criminal activities.

21. *American Psychiatric Association Statement on the Insanity Defense*, 11.

22. Ibid., 13.

23. This proposal would limit evidence of mental illness only to establishing whether or not the defendant acted with the state of mind or mental attitude required by the law the defendant is charged with breaking.

24. *First Tentative Draft, ABA Criminal Justice Mental Health Standards*, Standard 7–6.1 (American Bar Association, 1983), 7–262. The commentary asserts: "The basis for the insanity defense is a moral one and this standard retains insanity as a defense to criminal responsibility in order to preserve moral culpability as a fundamental premise for imputing guilt and imposing punishment."

25. *First Tentative Draft, ABA Criminal Justice Mental Health Standards*, Standard 7–6.1.

26. Ibid., Standard 7–263. The task force report was quite sensitive to the public's

perception of the insanity defense as being misused by criminal defendants who should be punished for their acts. One advantage of the *M'Naghten* test is the decreased likelihood of such "moral mistakes." Without the benefit of empirical evidence, the task force concluded that the insanity defense was not systematically abused, but that in close cases some persons are found not guilty by reason of insanity who should probably have been found responsible. Ibid., Standards 7–264–265.

27. The ABA Task Force was more blunt in reaching this conclusion. It stated: "Behavioral science has not yielded clinical tools for calibrating impairments of behavioral controls." Ibid., Standard 7–265.

28. *ABA Criminal Justice Mental Health Standards*, Standard 7–6.1 (1986, 1989).

29. Division of Psychology and Law, American Psychological Association, *More on Insanity Reform*, Newsletter 3 (1983): 8.

30. *Myths and Realities: A Report of the National Commission on the Insanity Defense* (Arlington, Va.: National Mental Health Association, 1983).

31. *The Insanity Defense in Criminal Trials and Limitations of Psychiatric Testimony*, 36–37.

32. Comprehensive Crime Control Act of 1984 (Insanity Defense Reform Act), Public Law No. 98–473, Chapter IV.

33. Ibid.

34. The American Psychiatric Association recommended that the insanity defense should be based only on serious mental disorders that psychiatrists normally diagnose as psychoses. See *American Psychiatric Association Statement on the Insanity Defense* (1982), 11. This change would ensure that offenders suffering simply from personality disorders would not avoid responsibility. Most psychiatrists generally consider such individuals able to control their behavior.

35. See, generally, P. Arenella, *Reflections on Current Proposals to Abolish or Reform the Insanity Defense*, Am. J.L. & Med. 8 (1983): 271–84.

36. Ibid.

37. See *Hearing on Bills to Amend Title 18 to Limit the Insanity Defense, Senate Judiciary Comm.*, 97th Cong., 2d Sess. 31–33 (1982) (Statement of Rudolph Giuliani, Associate Attorney General, Department of Justice).

38. Testimony of Attorney General William French Smith. *Insanity Defense: Hearings Before the Senate Judiciary Comm.*, 97th Cong., 2d Sess. 26–31 (1982). Testimony of Assistant Attorney General Rudolph Giuliani. *Insanity Defense: Hearings Before the Senate Judiciary Comm.*, 97th Cong., 2d Sess. 31–47 (1982).

Testimony of Associate Attorney General Rudolph Giuliani. *Insanity Defense in Federal Courts: Hearings Before the Subcomm. on Criminal Justice, House Judiciary Comm.*, 97th Cong., 2d Sess. 22–38 (1982).

39. *American Psychiatric Association Statement on the Insanity Defense* (1982). This was the first and only comprehensive position statement developed and adopted by the APA. *ABA Criminal Justice Mental Health Standards* (1986, 1989). The insanity test approved by the ABA was "almost identical to the proposal advanced by the American Psychiatric Association." Id., 335.

40. *Cal. Ev. Code* § 522; *Colo. Rev. Stat.* § 16–8–101(1)(*M'Naughten* plus irresistible impulse to *M'Naughten*); Conn. Gen. Stat. § 53a–13 (ALI to ALI modified); Del. Code Ann. 11, § 401; Ind. Code Ann. 35–41–3–6; Me. Rev. Stat. Ann. 17A, § 39 (ALI to ALI modified); N.D. Cert. Code 12.1–04.1–01 (ALI to ALI with the addition that "it is an essential element of the offense that the defendant acted willfully"); Tex. P.C. § 8.01. 18 U.S.C. § 17(a). See C. Mayer, "Insanity Defense Reforms Pre and Post Hinckley" (Unpublished article, Albany Law School, 1987).

41. *People* v. *Drew*, 149 Cal. Rptr. 275, 583 P.2d 1318 (1978).

42. Initiative measure popularly known as "Proposition 8" (voted on June 8, 1982).

43. Alaska Stat. § 12.47.010 (Supp. 1984).

44. Idaho: Idaho Code § 18–207 (1987); Montana: Montana Code Ann. § 46–14–102 (1989); Utah: Utah Code Ann. § 76–2–305 (Supp. 1987).

45. *State* v. *Korell*, 690 P.2d 992 (Mont. 1984); *State* v. *Searcy*, 798 P.2d 914 (Idaho 1990).

46. The Supreme Court upheld an Oregon statute requiring the defendant to prove insanity beyond a reasonable doubt; see *Leland* v. *Oregon*, 343 U.S. 790, 72 S. Ct. 1002, 96 L. Ed. 1302 (1952). In *Powell* v. *Texas*, 392 U.S. 514, 488 S. Ct. 2145, 20 L. Ed. 2d 125 (1968), the Supreme Court ruled that the significance of the insanity defense properly belongs to the states to determine. In *Rivera* v. *Delaware*, 429 U.S. 877, 97 S. Ct. 226, 50 L. Ed. 2d 160 (1976) the Court upheld a Delaware statute that burdened the defendant with proving insanity by a preponderance of the evidence. In *Patterson* v. *New York*, 432 U.S. 197, 97 S. Ct. 2319, 53 L. Ed. 2d 281 (1977), the Court ruled that a New York statute did not deprive a defendant of due process by placing on him the burden of proving by a preponderance of the evidence the defense of acting under extreme emotional distress, which reduced the crime charged to manslaughter. For more general information, see Morse, *Excusing the Crazy*; J. B. Sallet, *After Hinckley: The Insanity Defense Reexamined*, Yale L.J. 94 (1985): 1545–57.

47. The thirteen states are: Alaska, Delaware, Georgia, Illinois, Indiana, Kentucky, Michigan, Montana, New Mexico, Pennsylvania, South Carolina, South Dakota, and Utah. Alaska, Stat. § 12.47.040 (Supp. 1984); Del. Code Ann. Tit. II § 401(b) 408 (Supp. 1984); Ga. Code Ann. § 17–7–131 (Michie 1985); Ill. Rev. Stat. Ch. 38 § 115–2(b) (1981); Ind. Code § 35–36–2–3 (Supp. 1982); Ky. Rev. Stat. § 504.120 (Supp. 1982); Mich. Comp. Laws § 768.36 (1982); Mont. Code Ann. §46–14–312 (1987); N.M. Stat. Ann. § 31–9–3 (Supp. 1983); 18 P.A. Cons. Stat. § 314 (1983); S.C. Code Ann. § 17–24–20 (Law Co-op 1985); S.D. Codified Laws Ann. § 23A- 26–14; § 25A–25–13 (Rev. 1988) (Supp. 1983); Utah Code Ann. § 77–35–21.5 (Supp. 1988). Perhaps as many as twenty other states are considering enacting this legislation. See also C. Slobogin, *The Guilty But Mentally Ill Verdict: An Idea Whose Time Should Not Have Come*, Geo. Wash. L. Rev. 53 (1985): 494–527, 496; the *American Bar Association Criminal Justice Mental Health Standards*, the *American Psychiatric Association Statement on the Insanity Defense*, and the *National Mental Health Association's Report of the National Commission on the Insanity Defense* all recommended against adoption of the GBMI defense. Id., 496–97. Alaska Stat. 12.47.030 (1984), 12.47.050 (1984), 12.47.040 (1982); Del. Code Ann. Tit. II § 401(b), II § 408(b) (1987); Ga. Code Ann. § 27–1503 (1983); Idaho Code § 18–207, § 19–2523 (1987); Ill. Ann. Stat. Ch. 38 § 6–2(c)(d) (Smith-Hurd Supp. 1988).

48. Slobogin, *The Guilty But Mentally Ill Verdict*.

49. Idaho, Montana, and Utah have adopted the second version of the GBMI defense.

50. See, for example, *Robinson* v. *Solem*, 432 N.W.2d 246 (S.D. 1988).

51. Idaho Code § 18–207, 19–2523 (1987); Mont. Code Ann. § 46–14–311 (1987); Utah Code Ann. § 77–35–21.5 (Supp. 1988).

52. *People* v. *Ramsey*, 422 Mich. 500, 375 N.W.2d 297 (1985) (Levin, J., dissenting). One scholar has wryly noted in criticizing the GBMI verdict: "A jury verdict

is not the appropriate means to reach diagnoses or to insure treatment." See Morse, *Excusing the Crazy*, 804.

53. Ibid.

54. *U.S. Department of Justice, Attorney General's Task Force on Violent Crime: Final Report*, 54 (1981).

55. Most state GBMI statutes do not mandate treatment. For more information, see Slobogin, *The Guilty But Mentally Ill Verdict*, 513. Even those statutes that do mandate treatment are open to varying interpretations. See, for example, *People* v. *Mack*, 104 Mich. App. 560, 305 N.W.2d 264 (1981) and *People* v. *McLeod*, 407 Mich. 632, 288 N.W.2d 909 (1980). *Harris* v. *State*, 499 N.E.2d 723 (Ind. 1986) is a good example of the irrelevancy of a GBMI defense in sentencing. In this case the Indiana Supreme Court upheld the death sentence of a defendant who had pleaded GBMI, affirming an earlier ruling that finding a criminal GBMI "in reality adds nothing to a finding of guilty." The court made it eminently clear that this defense is not intended to have practical or symbolic consequences.

Without clear-cut instructions on the sentencing impact of a GBMI verdict, unwitting juries may now be misled as to the dispositional influence of this verdict. Nor does it make any sense to allow the existence of a special finding that has no significance in a criminal trial or at sentencing. At best, the GBMI defense is irrelevant to a jury's task; at worse, it may seriously confuse it. For discussion of this point, see Project, *Evaluating Michigan's Guilty But Mentally Ill Verdict: An Empirical Study*, U. Mich. J.L. Ref. 16 (1982): 77–114, 104–5.

56. *Harris* v. *State*, 499 N.E. 723 (Ind. 1986); *People* v. *Crews*, 122 Ill. 2d 266, 522 N.E.2d 1167 (1988).

57. Note, *The Guilty But Mentally Ill Verdict and Due Process*, Yale L.J. 92 (1983): 475–98.

58. See W. F. Smith, *Limiting the Insanity Defense: A Rational Approach to Irrational Crimes*, Mo. L. Rev. 47 (1982): 605–19.

59. For example, *United States* v. *Weismiller*, 815 F.2d 1106 (7th Cir. 1987), *citing Kirland* v. *State*, 166 Ga. App. 478, 304 S.E. 2d 561, 565 (1983); *People* v. *Marshall*, 114 Ill. App. 3d 217, 448 N.E.2d 969, 980 (1983); *Hardesty* v. *Michigan*, 447 U.S. 902, 106 S. Ct. 3269, 91 L. Ed. 2d 223 (1975).

60. For example, *United States* v. *Weismiller*, 815 F.2d 1106 (7th Cir. 1987); *People* v. *Ramsey*, 422 Mich. 500, 375 N.W.2d 297 (1985).

61. In all likelihood, a 1983 Supreme Court decision, *Jones* v. *United States*, 463 U.S. 354, 103 S. Ct. 3043, 77 L. Ed. 2d 694 (1983), authorizing indeterminate commitment of successful insanity acquittees has eliminated the need for the GBMI defense. This case is discussed later in this chapter.

62. See G. Morris, *The Insanity Defense: A Blueprint for Legislative Reform* (Lexington, MA: Lexington, Books, 1975), 97–126. Morris contends that twenty-six states have adopted some form of diminished capacity: Alaska, California, Colorado, Connecticut, Delaware, Hawaii, Idaho, Iowa, Kentucky, Missouri, Montana, Nebraska, Nevada, New Jersey, New Mexico, New York, Ohio, Oregon, Pennsylvania, Rhode Island, Tennessee, Texas, Utah, Virginia, Washington, and Wyoming. Eight states have dealt with the doctrine by statute: Alaska Stat. § 12.45.085 (1972); Ark. Stat. Ann. § 41–602 (1976); Colo. Rev. Stat. § 18–1–803 (1973); Haw. Rev. Stat. § 704–401 (Special Supp. 1975); Mo. Ann. Stat. § 552.030(3) (Vernon Supp. 1977); Mont. Rev. Codes Ann. § 95–502 (1969); Or. Rev. Stat. § 161.300 (1975); Wyo. Stat. §§ 7–242.4, 242.5 (Supp. 1975). See also, T. Lewin, *Psychiatric Evidence in Criminal*

Cases for Purposes Other than the Defense of Insanity, Syracuse L. Rev. 26 (1975): 1051–115.

63. G. E. Dix, *Psychological Abnormality as a Factor in Grading Criminal Liability: Diminished Capacity, Diminished Responsibility, and the Like*, J. Crim. L., Criminology & Police Sci. 62 (1971): 313–34. J. Dressler, *Reaffirming the Moral Legitimacy of the Doctrine of Diminished Capacity: A Brief Reply to Professor Morse*, J. Crim. L. & Criminology 75 (1984): 953–62; B. L. Diamond, *Criminal Responsibility of the Mentally Ill*, Stan. L. Rev. 14 (1961): 59–86.

64. H. Fingarette and A. Fingarette Hasse, *Mental Disabilities and Criminal Responsibility* (Berkeley: University of California Press, 1979).

65. Lewin, *Psychiatric Evidence in Criminal Cases for Purposes Other than the Defense of Insanity*, 1093.

66. R. W. Havel, *A Punishment Rationale For Diminished Capacity*, UCLA L. Rev. 18 (1971): 561–80, 567–72; P. Arenella, *The Diminished Capacity and Diminished Capacity and Responsibility Defenses: Two Children of a Doomed Marriage*, Colum. L. Rev. 77 (1977): 827–65; S. J. Morse, *Undiminished Confusion in Diminished Capacity*, J. Crim. L. & Criminology 75 (1984): 1–55; S. J. Morse, *Diminished Capacity: A Moral and Legal Conundrum*, Int'l J.L. & Psychiatry 2 (1979): 271–98.

67. § 28(b), California Penal Code provides in part: "As a matter of public policy there shall be no defense of diminished capacity, diminished responsibility, or irresistible impulse in a criminal action."

68. See, for example, *Johnson* v. *State*, 292 Md. 405, 439 A.2d 342 (1982), in which a divided Maryland Court of Appeals held that recognition of diminished capacity is essentially a legislative prerogative. See also 59 Del. L. Ch. 203, § 36.n8; *Bates* v. *State*, 386 A.2d 1139, 1143 (Del. 1978). In Delaware the legislature did enact a statute recognizing diminished capacity as a defense; however, it then repealed the provision prior to the date the statute was to go into effect.

69. See, for example, *State* v. *Bouwman*, Minn., 328 N.W.2d 703, 706 (1982), in which the Minnesota Supreme Court, adopting the reasoning of the D.C. Court of Appeals in *Bethea* v. *United States*, 365 A.2d 64, 83–92 (D.C. 1976), rejected the use of psychiatric evidence to show diminished capacity since this evidence "contradicts the presumptions inherent in the doctrine of *mens rea* and inevitably opens the door to variable or sliding scales of criminal responsibility." See also, *State* v. *Wilcox*, 76 Ohio St. 2d 182, 436 N.E.2d 523 (1982), in which the Ohio Supreme Court, relying on California's finding that it is judicially unjust for courts to consider psychiatric evidence because of its inherent uncertainty, concluded that admission of additional psychiatric evidence would lead to confusion and would not "bring the blurred lines of diminished capacity into proper focus so as to facilitate principled and consistent decision-making."

70. *United States* v. *Pohlot*, 827 F.2d 889 (3d Cir. 1987).

71. *Jones* v. *United States*, 463 U.S. 354, 103 S. Ct. 3043, 77 L. Ed. 2d 694 (1983).

72. Alan A. Stone, *Mental Health and the Law: A System in Transition* (Rockville, Md.: National Institute of Mental Health, Center for Studies of Crime and Delinquency, 1975), 33. See also, J. Monahan and D. B. Wexler, *A Definite Maybe: Proof and Probability in Civil Commitment*, Law & Hum. Behav. 2 (1978): 37–42.

73. W. LaFave and A. Scott, *Criminal Law*, 2d ed. (St. Paul, MN: West Publishing Co. 1986), § 4.5. See *State* v. *Pagano*, 294 N.C. 720, 242 S.E.2d 829 (1978); *Lilly* v. *People*, 148 Ill. 467, 36 N.E. 95 (1894); *People* v. *Kernaghan*, 72 Cal. 609, 14 P. 566 (1887).

74. Stone, *Mental Health and the Law*. See also, Monahan and Wexler, *A Definite*

Maybe: Proof and Probability in Civil Commitment. (Stone describes "preponderance of the evidence" as requiring a 51 percent level of certainty).

75. Comment, *Recent Changes in the Criminal Law: The Federal Insanity Defense,* La. L. Rev. 46 (1985): 337–60, 356, note 127. Comment, *Due Process and the Insanity Defense: The Supreme Court's Retreat from Winship and Mullaney,* Ind. L.J. 54 (1978): 95–107, 97. The number of jurisdictions that required the government to prove insanity was probably higher in the preceding years.

76. *Insanity Defense in Federal Courts,* Hearing on House of Representatives 6783 Before the Subcomm. on Criminal Justice, 98th Cong., 1st Sess. 152 (1982) (Statement of the Hon. Robert J. Lagomarsino of California).

77. Testifying before the House of Representatives, Rep. Robert J. Lagomarsino of California, in supporting his proposed legislation which would make criminal defendants prove insanity, said: "A moment's reflection reveals that it is not difficult to comprehend that to prove that there is nothing wrong with a person's mental capacity is an arduous task." Ibid.

78. *Reform of the Federal Insanity Defense, Hearings Before the Subcomm. on Criminal Justice, House Judiciary Comm.,* 98th Cong., 1st Sess. 553 (1983) (Statement of Rep. Lawrence Coughlin of Pennsylvania).

79. Comment, *Recent Changes in Criminal Law: The Federal Insanity Defense,* 357.

80. This instruction suggests the jury should be 75 percent certain the defendant was insane. Ariz. Rev. Stat. Ann. § 13– 502(b) (Supp. 1984). See also Stone, *Mental Health and the Law,* 33.

81. Comment, *Recent Changes in Criminal Law: The Federal Insanity Defense,* 356. Three states have abolished the insanity defense; consequently, neither the prosecution nor the defense are permitted to prove insanity.

82. L. Callahan, C. Mayer, and H. J. Steadman, *Insanity Defense Reform in the United States—Post Hinckley,* Mental & Phys. Disability L. Rep. 11(1) (1987): 54–59, 56.

83. Public Law 98–473, Chapter IV, Comprehensive Crime Control Act of 1984 [known as the "Insanity Defense Reform Act"], 18 USCA 20 provides: "(b) Burden of Proof—The defendant has the burden of proving the defense of insanity by clear and convincing evidence."

Some informed scholars thought that this procedural change in the law would have more impact on jury deliberations than a change in the insanity test itself. Professor Peter Arenella, a noted scholar of the insanity defense, thought that "[a] second reform that would insure that the defense would be raised successfully only in the most exceptional cases would be to shift the burden of proof from the Government to the defendant. This reform would probably influence jury deliberations far more significantly than a chance [*sic*] in the test's exculpatory criteria." *Insanity Defense in Federal Courts: Hearings Before the Subcomm. on Criminal Justice, House Judiciary Comm.,* 97th Cong., 2d Sess. 112 (1982). Senator Thad Cochran of Mississippi thought that John Hinckley would have been convicted if he had been required to prove his insanity. *Insanity Defense: Hearings Before the Senate Judiciary Comm.,* 97th Cong., 2d Sess. 81 (1982). Prior to enactment of the Insanity Defense Reform Act, the federal courts, relying on *Davis* v. *United States,* 160 U.S. 469, 16 S. Ct. 353, 40 L. Ed. 499 (1885), uniformly imposed on the prosecution the burden of proving the defendant was sane at the time of the offense. See Comment, *Recent Changes in Criminal Law: The Federal Insanity Defense,* 356, note 127.

84. Most states, usually by statute, require a defendant to specifically plead the

insanity defense, and states provide for pretrial examination of such defendants. S. L. Lefelt, *Pretrial Mental Examinations: Compelled Cooperation and the Fifth Amendment*, Am. Crim. L. Rev. 10 (1972): 431–64.

85. Defendants who refused to submit to examination by a government psychiatrist or to cooperate fully were penalized in a variety of ways. Some courts would not permit the defendant's own psychiatrist to testify about his insanity at trial. Others permitted the government to inform the jury that the defendant would not cooperate with the state physician. See, for example, *State* v. *Whitlow*, 45 N.J. 3, 210 A.2d 763 (1965); *Lee* v. *County* Court, 27 N.Y.2d 432, 442, 267 N.E.2d 452, 458, 318 N.Y.S.2d 705, 713, *cert. denied*, 404 U.S. 823 (1971); *State* v. *Obstein*, 52 N.J. 516, 529, 247 A.2d 5, 12 (1968); *State* v. *Huson*, 73 Wash. 2d 660, 667–68, 440 P.2d 192, 197–98 (1968), *cert. denied*, 393 U.S. 1096 (1969); *Johnson* v. *People*, 172 Colo. 72, 77, 470 P.2d 37, 40 (1970).

86. As stated by the court in *United States* v. *Albright*, 388 F.2d 719, 726 (4th Cir. 1968):

> From the intimate and personal nature of the examination, we are satisfied that, except in the unusual case, the presence of a third party, in a legal and non-medical capacity, would severely limit the efficacy of the examination, and that if the defendant's privilege against self-incrimination is given full effect with regard to his inculpatory statements to his examiner, the need for an attorney is obviated.

87. 384 U.S. 436 (1966).

88. *Brewer* v. *Williams*, 430 U.S. 387, 97 S. Ct. 1232, 51 L. Ed. 2d 424 (1977); *Massiah* v. *United States*, 37 U.S. 201 (1964) (police may not interrogate a criminal suspect who has been formally charged with a crime). In the 1967 case of *United States* v. *Wade*, the Court determined that a defendant had a right under the Sixth Amendment to have counsel present during a postindictment lineup. Although the theory of the case was not entirely clear, the Court intimated that only by having counsel present at this pretrial identification would the defendant be able to test effectively the reliability of the witness identification during the criminal trial.

89. See, for example, *United States* v. *Madrid*, 673 F.2d 1114 (10th Cir.), *cert. denied*, 459 U.S. 843 (1982); *United States* v. *Reifsteck*, 535 F.2d 1030 (8th Cir. 1976); *United States* v. *Cohen*, 530 F.2d 43 (5th Cir., 1976), *cert. denied*, 429 U.S. 855 (1976); *United States* v. *Bohle*, 445 F.2d 54 (7th Cir. 1971), overruled on other grounds; *United States* v. *Lawson*, 653 F.2d 299 (7th Cir. 1981); *United States* v. *Handy*, 454 F.2d 885 (9th Cir. 1971), *cert. denied*, 409 U.S. 846 (1972); *United States* v. *Weiser*, 428 F.2d 932 (2d Cir. 1969), *cert. denied*, 402 U.S. 949 (1971); *United States* v. *Baird*, 414 F.2d 700 (2d Cir. 1969), *cert. denied*, 396 U.S. 1005 (1970); *United States* v. *Albright*, 388 F.2d 719 (4th Cir. 1968); *Alexander* v. *United States*, 380 F.2d 33 (8th Cir. 1967). These cases stand for the general proposition that a defendant who raises the insanity defense and presents his or her own expert testimony voluntarily gives up the protection of the Fifth Amendment. See also, *United States* v. *Baird*, 414 F.2d 700, 709 (2d Cir. 1969); *United States* v. *Weiser*, 428 F.2d 932, 936 (2d Cir. 1971). Insanity defendants were "estopped" from denying government experts a reciprocal opportunity to gather evidence. See also, *United States* v. *Cohen*, 530 F.2d 43, 48 (5th Cir. 1976); *United States* v. *Handy*, 454 F.2d 885, 889 (9th Cir. 1971); *Battle* v. *Cameron*, 260 F. Supp. 804, 806 (D.D.C. 1966). (Evidence obtained from defendants during clinical evaluation are not "testimonial evidence" offered to prove guilt, but only "data" on which experts based their opinions.) See also, *United States* v. *Whitlock*, 663 F.2d 1094, 1107 (D.C. Cir. 1980); *United States* v. *Bohle*, 445 F.2d 54, 66–67 (7th

Cir. 1971); *United States* v. *Albright*, 388 F.2d 719, 725 (4th Cir. 1968). (Fifth Amendment only prevented prosecution from using defendant's statements to show he committed the crime charged; it did not prevent the prosecution from showing whether the defendant was sane.)

90. *French* v. *District Court*, 153 Colo. 10, 384 P.2d 268 (1963); *State* v. *Olson*, 274 Minn. 225, 143 N.W.2d 69 (1966); *Shepard* v. *Bowe*, 250 Or. 288, 442 P.2d 238 (1968); *Commonwealth* v. *Pomponi*, 447 Pa. 154, 284 A.2d 708 (1971). See Lefelt, *Pretrial Mental Examinations*.

91. See, for example, F. W. Danforth, *Death Knell for Pre-Trial Mental Examination? Privilege Against Self-Incrimination*, Rutgers L. Rev. 19 (1965): 489–505; Comment, *Requiring a Criminal Defendant to Submit to a Government Psychiatric Examination: An Invasion of the Privilege Against Self-Incrimination*, Harv. L. Rev. 83 (1970): 648–71; Lefelt, *Pretrial Mental Examinations*. But for a different perspective, see R. H. Aronson, *Should the Privilege Against Self-Incrimination Apply to Compelled Psychiatric Examinations?* Stan. L. Rev. 26 (1973): 55–93. Among the reasons for opposing forced cooperation with government mental examinations are

> (1) reluctance to subject an individual to the "cruel trilemma of self-accusation, perjury, or contempt"; (2) respect for the inviolability of the human personality, and "the right of each individual to a private enclave where he may lead a private life"; (3) fear that self-incriminatory statements result from inhumane treatment of the accused; (4) distrust of self-deprecatory statements; and (5) a commitment to an accusatorial rather than an inquisitorial trial process, which entails that the state should shoulder the load of convicting the defendant with independently acquired evidence.

See Comment, *Requiring a Criminal Defendant to Submit to a Government Psychiatric Examination*, 656.

92. 407 F.2d 695 (1969).

93. 407 F.2d 695, 702 (D.C. Cir.). See also Note, *Right to Counsel at the Pretrial Mental Examination of an Accused*, U. Pa. L. Rev. 118 (1970): 448–57. Judge Bazelon, however, thought that a broad range of alternatives might be available to protect a defendant's Sixth Amendment right and did not grant the defendant's request. In an earlier order, the federal appellate for the District of Columbia required hospital staff to record the senior staff conference on audiotape in case the defense counsel needed the tape to prepare for the trial cross-examination. See also, *State* v. *Whitlow*, 45 N.J. 3, 27–28, 210 A.2d 763, 776 (1965), which held that the trial court should permit defense psychiatrists to be present at the examination by a government expert if the defense so requested.

94. Danforth, *Death Knell for Pre-Trial Mental Examination?*, 491.

95. See, for example, *United States* v. *Madrid*, 673 F.2d 1114 (10th Cir. 1982), cert. denied, 459 U.S. 843; *United States* v. *Reifsteck*, 535 F.2d 1030 (8th Cir. 1976); *United States* v. *Cohen*, 530 F.2d 43 (5th Cir. 1976), *cert. denied*, 429 U.S. 855 (1976); *United States* v. *Bohle*, 445 F.2d 54 (7th Cir. 1971), overruled on other grounds in *United State* v. *Lawson*, 653 F.2d 299 (7th Cir. 1981); *United States* v. *Handy*, 454 F.2d 885 (1971), *cert. denied*, 409 U.S. 846, *United States* v. *Weiser*, 428 F.2d 932 (2d Cir. 1969); *United States* v. *Baird*, 414 F.2d 700 (2d Cir. 1969), *cert. denied*, 396 U.S. 1005 (1970); *United States* v. *Albright*, 388 F.2d 719 (4th Cir. 1968); *Alexander* v. *United States*, 380 F.2d 33 (8th Cir. 1967); *Pope* v. *United States*, 372 F.2d 710 (8th Cir. 1967) (*en banc*), *vacated and remanded on other grounds*, 392 U.S. 651 (1968).

96. 740 F.2d 1104 (D.C. Cir. 1984).

97. In a decision in which all members of the Court of Appeals for the District of Columbia participated, the court held that

when a defendant raises the defense of insanity, he may constitutionally be subjected to compulsory examination by court-appointed or government psychiatrists without the necessity of recording; and when he introduces into evidence psychiatric testimony to support his insanity defense, testimony of those examining psychiatrists may be received (on that issue) as well.

United States v. *Byers*, 740 F.2d 1104, 1113 (D.C. Cir. 1984).

98. Id, at 1113.

99. In 1981 the Supreme Court, in *Buchanan* v. *Kentucky*, 451 U.S. 454 (1981), reaffirmed the approach taken by the lower court in *Byers*. Congress has also endorsed this trend. The Insanity Defense Reform Act of 1984 modified 18 USCA 4244, deleting language which had guaranteed that "[no] statement made by the accused in the course of any examination into his sanity or mental competency . . . shall be admitted in evidence against the accused on the issue of guilt in any criminal proceeding." Comprehensive Crime Control Act of 1984, PL 98–473, 98 Stat. 2061, 18 USC § 4244(b) (1984).

100. See *State* v. *Hutchinson*, 111 Wash. 2d 872, 766 P.2d 447 (1989). The court held that compulsory psychiatric examinations do not violate defendants' Fifth Amendment rights. However, the constitutionality of permitting a defendant to use the diminished capacity defense only on the condition that he speak to a government psychiatrist was not addressed by the court. For cases with similar results, see *People* v. *Mangiapane*, 85 Mich. App. 379, 271 N.W.2d 240 (1978); *Commonwealth* v. *Stehley*, 350 Pa. Super. 311, 504 A.2d 854 (1986). But see, *Tarantino* v. *Superior Court*, 48 Cal. App. 3d 465, 122 Cal. Rptr. 61 (1975). See also, *State* v. *Vosler*, 216 Neb. 461, 345 N.W.2d 806 (1984); *Posner* v. *Superior Court*, 107 Cal. App. 3d 928, 166 Cal. Rptr. 123 (1980). See also Aronson, *Should the Privilege Against Self-Incrimination Apply to Compelled Psychiatric Examinations?*; Lefelt, *Pretrial Mental Examinations*; S. A. Saltzburg, *Privileges and Professionals: Lawyers and Psychiatrists*, Va. L. Rev. 66 (1980): 597–651.

101. However, the jury could not be told the expert had initially been retained by the defense, as this might unduly influence the jury.

102. See, for example, *United States* v. *Alvarez*, 519 F.2d 1036 (3d Cir. 1975); *State* v. *Toste*, 178 Conn. 626, 424 A.2d 293 (1979); *Ursury* v. *State*, 428 So.2d 713, 714, (Fla. Dist. Ct. App. 1983); *Pouncy* v. *State*, 353 So.2d 640, 642 (Fla. Dist. Ct. App. 1977); *State* v. *Pratt*, 284 Md. 516, 398 A.2d 421 (1979); *People* v. *Hilliker*, 29 Mich. App. 543, 185 N.W.2d 831 (1971); *State* v. *Moore*, 45 Or. App. 837, 609 P.2d 866, 869 (1980). See also R. P. Mosteller, *Discovery Against the Defense: Tilting the Adversarial Balance*, Calif. L. Rev. 74 (1986): 1569–1685.

103. The following are some examples. Iowa: *State* v. *Craney*, 347 N.W.2d 668, 676–77 (1984); Minnesota: *State* v. *Dodis*, 314 N.W.2d 233, 240–41 (1982); Missouri: *State* v. *Carter*, 641 S.W.2d 54, 58–59 (1982); New York: *United States ex rel Edney* v. *Smith*, 425 F. Supp. 1038, 1046 (E.D. N.Y. 1976), *aff'd mem.*, 556 F.2d 556 (2d Cir.), *cert. denied*, 431 U.S. 958 (1977); *People* v. *Edney*, 39 N.Y.2d 620, 350 N.E.2d 400, 385 N.Y.S.2d 23 (1976); Ohio: *Noggle* v. *Marshall*, 706 F.2d 1408, 1412 (6th Cir. 1983), *cert. denied*, 464 U.S. 1010 (1983); Texas: *Granviel* v. *Estelle*, 665 F.2d 673 (5th Cir, 1981), *cert. denied*, 455 U.S. 1003 (1982); *Granviel* v. *State*, 552 S.W.2d 107, 117 (Tex. Ct. Ap. 1976), *cert. denied*, 431 U.S. 933 (1977). As cited in Mosteller, *Discovery Against the Defense*; Washington: *State* v. *Pawlyk*, 115 Wash. 2d 457, 800 P.2d 338 (1990); *State* v. *Bonds*, 98 Wash. 2d 1, 22, 653 P.2d 1024 (1983). For further information, see Saltzburg, *Privileges and Professionals*.

104. Rule 704 was amended Oct. 12, 1984 by the Comprehensive Crime Control

Act of 1984 (the Insanity Defense Reform Act). Federal Rule of Evidence, Pub. L. No. 98–473 Title II, § 406, 98 Stat. 2067 (1984).

105. Cal. Penal Code § 25 (West 1988) Proposition 8 approved by voters on June 8, 1982.

106. All persons born or naturalized in the United States, and subject to the jurisdiction thereof, are citizens of the United States and of the state wherein they reside. No state shall make or enforce any law which shall abridge the privileges or immunities of citizens of the United States; nor shall any state deprive any person of life, liberty, or property, without due process of law; nor deny to any person within its jurisdiction the equal protection of the laws. U.S. Const. Amend. XIV, § 1.

107. 383 U.S. 107, 86 S. Ct. 760, 15 L. Ed. 2d 620 (1966).

108. In *Baxstrom*, the court stated, "[i]n order to accord to petitioner the equal protection of the laws, he was and is entitled to a review of the determination as to his sanity in conformity with the proceedings granted all others civilly committed under § 74 of the New York Mental Hygiene Law. He is also entitled to a hearing under the procedure granted all others by § 85 of the New York Mental Hygiene Law to determine whether he is so dangerously mentally ill that he must remain in a hospital maintained by the Department of Correction." *Baxstrom* v. *Herold*, 383 U.S. 107, 115 (1966).

109. *United States ex rel. Schuster* v. *Herold*, 410 F.2d 1071, 1082 (2d Cir. 1969).

110. In *Bolton* v. *Harris*, 395 F.2d 642 (D.C. Cir. 1968) the Court, relying on *Baxstrom*, held that a successful insanity defendant could be automatically committed temporarily to a psychiatric facility to determine if he presently was mentally ill or dangerous. The state could only keep him in the facility for an indefinite period if it committed him under standards and procedures "substantially similar to those in civil commitment proceedings." Id. at 651. It should be noted that the prosecution had failed to persuade the jury beyond a reasonable doubt that Bolton was insane as required under the law. Consequently, the court in *Bolton* concluded that there had never been a factual finding that the defendant was mentally ill. Id., at 650.

111. *Specht* v. *Patterson*, 386 U.S. 605, 87 S. Ct. 1209, 18 L. Ed. 2d 326 (1967).

112. After a person is found to constitute a threat of bodily harm to members of the public, or is a habitual offender and mentally ill, that person becomes punishable for an indeterminate term from one day to life as long as the conditions in Section 2 of the Sex Offenders Act are met. Section 2 requires that

(2) A complete psychiatric examination shall have been made of him by the psychiatrists of the Colorado psychopathic hospital or by psychiatrists designated by the district court; and

(3) A complete written report thereof submitted to the district court. Such report shall contain all facts and findings, together with recommendations as to whether or not the person is treatable under the provisions of this article; whether or not the person should be committed to the Colorado state hospital or to the state home and training schools as mentally ill or mentally deficient. Such report shall also contain the psychiatrist's opinion as to whether or not the person could be adequately supervised on probation.

113. In *Specht* the Court held the invocation of the Act entails the making of a new charge and possible additional criminal punishment. Due process therefore requires that petitioner be present with counsel, have an opportunity to be heard, be confronted with witnesses against him, have the right to cross-examine and to offer evidence of his own, and that there be findings adequate to make meaningful any appeal that is allowed.

114. 406 U.S. 715, 92 S. Ct. 1845, 32 L. Ed. 2d 435 (1972).

115. 441 U.S. 418, 99 S. Ct. 1804, 60 L. Ed. 2d 323 (1979).

116. 441 U.S. 418, 433 (1979)

117. This decision required the government to establish the criteria for civil commitment by "clear and convincing" evidence; not merely by a "preponderance of the evidence" before individuals could be civilly confined in psychiatric institutions for any length of time. *Addington* v. *Texas*, 441 U.S. 418, 433.

118. 395 F.2d 642 (1968).

119. Since the government had to prove the defendant's sanity beyond a reasonable doubt in the *Bolton* case, the jury verdict of NGRI did not establish that the defendant was mentally ill at the time of the offense but only reasonable doubt as to his sanity. "The jury's finding of a reasonable doubt as to defendant's sanity at the time of the offense provides sufficient warrant for further examination." Id at 642, 651. Thus, this particular verdict failed to find that the offender had ever been mentally ill.

120. *People* v. *McQuillan*, 392 Mich. 511, 221 N.W.2d 569 (1974). The court stated that "equal protection demands that differences in treatment of classes be based on a rational basis. The lack of a hearing cannot be justified by the contention that the defendant because of his acquittal by reason of insanity is so potentially dangerous at that time that he must be committed without further hearing. *Baxstrom* held that past criminal actions could not serve as a rational basis of classification for purposes of determining commitment procedure. . . . Thus, based on equal protection of the laws, we hold that defendant is entitled to a sanity hearing when found not guilty by reason of insanity after completion of observation and examination." Id at 569, 580.

121. *Benham* v. *Edwards*, 678 F.2d 511, (5th Cir. Unit B 1982) (striking down Georgia's NGRI disposition scheme because it denied NGRIs equal protection by: applying a presumption of continuing insanity to this class, denying the class the same number and kind of hearings provided civil committees, requiring the class to bear the burden of proof at release hearings, and requiring court approval for release of all NGRIs rather than only some). *Cert. granted* and *judgment vacated, Ledbetter* v. *Benham*, 463 U.S. 1222, 103 S. Ct. 3565, 77 L. Ed. 2d 1406 (1983); on remand to *Benham* v. *Edwards*, 719 F.2d 772 (5th Cir 1983), *on remand to Benham* v. *Ledbetter*, 609 F. Supp. 125 (N.D. Ga. 1985).

122. Comment, *Commitment Following an Insanity Acquittal*, Harv. L. Rev. 94 (1981): 605–25, note 3 and states listed therein.

123. *See also, Wilson* v. *State*, 259 Ind. 375, 287 N.E.2d 875 (1972); and *State* v. *Krol*, 68 N.J. 236, 344 A.2d 289 (1975).

124. Comment, *Commitment Following an Insanity Acquittal*.

125. California permits the trial judge to grant outpatient status to defendants found NGRI of less serious crimes. Cal. Penal Code § 1601(b) (West Supp. 1991).

126. See, for example, "Insane Risk," *New York Times*, April 15, 1987, p. A26, col. 1, editorial desk. The pass was later revoked because of adverse public reaction.

127. J. W. Ellis, *The Consequences of the Insanity Defense: Proposals to Reform Post-Acquittal Commitment Laws*, Cath. U. L. Rev. 35 (1986): 961–1020, 962. Ellis quotes N. Morris, *Psychiatry and the Dangerous Criminal*, S. Cal. L. Rev. 41 (1967–8): 514–47, 516.

128. 463 U.S. 354, 103 S. Ct. 3043, 77 L. Ed. 2d 694 (1983).

129. D.C. Code § 21–545(b) (1981).

130. 463 U.S. 354, 366 (1983).

131. Ibid., 364–65, note 13.

132. Ibid., 362, note 10.

133. Ibid., 364–66. Though of small consolation, the Court did conclude that the state could constitutionally commit an NGRI only to treat him and to protect the public. Ibid., 368. By implication, institutionalization for punishment would not be acceptable.

134. P. Margulies, *The "Pandemonium Between the Mad and the Bad": Procedures for the Commitment and Release of Insanity Acquittees After Jones v. United States*, Rutgers L. Rev. 36 (1984): 793–836; Ellis, *The Consequences of the Insanity Defense*.

135. This was also an open invitation to states to shift the burden of proof on insanity to the defendant since, under *Jones*, differential treatment was permissible only if there had been an affirmative finding of past mental illness.

136. The accuracy of behavioral predictions is positively correlated with the temporal immediacy of the past behavior on which the prediction is based. Morse, *Excusing the Crazy*, 832. The prediction that Jones continues to be dangerous more than six years after his last dangerous act is very likely to be wrong. The evidence for dangerousness (shoplifting) is acutely "stale." Evidently, the Supreme Court will impose no logical cut off on the use of past criminal acts as probative evidence establishing present dangerousness.

137. There is reason to believe that this hydraulic pressure from one system into the other system had already created back pressure both to stifle changes in civil commitment or to create new legal solutions to the problem. In particular, the Guilty But Mentally Ill Defense was enacted to cope with this very problem. Slobogin, *The Guilty But Mentally Ill Verdict*.

138. 463 U.S. 354, 370 (1983).

139. Margulies, *The "Pandemonium Between the Mad and the Bad,"* 804–5. In the past some courts have made this point. *Warren* v. *Harvey*, 632 F. 925, 932 (2d Cir.), *cert. denied*, 449 U.S. 902 (1980) (*citing U.S.* v. *Brown*, 478 F.2d 606, 611 (D.C. Cir. 1973).

140. Ellis, *The Consequences of the Insanity Defense*.

141. Callahan, Mayer, and Steadman, *Insanity Defense Reform in the United States—Post-Hinckley*. The authors find that the most common reform in insanity statutes throughout the country post-Hinckley and *Jones* occurred in provisions governing commitment and release (27 reforms in 26 states). Although the statutes vary from state to state, almost all states provide for some form of mandatory commitment following NGRI acquittal. For states adopting a *Jones*-like approach, see Md. Code Ann. § 12–111; Ariz. Crim. Code § 13–3944; Colo. Code Ann. § 16–8–105(4); S.D. Codified Laws § 23A–26–12.5; 15 Maine Rev. Stat. § 103.

142. 18 U.S.C.A. 4243(c) provides that a successful insanity acquittee charged with "an offense involving bodily injury to, or serious damage to the property of another person, or involving a substantial risk of such injury or damage, has the burden of proving by clear and convincing evidence that his release would not create a substantial risk of bodily injury to another person or serious damage of property of another due to present mental disease or defect." This section provides for mandatory, automatic commitment of a successful insanity defendant. A trial judge has no discretion. *United States* v. *Palesky*, 855 F.2d 34 (1st Cir. 1988).

143. *Phelps* v. *U.S.*, 831 F.2d 897 (9th Cir. 1987).

144. See *U.S.* v. *Cohen*, 733 F.2d 128 (D.C. Cir. 1984).

145. Mandatory initial commitment: *Arizona* - Ariz. Rev. Stat. Ann. § 13–3994 (1991 Supp.); *California* - Cal. Penal Code 1026(a) (West 1984); *Colorado* - Colo. Rev. Stat. § 16–8–105(4)(1986); *Connecticut* - Conn. Gen. Stat. Ann. § 17a–756 (1990);

D.C. - D.C. Code Ann. § 24–301(d)(1)(1981); *Hawaii* - Hawaii Rev. Stat. § 704–411(1)(a) (1985); *Iowa* - Iowa R.Cr.P. § 813.2(8) R. 21(8)(Rev. 1987); *Kansas* - Kan. Stat. Ann. § 22–3428(1)(1981); *Louisiana* - La. Code Crim. Proc. Ann. Art. 654 (West. Supp. 1988); *Maine* - Me. Rev. Stat. Ann. Tit. 15 § 103 (1980); *Maryland* - Md. [Health- General] Code Ann. § 12–111 (Supp. 1987); *Michigan* - Mich. Comp. Laws § 330.2050 (West 1980); *Missouri* - Mo. Ann. Stat. § 552.040(2) (Vernon 1987); *Nevada* - Nev. Rev. Stat. § 175.521(1)(1985); *N. Dakota* - N.D. Cent. Code § 2.1–04.1–21, § 2.1–04.1–22 (1985); *Oklahoma* - Okla. Stat. Ann. Tit. 22 § 1161 (West 1986); *S. Dakota* - S.D. Codified Laws Ann. § 23A–26–12 (Supp. 1987); *Texas* - Tex. Code Crim. Proc. Ann. Art. 46.03(4)(a), (d) (Vernon Supp. 1988).

146. Ariz. Rev. Stat. § 13–3994; Conn. Gen. Stat. 17a- 576; Iowa R. Cr. Proc. § 813.2(8) Rule 21; Md. Ann. Code Health-Gen. Art. 12–111 (from commitment for 30 days for evaluation followed by a due process hearing to automatic, mandatory commitment for 90 days); N.D. Cent. Code § 12.1–04.1–22; S.D. Codified Laws, § 23A–26–12; Tex. Code Crim. Proc. Ann. Art. 46.03.

147. Minn. Rules Cr. Pro. Rule 20.02 (8) [cited in Mayer, "Insanity Defense Reforms Pre and Post Hinckley."

148. Wash. Rev. Code Ann., § 10.77.110.

149. Tex. Code Crim. Proc. Ann., Art. 46.03 and Tex. Rev. Civ. Stat. Ann., Art. 5547–50 [cited in Mayer, "Insanity Defense Reforms Pre and Post Hinckley"].

150. Colo. Rev. Stat. 16–8–115; N.D. Cent. Code 12.1–04.1–22; Hawaii Rev. Stat § 704–415; S.D. Codified Laws, § 23A–26–12.3. Burden on acquittee, applicant, defendant - release: *Alaska* - Alaska Stat. § 12.47.090(c)(1984); *Arizona* - Ariz. Rev. Stat. Ann. § 13–3994(c)(Supp. 1987); *California* - Cal. Penal Code § 1026.2(k)(West 1984); *Colorado* - Colo. Rev. Stat. § 16–8–115(2)(1986); *Connecticut* - Conn. Gen. Stat. Ann. § 17a–576 (1990); *Delaware* - Del. Code Ann. Tit. 11 § 403 (1987); *D.C.* - D.C. Code § 24–301 (1981); *Georgia* - Ga. Code Ann. § 27–1503(f)(1983); *Hawaii* - Hawaii Rev. Stat. § 704–415 (1985); *Illinois* - Ill. Ann. Stat. Ch. 38 par. 1005 (Smith-Hurd 1987 Supp.); *Kansas* - Kan. Stat. Ann. § 22–3428 (1981); *Louisiana* - La. Code Cr. Proc. Ann. Art. 657 (West 1988 Supp.); *Maine* - Me. Rev. Stat. Ann. Tit. 15 § 104- A (1980); *Maryland* - Md. [Health-General] Code Ann. § 12–113(d)(1987); *Missouri* - Mo. Ann. Stat § 552.040 (1987); *Montana* - Mont. Code Ann. § 46–14–301, § 46–14–302 (1981); *N. Dakota* - N.D. Cent. Code § 12.1–04.1–22 (1985); *Oregon* - Or. Rev. Stat. § 161.341 (1985); *S. Dakota* - S.D. Codified Laws Ann. § 23A-26–12.3 (Supp. 1987); *Utah* - Utah Code Ann. § 77–14–5(2) (Supp. 1987); *Virginia* - Va. Code 19.2–181 (Supp. 1987); *Washington* - Wash. Rev. Code Ann. § 10.77.200 (1980); *Wisconsin* - Wis. Stat. Ann. § 971.17 (West 1985).

151. Court ordered release is required in these states: *California* - Cal. Penal Code § 1026.2 (West 1984); *Colorado* - Colo. Rev. Stat. § 16–8–115 (1986); *Connecticut* - Conn. Gen. Stat. § 17a–576 (1990); *Delaware* - Del. Code Ann. Tit. 11 § 403 (1987); *D.C.* - *D.C.* Code Ann. § 24–301 (1981); *Florida* - Fla. Stat. Ann. § 916.15(3) (West 1985); *Georgia* - Ga. Code Ann. § 27–1503(f) (1983); *Hawaii* - Hawaii Rev. Stat. § 704–415 (1985); *Illinois* - Ill. Ann. Stat. Ch. 38 par. 1005–2–4(d), (e) (Smith-Hurd 1987 Supp.); *Iowa* - Iowa R. Cr. P. § 813.2(8) R. 21(8) (Rev. 1987); *Kansas* - Kan. Stat. Ann. § 22–3428 (1981); *Louisiana* - La. Code Cr. Proc. Ann. Art. 657 (West 1988 Supp.); *Maine* - Me. Rev. Stat. Ann. Tit. 15, § 104-A (1980); *Maryland* - Md. [Health-General] Code Ann. § 12–114 (1987 Supp.); *Missouri* - Mo. Ann. Stat. § 552.040; *Montana* - Mont. Code Ann. § 46–14- 301, 46–14–302; *Nebraska* - Neb. Rev. Stat. § 29–3703 (1985); *New Jersey* - N.J. Stat. § 2C:4–9 (West 1982); *New York* - N.Y. Crim. Proc. Law § 330.20 (McKinney 1987); *N. Carolina* - N.C. Gen. Stat. §

122C–277 (1987 Supp.); *Ohio* - Ohio Rev. Code Ann. 2945.40 (Baldwin 1987); *Rhode Island* - R.I. Gen. Laws § 40.1–5.3–4 (1984); *Texas* - Tex. Code Crim. Proc. Ann. Art. 46.03 (Vernon Supp. 1988); *Utah* - Utah Code Ann. § 77–14–5(2)(1987 Supp.); *Vermont* - Vt. Stat. Ann. Tit. 13 § 4822 (1974); *Virginia* - Va. Code 19.2–181 (Supp. 1987); *Washington* - Wash. Rev. Code Ann. § 10.77.150, § 10.77.200 (1980); *Wisconsin* - Wis. Stat. Ann. § 51.37(8)(a) (1987); *Wyoming* - Wyo. Stat. § 7–11–306 (1987).

152. See, for example, Conn. Gen. Stat. § 17a–571 (1990).

153. Ariz. Rev. Stat. § 36–540.01 (I); Colo. Rev. Stat. 16–8–115.5; Hawaii Rev. Stat. § 704–416.5; 18 U.S.C.S. 4243(e) and (g).

154. Ind. Code Ann. § 16–14–9.1–20(c); N.D. Cent. Code § 25–03.1–22. Mayer, "Insanity Defense Reforms Pre and Post Hinckley."

155. J. L. Rogers and J. D. Bloom, *The Insanity Sentence: Oregon's Psychiatric Security Review Board*, Behav. Sci. & L. 3(1) (1985): 69–84.

156. Ibid., 84.

157. Connecticut has adopted this approach. See, generally, Conn. Gen. Stat. § 17a–580–§ 17a–604 (1990).

158. Mayer, "Insanity Defense Reforms Pre and Post Hinckley."

Chapter 4

1. W. Vogel, *A Personal Memoir of the State Hospitals of the 1950s*, Hosp. & Commun. Psychiatry 42(6) (1991): 593–97.

2. Prominent lawsuits, such as *In re Oakes* in 1845, brought the fear of wrongful commitment into public view and encouraged enactment of more restrictive commitment laws. A habeas corpus petition was filed on behalf of Josiah Oakes for his release from McLean Asylum in Massachusetts on grounds that he had been illegally committed by his family. *Matter of Josiah Oakes*, Law Rep. 8 (1845): 122–29. In another case, Mrs. E.P.W. Packard, who had been committed for three years to the Illinois State Hospital in 1860 by her husband, launched an effective public campaign to prevent commitment because of one's personal or political beliefs.

3. Gerald Grob, *Mental Illness and American Society, 1875–1940* (Princeton, N.J.: Princeton University Press, 1983).

4. The number reported here represents inpatient episodes as opposed to a simple one-day census of the hospital population (see Charles A. Kiesler and Amy E. Sibulkin, *Mental Hospitalization: Myths and Facts About a National Crisis* [Beverly Hills, Calif.: Sage Publications, 1987]).

5. According to the National Institute of Mental Health, a one-day census of residents in mental hospitals in 1955 was about 559,000. This compares with approximately 180,000 individuals in prisons during the same year.

6. A writ of habeas corpus was usually the only method available to challenge the detention of a mentally disabled person. However, it could only challenge the legality of an initial commitment decision—not the readiness of a patient for release.

7. Grob, *Mental Illness and American Society*.

8. S. J. Brakel, J. Parry, and B. A. Weiner, *The Mentally Disabled and the Law*, 3d ed. (Chicago: American Bar Foundation, 1985).

9. Ibid.

10. Ibid.

11. As late as 1971, commitment laws of most states failed to make a proper distinction between involuntary commitment and incompetency. In 1985, Brakel,

Parry, and Weiner (*The Mentally Disabled and the Law*, p. 375) noted that forty-two jurisdictions currently specified that an individual's competency is not affected by institutionalization.

12. Gerald Grob, however, argues that the Great Depression had less impact on mental hospitals than on other institutions. He claims that many impoverished mentally ill people could retreat from disorganized communities into hospitals, there receiving shelter and protection while many mentally intact people were starving (Grob, *Mental Illness and American Society*).

13. Albert Deutsch, *The Mentally Ill in America: A History of Their Care and Treatment from Colonial Times*, 2d ed. (New York: Columbia University Press, 1949), 449.

14. E. F. Torrey, *Nowhere to Go: The Tragic Odyssey of the Homeless Mentally Ill* (New York: Harper & Row, 1988).

15. The term "snake pit" was first used by Mary Jane Ward in her novel *The Snake Pit* (New York: Random House, 1949) to describe the experiences of a fictional character, Virginia Stuart, who was confined to a mental hospital against her will.

16. W. Gronfein, *Incentives and Intentions in Mental Health Policy: A Comparison of the Medicaid and Community Mental Health Program*, J. Health & Soc. Behav. 26 (1985): 192–206.

17. Erving Goffman, *Asylums* (New York: Doubleday, 1961).

18. Joint Commission on Mental Illness and Health, *Action for Mental Health* (New York: Basic Books, 1961).

19. Goffman, *Asylums*.

20. Andrew T. Scull, *Decarceration: Community and the Deviant—A Radical View* (Englewood Cliffs, N.J.: Prentice-Hall, 1977; rev. ed., 1984).

21. T. Szasz, *The Myth of Mental Illness* (New York: Hoeber-Harper, 1961). See also, R. D. Laing, *The Divided Self* (Baltimore: Penguin, 1960).

22. Joint Commission on Mental Illness and Health, *Action for Mental Health*, 3.

23. John Talbott, *The Death of the Asylum* (New York: Grune & Stratton, 1979); B. Pepper and H. Ryglewicz, *The Role of the State Hospital: A New Mandate for a New Era*, Psychiatric Q. 57(3–4) (Fall/Winter 1985): 230–51.

24. Although the implementation of deinstitutionalization policies varied widely from state to state, only 1.5 percent of all patients in the United States were discharged in each of the years between 1955 and 1965. Gronfein, *Incentives and Intentions in Mental Health Policy*.

25. Pepper and Ryglewicz, *The Role of the State Hospital*.

26. Andrew T. Scull, *A New Trade in Lunacy: The Recommodification of the Mental Patient*, Am. Behav. Sci. 24 (6) (July/August 1981): 741–54.

27. Comptroller General of the United States, *Returning the Mentally Disabled to the Community: Government Needs to Do More* (Washington, D.C.: Government Accounting Office, 1977).

28. This tremendous cost differential between outpatient and inpatient care was partially offset by the likelihood that a person released from a hospital probably received income from Social Security Insurance. Even that cost (about $400 in 1974) was split between the state and the federal government.

29. S. M. Rose, *Deciphering Deinstitutionalization: Complexities in Policy and Program Analysis*, Milbank Memorial Fund Q. 57 (1979): 429–60.

30. According to M. Derthick, California was the first and, for several years, the only state to take advantage of federal funding programs in a big way. From 1967 to 1971, California showed its skill in promoting and subsidizing state objectives through

the use of federal funds by receiving from 25 to 36 percent of the nation's total expenditures for social services and training grants (M. Derthick, *Uncontrollable Spending for Social Service Grants* [Washington, D.C.: Brookings Institute, 1975]). California led all states between 1955 and 1970 in reducing its hospitalized population; however, by 1975, the rest of the country had achieved similar population reductions for patients under sixty-five years of age (Paul Lerman, *Deinstitutionalization and the Welfare State* [New Brunswick, N.J.: Rutgers University Press, 1982]).

31. Although Social Security benefits were available long before the Liberal Era to provide a monthly income to all insured people over sixty-five years of age, the Social Security Act had little impact on aged patients who had lived in hospitals for years and had never paid into the system. Old Age Assistance (OAA) and Aid to Permanently and Totally Disabled (APTD) were also established. These programs were eventually replaced by Supplementary Security Income for the Aged, Blind, and Disabled (SSI), which provided a national standard of minimum payments to eligible persons fully funded by the federal government (Lerman, *Deinstitutionalization and the Welfare State*).

32. Medicare (Title XVIII) pays primarily for hospital coverage for the elderly, with only a tiny portion of its reimbursement going to skilled nursing home facilities. Medicaid (Title XIX) provides matching funds to states to pay medical expenses for qualified low-income people of any age; funds cover services of many types, including unlimited stays in nursing homes.

33. *Lessard* v. *Schmidt*, 349 F. Supp. 1078 (E.D. Wis. 1972), *vacated* and *remanded*, 414 U.S. 473 (1974), *order on remand*, 379 F. Supp. 1376 (1974), *vacated* and *remanded on other grounds*, 421 U.S. 957 (1975), order *reinstated on remand*, 413 F. Supp. 1318 (1976).

34. Loren H. Roth, *Mental Health Commitment: The State of the Debate, 1980*, Hosp. & Commun. Psychiatry 31(6) (June 1980): 385–96.

35. See, for example, *Stamus* v. *Leonhart*, 414 F. Supp. 439 (S.D. Iowa 1976); *Bension* v. *Meredith*, 455 F. Supp. 662 (D.C.C. 1978); *Suzuki* v. *Yuen*, 438 F. Supp. 1106 (D. Haw. 1977), *modified*, 617 F.2d 173 (1980); *Lynch* v. *Baxley*, 386 F. Supp. 378 (M.D. Ala. 1974), rev'd 651 F.2d 387 (1981); *Warren* v. *Harvey*, 472 F. Supp. 1061 (D. Conn. 1979), *cert. denied*, 449 U.S. 902 (1980). For further discussion, see J. Q. La Fond, *An Examination of the Purposes of Involuntary Civil Commitment*, Buff. L. Rev. 30 (1981): 499–535.

36. *Colyar* v. *Third Judicial District Court*, 469 F. Supp. 424 (D. Utah 1979).

37. See, for example, *Lynch* v. *Baxley*, 386 F. Supp. 378 (M.D. Ala. 1974), rev'd 651 F.2d 387 (1981); *Suzuki* v. *Yuen*, 438 F. Supp. 1106 (D. Haw. 1977), *modified*, 617 F.2d 173 (1980); *Doremus* v. *Farrell*, 407 F. Supp. 509 (D. Neb. 1975); *Warren* v. *Harvey*, 472 F. Supp. 1061 (D. Conn. 1979), *cert. denied*, 449 U.S. 902 (1980). See also, La Fond, *An Examination of the Purposes of Involuntary Civil Commitment*; Comment, *Overt Dangerous Behavior as a Constitutional Requirement for Involuntary Commitment of the Mentally Ill*, U. Chi. L. Rev. 44 (1977): 562–93.

38. For an excellent discussion of state statutes that were revised after *Lessard*, see Note, *Lessard* v. *Schmidt: Due Process and Involuntary Civil Commitment*, U. Chi. L. Rev. 68 (1977): 562.

39. For a thorough review of laws during the Pre-Liberal Era, see S. J. Brakel and R. Rock, *The Mentally Disabled and the Law*, 2d ed. (Chicago, Il: University of Chicago Press, 1971).

40. Most states authorize temporary emergency commitment of persons determined mentally ill and dangerous to others. See Alaska Stat. § 47.30.705 (Supp. 1990);

Ariz. Rev. Stat. Ann. § 36–526 (Supp. 1990); Ark. Stat. Ann § 20–47–210 (Supp. 1987); Cal. Welf. & Inst. Code § 5150 (West Supp. 1991); Colo. Rev. Stat. § 27–10–105 (Supp. 1990); Conn. Gen. Stat. Ann. § 17a-502 (West Supp. 1990); Del. Code Ann. Tit. 16, § 5122 (Supp. 1990); Fla. Stat. Ann. § 394.463 (West Supp. 1990); Official Code Ga. Ann. § 37–3–63 (Supp. 1982); Hawaii Rev. Stat. § 334–59 (Supp. 1990); Idaho Code Ann. § 66–326 (Supp. 1990); Ill. Rev. Stat. Ch. 91 1/2 § 3–600 (Supp. 1989); Ind. Code Ann. § 16–14–9.1–7 (Burns Supp. 1990); Iowa Code Ann. § 229.22 (West Supp. 1989); Kan. Stat. Ann. § 59–2908 (Supp. 1989); La. Rev. Stat. § 28:53 (Supp. 1990); Md. Ann. Code HG § 10–625 (Supp. 1990); Mass. Gen. Laws Ch. 123 § 12 (Lawyer's Coop. 1991); Mich. Comp. Laws § 330.1427 (Supp. 1991); Miss. Code Ann. § 41–21–71 (Supp. 1990); Mont. Rev. Code Ann. § 53–21–129 (1990); Neb. Rev. Stat. §§ 83–1020, 1021 (Supp. 1989); Nev. Rev. Stat. § 433A.160 (Supp. 1986–89); N.H. Rev. Stat. Ann. § 135-C:27 (Supp. 1990); N.J. Stat. Ann. § 30:4–26.3 (West Supp. 1983); N.M. Stat. Ann. § 43–1–10 (Supp. 1990); N.Y. Mental Hyg. Law § 9.39 (Supp. 1991); N.C. Gen Stat. § 122C–262 (1990); N.D. Cent. Code § 25–03.1–25 (Supp. 1989); Ohio Rev. Code Ann. § 5122.10 (Baldwin Supp. 1991); Okla. Stat. Ann. Tit. 43A § 5–205 (Supp. 1990); Ore. Rev. Stat. §§ 426.175, .215 (1989); Pa. Stat. Ann. Tit. 50 §§ 7301, 7302 (Supp. 1989); S.C. Code § 44–17–410 (Supp. 1991); S.D. Codified Laws § 27A–10–3 (Supp. 1991); Tenn. Code Ann. § 33–6–103 (Supp. 1984); Tex. Rev. Civ. Stat. Art. 5547-28 (Supp. 1991); Utah Code Ann. § 62A–12–235 (Supp. 1986); Vt. Stat. Ann. Tit. 18 §§ 7504, 7505 (Supp. 1990); Wash. Rev. Code Ann. § 71.05.150 (Supp. 1990); Wis. Stat. Ann. § 51.15 (Supp. 1989–90); Wyo. Stat. § 25–10–109 (1991).

41. B. Ennis and P. Litwack, *Psychiatry and the Presumption of Expertise: Flipping Coins in the Courtroom*, Calif. L. Rev. 62 (1974): 693–752; J. Cocozza and H. J. Steadman, *The Failure of Psychiatric Predictions of Dangerousness: Clear and Convincing Evidence*, Rutgers L. Rev. 29 (1976): 1084–101; H. J. Steadman, *Some Evidence on the Inadequacy of the Concept and Determination of Dangerousness in Law and Psychiatry*, J. Psychiatry & L. 1 (1973): 409–426; Bernard Rubin, *Prediction of Dangerousness in Mentally Ill Criminals*, Arch. Gen. Psychiatry 27 (1972): 397–407.

42. A. Beigel, K. Hegland, and D. Wexler, "Implementing a New Commitment Law in the Community: Practical Problems for Professionals," in *Law and the Mental Health Professions: Friction at the Interface*, ed. W. E. Barton and C. J. Sanborn (New York: International Universities Press, 1978), 273–95.

43. Emergency detention could last no longer than 72 hours, excluding weekends and holidays. A judicial hearing was required for detention to continue beyond that point (Revised Code of Washington, 71.05).

44. *Covington* v. *Harris*, 419 F.2d 617 (D.C. Cir. 1969).

45. A few examples include: Ala. Code § 22–52–10(a)(5) (1982 Supp.); Ariz. Rev. Stat. Ann. § 36–540 (West Supp.1983); Ill. Rev. Stat. Ch. 91–1/2, § 3–812 (1979); Mich. Comp. Laws § 330.1468(2)(c) (West Supp. 1982); Va. Code §§ 37.1–84.1(6)(c) (1976); West's Wash. Rev. Code Ann. 71.05.320(1) (1983). See also, P. B. Hoffman and L. L. Foust, *Least Restrictive Treatment of the Mentally Ill: A Doctrine in Search of Its Senses*, San Diego L. Rev. 14 (1977): 1100–54, for an excellent discussion of various state statutes incorporating the least restrictive standard.

46. *Lake* v. *Cameron*, 364 F.2d 657 (D.C. Cir. 1966) (the court required an exploration for least restrictive alternative). For further discussion, see Gerald E. Frug, *The Judicial Power of the Purse*, U. Pa. L. Rev. 126 (1978): 715–94, 792. See also, S. H. Lipsius, *Judgments of Alternatives to Hospitalization*, Am. J. Psychiatry

130(8) (1973): 892–96; Hoffman and Foust, *Least Restrictive Treatment of the Mentally Ill*.

47. *Wyatt* v. *Stickney*, 325 F. Supp. 781 (M.D. Ala. 1971), 334 F. Supp. 1341 (M.D. Ala.), 344 F. Supp. 387 (M.D. Ala. 1972), *aff'd sub nom. Wyatt* v. *Aderholt*, 503 F.2d 1305 (5th Cir. 1974). See also, M. Perlin, "Other Rights of Residents in Institutions," in *Legal Rights of Mentally Disabled Persons*, vol. 2, ed. P. Friedman (New York: Practicing Law Institute, 1979), 1011.

48. Bruce Ennis, "Judicial Involvement in the Public Practice of Psychiatry," in *Law and the Mental Health Professions*, 6.

49. J. Brant, *The Hostility of the Burger Court to Mental Health Law Reform Litigation*, Bull. Am. Acad. L. & Psychiatry 11 (1983): 77–90; A. Chayes, *The Role of the Judge in Public Law Litigation*, Harv. L. Rev. 89 (1976): 1281–316.

50. See, for example, *Wyatt* v. *Stickney*, 325 F. Supp. 781 (M.D. Ala. 1971); *Rone* v. *Fireman*, 473 F. Supp. 92 (N.D. Ohio 1979).

51. See, for example, *Wyatt* v. *Stickney*, 325 F. Supp. 781.

52. *Rone* v. *Fireman*, 473 F. Supp. 92.

53. P. S. Appelbaum, *The Supreme Court Looks at Psychiatry*, Am. J. of Psychiatry 141(7) (1984): 827–35.

54. *Wyatt* v. *Stickney*, 325 F. Supp. 781 (M.D. Ala. 1971), 334 F. Supp. 1341 (M.D. Ala.), 344 F. Supp. 387 (M.D. Ala. 1972), *aff'd sub nom. Wyatt* v. *Aderholt*, 503 F.2d 1305 (5th Cir. 1974).

55. Brakel, Parry, and Weiner, *The Mentally Disabled and the Law*.

56. Other judges also took this approach with other institutions. *Pennhurst State School and Hospital* v. *Halderman*, 451 U.S. 1 (1981), *on remand*, 673 F.2d 647 (3d Cir. 1982), *rev'd*, 104 S. Ct. 900 (1984), is another example of a series of judicial decisions regarding the ability of a hospital for the mentally retarded to provide adequate treatment. The case was appealed and several years later the U.S. Supreme Court finally upheld a federal Court of Appeals decision to reverse a District Judge's findings that the hospital was unable to provide adequate treatment.

57. American Psychiatric Association, *Position Statement on the Question of Adequacy of Treatment*, Am. J. Psychiatry 123(11) (1967): 1458–60, 1458.

58. American Psychiatric Association, *Position Statement on the Right to Adequate Care and Treatment for the Mentally Ill and Mentally Retarded*, Am. J. Psychiatry 134(3) (1977): 354–55.

59. Selected state court cases include the following: Arizona: *Large* v. *Superior Court*, 148 Ariz. 229, 714 P.2d 399 (1986); *Anderson* v. *State*, 663 P.2d 570 (Ariz. App. 1982); California: *Keyhea* v. *Rushen*, 178 Cal. App. 3d 526, 223 Cal. Rptr. 746 (1986); *Foy* v. *Greenblot*, 141 Cal. App. 3d 1, 190 Cal. Rptr. 84 (1983); Colorado: *Goedecke* v. *State Department of Institutions*, 198 Colo. 407, 603 P.2d 123 (1979); *People in Interest of Medina*, 662 P.2d 184 (Colo. App. 1982); District of Columbia: In re *Boyd*, 403 A.2d 744 (D.C. 1979); Illinois: *People* v. *Schyve*, 113 Ill. App. 255, 445 N.E.2d 1260 (Ill. App. 1 Dist. 1983); Indiana: In re *The Mental Commitment of M.P.*, 500 N.E.2d 216 (Ind. App. 2 Dist. 1986); Iowa: *Clites* v. *State*, 322 N.W.2d 917 (1982); Kansas: *Durflinger* v. *Artiles*, 234 Kan. 484, 673 P.2d 86 (Kan. 1983); Kentucky: *Gundy* v. *Pauley*, 619 S.W.2d 730 (Ky. App. 1981); Minnesota: *Matter of Kennedy*, 350 N.W.2d 484 (Minn. App. 1984); Missouri: *Kolocotronis* v. *Ritterbusch*, 667 S.W.2d 430 (Mo. App. 1984); New York: *Rivers* v. *Katz*, 67 N.Y.S.2d 485, 495 N.E.2d 337, 504 N.Y.S.2d 74 (Ct. App. 1986); *Savastano* v. *Saribeyoglu*, 480 N.Y.S.2d 977 (Sup. 1984); New Hampshire: *Opinion of the Justices*, 123 N.H. 554, 465 A.2d

484 (N.H. 1983); Oklahoma: In re *Mental Health of K.K.B.*, 609 P.2d 747 (Okla. 1980); Vermont: *J.L.* v. *Miller*, No. S–418–84-WnC (Vt. Super. Ct., Washington County, May 20, 1985), reported in *Mental & Phys. Disab. L. Rep.* 9 (1985): 261; Washington: In re *Guardianship of Ingram*, 102 Wash. 2d 827, 689 P.2d 1363 (1984); West Virginia: *E. H.* v. *Matin*, 284 S.E.2d 232 (W. Va. 1981); Wisconsin: *State* ex rel. *Jones* v. *Gerhardstein*, 135 Wis. 2d 161, 400 N.W.2d 1 (Wis. App.1986).

60.

Severe and potentially permanent is tardive dyskinesia, an irreversible neurological disorder characterized by involuntary, uncontrollable movements of the tongue, mouth or jaw. Fingers, arms and legs may also be affected. Tardive Dyskinesia can be masked by the drug causing the condition, and can manifest itself years after treatment has occurred.

D. J. Kemna, *Current Status of Institutionalized Mental Health Patients' Right to Refuse Psychotropic Drugs*, J. Legal Med. 6 (1985): 107–38, 111–13. Neuroleptic malignant syndrome, a recently identified side effect, can be fatal if not correctly diagnosed and treated. Harrison G. Pope, Paul E. Keck, and Susan L. McElroy, *Frequency and Presentation of Neuroleptic Malignant Syndrome in a Large Psychiatric Hospital*, Am. J. Psychiatry 143 (1986): 1227–33.

61. Several courts have concluded that a hospital staff used psychotropic drugs to punish and control patients. See, for example, *Davis* v. *Hubbard*, 506 F. Supp. 915, 926–27 (N.D. Ohio 1980); *Rennie* v. *Klein*, 476 F. Supp. 1294, 1299–1302 (D.N.J. 1979), *vacated* and *remanded*, 458 U.S. 1119 (1982). For further discussion, see J. Litman, *A Common Law Remedy for Forcible Medication of the Institutionalized Mentally Ill*, Colum. L. Rev. 82 (1982): 1720– 51.

62. Brakel, Parry, and Weiner, *The Mentally Disabled and the Law*; A. Meisel, *The Rights of the Mentally Ill Under State Constitutions*, L. & Contemp. Probs 45 (1982): 7– 40.

63. 422 U.S. 563, 95 S. Ct. 2486, 45 L. Ed. 2d 396 (1975). The earliest cases pertaining to the mentally ill that came before the Supreme Court dealt with criminal or quasicriminal commitments. Those matters often dealt with procedural issues such as the rights of prisoners subject to civil commitment (*Baxstrom* v. *Herold*, 1966; In re *Gault*, 1967; *Specht* v. *Patterson*, 1967; *Humphrey* v. *Cady*, 1972; *Jackson* v. *Indiana*, 1972; *McNeil* v. *Director, Pautuxent Institution*, 1972).

64. For a powerful description of Donaldson's travails, see Kenneth Donaldson, *Insanity Inside Out* (New York: Crown, 1976.)

65. This discussion was not essential to deciding the case and therefore was not binding on lower courts.

66. 422 U.S. at 576. With this rather awkward sentence, the justices concluded that involuntary detention of a nondangerous person requires some purpose other than improvement of a person's quality of life. If a nondangerous person can survive in the community with the help of family or friends, the Court decided, detention should not be sought.

67. 422 U.S. at 575.

68. *O'Connor* v. *Donaldson*, 422 U.S. 563, 573 (1975).

69. A. A. Stone, *Law, Psychiatry, and Morality* (Washington, D.C.: American Psychiatric Press, 1984); A. A. Stone, *The Commission on Judicial Action of the American Psychiatric Association: Origins and Prospects—A Personal View*, Bull. Am. Acad. Psychiatry & L. 3 (1975): 119–22.

70. P. Chodoff, *The Case for Involuntary Hospitalization of the Mentally Ill*, Am.

J. Psychiatry 133(5) (1967): 496–501; R. Slovenko, *Civil Commitment in Perspective*, J. Pub. L. 20 (1971): 3–32; and J. Katz, *The Right to Treatment—An Enchanting Legal Fiction*, U. Chi. L. Rev. 36 (1969): 755–83.

71. S. Rachlin, *When Schizophrenia Comes Marching Home*, Psychiatric Q. 50(3) (1978): 202–10; S. Rachlin, *With Liberty and Psychosis for All*, Psychiatric Q. 48 (1974): 410–20.

Chapter 5

1. David Rothman, *Conscience and Convenience: The Asylum and its Alternatives in Progressive America* (Boston: Little, Brown and Co., 1971.)

2. As we saw in Chapter 4, the number of inpatient episodes in state mental hospitals fell from a high of 819,000 in 1955 to 499,000 in 1981. Moreover, the 379,000 clinical episodes of outpatient care in 1955 mushroomed to 4.6 million in 1975—a twelvefold increase in that twenty-year period. Charles A. Kiesler, "Mental Hospitals and Alternative Care: Noninstitutionalization as Potential Public Policy," in *Mental Health Care and Social Policy*, ed. Phil Brown (Boston: Routledge and Kegan Paul, 1985), 292–315.

3. Aviram and Segal refer to the inner-city areas where chronically mentally ill people congregate as "psychiatric ghettos." U. Aviram and S. P. Segal, *Exclusion of the Mentally Ill: Reflection of an Old Problem in a New Context*, Arch. Gen. Psychiatry 29 (1973): 126–31.

4. H. H. Goldman and J. P. Morrissey, *The Alchemy of Mental Health Policy: Homelessness and the Fourth Cycle of Reform*, Am. J. Pub. Health 75(7) (1985): 727–31.

5. Family members: A. C. Dunham, *APA's Model Law: Protecting the Patient's Ultimate Interests*, Hosp. & Commun. Psychiatry 36(9) (1985): 973–75. Professionals: L. L. Bachrach, *Asylum and Chronically Ill Psychiatric Patients*, Am. J. Psychiatry 141(8) (1984): 975–78; H. R. Lamb and J. A. Talbott, *The Homeless Mentally Ill: The Perspective of the American Psychiatric Association*, J. Am. Med. A. 256(4) (1986): 498–501; A. A. Stone, *A Reponse to Comments on APA's Model Commitment Law*, Hosp. & Commun. Psychiatry 36(9) (1985): 984–89; E. F. Torrey, *Nowhere to Go: The Tragic Odyssey of the Homeless Mentally Ill* (New York: Harper & Row, 1988). The popular press: A. B. Johnson, *Out of Bedlam* (New York: Basic Books, 1990); R. J. Isaac and V. C. Armat, *Madness in the Streets* (New York: Free Press, 1990). The media: D. C. Drake, "The Forsaken," *Philadelphia Inquirer*, July 18–24, 1982; P. Earley, "Jails Are Becoming 'Dumping Grounds,' Federal Government Advisory Panel Told," *Washington Post*, June 17, 1983, p. A12; E. A. Gargan, "Ducking for Cover Over the Homeless," *New York Times*, November 27, 1983, sec. 4, p. E7, col. 1; I. Peterson, "Warm Season Masks but Doesn't End Problem of the Homeless," *New York Times*, June 3, 1983, p. A16, col. 1; "Homeless in America," *Newsweek*, January 2, 1984, p. 21.

6. J. Abramson, *The Criminalization of Mentally Disordered Behavior: Possible Side Effects of a New Mental Health Law*, Hosp. & Commun. Psychiatry 23(4) (1972): 101–5.

7. J. C. Bonovitz and E. B. Guy, *Impact of Restrictive Civil Commitment Procedures on a Prison Psychiatric Service*, Am. J. Psychiatry 136 (1979): 1045–48; J. C. Bonovitz and J. S. Bonovitz, *Diversion of the Mentally Ill Into the Criminal Justice System: The Police Intervention Perspective*, Am. J. Psychiatry 138(7) (1981): 973–76; A. A. Stone, *A Reponse to Comments on APA's Model Commitment Law*.

8. An excellent synthesis of the literature may be found in L. A Teplin, *The Criminalization of the Mentally Ill: Speculation in Search of Data*, Psychological Bull. 94 (1983): 54–67.

9. E. Bittner, *Police Discretion in Emergency Apprehension of Mentally Ill Persons*, Soc. Probs. 14 (1967): 278–92; R. Rock, M. Jacobson, and R. Janepaul, "Police Participation in Initiating Hospitalization Procedures," in *Hospitalization and Discharge of the Mentally Ill* (Chicago: University of Chicago Press, 1968); E. Sheridan and L. A. Teplin, *Police-Referred Psychiatric Emergencies: Advantages of Community Treatment*, J. Commun. Psychology 9 (1981): 140–47; L. A. Teplin, W. Filstead, G. Hefter, and E. Sheridan, *Police Involvement with the Psychiatric Emergency Patient*, Psychiatric Annals 10(5) (1980): 202–7; C. A. B. Warren, *The Social Construction of Dangerousness* (Los Angeles: University of Southern California Press, 1977).

10. In fact, according to L. A. Teplin, police contact with mentally ill persons is most likely *not* to have been the result of that person having committed a crime. Teplin shows that mentally ill persons were involved as suspects only slightly more often than would be expected by their numbers in the population. Those deemed mentally unstable are more likely to engage in behavior harmful to themselves than to others. See L. A. Teplin, *The Criminality of the Mentally Ill: A Dangerous Misconception*, Am. J. Psychiatry 142(5) (1985): 593–99.

11. Teplin, *The Criminalization of the Mentally Ill: Speculation in Search of Data*, 55. According to Teplin's research, mentally ill people are jailed, even though they do not commit serious crimes, at a rate disproportionate to their numbers in the general population. In Teplin's 1985 study, *The Criminality of the Mentally Ill*, mentally disordered people had a significantly greater chance of being arrested than nonmentally disordered citizens for similar offenses. See also, L. A. Teplin, *Criminalizing Mental Disorders: The Comparative Arrest Rate of the Mentally Ill*, Am. Psychologist 39(7) (1984): 794–803.

12. Teplin, *The Criminalization of the Mentally Ill: Speculation in Search of Data*. Most calls to the police involving the mentally ill are for minor disturbances. With informal dispositions accounting for the vast majority of all police encounters with the mentally ill, arrest is reserved for the relatively small proportion of police contacts where a mentally ill person is believed to be "unacceptable" to a hospital, intolerable to community members, or when the disturbing behavior is likely to continue unless an arrest is made. Teplin, *Criminalizing Mental Disorders: The Comparative Arrest Rate of the Mentally Ill*.

13. Teplin, *The Criminalization of the Mentally Ill: Speculation in Search of Data*.

14. Ibid.

15. S. M. Rose, *Deciphering Deinstitutionalization: Complexities in Policy and Program Analysis*, Milbank Memorial Fund Q. Health & Soc. 57(4) (1979): 429–60.

16. Aviram and Segal, *Exclusion of the Mentally Ill*.

17. J. A. Gilboy and J. R. Schmidt, *"Voluntary" Hospitalization of the Mentally Ill*, Nw. U.L. Rev. 66 (1971): 429–53.

18. Charles A. Kiesler and Amy E. Sibulkin, *Mental Hospitalization: Myths and Facts About a National Crisis* (Beverly Hills, Calif.: Sage Publications, 1987).

19. P. H. Rossi, J. D. Wright, G. A. Fisher, and G. Willis, *The Urban Homeless: Estimating Composition and Size*, Science 235 (1987): 1336–41.

20. F. Barringer, "Federal Count of Homeless is Far Below Other Figures," *New York Times*, April 12, 1991, p. A14.

21. Charles A. Kiesler and Amy E. Sibulkin, *Mental Hospitalization*.

22. J. K. Langdon and M. A. Kass, *Homelessness in America: Looking for the*

Right to Shelter, Colum. J.L. & Soc. Probs. 19 (1985): 305–92; J. Kozol, *Rachael and Her Children: Homeless Families in America* (New York: Crown Publishers, 1988).

23. E. F. Torrey, *Nowhere to Go: The Tragic Odyssey of the Homeless Mentally Ill* (1988); L. L. Bachrach, *Asylum and Chronically Ill Psychiatric Patients*, Am. J. Psychiatry 141(8) (1984): 975–78.

24. The media is represented by: Drake, "The Forsaken"; Earley, "Jails Are Becoming 'Dumping Grounds' "; Peterson, "Warm Season Masks but Doesn't End Problem of the Homeless." The sentiment of the American Psychiatry Association was expressed by C. D. Stromberg and A. A. Stone, *A Model State Law on Civil Commitment of the Mentally Ill*, Harv. J. on Legis. 20 (1983): 275–396.

25. E. L. Bassuk, L. Rubin, and A. Lauriat, *Is Homelessness a Mental Health Problem?* Am. J. Psychiatry 141(2) (1984): 1546–50.

26. L. L. Bachrach, "Asylum for Chronic Mental Patients," in L. L. Bachrach, *Leona Bachrach Speaks: Selected Speeches and Lectures*, vol. 35, *New Directions for Mental Health Services* (San Francisco, Calif.: Jossey-Bass, 1987).

27. H. H. Goldman and J. Morrissey, "Homelessness and Mental Illness in America: Emerging Issues in the Construction of a Social Problem," in *Location and Stigma, Contemporary Perspectives on Mental Health and Mental Health Care*, ed. C. J. Smith and J. A. Giggs (Boston: Allen & Unwin, 1988); D. J. Roth and G. J. Bean, *New Perspectives on Homelessness: Findings from a Statewide Epidemological Study*, Hosp. & Commun. Psychiatry 37 (1985): 712–14.

28. Part of the reason for the difficulty in obtaining an estimate is that the homeless population is so diverse that the only common denominator is their lack of a home. Most researchers have counted the homeless population in slightly different ways, thus accounting for the wide differences in estimates of the population size. As a result, one of the fundamental inquiries in understanding homelessness is to determine what proportion of homeless people are mentally ill and what proportion of the mentally ill are homeless. More generally, it is essential to examine the issue of whether homelessness is a medical or a social problem.

It was not until the mid-1980s that researchers began to approach the description of homelessness more systematically and scientifically. Early studies, which had characterized the homeless based only on interviews with or observation of people who were residents of missions, shelters, or other cheap lodgings, are responsible for some of the misconceptions about the homeless. Such sampling methods resulted in significant distortions in counting the number of certain types of homeless people, notably the mentally ill. Even when researchers made clear reference to the limitations of their study data (e.g., D. Roth, G. J. Bean, and P. S. Hyde, *Homelessness and Mental Health Policy: Developing an Appropriate Role for the 1980s*, Commun. Mental Health J. 22(3) (1986): 203–14), their findings have been used by others to generalize the homeless population at large. Recent estimates project the number of homeless to be in the range of 300,000 to 735,000. See Martha R. Burt and Barbara E. Cohen, *America's Homeless: Numbers, Characteristics, and Programs that Serve Them* (Washington, D.C., Urban Institute Press, 1989); Peter H. Rossi, *Down and Out in America: The Origins of Homelessness* (Chicago: University of Chicago Press, 1989). The 1990 U.S. Census made an attempt for the first time to count the number of homeless people in America.

29. For example, between 1970 and 1982 the number of low-cost single room occupancy dwellings (SROs) in the U.S. decreased by 1 million units. N. K. Rhoden, *The Limits of Liberty: Deinstitutionalization, Homelessness, and Libertarian Theory*, Emory L.J. 31 (1982): 375– 440.

30. See, generally, *Homelessness in America: Hearings Before the Subcomm. on Housing and Community Development of the House Comm. on Banking, Finance, and Urban Affairs*, 97th Cong., 2d Sess. (1982); *Homelessness in America-II: Hearings Before the Subcomm. on Housing and Community Development of the House Comm. on Banking, Finance, and Urban Affairs*, 98th Cong., 2d Sess. (1984). *Sewell Associates* v. *City of New York*, 534 N.Y.S.2d 958, 142 A.D.2d 72 (1988) [upholding as constitutional a New York City law providing for a five-year moratorium on the demolition or conversion of SRO—single room occupancy—housing].

31. K. Hopper, *Homelessness: Reducing the Difference*, New Eng. J. Hum. Serv. 3(4) (1983): 30–47.

32. Lamb and Talbott, *The Homeless Mentally Ill*, 498–501.

33. David Mechanic, *Correcting Misconceptions in Mental Health Policy: Strategies for Improved Care of the Seriously Mentally Ill*, Milbank Q. 65(2) (1987): 203–30.

34. Morton Kramer, *Psychiatric Services and the Changing Institutional Scene* (Rockville, Md.: U.S. Dept. of Health, Education, and Welfare, Public Health Service, Alcohol, Drug Abuse, and Mental Health Administration, 1977, DHEW publication no. (ADM) 77–433, Mental Health Statistics: Series B, Analytical and Special Study reports; no. 12).

35. Mechanic, *Correcting Misconceptions in Mental Health Policy*, 211.

36. Ibid., 213.

37. Bachrach, *Asylum and Chronically Ill Psychiatric Patients*.

38. A. S. Bellack and K. T. Meuser, *A Comprehensive Treatment Program for Schizophrenia and Chronic Mental Illness*, Commun. Mental Health J. 22(3) (1986): 175–89; Rhoden, *The Limits of Liberty*.

39. Lamb and Talbott, *The Homeless Mentally Ill*.

40. In *Donaldson*, the Supreme Court clearly indicated that it was unconstitutional to commit a mentally ill person for the reason of "pure asylum"; that is, to improve the person's standard of living. For a discussion of the *Donaldson case*, see Chapter 4.

41. This recommendation is in line with the APA's Model Commitment Law and its focus on therapeutic commitments. For example, both the Task Force and the Model Law would allow commitment of a homeless, mentally ill bag lady if she cannot make an informed treatment decision, is treatable, and refuses to seek therapy.

42. The APA did express its concern that public haste to solve the problem of homelessness might result in large-scale reinstitutionalization or inappropriate reliance on shelters.

43. Although some states require that attempts be made to collect the cost of inpatient care from patients, these attempts are rarely successful. Over 90 percent of involuntarily committed patients are unemployed at the time of their detention. See M. L. Durham and J. Q. La Fond, *The Empirical Consequences and Policy Implications of Broadening the Statutory Criteria for Civil Commitment*, Yale L. & Pol'y Rev. 3, (1985): 395–446; L. R. Faulkner, J. D. Bloom, B. H. McFarland, and T. O. Stern, *The Effect of Mental Health System Changes on Civil Commitment*, Bull. Am. Acad. Psychiatry & L. 13(4) (1985): 345–57. The states rely on Medicaid as well as state resources to support patients' hospitalization. They cannot obtain Social Security funds, since these payments stop when a person is hospitalized because of the requirement that the recipient have a home address other than an institution in order to receive benefits.

44. Quoted in H. R. Lamb and M. J. Mills, *Needed Changes in Law and Procedure for the Chronically Mentally Ill*, Hosp. & Commun. Psychiatry 37(5) (1986): 475–80, 475.

45. L. S. Rubenstein, *APA's Model Law: Hurting the People It Seeks to Help*, Hosp.& Commun. Psychiatry 36(9) (1985): 968–72.

46. W. K. Bentz and J. W. Edgerton, *Consensus on Attitudes Toward Mental Illness*, Arch. Gen. Psychiatry 22 (1970): 468–73.

47. S. Rachlin, "The Influence of Law on Deinstitutionalization," in *Deinstitutionalization*, ed. Leona L. Bachrach, vol. 17, *New Directions for Mental Health Services* (San Francisco, Calif.: Jossey-Bass, 1983), 41–54.

48. J. P. Morrissey and H. H. Goldman, *Cycles of Reform in the Care of the Chronically Mentally Ill*, Hosp. & Commun. Psychiatry 35(8) (1984): 785–93; Rothman, *Conscience and Convenience*; Gerald N. Grob, "Historical Origins of Deinstitutionalization," in *Deinstitutionalization*, vol. 17, *New Directions for Mental Health Services*.

49. G. E. Hogarty, N. R. Schooler, R. Ulrich, et al., *Fluphenazine and Social Therapy in the Aftercare of Schizophrenic Patients*, Arch. Gen. Psychiatry 36(12), (1979): 1283–94.

50. American Psychiatric Association, *Diagnostic and Statistical Manual of Mental Disorders: DSMIII-R*, 3d ed. rev. (Washington, D.C.: American Psychiatric Association, 1987).

51. See, for example, *Stamus* v. *Leonhardt*, 414 F. Supp. 439 (S.D. Iowa 1976); *Bension* v. *Meredith*, 455 F. Supp. 662 (D.D.C. 1978); *Suzuki* v. *Alba*, 438 F. Supp. 1106 (D. Haw. 1977), *modified*, 617 F.2d 173, (1980); *Lynch* v. *Baxley*, 386 F. Supp. 378 (M.D. Ala. 1974), *rev'd*, 651 F.2d 387 (1981); *Warren* v. *Harvey*, 472 F. Supp. 1061 (D. Conn. 1979), *cert. denied*, 449 U.S. 902 (1980).

52. Robert D. Miller, *Involuntary Civil Commitment of the Mentally Ill in the Post-Reform Era* (Springfield, Ill.: Charles C Thomas, 1987).

53. Rhoden, *The Limits of Liberty*.

54. S. Rachlin, *When Schizophrenia Comes Marching Home*, Psychiatric Q. 50(3) (1978): 202–10.

55. Z. M. Lebensohn, *Pilgrim's Progress, or the Tortuous Road to Mental Health*, Comprehensive Psychiatry 16(5) (1975): 415–26.

56. See, for example, *Wyatt* v. *Stickney*, 325 F. Supp. 781 (M.D. Ala. 1971); *Rone* v. *Firemen*, 473 F. Supp. 92 (N.D. Ohio 1979).

57. The American Federation of State, County and Municipal Employees (AFL-CIO) launched an all-out attack on state plans to close hospitals in California. See H. Santiestevan, *Out of Their Beds and Into the Streets* (Washington, D.C.: American Federation of State, County and Municipal Employees, 1975). North Carolina encountered a similar experience when public pressure stopped the closure of the Dorothea Dix Psychiatric Hospital. See W. A. Harrington, "Deinstitutionalization: Organizational Change in Dorothea Dix Psychiatric Hospital," in *Multi-Institutional Systems Management: Concepts and Cases*, ed. B. J. Jaeger, A. D. Kaluzny, and K. Magruder-Habib (Owings Mills, Md.: AUPHA Press, 1987), 41–52. The same story can be told for many states across America.

58. Kiesler and Sibulkin, *Mental Hospitalization*.

59. Stone, *A Reponse to Comments on APA's Model Commitment Law*, 985. Stone acknowledges the fundamental role economic factors have on the plight of the mentally ill.

60. Neal Milner, "Viewing and Assessing the Mental Patient Rights Movement" (Paper presented at Law and Society Association Meeting, San Diego, Calif., June 6–9, 1985).

61. D. Mechanic, *Mental Health and Social Policy: Initiatives for the 1980s*, Health Affairs (Project Hope) 4 (1985): 75–88.

62. Ironically, during the Liberal Era psychiatrists had often blamed families for the mental illness of one of their members. J. A. Talbott, *Response to the Presidential Address: Psychiatry's Unfinished Business in the 20th Century*, Am. J. Psychiatry 141(8) (1984): 927–30.

63. Durham and La Fond, *The Empirical Consequences and Policy Implications of Broadening the Statutory Criteria for Civil Commitment*; V. A. Hiday, *Court Decisions in Civil Commitment: Independence or Deference*, Int'l J.L. & Psychiatry 4 (1/2) (1981): 159–70.

64. D. A. Treffert, *Dying With Their Rights On*, Am. J. Psychiatry 141 (1981): 1041.

65. Neal Milner, "The Denigration and Diminishing of Rights" (Paper presented at the 14th International Congress on Law and Psychiatry, Montreal, Canada, June, 1988).

66. "Delusions About Mental Health," *New York Times*, Aug. 1, 1986, p. A26, col. 1, editorial desk; R. Sullivan, "Ferry Slashing Report Assails Hospital for Freeing Suspect," *New York Times*, July 12, 1986, p. A1, col. 1.

67. Durham and La Fond, *The Empirical Consequences and Policy Implications of Broadening the Statutory Criteria for Civil Commitment*.

68. H. Santiestevan, *Out of Their Beds and into the Streets*; Gargan, "Ducking for Cover Over the Homeless"; "Homeless in America."

69. Alaska Stat. § 47.30.915(7)(B) (1984); Ariz. Rev. Stat. Ann. § 36–501(5), (6), (14), (15) (1986, revised 1989); Hawaii Rev. Stat. Ann. § 334–1 (1988); Kan. Stat. Ann. § 59.2902(a)(2) (K.S.A. 1986 Supp.); N.C. Gen. Stat. § 122–58.2 (1981); Ore. Laws Adv. Sh. No. 2324 (1987); Tex. Civ. Ann. Art. 5547–50(b)(2)(iii) (Vernon 1987); Wash. Rev. Code Ann. § 71.05.010 (West 1975).

70. Durham and La Fond, *The Empirical Consequences and Policy Implications of Broadening the Statutory Criteria for Civil Commitment*.

71. Kiesler, "Mental Hospitals and Alternative Care."

72. N. Darnton, "Committed Youth: Why Are So Many Teens Being Locked up in Private Mental Hospitals?" *Newsweek*, July 31, 1989, pp. 66–72; John Kass, "Teen Trap: Treating Adolescents in Psychiatric Clinics: More Profit Motive than Actual Concern?" *Seattle Times*, July 9, 1989, pp. K1–2.

73. Darnton, "Committed Youth," p. 67.

74. Lois A. Wiethorn, *Mental Hospitalization of Troublesome Youth: An Analysis of Skyrocketing Admission Rates*, Stanford Law Review 40(3) (1988): 773–838.

Chapter 6

1. P. S. Appelbaum, *Civil Commitment: Is the Pendulum Changing Direction?* Hosp. & Commun. Psychiatry 33(9) (1982): 703–4; S. J. Brakel, J. Parry, and B. A. Weiner, *The Mentally Disabled and the Law*, 3d ed. (Chicago: American Bar Foundation, 1985).

2. See J. Q. La Fond, *An Examination of the Purposes of Involuntary Civil Com-*

mitment, Buffalo L. Rev. 30 (1982): 499–535; Comment, *Overt Dangerous Behavior as a Constitutional Requirement for Involuntary Civil Commitment of the Mentally Ill*, U. Chi. L. Rev. 44 (1977): 562–93.

3. Brakel, Parry, and Weiner, *The Mentally Disabled and the Law*.

4. See Chapter 5.

5. Alaska Stat. § 47.30.915(7)(B) (1984); Ariz. Rev. Stat. Ann. § 36–501(5), (6), (14), (15) (1986, revised 1989); Hawaii Rev. Stat. § 334–1 (1988); Wash. Rev. Code Ann. § 71.05.020 (West Suppl. 1991). See also, M. L. Durham and J. Q. La Fond, *The Empirical Consequences and Policy Implications of Broadening the Statutory Criteria for Civil Commitment*, Yale L. & Pol'y Rev. 3 (1985): 395– 446. Other states, including California, considered doing this, but in the end decided against it because the cost would be prohibitive.

6. Wash. Rev. Code Ann. § 71.05.020 (West 1975). Revised in 1979 Wash. Rev. Code Ann. § 71.05.012 (West Supp. 1991). See also, Durham and La Fond, *The Empirical Consequences and Policy Implications of Broadening the Statutory Criteria for Civil Commitment*.

7. See J. Gillie, "Murder Suspect was Refused Entry at Steilacoom," *Tacoma News Tribune*, Aug. 10, 1978, p. B12; M. Friedman and N. Modie, "Suspect in Slayings Tried to Get Treatment," *Seattle Post-Intelligencer*, Aug. 10, 1978, p. A1; G. Foster, "Parents Claim Law Fails the 'Chronic' Patient," *Seattle Post- Intelligencer*, Aug. 27, 1978, p. B3; T. L. Rothstein, "Care Denied to Mentally Ill," *Seattle Post-Intelligencer*, Sept. 28, 1978, p. B3; J. Hahn, "A Trail of Anguish," *Seattle Post-Intelligencer*, Nov. 4, 1978, p. A1; J. Gillie, "Group Pushes Family Action," *Tacoma News Tribune*, Nov. 5, 1978, p. F1.

8. The 1979 Involuntary Treatment Act did broaden police power commitment authority slightly by expanding the definition of "likelihood of serious harm" to include destruction of property. Thus, mentally disturbed persons who posed a "substantial risk" to the property of others could be forcibly put in hospitals. This legislation was revised, even though in *Suzuki* v. *Yuen*, 617 F.2d 173 (9th Cir. 1980), the Federal Court of Appeals for the Ninth Circuit had previously struck down a very similar Hawaii statute.

9. See Wash. Rev. Code Ann. § 71.05.020(1) (West Supp. 1984). Grave disability was defined as

> a condition in which a person, as a result of a mental disorder; (a) Is in danger of serious physical harm resulting from a failure to provide for his essential human needs of health or safety, or (b) Manifests severe deterioration in routine functioning evidenced by repeated and escalating loss of cognitive or volitional control over his or her actions and is not receiving such care as is essential for his or her health or safety.

10. The 1979 ITA was attacked as unconstitutionally vague and overbroad. The Washington Supreme Court upheld the statute; however, it effectively revised the statutory commitment criteria by requiring the government to prove that a person was "*unable* because of severe deterioration of mental functioning, to make a rational decision with respect to his need for treatment." *In re LaBelle*, 107 Wash. 2d 196, 208, 728 P.2d 138 (1986). The court affirmed the commitment of several individuals who were homeless and had planned to live in public shelters or camp in public forests.

11. *Project Release* v. *Prevost*, 551 F. Supp. 1298 (E.D.N.Y. 1982)

12. N.Y. Mental Hyg. Law § 9.27 (McKinney 1991).

13. *Project Release* v. *Prevost*, 722 F.2d 960, 972 (1983).

14. C. D. Stromberg and A. A. Stone, *A Model State Law on Civil Commitment*

of the Mentally Ill, Harv. J. Legis. 20 (1983): 275–396, 330. Model Statute, Section 6.C.

15. Stromberg and Stone, *A Model State Law on Civil Commitment of the Mentally Ill.*

16. Ibid. 281.

17. Arizona Rev. Stat. Ann. 36–520 (West Supp. 1986).

18. Arizona Rev. Stat. Ann. 36–501(29).

19. A. Arneill, *Comprehensive Analysis of Proposed Revisions to the Lanterman-Petris-Short Act*, (Sacramento, Calif.: Council on Mental Health, 1987).

20. Ibid., 8.

21. Durham and La Fond, *The Empirical Consequences and Policy Implications of Broadening the Statutory Criteria for Civil Commitment.*

22. Arneill, *Comprehensive Analysis of Proposed Revisions to the Lanterman-Petris-Short Act*; Durham and La Fond, *The Empirical Consequences and Policy Implications of Broadening the Statutory Criteria for Civil Commitment.*

23. Only 28 beds are available at Bellevue Hospital in New York City for the mentally ill homeless, even though estimates of this population are as high as 40,000 people. See S. Daley, "Koch Policy for Homeless Creates Fears," *New York Times*, October 12, 1987, p. B1, col. 6.

24. Most state laws have required that involuntary treatment be provided in the least restrictive possible settings, such as a nursing home, instead of a state hospital. Placement in the least restrictive alternative has not been widely used, however.

25. North Carolina does not permit outpatients to be given medication if they refuse. Only persuasion by a mental health professional is permitted. This system has been criticized because it does not authorize compelled treatment of a recalcitrant outpatient. See V. A. Hiday and T. L. Scheid-Cook, *The North Carolina Experience With Outpatient Commitment: A Critical Appraisal*, Int'l J.L. & Psychiatry 10(3) (1987): 215–32.

26. I. Keilitz and T. Hall, *State Statutes Governing Involuntary Outpatient Civil Commitment*, Mental & Phys. Disability L. Rep. 9(5) (1985): 378–400. See also, R. D. Luskin, *Compulsory Outpatient Treatment for the Mentally Ill*. Report to the American Psychiatric Association Task Force on Involuntary Outpatient Treatment (March 1983).

27. N.C. Gen. Stat. §§ 122C–267; See also, Hiday and Scheid-Cook, *The North Carolina Experience With Outpatient Commitment.*

28. R. D. Miller, *Involuntary Civil Commitment of the Mentally Ill in the Post-Reform Era* (Springfield, Ill.: Thomas, 1987).

29. S. Stefan, *Preventive Commitment: The Concept and Its Pitfalls*, Mental & Phys. Disability L. Rep. 11(4) (1987): 288– 304.

30. In Georgia, for example, if outpatient services are not available, a person who would otherwise meet standards for outpatient commitment but *not* inpatient hospitalization may be held in an institution until a court hearing. Ga. Code Ann. 37– 3–90 (c) (2) (1986). In North Carolina, an outpatient may be forcibly transported to a clinic appointment if he or she fails to attend voluntarily. N.C. Gen. Stat. § 122C–265 (1990).

31. Stefan, *Preventive Commitment.*

32. Miller, *Involuntary Civil Commitment.*

33. D. A. Treffert, *The Obviously Ill Patient in Need of Treatment: A Fourth Standard for Civil Commitment*, Hosp. & Commun. Psychiatry 36 (1985): 259–64.

34. *Rennie* v. *Klein*, 653 F.2d 836, 851 (3d Cir. 1981).

35. Ralph Slovenko, *Psychiatry and Law* (Boston: Little, Brown and Co., 1973), 205.

36. Brakel, Parry, and Weiner, *The Mentally Disabled and the Law*.

37. Appelbaum, *Civil Commitment*; S. Rachlin, *When Schizophrenia Comes Marching Home*, Psychiatric Q. 50(3) (1978): 202–10; Miller, *Involuntary Civil Commitment*; A. Stone, *Recent Mental Health Litigation: A Critical Perspective*, Am. J. Psychiatry 134(3) (1977): 273–79.

38. V. A. Hiday, *Civil Commitment: A Review of Empirical Research*, Behav. Sci. & L. 6(1) (1988): 15–43; C. A. B. Warren, *Involuntary Commitment for Mental Disorder: The Application of California's Lanterman-Petris-Short Act*, Law & Soc'y Rev. 11 (1977): 629–49; C. A. B. Warren, *The Social Construction of Dangerousness*, Urban Life 8 (1979): 359–84; C. A. B. Warren, *Court of Last Resort: Mental Illness and the Law* (Chicago: University of Chicago Press, 1982); Note, *Involuntary Hospitalization of the Mentally Ill in Iowa: The Failure of the 1975 Legislation*, Iowa L. Rev. 64 (1979): 1284–458.

39. Stromberg and Stone, *A Model State Law on Civil Commitment of the Mentally Ill*, 340.

40. Ibid., 323.

41. Brakel, Parry, and Weiner, *The Mentally Disabled and the Law*. Alaska has increased the length of initial detention from 72 hours to 30 days; subsequent detentions have been increased from 21 to 30 additional days, and from 120 to 180 additional days. Alaska Stat. 47.30.715 (1990).

42. Appelbaum, *Civil Commitment*.

43. 441 U.S. 418, 99 S. Ct. 1804, 60 L. Ed. 2d 323 (1979).

44. Although it is impossible to quantify the degree of certainty embodied in various standards of proof, Alan Stone has suggested that the "beyond a reasonable doubt" standard requires certainty approaching 90 percent in contrast to the 75 percent certainty required by "clear and convincing evidence." A. Stone, *Mental Health and the Law: A System in Transition* (Rockville, Md.: National Institute of Mental Health, Center for Studies of Crime and Delinquency, 1975).

45. *Addington* v. *Texas*, 441 U.S. at 428, 99 S. Ct. 1804 60 L. Ed. 2d 323 (1979).

46. *Addington* v. *Texas*, 441 U.S. at 429.

47. A handful of states insert an additional word ("clear, cogent, and convincing"—North Carolina, Washington; "clear, unequivocal, and convincing"—Alabama, Tennessee) which suggests a slightly higher standard but probably does not make any real difference. About a dozen states do not even have provisions that cover the burden of proof for the commitment process (Brakel, Parry, and Weiner, *The Mentally Disabled and the Law*), and only two states (Rhode Island and Hawaii) retain the requirement of proof beyond a reasonable doubt. (In 1986, Hawaii changed its standard so that mental illness must be proved beyond a reasonable doubt, but imminent dangerousness to self or others or grave disability may be proved by clear and convincing evidence. Hawaii Rev. Stat. Ann. 334–60.5 [1986].)

48. *Parham* v. *J. R.*, 442 U.S. 584, 99 S. Ct. 2493 61, L. Ed. 2d 101 (1979).

49. Ibid.

50. Ibid.

51. Inpatient hospitalization of adolescents increased from 82,000 in 1980 to more than 112,000 in 1986. Most of the increase was in admissions to private hospitals. N. Darnton, "Committed Youth: Why Are so Many Teens Being Locked Up in Private Mental Hospitals?" *Newsweek*, July 31, 1989, pp. 66–72.

52. Dr. Morton Birnbaum is regarded as the father of the concept of the right-

to-treatment for mental patients. In 1960 he wrote an influential article advocating recognition and enforcement of the right to adequate medical treatment for mental patients. See M. Birnbaum, *The Right to Treatment*, A.B.A.J. 46 (1960): 499–505.

53. *Rouse* v. *Cameron*, 373 F.2d 451 (D.C. Cir. 1966). In explicating this standard more fully, Judge Bazelon wrote:

> The hospital need not show that the treatment will cure or improve him but only that there is a bona fide effort to do so. This requires the hospital to show that initial and periodic inquiries are made into the needs and conditions of the patient with a view to providing suitable treatment for him and that the program provided is suited to his particular needs.

Id., 456.

54. *Wyatt* v. *Stickney*, 325 F. Supp. 781 (M.D. Ala. 1971).

55. *Donaldson* v. *O'Connor*, 493 F.2d 507 (1974), *vacated and remanded*, 422 U.S. 563 (1975).

56. It did not decide whether patients committed as dangerous to themselves or others had a "constitutional right to treatment."

57. 457 U.S. 307, 102 S. Ct. 2452, 73 L. Ed. 2d 28 (1982).

58. Ibid., 307.

59. Ibid., 323.

60. *Pennhurst* v. *Halderman*, 465 U.S. 89, 104 S. Ct. 900, 79 L. Ed. 2d 67 (1984).

61. Psychoactive drugs are given for the primary control of psychiatric symptoms. Major categories include antidepressants, antianxiety medications, antipsychotic drugs, and mood-altering agents.

62. M. L. Durham and J. Q. La Fond, *A Search for the Missing Premise of Involuntary Therapeutic Commitment: Effective Treatment of the Mentally Ill*, Rutgers L. Rev. 40 (1988): 303–68. See also, *Rennie* v. *Klein*, 462 F. Supp. 1131, 1137 (D.N.J. 1978).

63. Bruce J. Winick, *Psychotropic Medication and Competence to Stand Trial*, Am. B. Found. Res. J. 1977(3) (1977):769–816, 773– 74. *Rennie* v. *Klein*, 462 F. Supp. 1131, 1137 (D.N.J. 1978) (testimony of Dr. Stinnet).

64. For an excellent discussion of the adverse side effects of psychotropic drugs and the development of the right to refuse treatment, see A. D. Brooks, *The Right to Refuse Antipsychotic Medications: Law and Policy*, Rutgers L. Rev. 39 (1987): 339–76. See also, A. D. Brooks, *The Constitutional Right to Refuse Antipsychotic Medications*, Bull. Am. Acad. Psychiatry & L. 8 (1980): 179–221; A. D. Brooks, "The Effect of Law on the Administration of Antipsychotic Medications," in *Ethical Issues in Epidemiological Research*, ed. L. Tancredi (New Brunswick, N.J.: Rutgers University Press, 1986); A. D. Brooks, *Law and Antipsychotic Medications*, Behav. Sci. & L. 4 (1986): 247–63.

65. Brooks, *The Right to Refuse Antipsychotic Medications*. Ironically, some of these side effects mimic the symptoms of mental illness. A new side effect, called neuroleptic malignant syndrome, has recently been identified. Death can result if it is not correctly diagnosed and treated. See H. G. Pope, P. E. Keck, and S. L. McElroy, *Frequency and Presentation of Neuroleptic Malignant Syndrome in a Large Psychiatric Hospital*, Am. J. Psychiatry 143(10) (1986): 1227–33.

66. Brooks, *The Right to Refuse Antipsychotic Medications*, 348. See also, Chapter 4 for discussion of patients retaining their general legal competency even after commitment.

67. *Rennie* v. *Klein*, 462 F. Supp. 1131 (D.N.J. 1979); *Rennie* v. *Klein*, 476 F.

Supp. 1294 (D.N.J. 1979); Rogers v. Okin, 478 F. Supp. 1342 (D. Mass. 1979). Initially, in the *Rennie* case, the trial court held that a patient was entitled to the assistance of a lawyer. 462 F. Supp. at 1147. In the subsequent opinion, the trial court held that a "patient advocate," who did not have to be a lawyer, was sufficient. 478 F. Supp. at 1311–12.

68. *Rennie* v. *Klein*, 653 F.2d 836 (3d Cir. 1981).

69. Ibid., 848.

70. 478 F. Supp. 1342 (D. Mass. 1979).

71. The court said:

The First Amendment protects the communication of ideas. That protected right of communication presupposes a capacity to produce ideas. . . . Whatever powers the Constitution has granted our government, involuntary mind control is not one of them, absent extraordinary circumstances.

478 F. Supp. at 1367 (1979).

72. 457 U.S. 307, 102 S. Ct. 2452, 73 L. Ed. 2d 28 (1982).

73. Ibid.

74. *Rennie* v. *Klein*, 720 F.2d 266 (3d Cir. 1983). *On remand* from the U.S. Supreme Court.

75. *Rogers* v. *Commissioner of the Department of Mental Health*, 390 Mass. 489, 458 N.E.2d 308 (1983).

76. Cases using the "substituted judgment" approach include: *Harper* v. *State*, 110 Wash. 2d 873, 759 P.2d 358 (1988); *Riese* v. *St. Mary's Hospital and Medical Center*, 209 Cal. App. 3d 1303, 271 Cal. Rptr. 199 (1987); *Commonwealth* v. *Del Verde*, 398 Mass. 288, 496 N.E.2d 1357 (1986); *In re Schuoler*, 106 Wash. 2d 500, 723 P.2d 1103 (1986); *Matter of Guardianship of Ingram*, 102 Wash. 2d 827, 689 P.2d 1363 (1984); *In re Caulk*, 125 N.H. 226, 480 A.2d 93 (1984); *Rogers* v. *Commissioner of Dept. of Mental Health*, 390 Mass. 489, 458 N.E.2d 308(1983); *Matter of A.W.*, 637 P.2d 366 (1981); *Guardianship of Roe*, 383 Mass. 415, 421 N.E.2d 40 (1982); *Matter of Storar*, 438 N.Y.S.2d 266, 53 N.Y.2d 363, 420 N.E.2d 64 (1981); *In re K.K.B.*, 609 P.2d 747 (1980), *Mills* v. *Rogers*, 457 U.S. 291, 102 S. Ct. 244, 273 L. Ed. 2d 16 (1982); *Rogers* v. *Okin*, 738 F.2d 1 (1st Cir. 1984); *Project Release* v. *Prevost*, 722 F.2d 960 (2d Cir. 1982); *Lojuk* v. *Quandt*, 706 F.2d 1456 (7th Cir. 1982); *Rogers* v. *Okin*, 634 F.2d 650 (1st Cir. 1982); *Ross* v. *Hilltop Rehabilitation Hospital*, 676 F. Supp. 1528, 56 U.S.L.W. 2398 (D.D. Colo. 1988).

77. See *R.A.J.* v. *Miller*, 590 F. Supp. 1319 (N.D. Tex. 1984).

78. *Washington* v. *Harper*, 489 U.S. 1064, 109 S. Ct. 1337, 103 L. Ed. 2d (1989).

79. In order to be committed for thirty days under the model statute, the court must determine on the basis of clear and convincing evidence that

1. The person is suffering from a severe mental disorder; and
2. There is a reasonable prospect that his disorder is treatable at or through the facility to which he is to be committed, and such commitment would be consistent with the least restrictive alternative principle; and
3. The person either refuses or is unable to consent to voluntary admission for treatment; and
4. The person lacks capacity to make an informed decision concerning treatment; and
5. As the result of the severe mental disorder, the person is (a) likely to cause harm to himself or to suffer substantial mental or physical deterioration, or (b) likely to cause harm to others.

See Stromberg and Stone, *A Model State Law on Civil Commitment of the Mentally Ill.*

80. Section 4 of the Model Law permits an examining psychiatrist to confine a person in an evaluation and treatment facility if he determines that "the person suffers from a severe mental disorder as the result of which: he *lacks capacity to make an informed decision concerning treatment*" [emphasis added]. Stromberg and Stone, *A Model State Law on Civil Commitment of the Mentally Ill*, 302–3.

81. Psychiatrists would still be liable in tort for any damage done through their conduct that is either negligent or grossly negligent, depending on what standard of care is used by the jurisdiction. Nor could they perform psychosurgery on involuntary patients.

82. Stromberg and Stone, pp. 349–57, also discuss the arguments against the right to refuse treatment.

83. *Shelton* v. *Tucker*, 364 U.S. 479, 81 S. Ct. 247, 5 L. Ed. 2d 231 (1960).

84. *Lake* v. *Cameron*, 364 F.2d 657 (D.C. Cir. 1966); *Lynch* v. *Baxley*, 386 F. Supp. 378, 392, note 10 (M.D. Ala. 1974); *Stamus* v. *Leonhardt*, 414 F. Supp. 439 (S.D. Iowa 1976); *Lessard* v. *Schmidt*, 349 F. Supp. 1078 (E.D. Wis. 1972), *vacated on other grounds and remanded*, 414 U.S. 473, *judgment modified on other grounds and reinstated*, 379 F. Supp. 1376 (E.D. Wis. 1974), 421 U.S. 957 (1975). See also, D. L. Chambers, *Alternatives to Civil Commitment of the Mentally Ill: Practical Guides and Constitutional Imperatives*, Mich. L. Rev. 70 (1972): 1107–200; P. B. Hoffman and L. L. Foust, *Least Restrictive Treatment of the Mentally Ill: A Doctrine in Search of Its Sense*, San Diego L. Rev. 14 (1977): 1100–54; R. G. Spece, *Preserving the Right to Treatment: A Critical Assessment and Constructive Development of Constitutional Right to Treatment Theories*, Ariz. L. Rev. 20 (1978): 1–47.

85. Brakel, Parry, and Weiner, *The Mentally Disabled and the Law*, 266. For a more thorough discussion of this doctrine, see Hoffman and Foust, *Least Restrictive Treatment of the Mentally Ill.*

86. *Lake* v. *Cameron*, 364 F.2d 657 (D.C. Cir. 1966); *In re Walls*, 442 F.2d 749 (D.C. Cir. 1971); *Stamus* v. *Leonhardt*, 414 F. Supp. 439 (S.D. Iowa 1976); *Dixon* v. *Attorney General*, 325 F. Supp. 966 (M.D. Pa. 1971).

87. *Eubanks* v. *Clarke*, 434 F. Supp. 1022 (E.D. Pa. 1977). *Ploof* v. *Brooks*, 342 F. Supp. 999 (D. Vt. 1972); *In re D.D.*, 118 N.J. Super. 1, 285 A.2d 283 (1971); *Keeselbrenner* v. *Anonymous*, 33 N.Y.2d 161, 305 N.E.2d 903, 350 N.Y.S.2d 893 (1973).

88. *Brewster* v. *Dukakis*, 786 F.2d 16 (1st Cir. 1986). See also, *Wuori* v. *Zitnay*, No. 75-80-SD (D. Me. July 14, 1978), Mental Disability L. Rep. 2 (1978): 693, 729; *New York State Association for Retarded Children and Parisi* v. *Rockefeller*, 357 F. Supp. 752 (E.D.N.Y. 1973); *NYSARC* v. *Carey*, No. 72-C-356/357 (E.D.N.Y. April 30, 1975), *approved* 393 F. Supp. 715 (E.D.N.Y. 1975); *Klosterman* v. *Cuomo*, 463 N.E.2d 588, 61 N.Y.2d 525, 475 N.Y.S.2d 247 (1984); *Morales* v. *Turman*, 364 F. Supp. 166 (E.D. Tex. 1973).

89. See *United States* v. *Charters*. 829 F.2d 479, 493 (4th Cir. 1987); *Bee* v. *Greaves*, 744 F.2d 1387,1396 (10th Cir. 1984).

90. *Rone* v. *Fireman*, 473 F. Supp. 92 (D. Ohio 1979); *Garrity* v. *Gallen*, 522 F. Supp. 171 (D.N.H. 1981); *Society for Goodwill to Retarded Children, Inc.* v. *Cuomo*, No. 83–7621 (2d Cir. June 13, 1984); *Johnson* v. *Brelje*, 701 F.2d 1201 (7th Cir. 1983); *Phillips* v. *Thompson*, 715 F.2d 365 (7th Cir. 1983).

91. Brakel, Parry, and Weiner, *The Mentally Disabled and the Law*, 621, citing

Halderman v. *Pennhurst State School & Hosp.*, No. 78–1490 (3d Cir. *filed* Apr. 24, 1984), Mental & Phys. Disability L. Rep. 8(3) (1984): 296–97.

92. *Youngberg* v. *Romeo*, 457 U.S. 307, 102 S. Ct. 2452, 73 L. Ed. 2d 28 (1982).

93. Miller, *Involuntary Civil Commitment*, 119. See also, J. Parry, *Youngberg and Pennhurst II Revisited—Part I*, Mental & Phys. Disability L. Rep. 10(3) (1986): 154–258, 213.

94. *Goebel* v. *Colorado Dept. of Institutions*, 764 P.2d 785 (Colo. 1988).

95. See Durham and La Fond, *A Search for the Missing Premise of Involuntary Therapeutic Commitment*, 313–17. Treatment for involuntary mental patients is required by statute in forty-nine states and the District of Columbia.

Chapter 7

1. R. A. Pasewark, *Insanity Plea: A Review of the Research Literature*, J. Psychiatry & L. 9 (1981): 357–401; A. R. Matthews, *Mental Disability and the Law*, (Chicago: American Bar Association, 1970); R. A. Pasewark and P. L. Craig, *Insanity Plea: Defense Attorneys' Views*, J. Psychiatry & L. 8 (1980): 413–41; M. L. Criss and D. R. Racine, *Impact of Change in Legal Standard for Those Adjudicated Not Guilty by Reason of Insanity, 1975–1979*, Bull. Am. Acad. Psychiatry & L. 8 (1980): 261–71. The actual number of insanity pleas are unknown because of pleading practices in the United States and the lack of interest shown by states in maintaining any systematic record of the use of NGRI pleas. For this, see Pasewark, *Insanity Plea*; B. Sales and T. Hafemeister, "Empiricism and Legal Policy on the Insanity Defense," in *Mental Health and Criminal Justice*, ed. L. Teplin (Beverly Hills, Calif.: Sage Publications, 1984), 253–78. Actual estimates of the success rate of the NGRI plea range from less than 1 percent (R. A. Pasewark and J. L. Pantle, *Insanity Plea: Legislators' View*, Am. J. Psychiatry 136(2) (1979): 222–23) to 25 percent (H. J. Steadman et. al. *Factors Associated with a Successful Insanity Defense*, Am. J. Psychiatry 140(4) (1983): 401–5); to a high of 36 percent (M. Perlin, *Whose Plea Is It Anyway? Insanity Defense Myths and Realities*, Philadelphia Medicine 79 (1983): 5–10).

2. Pasewark and Craig, *Insanity Plea: Defense Attorneys' Views*; N. M. Burton and H. J. Steadman, *Legal Professionals' Perceptions of the Insanity Defense*, J. Psychiatry & L. 6 (1978): 173–87; Pasewark and Pantle, *Insanity Plea: Legislators' View*; Pasewark, *Insanity Plea*; R. A. Pasewark and D. Seidenzahl, *Opinions Concerning the Insanity Plea and Criminality Among Mental Patients*, Bull. Am. Acad. Psychiatry & L. 7 (1979): 199–202; R. A. Pasewark, D. Seidenzahl, and J. L. Pantle, *Opinions About the Insanity Plea*, J. Forensic Psychology 8 (1981): 63. See also, V. Hans, *An Analysis of Public Attitudes Toward an Insanity Defense*, Criminology 24 (1986): 393–414; I. Arafat and K. McCahery, *The Insanity Defense and the Juror*, Drake L. Rev. 23 (1973): 538–49; H. J. Steadman and J. J. Cocozza, *Selective Reporting and the Public's Misconceptions of the Criminally Insane*, Pub. Opinion Q. 41 (1978): 523.

3. J. Petrila, *The Insanity Defense and Other Mental Health Dispositions in Missouri*, Int'l J.L. & Psychiatry 5 (1982): 81–101; J. L. Rogers, W. H. Sack, J. D. Bloom, and S. M. Manson, *Women in Oregon's Insanity Defense System*, J. Psychiatry & L. 11 (1983): 515; J. L. Rogers and J. D. Bloom, *Characteristics of Persons Committed to Oregon's Psychiatric Security Review Board*, Bull. Am. Acad. Psychiatry L. 10(3)

(1982): 155–64. Studies have been conducted in Michigan: G. Cooke and C. Sikorski, *Factors Affecting Length of Hospitalization in Persons Adjudicated Not Guilty by Reason of Insanity*, Bull. Am. Acad. Psychiatry & L. 2 (1974): 251– 61; New York: H. J. Steadman, *Insanity Acquittals in New York: 1965–1978*, Am. J. Psychiatry 137(3) (1980): 321–26; Connecticut: B. L. Phillips and R. A. Pasewark, *Insanity Pleas in Connecticut*, Bull. Am. Acad. Psychiatry & L. 8(3) (1980): 335–44; and New Jersey: A. Singer, *Insanity Acquittals in the Seventies: Observations and Empirical Analysis of One Jurisdiction*, Mental Disability L. Rep. 2 (1978): 406–17. For a general discussion of the empirical research in this area, see C. E. Boehnert, *Psychological and Demographic Factors Associated with Individuals Using the Insanity Defense*, J. Psychiatry L. 13 (1985): 9; H. J. Steadman, *Empirical Research on the Insanity Defense*, Annals Am. Acad. Pol. & Soc. Sci. 477 (1985): 58–71; H. J. Steadman and J. Braff, "Defendants Not Guilty by Reason of Insanity," in *Mentally Disordered Offenders*, ed. J. Monahan and H. J. Steadman (New York: Plenum, 1983), 109– 29; I. Keilitz, *Researching and Reforming the Insanity Defense*, Rutgers L. Rev. 39 (1987): 289–322; H. J. Steadman, *Mental Health Law and the Criminal Offender: Research Directions for the 1990's*, Rutgers L. Rev. 39 (1987): 323–37; R. A. Pasewark and H. McGinley, *Insanity Plea: National Survey of Frequency and Success*, J. Psychiatry & L. 13 (Spring–Summer 1985): 101–8; Sales and Hafemeister, "Empiricism and Legal Policy on the Insanity Defense," 253–70; Pasewark, *Insanity Plea*, 357.

4. Phillips and Pasewark, *Insanity Pleas in Connecticut*; R. A. Pasewark, R. L. Pantle, and H. J. Steadman, *Characteristics and Disposition of Persons Found Not Guilty by Reason of Insanity in New York State, 1971–1976*, Am. J. Psychiatry 136 (1979): 655– 60; M. Perlin, *Mental Disability Law: Civil and Criminal*, vol. 3 (Charlottesville, Va.: Michie Company, 1989); Cooke and Sikorski, *Factors Affecting Length of Hospitalization in Persons Adjudicated Not Guilty by Reason of Insanity*; Criss and Racine, *Impact of Change in Legal Standard*; W. R. Morrow and D. B. Peterson, *Follow-up on Discharged Offenders—"Not Guilty by Reason of Insanity" and "Criminal Sexual Psychopaths,"* J. Crim. L., Criminology & Police Sci. 57 (1966): 31–34; R. A. Pasewark, M. L. Pantle, and H. J. Steadman, *The Insanity Plea in New York State, 1965–1976*, N.Y. St. Bar J. 53 (1979): 186–89, 217–225; Rogers and Bloom, *Characteristics of Persons Committed to Oregon's Psychiatric Security Review Board*; Singer, *Insanity Acquittals in the Seventies*; Petrila, *The Insanity Defense and Other Mental Health Dispositions in Missouri*; Steadman, *Empirical Research on the Insanity Defense*; Sales and Hafemeister, "Empiricism and Legal Policy on the Insanity Defense."

5. Pasewark, *Insanity Plea*.

6. H. J. Steadman, *Beating a Rap? Defendants Found Incompetent to Stand Trial* (Chicago: University of Chicago Press, 1981).

7. Steadman, *Empirical Research on the Insanity Defense*. Dr. Henry Steadman gives a straightforward discussion of the difficulties in estimating how long defendants acquitted by reason of insanity are detained. See also, J. H. Rodriguez, L. M. LeWinn, and M. Perlin, *The Insanity Defense Under Siege: Legislative Assaults and Legal Rejoinders*, Rutgers L.J. 14 (1983): 397–430; Steadman and Braff, "Defendants Not Guilty by Reason of Insanity"; M. Perlin, *The Supreme Court, the Mentally Disabled Criminal Defendant, and Symbolic Values: Random Decisions, Hidden Rationales, or "Doctrinal Abyss"?* Ariz. L. Rev. 29 (1987): 1–98.

8. Steadman, *Empirical Research on the Insanity Defense*, 66.

9. J. Braff, T. Arvanites, and H. J. Steadman, *Detention Patterns of Successful and Unsuccessful Insanity Defendants*, Criminology 21 (1983): 439–48.

10. Rogers and Bloom, *Characteristics of Persons Committed to Oregon's Psychiatric Security Review Board*; R. L. Pantle, R. A. Pasewark, and H. J. Steadman, *Comparing Institutionalization Periods and Subsequent Arrests of Insanity Acquittees and Convicted Felons*, J. Psychiatry & L. 8 (1980): 305–16; R. A. Pasewark, S. Bieber, K. J. Bosten, M. Kiser, and H. J. Steadman, *Criminal Recidivism Among Insanity Acquittees*, Int'l J.L. & Psychiatry 5 (1982): 365–75; Steadman, *Empirical Research on the Insanity Defense*.

11. Steadman, *Empirical Research on the Insanity Defense*; Steadman et al., *Factors Associated with a Successful Insanity Defense*. A number of studies have described the general characteristics of the NGRI population and found that they tend to be unmarried males in their late twenties to mid-thirties and disproportionately white when compared with state prison inmates. Many lack a high school education and are unskilled or unemployed at the time of their arrest. Since states are not required to keep statistics on either the number or characteristics of individuals who plead insanity or those who are excused from their crimes for this reason, it has been extremely difficult to learn much about this group of offenders.

At least one major study is currently being funded by the National Institute of Mental Health to study insanity defense reforms since the *Hinckley* decision. The study team, led by Dr. Henry Steadman, should accumulate the best data to date on many of these issues. However, this still will not provide a nationwide, ongoing count and description of insanity acquittees and other mentally ill offenders.

12. For a discussion of the insanity defense throughout history, see Perlin, *Mental Disability Law*, 279–317. See also, *American Psychiatric Association Statement on the Insanity Defense, Issues in Forensic Psychiatry: Insanity Defense, Hospitalization of Adults, Model Civil Commitment Law, Sentencing Process, Child Custody*, Consultation 5 (1984): 15– 16.

13. I. Keilitz, *Researching and Reforming the Insanity Defense*, Rutgers L. Rev. 39 (1987): 289–322, 299.

14. Ibid.

15. R. Arens, *The Durham Rule in Action: Judicial Psychiatry and Psychiatric Justice*, Law & Soc. Rev. 1(2) (1967): 41–80. It is important to note that Arens's data cannot rule out a number of other factors that may have resulted in the irregular pattern of increases observed between 1954 and 1962. Most important, the largest increases occurred more than five years after the *Durham* decision, after court rulings and legislation had already limited the scope of the *Durham* test.

16. S. E. Reynolds, *Battle of the Experts Revisited: 1983 Oregon Legislation on the Insanity Defense*, Willamette L. Rev. 20 (1984): 303–17; R. H. Sauer and P. M. Mullins, *The Insanity Defense: McNaughtan [sic] vs. ALI*, Bull. Am. Acad. Psychiatry & L. 4 (1976): 73. The Sauer and Mullins study had a very weak research design because it used a single point in time on either side of the legal change to represent insanity defense practices. There is absolutely no way to rule out alternative explanations for the changes that were observed after the ALI test was adopted.

17. Pasewark, *Insanity Plea*; Keilitz, *Researching and Reforming the Insanity Defense*.

18. This is especially true when demographic changes result in the growth of specific populations who are at higher risk for both criminal behavior and psychiatric impairment; for example, young adults are at higher risk for schizophrenia and many types of criminal behavior.

19. Pasewark, Pantle, and Steadman, *The Insanity Plea in New York State, 1965–1976*.

20. Singer, *Insanity Acquittals in the Seventies*. This is not to suggest that court decisions always lead to measurable changes in insanity acquittal practices. In a study of 200 years of NGRI pleas in Great Britain, researchers found that the success rate of such pleas did not vary significantly following important court decisions. Although a national study to observe these types of patterns in the United States would be illuminating, it would be impossible because no data are kept to track such cases. See also, Nigel Walker, *Crime and Insanity in England*, vol. 1 (Edinburgh: Edinburgh University Press, 1968); Nigel Walker and Sarah McCabe, *Crime and Insanity in England*, vol. 2 (Edinburgh: Edinburgh University Press, 1973).

21. Michigan (1975), Indiana (1980), and Illinois (1981) passed legislation providing for a guilty but mentally ill verdict prior to the *Hinckley* verdict.

22. As Callahan and her colleagues point out, it is a moot question as to whether or not the legal changes that occurred after *Hinckley* were precipitated by that case or if they were due to other developments. See L. A. Callahan, C. Mayer, and H. J. Steadman, *Insanity Defense Reform in the United States—Post-Hinckley*, Mental & Phys. Disability L. Rep. 11(1) (1987): 54–59; Also see, G. Geis and R. F. Meier, *Abolition of the Insanity Plea in Idaho: A Case Study*, Annals Am. Acad. Pol. & Soc. Sci. 477 (1985): 72–83; T. Gest, "Hinckley Bombshell: End of Insanity Pleas?" *U.S. News and World Report*, July 5, 1982, p. 12; E. R. Isaacson, "Insane on All Counts; After Tortuous Deliberations, Jury Acquits John Hinckley," *Time*, July 5, 1982, p. 22.

For a discussion of how cases such as *People* v. *McQuillan* (392 Mich. 511, 221 N.W. 2d 569 [1974]) become catalysts for reform, see Keilitz, *Researching and Reforming the Insanity Defense*; and I. Keilitz et al., "Catalysts for Reform," in *The Guilty But Mentally Ill Verdict: An Empirical Study, Final Report of the Guilty But Mentally Ill Project*, Part 2 (Williamsburg, Va.: Institute on Mental Disability and the Law, 1984).

23. The effective dates of GBMI legislation are: Michigan, August 6, 1975; Indiana, September 1, 1980; Illinois, September 17, 1981; New Mexico, May 19, 1982; Georgia, July 1, 1982; Delaware, July 2, 1982; Kentucky, July 15, 1982; Alaska, October 1, 1982; Pennsylvania, March 15, 1983; South Dakota, March 19, 1983; Utah, March 31, 1983. The federal courts made several revisions in 1984. *People* v. *McQuillan* was decided in 1974; John Hinckley attempted to assassinate Ronald Reagan on March 30, 1981. He was found not guilty by reason of insanity on June 21, 1982. See Keilitz, *Researching and Reforming the Insanity Defense*.

24. Keilitz, *Researching and Reforming the Insanity Defense*.

25. Attorneys, judges, and juries in eleven states used the GBMI option in about 800 cases between 1975 and 1984. Keilitz et al., "Catalysts for Reform." See also, Steadman, *Empirical Research on the Insanity Defense*. Even though no decrease appears to have occurred in the number of insanity acquittals, Keilitz believes that the availability of the GBMI alternative may have influenced the type of person who is acquitted by reason of insanity. In Illinois, fewer successful NGRI defendants were diagnosed as psychotic than before the enactment of the GBMI law (70 versus 51 percent), and the average length of confinement dropped from just over two years to slightly over six months. Keilitz, *Researching and Reforming the Insanity Defense*.

26. M. A. McGreevy, H. J. Steadman, and L. A. Callahan, *The Negligible Effects of California's 1982 Reform of the Insanity Defense Test*, Am. J. Psychiatry 148(6) (June 1991): 744–50.

27. Keilitz, *Researching and Reforming the Insanity Defense*.

28. Ibid.

29. H. J. Steadman, L. A. Callahan, P. C. Robbins, and J. P. Morrissey, *Maintenance of an Insanity Defense Under Montana's "Abolition" of the Insanity Defense*, Am. J. Psychiatry 146 (1989): 357–60, 357.

30. Callahan, Mayer, and Steadman, *Insanity Defense Reform in the United States—Post-Hinckley*.

31. Rodriguez, LeWinn, and Perlin, *The Insanity Defense Under Siege*.

32. According to estimates from the National Institute of Mental Health (NIMH), in 1980 there were 306,468 involuntary and 838,317 voluntary commitments to the inpatient psychiatric services of state and county mental hospitals, private psychiatric hospitals, and the inpatient psychiatric services of nonfederal general hospitals. An additional 31,773 involuntary criminal commitments also took place in these hospitals during 1980. Males make up 62 percent of the committed population, with nonwhites overrepresented relative to the general population (37 percent of committees). Schizophrenia is the most frequent diagnosis, comprising 42 percent of all state and county mental hospital admissions. M. Rosenstein, H. J. Steadman, R. MacAskill, and R. Manderscheid, *Legal Status of Admission to Three Inpatient Psychiatric Settings, United States (1980)*, Mental Health Statistical Note No. 178 (Washington, D.C.: U.S. Dept. of Health and Human Services, 1986). A large number of studies have found that 90 percent or more of state mental patients are unemployed. M. L. Durham and J. Q. La Fond, *The Empirical Consequences and Policy Implications of Broadening the Statutory Criteria for Civil Commitment*, Yale L. & Pol'y Rev. 3 (1985): 395–446; L. R. Faulkner, J. D. Bloom, B. H. McFarland, and T. O. Stern, *The Effect of Mental Health System Changes on Civil Commitment*, Bull. Am. Acad. Psychiatry & L. 13 (1985): 345–57.

33. The evidence has been summarized in J. K. Myers, M. M. Weissman, G. L. Tischler, C. E. Holzer, P. J. Leaf, H. Orvaschell, J. C. Anthony, J. H. Boyd, J. D. Burke, M. Kramer, and R. Stoltzman, *Six-Month Prevalence of Psychiatric Disorders in Three Communities*, Arch. Gen. Psychiatry 41(10) (1984): 959–67.

34. V. A. Hiday, *Civil Commitment: A Review of the Empirical Research*, Behav. Sci. & L. 6 (1988): 15–43.

35. V. A. Hiday, *Judicial Decisions in Civil Commitment*, Law & Soc. Rev. 17 (1983): 517–30; S. Splane, J. Monahan, D. Prestholt, and H. D. Friedlander, *Patients' Perceptions of the Family Role in Involuntary Commitment*, Hosp. & Commun. Psychiatry 33(7) (1982): 569–72; C. A. B. Warren, *Court of Last Resort: Judicial Review of Involuntary Civil Commitment in California* (Chicago: University of Chicago Press, 1982); M. L. Durham, H. D. Carr, and G. L. Pierce, *Police Involvement in Involuntary Civil Commitment*, Hosp. & Commun. Psychiatry 35(6) (1984): 580–84.

36. V. A. Hiday, and T. L. Scheid-Cook, *The North Carolina Experience with Outpatient Commitment: A Critical Appraisal*, Int'l J.L. & Psychiatry 10(3) (1987): 215–32; S. K. Hoge, P. S. Appelbaum, and A. Greer, *An Empirical Comparison of the Stone and Dangerousness Criteria for Civil Commitment*, Am. J. Psychiatry 146(2) (1989): 170–75; H. Mahler and B. T. Co, *Who Are the "Committed"?: Update*, J. Nervous & Mental Disease 172(4) (1984): 189–96; R. A. Nicholson, *Correlates of Commitment Status in Psychiatric Patients*, Psychological Bull. 100 (1986): 241–50; E. S. Rofman, C. Askinazi, and E. Fant, *The Prediction of Dangerous Behavior in Emergency Civil Commitment*, Am. J. Psychiatry 137(9) (1980): 1061–64; S. P. Segal, M. A. Watson, S. M. Goldfinger, and D. S. Averbuck, Civil commitment in the psychiatric emergency room. II: Mental disorder indicators and three dangerousness criteria. Arch. Gen. Psychiatry 45 (1988): 753–8; J. H. Shore, W. Breakey, and B.

Arvidson, *Morbidity and Mortality in the Commitment Process*, Arch. Gen. Psychiatry 38 (1981): 930–34; Warren, *Court of Last Resort: Judicial Review*; Hiday, *Civil Commitment*.

37. M. L. Durham and G. L. Pierce, *Legal Intervention in Civil Commitment: The Impact of Broadened Commitment Criteria*, Annals Am. Acad. Pol. & Soc. Sci. 414 (1986): 42–55; Hiday, *Civil Commitment*; V. A. Hiday, *Reformed Commitment Procedures: An Empirical Study in the Courtroom*, Law & Soc. Rev. 11 (1977): 652–66; V. A. Hiday, *The Role of Counsel in Civil Commitment: Changes, Effects, Determinants*, J. Psychiatry & L. 5 (1977): 551– 69; Mahler and Co, *Who Are the "Committed"?*; G. L. Pierce, M. L. Durham, and W. H. Fisher, *The Impact of Broadened Civil Commitment Standards on Admission to State Mental Hospitals*, Am. J. Psychiatry 142 (1985): 104–7; Warren, *Court of Last Resort: Judicial Review*; J. A. Yesavage, P. D. Werner, J. M. T. Becker, and M. J. Mills, *The Context of Involuntary Commitment on the Basis of Danger to Others*, J. Nervous & Mental Disease 170(10) (1982): 622–27; J. A. Yesavage, P. D. Werner, J. M. T. Becker, and M. J. Mills, *Short-Term Civil Commitment and the Violent Patient: A Study of Legal Status and Inpatient Behavior*, Am. J. Psychiatry 139(9) (1982): 1145–49.

38. A few courts have required proof of a recent overt dangerous act before permitting commitment of a citizen as dangerous. Comment, *Overt Dangerous Behavior as a Constitutional Requirement for Involuntary Civil Commitment of the Mentally Ill*, U. Chi. L. Rev. 44 (1977): 562–93.

39. Danger to property is a criterion for commitment in some states, although its constitutionality has been disputed. See *Suzuki* v. *Yuen*, 617 F.2d 173 (9th Cir. 1980).

40. Although medical and legal records might be expected to contain accurate notations of the behavior that prompted commitment proceedings, they contain serious biases in reporting. Legal records contain allegations and conclusory statements that may be unsubstantiated in the courtroom. Medical records often report behavior that physicians or hospital officials have not observed firsthand. Research studies that collect data through courtroom observation are limited to those cases which reach a judge and exclude uncontested cases or those patients who, faced with involuntary commitment, agree to voluntary detention. For a discussion of the sources of bias in research of this nature, see Hiday, *Civil Commitment*. See also, J. Monahan, M. Ruggiero, and H. D. Friedlanger, *Stone-Roth Model of Civil Commitment and the California Dangerousness Standard*, Arch. Gen. Psychiatry 39 (1982): 1267–71; M. J. Mills, *Civil Commitment of the Mentally Ill: An Overview*, Annals Am. Acad. Pol. Soc. Sci. 484 (1986): 28–41; L. C. Rubin and M. J. Mills, *Behavioral Precipitants to Civil Commitment*, Am. J. Psychiatry 140(5) (1983): 1061–64; Warren, *Court of Last Resort: Judicial Review*; C. A. B. Warren, *The Social Construction of Dangerousness*, Urban Life 8 (1979): 359–84; Rofman, Askinazi, and Fant, *The Prediction of Dangerous Behavior in Emergency Civil Commitment*.

41. R. Peters, K. S. Miller, W. Schmidt, and D. Meeter, *The Effects of Statutory Change on the Civil Commitment of the Mentally Ill*, Law & Hum. Behav. 11 (1987): 73–99. See also, Durham, Carr, and Pierce, *Police Involvement in Involuntary Civil Commitment*; Hiday, *Civil Commitment*; Warren, *The Social Construction of Dangerousness*; Rofman, Askinazi, and Fant, *The Prediction of Dangerous Behavior in Emergency Civil Commitment*.

42. V. A. Hiday, *Arrest and Incarceration of Civil Commitment Candidates*, Hosp. & Commun. Psychiatry 42(7) (1991): 729–34.

43. Rofman, Askinazi, and Fant, *The Prediction of Dangerous Behavior in Emergency Civil Commitment*; J. A. Yesavage, *A Study of Mandatory Review of Civil*

Commitment, Arch. Gen. Psychiatry 41 (1984): 305–8; Yesavage, Werner, Becker, and Mills, *The Context of Involuntary Commitment on the Basis of Danger to Others*; Yesavage, Werner, Becker, and Mills, *Short-Term Civil Commitment and the Violent Patient*; D. E. McNeil and R. L. Binder, *Violence, Civil Commitment and Hospitalization*, J. Nervous & Mental Disease 174(2) (1986): 107–11; P. D. Werner, J. A. Yesavage, J. M. T. Becker, D. W. Brunsting, and J. Issacs, *Hostile Worlds and Assaultive Behavior on an Acute Inpatient Unit*, J. Nervous & Mental Disease 171(6) (1983): 385–87; Hiday, *Civil Commitment*.

44. J. Rabkin, *Criminal Behavior of Discharged Mental Patients: A Critical Appraisal of the Research*, Psychological Bull. 86 (1979): 1–27; and J. Monahan and H. J. Steadman, "Crime and Mental Disorder: An Epidemiological Approach," in *Crime and Justice: An Annual Review of Research*, ed. M. Tonrey and N. Morris (Chicago: University of Chicago Press, 1982). This compares with an arrest rate of approximately two times greater than the general population for inpatients admitted to community mental health centers.

45. Shore, Breakey, and Arvidson, *Morbidity and Mortality in the Commitment Process*. While the suicides clearly signified that a subgroup of ex-patients were dangerous to themselves, the authors did not consider the deaths from medical causes to be the result of psychiatric problems.

46. Stjepan Mestrovic, *Admission Patterns at South Carolina's State Psychiatric Hospitals Following Legislative Reform*, J. Psychiatry & L. 10 (1982): 457–69; D. Wexler, *Mental Health Law: Major Issues*, Perspectives in Law and Psychology Series (New York: Plenum Press, 1981); C. A. B. Warren, *Involuntary Commitment for Mental Disorder: The Application of California's Lanterman-Petris-Short Act*, Law & Soc. Rev. 11 (1977): 629–50.

47. The studies whose research designs actually allow measurement of the effects of a statutory commitment scheme are those which compare data collected during a period prior to implementation of the new law with data obtained after the revised law is in place. The clinical literature is full of observational reports that describe committed patients and their confinement and treatment experiences. Unfortunately, those studies have little to offer on the question of whether or not the law had any impact on involuntary commitment practices. See P. S. Appelbaum, *Standards for Civil Commitment: A Critical Review of Empirical Research*, Am. J.L. & Psychiatry 7 (1984): 133–44; R. Michael Bagby and Leslie Atkinson, *The Effects of Legislative Reform on Civil Commitment Admission Rates: A Critical Analysis*, Behav. Sci. & L. 6(1) (1988): 45–61; M. L. Durham and J. Q. La Fond, *A Search for the Missing Premise of Involuntary Therapeutic Commitment: Effective Treatment of the Mentally Ill*, Rutgers L. Rev. 40 (1987): 303–68.

48. Bagby and Atkinson, *The Effects of Legislative Reform on Civil Commitment Admission Rates*.

49. V. A. Hiday, "New Involuntary Commitment Legislation: Impact on State Mental Hospitals" (Unpublished manuscript, Department of Psychiatry, Duke University, 1979); H. R. Lamb, A. P. Sorkin, and J. Zusman, *Legislating the Control of the Mentally Ill in California*, Am. J. Psychiatry 138(3) (1981): 334–39; L. R. Faulkner, J. D. Bloom, and K. Kuhndahl-Stanley, *Effects of a New Involuntary Civil Commitment Law: Expectations and Reality*, Bull. Amer. Acad. Psychiatry & L. 10(4) (1982): 249–59; R. M. Bagby, *The Effects of Legislative Reform on Admission Rates to Psychiatric Units of General Hospitals*, Int'l J.L. & Psychiatry 10 (1987): 383–94; R. M. Bagby, I. Silverman, D. P. Ryan, and S. E. Dickens, *The Effects of Legislative Reform in Ontario*, Canadian Psychology 28 (1987): 21–29.

50. Bagby and Atkinson, *The Effects of Legislative Reform on Civil Commitment Admission Rates*; Bagby, Silverman, Ryan, and Dickens, *The Effects of Legislative Reform in Ontario*.

51. Warren, *Involuntary Commitment for Mental Disorder*; V. A. Hiday, *The Sociology of Mental Health Law*, Sociol. & Soc. Res. 67(2) (1983): 111–28; Peters, Miller, Schmidt, and Meeter, *The Effects of Statutory Change on the Civil Commitment of the Mentally Ill*; S. Page, *Civil Commitment: Operational Definition of New Criteria*, Canadian J. Psychiatry 26 (1981): 419– 20; Hiday, "New Involuntary Commitment Legislation"; J. W. Luckey and J. D. Berman, *Effects of a New Commitment Law on Involuntary Admissions and Service Utilization Patterns*, L. & Hum. Behav. 3 (1979): 149–61; Lamb, Sorkin, and Zusman, *Legislating the Control of the Mentally Ill in California*; M. Bagby, and L. Atkinson, *The Effects of Legislative Reform on Civil Commitment Admission Rates*.

52. C. A. Kiesler and A. E. Sibulkin, *Mental Hospitalization: Myths and Facts About a National Crisis* (Beverly Hills, Calif.: Sage Publications, 1987).

53. C. A. Kiesler and A. E. Sibulkin, *Mental Hospitalization*; A. Sirrocco, *Inpatient Health Facilities as Reported from the 1971 MFI Survey*, Vital and Health Statistics Series 14, No. 12. DHEW No. HRA 74–1807 (Rockville, Md.: National Center for Health Statistics, 1974); J. F. Sutton and A. Sirrocco, *Inpatient Health Facilities as Reported from the 1976 MFI Survey*, Vital and Health Statistics Series 14, No. 23. DHEW No. PHS 80–1818 (Hyattsville, Md.: National Center for Health Statistics, 1980).

54. A. L. McGarry, R. K. Schwitzgebel, P. D. Lipsett, and D. Delos, *Civil Commitment and Social Policy: An Evaluation of the Massachusetts Mental Health Reform Act of 1970*, Final Research Report (National Institute of Mental Health, Center for Studies on Crime and Delinquency, U.S. Dept. of Health and Human Services, ADM 81–1011, 1981); P. Lerman, *Deinstitutionalization and the Welfare State* (New Brunswick, N.J.: Rutgers University Press, 1982).

55. Nicholson, *Correlates of Commitment Status in Psychiatric Patients*.

56. ENKI Research Institute, *A Study of California's New Mental Health Law (1969–71)* (Los Angeles: ENKI Corp., 1972); McGarry, Schwitzgebel, Lipsett, and Delos, *Civil Commitment and Social Policy*; Faulkner, Bloom, McFarland, and Stern, *The Effect of Mental Health System Changes on Civil Commitment*; M. R. Munetz, K. R. Kaufman, and C. L. Rich, *Modernization of a Mental Health Act I: Commitment Patterns*, Bull. Am. Acad. Psychiatry & L. 8 (1980): 83–93; H. E. Gudeman, M. I. Nelson, L. J. Kux, and L. F. Sine, *Changing Admission Patterns at Hawaii State Hospital Following the 1976 Revision of the Hawaii Mental Health Statutes*, Hawaii Med. J. 38 (1979): 65–71. However, Peters and colleagues found a slightly larger proportion of schizophrenics among civil detainees in Florida after commitment criteria were narrowed. It should be noted that their conclusions were based on *evidence* submitted at the commitment hearing to prove dangerousness—a factor that severely limits the usefulness of these findings. See Peters, Miller, Schmidt, and Meeters, *The Effects of a Statutory Change on the Civil Commitment of the Mentally Ill*.

57. Monahan and Steadman, "Crime and Mental Disorder: An Epidemiological Approach"; Rabkin, *Criminal Behavior of Discharged Mental Patients*; H. J. Steadman, J. J. Cocozza, and M. E. Melick, *Explaining the Increased Arrest Rate Among Mental Patients: The Changing Clientele of State Hospitals*, Am. J. Psychiatry 135(7) (1978): 816–20; J. P. Morrissey and H. H. Goldman, *Care and Treatment of the*

Mentally Ill in the United States: Historical Developments and Reforms, Annals Am. Acad. Pol. & Soc. Sci. 484 (1986): 12–27; V. A. Hiday and S. J. Markell, *Components of Dangerousness: Legal Standards in Civil Commitment*, Int'l J.L. & Psychiatry 3 (1981): 405–19; J. M. Lagos, K. Perlmutter, and H. Saexinger, *Fear of the Mentally Ill: Empirical Support for the Common Man's Response*, Am. J. Psychiatry 134(10) (1977): 1134–37; J. Monahan, C. Calderia, and H. D. Friedlander, *Police and the Mentally Ill: A Comparison of Committed and Arrested Persons*, Int'l J.L. & Psychiatry 2 (1979): 509–18.

58. Appelbaum, *Standards for Civil Commitment*.

59. Warren, *Involuntary Commitment for Mental Disorder*; Warren, *The Social Construction of Dangerousness*; Warren, *Court of Last Resort: Judicial Review*; D. L. Wenger and C. R. Fletcher, *The Effect of Legal Counsel on Admissions to a State Mental Hospital: A Confrontation of Professions*, J. Health & Soc. Behav. 10 (1969): 66–72; R. D. Miller and P. B. Fiddleman, *Emergency Involuntary Commitment: A Look at the Decision-Making Process*, Hosp. & Commun. Psychiatry 34(3) (1983): 249–54; R. D. Miller and P. B. Fiddleman, *Involuntary Civil Commitment in North Carolina: The Results of the 1979 Statutory Changes*, N.C.L. Rev. 60 (1982): 985–1026; R. D. Miller and P. B. Fiddleman, *Changes in North Carolina Commitment Statutes: The Impact of Attorneys*, Bull. Am. Acad. Psychiatry & L. 11(1) (1983): 43–50; R. D. Miller, R. M. Ionescu-Pioggia, and P. B. Fiddleman, *The Effects of Witnesses, Attorneys, and Judges Upon Civil Commitment in North Carolina: A Prospective Study*, J. Forensic Sci. 28 (1983): 829–38; Hiday, *Reformed Commitment Procedures*; Hiday, *The Role of Counsel in Civil Commitment*; V. A. Hiday, *Court Decisions in Civil Commitment: Independence or Deference*, Int'l J.L. & Psychiatry 4 (1981): 159–70; V. A. Hiday, *The Attorney's Role in Involuntary Civil Commitment*, N.C.L. Rev. 60 (1982): 1027–56; V. A. Hiday and R. R. Goodman, *The Least Restrictive Alternative to Involuntary Hospitalization, Out-Patient Commitment: Its Use and Effectiveness*, J. Psychiatry & L. 10 (1982): 81–96.

60. V. A. Hiday, *Civil Commitment*; N. G. Poythress, *Psychiatric Expertise in Civil Commitment: Training Attorneys to Cope with Expert Testimony*, L. & Hum. Behav. 2 (1978): 1–23.

61. D. N. Haupt and S. M. Erlich, *The Impact of a New State Commitment Law on Psychiatric Patients' Careers*, Hosp. & Commun. Psychiatry 31 (1980): 745–51; M. R. Munetz, *Pennsylvania's Commitment Law: Problems in Implementation, Differences in Interpretation*, Hosp. & Commun. Psychiatry 32 (1981): 283–84; Munetz, Kaufman, and Rich, *Modernization of a Mental Health Act I: Commitment Patterns*; M. R. Munetz, K. R. Kaufman, and C. L. Rich, *Modernization of a Mental Health Act II: Outcome Effects*, J. Clin. Psychology 49(2) (1981): 333–37; Note, *Involuntary Hospitalization of the Mentally Ill in Iowa: The Failure of the 1975 Legislation*, Iowa L. Rev. 64 (1979): 1284–458.

62. Durham and La Fond, *The Empirical Consequences and Policy Implications of Broadening the Statutory Criteria for Civil Commitment*; Pierce, Durham, and Fisher, *The Impact of Broadened Civil Commitment Standards on Admission to State Mental Hospitals*.

63. Miller and Fiddleman, *Involuntary Civil Commitment in North Carolina*; Miller, Ionescu-Pioggia, and Fiddleman, *The Effects of Witnesses, Attorneys and Judges Upon Civil Commitment in North Carolina*; Munetz, *Pennsylvania's Commitment Law*; Munetz, Kaufman, and Rich, *Modernization of a Mental Health Act I: Commitment Patterns*; Munetz, Kaufman, and Rich, *Modernization of a Mental Health*

Act II: Outcome Effects; Haupt and Erlich, *The Impact of a New State Commitment Law on Psychiatric Patients' Careers*; B. Wanck, *Two Decades of Involuntary Hospitalization Legislation*, Am. J. Psychiatry 141 (1984): 33–38.

64. *Pierce County* v. *Western State Hospital*, 97 Wash. 2d 264, 268, 644 P.2d 131, 133–34 (1982).

65. Durham and La Fond, *The Empirical Consequences and Policy Implications of Broadening the Statutory Criteria for Civil Commitment*.

66. Ibid. There have been two studies that have attempted to evaluate on a simulated basis what would happen to commitment rates if paternalistic commitment criteria were substituted for existing dangerousness standards. One study applied the criteria developed by Alan Stone that patients be forcibly hospitalized only if the following conditions were satisfied: (1) the patient demonstrated the presence of severe mental disorder; (2) a health professional could give an immediate prognosis of major distress; (3) effective treatment existed, and (4) the patient was incompetent to refuse treatment. In the other study, Monahan and colleagues evaluated a single group of patients, using both the dangerousness criteria and the "need-for-treatment" criteria suggested by Stone. The researchers concluded that significantly fewer candidates would be committed under Stone's paternalistic criteria than under California's dangerousness standard. The requirement of severe mental illness (psychosis) appears to limit the number of persons who would have been detained. Monahan, Ruggiero, and Friedlander, *Stone-Roth Model of Civil Commitment and the California Dangerousness Standard*; A. A. Stone, *Mental Health and the Law: A System in Transition* (Rockville, Md.: Center for Studies of Crime and Delinquency, NIMH, DHEW, Publication No. (ADM) 76–176, 1976).

Using a similar approach, Hoge and his colleagues evaluated a group of candidates using the Massachusetts dangerousness standard versus the Stone criteria. Stone's criteria once again proved more restrictive than the dangerousness standard due to Stone's requirement of the presence of major patient distress and incompetence. Hoge, Appelbaum, and Greer, *An Empirical Comparison of the Stone and Dangerousness Criteria for Civil Commitment*; S. K. Hoge, G. Sachs, P. S. Appelbaum, A. Greer, and C. Gordon, *Limitations on Psychiatrists' Discretionary Civil Commitment Authority by the Stone and Dangerousness Criteria*, Arch. Gen Psychiatry 45(8) (1988): 764–69.

While these theoretical comparisons are interesting and thought-provoking, the implementation of Stone's need-for-treatment criteria has never been evaluated in a real-life setting where clinicians not participating in a research study apply the criteria to the decision to commit. We saw earlier that the actual application of dangerousness criteria may be influenced more by the *intentions* of mental health authorities than by the statutory criteria for commitment. One cannot help but wonder if in actual practice Stone's need-for-treatment criteria might not lead to a situation similar to the more broadly defined need-for-treatment criteria in Washington State.

67. Bagby and Atkinson, *The Effects of Legislative Reform on Civil Commitment Admission Rates*.

68. There is widespread acknowledgment that significant limitations exist in the quality, depth, and abundance of research on the insanity defense and civil commitment. The shortcomings of research designs to measure the impact of legal change— including the quality and availability of data, the choice of statistical techniques, the impossibly short time-frames, and the confounding effects of extralegal factors—have been discussed elsewhere. More research is clearly needed to untangle the plethora of questions that have had little attention via systematic study. See especially, Ap-

pelbaum, *Standards for Civil Commitment*; Bagby and Atkinson, *The Effects of Legislative Reform on Civil Commitment Admission Rates*.

Chapter 8

1. D. J. Rothman, *Conscience and Convenience: The Asylum and Its Alternative in Progressive America* (Boston: Little, Brown & Co., 1971).

2. C. A. B. Warren, *New Forms of Social Control: The Myth of Deinstitutionalization*, Am. Behav. Sci. 24(6) (1981): 724–40; S. Cohen, *Visions of Social Control* (Cambridge: Polity Press, 1985).

3. N. N. Kittrie, *The Right to Be Different: Deviance and Enforced Therapy* (Baltimore: Johns Hopkins University Press, 1971).

4. J. W. Schneider and P. Conrad, "The Medical Control of Deviance: Contests and Consequences," in *Research in the Sociology of Health Care*, vol. 1, ed. J. Roth (Greenwich, Conn.: JAI Press, 1980), 1–53; P. Conrad and J. W. Schneider, *Deviance and Medicalization: From Badness to Sickness* (St. Louis: Mosby, 1980).

5. Rothman, *Conscience and Convenience*.

6. See, for example, *People* v. *Ramsey*, 422 Mich. 500, 375 N.W.2d 298 (1985), in which the Michigan Supreme Court upheld the guilty but mentally ill statute against various constitutional challenges; *State* v. *Korell*, 690 P.2d 992 (Mont. 1984), in which the Montana Supreme Court upheld legislative abolition of the insanity defense against constitutional attack.

7. Alan A. Stone, *Mental Health and the Law: A System in Transition* (Washington, D.C.: National Institute of Mental Health, 1975).

8. M. S. Moore, *Law and Psychiatry: Rethinking the Relationship* (New York: Cambridge University Press, 1984); S. J. Morse, *Crazy Behavior, Morals, and Science; An Analysis of Mental Health Law*, So. Calif. L. Rev. 51 (1978): 527–654.

9. R. J. Bonnie and C. Slobogin, *The Role of Mental Health Professionals in the Criminal Process: The Case for Informed Speculation*, Va. L. Rev. 66 (1980): 427–522.

10. 63 U.S. 354 (1983).

11. J. L. Rogers and J. D. Bloom, *The Insanity Sentence: Oregon's Psychiatric Security Review Board*, Behav. Sci. & L. 3(1) (1985): 69–84. See also Chapter 3.

12. Note, *The Guilty But Mentally Ill Verdict and Due Process*, Yale L.J. 92 (1983): 475–498; R. A. Burt, *Of Mad Dogs and Scientists: The Perils of the "Criminal-Insane,"* U. Pa. L. Rev. 123 (1974): 258–96.

13. Laws of 1990, Chapter 3, §§ 1001–1013.

14. See Comment, *Washington's New Sexual Offender Civil Commitment System: An Unconstitutional Commitment System and Unwise Policy Choice*, U. Puget Sound L. Rev. 14 (1990): 105–41.

15. E2 S.S.B. 6259, 51st Leg., Reg. Sess., 1990 Wash. Laws Chap. 3; *Task Force on Community Protection, Final Report to Governor Booth Gardner, Governor, State of Washington* (1989).

16. J. Q. La Fond, *An Examination of the Purposes of Involuntary Civil Commitment*, Buffalo L. Rev. 30 (1981): 499–535; Note, *Developments in the Law: Civil Commitment of the Mentally Ill*, Harv. L. Rev. 87 (1974): 1190–406.

17. E. F. Torrey, *Nowhere to Go: The Tragic Odyssey of the Homeless Mentally Ill* (New York: Harper & Row, 1988).

18. La Fond, *An Examination of the Purposes of Involuntary Civil Commitment*. See also, *In re La Belle*, 107 Wash. 2d 196, 728 P.2d 138 (1986).

19. M. L. Durham and J. Q. La Fond, *A Search for the Missing Premise of Involuntary Therapeutic Commitment: Effective Treatment of the Mentally Ill*, Rutgers L. Rev. 40 (1988): 303–68.

20. *Rennie* v. *Klein*, 476 F. Supp. 1294 (D.N.J. 1979).

21. See E. Goffman, *Asylums: Essays on the Social Situation of Mental Patients and Other Inmates* (Garden City, N.Y: Doubleday, 1961).

22. M. L. Durham and J. Q. La Fond, *The Empirical Consequences and Policy Implications of Broadening the Statutory Criteria for Civil Commitment*, Yale L. & Pol'y Rev. 3 (1985): 395–446.

23. Ibid.

24. We are well aware that important and legitimate questions should be raised about the "voluntary" nature of voluntary commitments. For this, see J. A. Gilboy and J. R. Schmidt, *"Voluntary" Hospitalization of the Mentally Ill*, Nw. U.L. Rev. 66 (1971): 429–53. See also, B. J. Winnick, *Competency to Consent to Voluntary Hospitalization: A Therapeutic Jurisprudence Analysis of Zinermon v. Burch*, Int'l J.L. & Psychiatry 14 (1991): 169–214. However, without a mechanism for truly voluntary patients to seek assistance, there is absolutely nowhere for them to go.

25. Durham and La Fond, *A Search for the Missing Premise of Involuntary Therapeutic Commitment*.

26. A. Gralnick, *Build a Better State Hospital: Deinstitutionalization Has Failed*, Hosp. & Commun. Psychiatry 36(7) (1985): 738–741; L. L. Bachrach, *Asylum and Chronically Ill Psychiatric Patients*, Am. J. Psychiatry 141(8) 1984: 975–78.

27. *Donaldson* v. *O'Connor*, 422 U.S. 563, 575 (1975).

28. D. J. Roth and G. J. Bean, *New Perspectives on Homelessness: Findings from a Statewide Epidemiological Study*, Hosp. &. Commun. Psychiatry 37 (1985): 712–14.

29. Ibid.; H. H. Goldman and J. Morrissey, "Homelessness and Mental Illness in America: Emerging Issues in the Construction of a Social Problem," in *Location and Stigma: Contemporary Perspectives on Mental Health and Mental Health Care*, ed. C. J. Smith and J. A. Giggs (Boston: Allen & Unwin, 1988).

30. Roth and Bean, *New Perspectives on Homelessness*; Goldman and Morrissey, "Homelessness and Mental Illness in America"; K. H. Dockett, *Street Homeless People in the District of Columbia, Characteristics and Service Needs* (Washington, D.C.: University of the District of Columbia, 1984).

31. V. A. Hiday and T. L. Scheid-Cook, *The North Carolina Experience with Outpatient Commitment: A Critical Appraisal*, Int'l J.L. & Psychiatry 10 (1989): 215–32.

32. Ibid.

33. Unpublished estimates, Statistical Research Branch, Division of Applied and Service Research, National Institute of Mental Health, August 1991. Approximately two-thirds of state mental health budgets go to support public mental hospitals, although the proportion varies across states. Georgia, for example, spends over 90 percent of its state mental health budget on public mental hospitals, while California spends less than 50 percent. P. Lerman, *Deinstitutionalization and the Welfare State* (New Brunswick, N.J.: Rutgers University Press, 1982).

34. *In re Mental Commitment of M.P.*, 500 N.Ed.2d 216, 225 (Ind. App. 1986) (Sullivan, J., dissenting).

35. Wash. Rev. Code Ann. 71.05.360(2) (West Supp. 1985).

36. *Pierce County* v. *Western State Hospital*, 97 Wash. 2d. 264, 268, 644 P.2d 131, 133–34 (1982).

37. See, for example, Revised Code of Washington (RCW) 71.05.020(1). Durham

and La Fond, *The Empirical Consequences and Policy Implications of Broadening the Statutory Criteria for Commitment*. See also, C. D. Stromberg and A. A. Stone, *A Model State Law on Civil Commitment of the Mentally Ill*, Harv. J. on Legis. 20 (1983): 275–396.

38. For a thorough review of the clinical studies and political response to the new drug clozapine, see Hosp. & Commun. Psychiatry 41(8) (1990), which is devoted entirely to this complex topic.

39. The drug costs about $8,944 per year per patient because the manufacturer insists that patients also pay for an expensive blood-monitoring program to detect a possible fatal side effect. Only recently has the manufacturer promised to reduce the drug's price and let other providers monitor patients who take the drug. M. Freudenheim, "Maker of Schizophrenia Drug Bows to Pressure to Cut Cost," *New York Times*, Dec. 6, 1990, p. A1, col. 1.

40. Durham and La Fond, *The Empirical Consequences and Policy Implications of Broadening the Statutory Criteria for Civil Commitment*. Washington State enacted its 1979 Involuntary Treatment Act after a young man, denied voluntary admission to a state mental hospital, killed an elderly couple who lived next door. Pennsylvania considered revising its commitment statute after Sylvia Secrest, a woman with a history of psychiatric treatment, killed seven people in a shopping mall.

Bibliography

Abrahamsen, David. *Confessions of Son of Sam*. New York: Columbia University Press, 1985.

Abrahamson, J. *The Criminalization of Mentally Disordered Behavior: Possible Side Effects of a New Mental Health Law*. Hosp. & Commun. Psychiatry 23(4) (1972): 101–5.

Abrahamson, S. *Redefining Roles: The Victim's Rights Movement*. Utah L. Rev. (1985): 517–67.

Allen, F. A. *Criminal Justice, Legal Values and the Rehabilitative Ideal*. J. Crim. L., Criminology & Police Sci. 50 (1959): 226–36.

American Friends Service Committee. *Struggle for Justice: A Report on Crime and Punishment in America*. New York: Hill and Wang, 1971.

American Psychiatric Association. *Diagnostic and Statistical Manual of Mental Disorders: DSM-III-R*, 3d ed. rev. Washington, D.C.: APA, 1980.

American Psychiatric Association. *Position Statement on the Right to Adequate Care and Treatment for the Mentally Ill and Mentally Retarded*. Am. J. Psychiatry 134(3) (1977): 354–55.

American Psychiatric Association. *Position Statement on the Question of Adequacy of Treatment*. Am. J. Psychiatry 123(11) (1967): 1458–60.

American Psychiatric Association Statement on the Insanity Defense. Washington, D.C.: APA, 1982.

Anderson, J. R., and P. L. Woodard. *Victim and Witness Assistance: New State Laws and the System's Response*. Judicature 68(2) (1985): 221–44.

Appelbaum, P. S. *Civil Commitment: Is the Pendulum Changing Direction?* Hosp. & Commun. Psychiatry 33(9) (1982): 703–4.

Appelbaum, P. S. *The Supreme Court Looks at Psychiatry*. Am. J. Psychiatry 141(7) (1984): 827–35.

Arafat, I., and K. McCahery. *The Insanity Defense and the Juror*. Drake L. Rev. 23 (1973): 538–49.

Arenella, P. *The Diminished Capacity and Diminished Responsibility Defenses: Two Children of a Doomed Marriage*. Colum. Law Rev. 77 (1977): 827–65.

Arenella, P. *Reflections on Current Proposals to Abolish or Reform the Insanity Defense*. Am. J. L. & Med. 8 (1983): 271–84.

Arens, R. *The Durham Rule in Action: Judicial Psychiatry and Psychiatric Justice*. Law & Soc. Rev. 1(2) (1967): 41–80.

Arens, R. *Insanity Defense*. New York: Philosophical Library, 1974.

Arneill, A. *Comprehensive Analysis of Proposed Revisions to the Lanterman-Petris-Short Act*. Sacramento, Calif.: Council on Mental Health, 1987.

Arnonson, R. H. *Should the Privilege Against Self-Incrimination Apply to Compelled Psychiatric Examinations?* Stan. L. Rev. 26 (1973): 55–93.

Asinof, E. *The Fox Is Crazy Too: The True Story of Garrett Trapnell, Adventurer, Skyjacker, Bankrobber, Con-Man, Lover*. New York: Morrow, 1976.

Aviram, U., and S. P. Segal. *Exclusion of the Mentally Ill: Reflection of an Old Problem in a New Context*. Arch. Gen. Psychiatry 29 (1973): 126–31.

Ayd, Frank J., Jr., *Medical, Moral and Legal Issues in Mental Health Care*. Baltimore: Williams & Wilkins, 1974.

Aynes, R. L., *Constitutional Considerations: Government Responsibility and the Right Not to Be a Victim*. Symposium Issue, Pepperdine L. Rev. 11 (1984).

Bachrach, L. L. *Asylum and Chronically Ill Psychiatric Patients*. Am. J. Psychiatry 141(8) (1984): 975–78.

Bachrach, L. L. "Asylum for Chronic Mental Patients," in L. L. Bachrach, *Leona Bachrach Speaks: Selected Speeches and Lectures*, vol. 35, *New Directions for Mental Health Services*. San Francisco, Calif.: Jossey-Bass, 1987.

Bagby, R. M., *The Effects of Legislative Reform on Admission Rates to Psychiatric Units of General Hospitals*. Int'l J. L. & Psychiatry 10 (1987): 383–94.

Bagby, R. M. and L. Atkinson. *The Effects of Legislative Reform on Civil Commitment Admission Rates: A Critical Analysis*. Behav. Sci. & L. 6(1) (1988): 45–61.

Bagby, R. M., I. Silverman, D. P. Ryan, and S. E. Dickens. *The Effects of Legislative Reform in Ontario*. Canadian Psychology 28 (1987): 21–29.

Ball, F. L., and B. E. Havassy. *A Survey of the Problems and Needs of Homeless Consumers of Acute Psychiatric Services*. Hosp. & Commun. Psychiatry 35(9) (1984): 917–21.

Barringer, F. "Federal Count of Homeless is Far Below Other Figures," *New York Times*, April 12, 1991, p. A14.

Bassuk, E. L. *The Homelessness Problem*. Sci. Am. 241 (1984): 40–45.

Bassuk, E. L., L. Rubin, and A. Lauriat. *Is Homelessness a Mental Health Problem?* Am. J. Psychiatry 141(2) (1984): 1546–50.

Bazelon, D. *The Concept of Responsibility*. Geo. L. J. 53 (1964): 5–18.

Bazelon, D. *The Morality of the Criminal Law*. S. Cal. L. Rev. 49 (1975): 385–405.

Bazelon, D. *Psychiatrists and the Adversary Process*. Sci. Am. 230(6) (1974): 18–23.

Bazelon, D. *Questioning Authority*. New York: Knopf, 1987.

Beigel, A., K. Hegland, and D. Wexler. "Implementing a New Commitment Law in the Community: Practical Problems for Professionals," in *Law and the Mental Health Professions: Friction at the Interface*, ed. W. E. Barton and C. J. Sanborn. New York: International Universities Press, 1978.

Bell, D. *The Cultural Contradictions of Capitalism*. New York: Basic Books, 1976.

Bellack, A. S., and K. T. Meuser. *A Comprehensive Treatment Program for Schizophrenia and Chronic Mental Illness*. Commun. Mental Health J. 22(3) (1986): 175–89.

Bentz, W. K., and J. W. Edgerton. *Consensus on Attitudes Toward Mental Illness*. Arch. Gen. Psychiatry 22 (1970): 468–73.

Berger, V. *Man's Trial, Woman's Tribulation: Rape Cases in the Courtroom*. Colum. L. Rev. 77 (1977): 1–103.

Birnbaum, M. *The Right to Treatment*. A. B. A. J. 46 (1960): 499–505.

Bittner, E. *Police Discretion in Emergency Apprehension of Mentally Ill Persons*. Soc. Probs. 14 (1967): 278–92.

Boehnert, C. E. *Psychological and Demographic Factors Associated with Individuals Using the Insanity Defense*. J. Psychiatry & L. 13 (1985): 9.

Bonnie, R. J., and C. Slobogin. *The Role of Mental Health Professionals in the Criminal Process: The Case for Informed Speculation*. Va. L. Rev. 66 (1980): 427–522.

Bonnie, R. J. *The Moral Basis of the Insanity Defense*. A. B. A. J. 69 (1983): 194–97.

Bonovitz, J. C., and E. B. Guy. *Impact of Restrictive Civil Commitment Procedures on a Prison Psychiatric Service*. Am. J. Psychiatry 136(8) (1979): 1045–48.

Bonovitz, J. C., and J. S. Bonovitz. *Diversion of the Mentally Ill into the Criminal Justice System: The Police Intervention Perspective*. Am. J. Psychiatry 138(7) (1981): 973–76.

Bowerman, L. *Victim's Rights: Vermont's New Law*. Vt. L. Rev. 11 (1986): 695–704.

Braff, J., T. Arvanites, and H. J. Steadman. *Detention Patterns of Successful and Unsuccessful Insanity Defendants*. Criminology 21 (1983): 439–48.

Brakel, S. J., and R. Rock. *The Mentally Disabled and the Law*, 2d ed. Chicago: American Bar Foundation, 1971.

Brakel, S. J., J. Parry, and B. A. Weiner. *The Mentally Disabled and the Law*, 3d ed. Chicago: American Bar Foundation, 1985.

Brancale, R. *Diagnostic Techniques in Aid of Sentencing*. Law & Contemp. Probs. 23 (1958): 442–60.

Branch, T. *Parting the Waters: America in the King Years, 1954–63*. New York: Simon and Schuster, 1988.

Brant, J. *The Hostility of the Burger Court to Mental Health Law Reform Litigation*. Bull. Am. Acad. L. & Psychiatry 11 (1983): 77–80.

Brooks, A. D. *The Constitutional Right to Refuse Antipsychotic Medications*. Bull. Am. Acad. Psychiatry & L. 8 (1980): 179–221.

Brooks, A. D. "The Effect of Law on the Administration of Antipsychotic Medications," in *Ethical Issues in Epidemiological Research*, ed. L. Trancredi. New Brunswick, N.J.: Rutgers University Press, 1986.

Brooks, A. D. *Law and Antipsychotic Medications*. Behav. Sci. & L. 4 (1986): 247–63.

Brooks, A. D. *The Right to Refuse Antipsychotic Medications: Law and Policy*. Rutgers L. Rev. 39 (1987): 339–76.

Brownmiller, S. *Against Our Will: Men, Women, and Rape*. New York: Simon & Schuster, 1975.

Bryant, R. P., and C. B. Hume. *Recent Developments, Diminished Capacity—Recent Decisions and an Analytic Approach*. Vand. L. Rev. 30 (1977): 213–257.

Burt, M. R., and B. E. Cohen. *America's Homeless: Numbers, Characteristics, and Programs that Serve Them*. Washington, D.C.: Urban Institute Press, 1989.

Burt, R. A. *Of Mad Dogs and Scientists: The Perils of the"Criminal-Insane."* U. Pa. L. Rev. 123 (1974): 258–96.

Burton, N. M., and H. J. Steadman. *Legal Professionals' Perceptions of the Insanity Defense*. J. Psychiatry & L. 6 (1978): 173–87.

Callahan, L., C. Mayer, and H. J. Steadman. *Insanity Defense Reform in the United States—Post Hinckley*. Mental & Phys. Disability L. Rep. 11(1) (1987): 54–59.

Chafe, W.H. *The Unfinished Journey: America Since World War II*. New York: Oxford University Press, 1986.

Chambers, D. L. *Alternatives to Civil Commitment of the Mentally Ill: Practical Guides and Constitutional Imperatives*. Mich. L. Rev. 70 (1972): 1107–1200.

Chayes, A. *The Role of the Judge in Public Law Litigation*. Harv. L. Rev. 89 (1976): 1281–1316.

Chodoff, P. *The Case for Involuntary Hospitalization of the Mentally Ill*. Am. J. Psychiatry 133(5) (1967): 496–501.

Clark, R. *Crime in America*. New York: Simon & Schuster, 1970.

Cloward, R. A., and L. E. Ohlin. *Delinquency and Opportunity: A Theory of Delinquent Gangs*. New York: Free Press, 1960.

Cocozza, J., and H. J. Steadman. *The Failure of Psychiatric Predictions of Dangerousness: Clear and Convincing Evidence*. Rutgers L. Rev. 29 (1976): 1084–1101.

Cohen, S. *Visions of Social Control*. Cambridge: Polity Press, 1985.

Collier, P., and D. Horowitz. *Destructive Generation: Second Thoughts About the '60s*. New York: Summit Books, 1989.

Comptroller General of the United States. *Returning the Mentally Disabled to the Community: Government Needs to Do More*. Washington, D.C.: Government Accounting Office, 1977.

Conrad, P., and J. W. Schneider. *Deviance and Medicalization: From Badness to Sickness*. St. Louis: Mosby, 1980.

Cooke, G., and C. Sikorski. *Factors Affecting Length of Hospitalization in Persons Adjudicated Not Guilty By Reason of Insanity*. Bull. Am. Acad. Psychiatry & L. 2 (1974): 251–61.

Coser, L.A., and I. Howe, eds. *The New Conservatives: A Critique from the Left*. New York: Quadrangle, 1974.

Cox, A. *Federalism and Individual Rights Under the Burger Court*. Nw. U.L. Rev. 73 (1978): 1–25.

Criss, M. L., and D. R. Racine. *Impact of Change in Legal Standard for Those Adjudicated Not Guilty by Reason of Insanity, 1975–1979*. Bull. Am. Acad. Psychiatry & L. 8 (1980): 261–71.

Daley, S. "Koch Policy for Homeless Creates Fears," *New York Times*, October 12, 1987, p. Bl, col. 6.

Danforth, F. W. *Death Knell for Pre-Trial Mental Examination? Privilege Against Self-Incrimination*. Rutgers L. Rev. 19 (1965): 489–505.

Darnton, N. "Committed Youth: Why Are So Many Teens Being Locked Up in Private Mental Hospitals?" *Newsweek*, July 31, 1989, pp. 66–72.

De Grazia, E. *The Distinction of Being Mad*. U. Chi. L. Rev. 22 (1955): 339–55.

Delgado, R. *"Rotten Social Background": Should the Criminal Law Recognize a Defense of Severe Environmental Deprivation?* Law & Inequality 3 (1985): 9–90.

"Delusions About Mental Health," *New York Times*, Aug. 1, 1986, p. A26, col. 1, editorial desk.

Dershowitz, A. *The Law of Dangerousness: Some Fictions About Predictions*. J. Legal Educ. 23 (1970): 24–47.

Dershowitz, A. *The Origins of Preventive Confinement in Anglo-Saxon American Law—Part I: The English Experience*. U. Cin. L. Rev. 43 (1974): 1–60.

Dershowitz, A. *The Origins of Preventive Confinement in Anglo-Saxon American Law—Part II: The American Experience*. U. Cin. L. Rev. 43 (1974): 781–846.

Dershowitz, A. *Preventive Confinement: A Suggested Framework for Constitutional Analysis*. Tex. L. Rev. 51 (1973): 1277–1324.

Deutsch, A. *The Mentally Ill in America: A History of Their Care and Treatment from*

Colonial Times, 2d ed., rev. and enl. New York: Columbia University Press, 1949.

Developments in the Law: Civil Commitment of the Mentally Ill. Harv. L. Rev. 87 (1974): 1190–406.

Diamond, B. L. *Criminal Responsibility of the Mentally Ill*. Stan. L. Rev. 14 (1961): 59–86.

Diamond, B. L. *The Fallacy of the Impartial Expert*. Arch. Crim. Psychodynamics 3(2) (1959): 221.

Diamond, B. L. *From Durham to Brawner, A Futile Journey*. Wash. L. Q. (1973): 109–25.

Diamond, B. L. *From M'Naghten to Currens, and Beyond*. Calif. L. Rev. 50 (1962): 189–205.

Diamond, B. L. *The Psychiatrist as Advocate*. J. Psychiatry & L. 1 (1973): 5–21.

Diver, C. S. *The Judge as Political Powerbroker: Superintending Structural Change in Public Institutions*. Va. L. Rev. 65 (1979): 43–106.

Dix, G. E. *Psychological Abnormality as a Factor in Grading Criminal Liability: Diminished Capacity, Diminished Responsibility, and the Like*. J. Crim. L., Criminology & Police Sci. 62 (1971): 313–34.

Dockett, K. H. *Street Homeless People in the District of Columbia, Characteristics and Service Needs*. Washington, D.C.: University of the District of Columbia, 1984.

Donaldson, K. *Insanity Inside Out*. New York: Crown, 1976.

Drake, D. C. "The Forsaken," *Philadelphia Inquirer*, July 18–24, 1982.

Dressler, J. *Reaffirming the Moral Legitimacy of the Doctrine of Diminished Capacity: A Brief Reply to Professor Morse*. J. Crim. L. & Criminology 75 (1984): 953–62.

Dunham, A. C. *APA's Model Law: Protecting the Patient's Ultimate Interests*. Hosp. & Commun. Psychiatry 36(9) (1985): 973–75.

Durham, M. L., and J. Q. La Fond. *The Empirical Consequences and Policy Implications of Broadening the Statutory Criteria for Civil Commitment*. Yale L. & Pol'y Rev. 3 (1985): 395–446.

Durham, M. L. and J. Q. La Fond. *A Search for the Missing Premise of Involuntary Therapeutic Commitment: Effective Treatment of the Mentally Ill*. Rutgers L. Rev. 40 (1988): 303–68.

Durham, M. L., and G. L. Pierce. *Legal Intervention in Civil Commitment: The Impact of Broadened Commitment Criteria*. Annals Am. Acad. Pol. & Soc. Sci. 414 (1986): 42–55.

Durham, M. L., H. D. Carr, and G. L. Pierce. *Police Involvement in Involuntary Civil Commitment*. Hosp. & Commun. Psychiatry 35(6) (1984): 580–84.

Earley, P. "Jails Are Becoming 'Dumping Grounds,' Federal Government Advisory Panel Told," *Washington Post*, June 17, 1983, p. A12.

Ellis, J. W. *The Consequences of the Insanity Defense: Proposals to Reform Post-Acquittal Commitment Laws*. Cath. U. L. Rev. 35 (1986): 961–1020.

ENKI Research Institute. *A Study of California's New Mental Health Law (1969–71)*. Los Angeles: ENKI Corp., 1972.

Ennis, B., and T. Litwack. *Flipping Coins in the Courtroom: Psychiatry and the Presumption of Expertise*. Calif. L. Rev. 62 (1974): 693–752.

Faulkner, L. R., J. D. Bloom, and K. Kuhndahl-Stanley. *Effects of a New Involuntary Civil Commitment Law: Expectations and Reality*. Bull. Amer. Acad. Psychiatry & L. 10(4) (1982): 249–59.

Faulkner, L. R., J. D. Bloom, B. H. McFarland, and T. O. Stern. *The Effect of Mental Health System Changes on Civil Commitment*. Bull. Am. Acad. Psychiatry & L. 13(4) (1985): 345–57.

Feinberg, J. *Doing and Deserving*. Princeton, N.J.: Princeton, 1970.

Fingarette, H., and A. Fingarette Hasse. *Mental Disabilities and Criminal Responsibility*. Berkeley: University of California Press, 1979.

Fiss, O. *Foreword: The Forms of Justice*. Harv. L. Rev. 93 (1979): 1–58.

Fiss. O. *The Social and Political Foundations of Adjudication*. Law & Hum. Behav. 6 (1982): 121–28.

Fletcher, G. P. *A Crime of Self Defense: Bernhard Goetz and the Law on Trial*. New York: Free Press, 1988.

Fletcher, G. P. *Rethinking Criminal Law*, Boston: Little, Brown, 1978.

Foster, G. "Parents Claim Law Fails the 'Chronic' Patient," *Seattle Post-Intelligencer*, Aug. 27, 1978, p. B3.

Foucault, M. *Madness and Civilization: A History of Insanity in the Age of Reason*. New York: Pantheon Books, 1965.

Fox, S. J. *Juvenile Justice Reform: An Historical Perspective*. Stan. L. Rev. 22 (1970): 1187–1239.

Freudenheim, M. "Maker of Schizophrenia Drug Bows to Pressure to Cut Cost." *New York Times*, Dec. 6, 1990, p. A1, col. 1.

Friedman, M., and N. Modie. "Suspect in Slayings Tried to Get Treatment," *Seattle Post-Intelligencer*, Aug. 10, 1978, p. A1.

Friendly, H. *The Courts and Social Policy: Substance and Procedure*. U. Miami L. Rev. 33 (1978): 21–42.

Frug, G. *The Judicial Power of the Purse*. U. Pa. L. Rev. 126 (1978): 715–94.

Galbraith, J. K. *The Affluent Society*. Boston: Houghton-Mifflin, 1958.

Gardner, M. R. *Punitive Juvenile Justice: Some Observations on a Recent Trend*. Int'l J. L. & Psychiatry 10 (1987): 129–51.

Gardner, M. R. *The Renaissance of Retribution—An Examination of Doing Justice*. Wis. L. Rev. 1976 (1976): 781–815.

Gargan, E. A. "Ducking for Cover Over the Homeless," *New York Times*, November 27, 1983, sec. 4, p. E7, col. 1.

Gaskins, R. *Second Thoughts on "Law as an Instrument of Social Change"*. Law & Hum. Behav. 6 (1982): 153–68.

Geis, G., and R. F. Meier. *Abolition of the Insanity Plea in Idaho: A Case Study*. Annals Am. Acad. Pol. & Soc. Sci. 477 (1985): 72–83.

Gest, T. "Hinckley Bombshell: End of Insanity Pleas?" *U.S. News and World Report*, July 5, 1982, p. 12.

Gilboy, J. A., and J. R. Schmidt. *"Voluntary" Hospitalization of the Mentally Ill*. Nw. U.L. Rev. 66 (1971): 429–53.

Gilder, G. *Wealth and Poverty*. New York: Basic Books, 1981.

Gilder, G. "Why I Am Not a Neo-Conservative". *National Review*, March 5, 1982, 218–22.

Gillie, J. "Group Pushes Family Action," *Tacoma News Tribune*, Nov. 5, 1978, p. F1.

Gillie, J. "Murder Suspect was Refused Entry at Steilacoom," *Tacoma News Tribune*, Aug. 10, 1978, p. B12.

Gitlin, T. *The Sixties: Years of Hope, Days of Rage*. New York: Bantam, 1987.

Gittler, J. *Expanding the Role of the Victim in a Criminal Action: An Overview of Issues and Problems*. Symposium Issue, Pepperdine L. Rev. 11 (1984): 117–82.

Goffman, E. *Asylums: Essays on the Social Situation of Mental Patients and Other Inmates*. Garden City, N.Y.: Doubleday, 1961.

Goldman, H. H., and J. P. Morrissey. *The Alchemy of Mental Health Policy: Homelessness and the Fourth Cycle of Reform*. Am. J. Pub. Health 75(7) (1985): 727–31.

Goldman, H. H., and J. P. Morrissey. "Homelessness and Mental Illness in America: Emerging Issues in the Construction of a Social Problem," in *Location and Stigma, Contemporary Perspectives on Mental Health and Mental Health Care*, ed. C. J. Smith and J. A. Griggs. Boston: Allen & Unwin, 1988.

Goldman, S. *Reagan's Judicial Legacy: Completing the Puzzle and Summing Up*. Judicature 72 (1989): 318–30.

Goldstein, A. *Defining the Role of the Victim in Criminal Prosecution*. Miss. L. J. 52 (1982): 515–61.

Goldstein, A. *The Insanity Defense*. New Haven: Yale University Press, 1967.

Goldstein, J., and J. Katz. *Abolish the Insanity Defense—Why Not?* Yale L. J. 72 (1963): 853–76.

Gould, R. E., and R. Levy. "Psychiatrists as Puppets of Koch's Roundup Policy," *New York Times*, Nov. 27, 1988, p. A3, col. 4.

Graham, H. D. *The Civil Rights Era: Origins and Development of National Policy, 1960–1972*. New York: Oxford University Press, 1990.

Gralnick, A. *Build a Better State Hospital: Deinstitutionalization Has Failed*. Hosp. & Commun. Psychiatry 36(7) (1985): 738–41.

Grob, G. *The Forging of Mental Health Policy in America: World War II to New Frontier*. J. Hist. Med. & Allied Sci. 42 (October 1987): 410–46.

Grob, G. *Mental Illness and American Society, 1875–1940*. Princeton, N.J.: Princeton University Press, 1983.

Gronfein, W. *Incentives and Intentions in Mental Health Policy: A Comparison of the Medicaid and Community Mental Health Program*. J. Health & Soc. Behav. 26 (1985): 192–206.

Gross, H. *A Theory of Criminal Justice*. New York: Oxford University Press, 1979.

Gudeman, H. E., M. I. Nelson, L. J. Kux, and L. F. Sine. *Changing Admission Patterns at Hawaii State Hospital Following the 1976 Revision of the Hawaii Mental Health Statutes*. Hawaii Med. J. 38 (1979): 65–71.

Guttmacher, M. S. *The Psychiatrist as an Expert Witness*. U. Chi. L. Rev. 22 (1955): 325–30.

Guttmacher, M. S., and H. Weihofen. *Psychiatry and the Law*. New York: Norton, 1952.

Hahn, J. "A Trail of Anguish," *Seattle Post-Intelligencer*, Nov. 4, 1978, p. A1.

Hall, J. *Justice in the 20th Century*. Calif. L. Rev. 59 (1971): 752–68.

Halleck, C. W. *The Insanity Defense in the District of Columbia—A Legal Lorelei*. Geo. L. J. 49 (1960): 294–320.

Halleck, S. *Psychiatry and the Dilemmas of Crime: A Study of Causes, Punishment, and Treatment*. New York: Harper, 1967.

Hans, V. *An Analysis of Public Attitudes Toward an Insanity Defense*. Criminology 24 (1986): 393–414.

Hardisty, J. H. *Mental Illness: A Legal Fiction*. Wash. L. Rev. 48 (1973): 735–62.

Harrington, W. A. "Deinstitutionalization: Organizational Change in Dorothea Dix Psychiatric Hospital," in *Multi-Institutional Systems Management: Concepts and Cases*, ed. B. J. Jaeger, A. D. Kaluzny, and K. Magruder-Habib. Owings Mills, Md.: AUPHA Press, 1987, 41–52.

Hart, H. L. A. *The Morality of the Criminal Law*. Jerusalem: Magnes Press, 1964.

Hart, H. L. A. *Punishment and Responsibility*. New York: Oxford University Press, 1968.

Hart, H. M. *The Aims of the Criminal Law*. Law & Contemp. Probs. 23 (1958): 401–41.

Haupt, D. N., and S. M. Erlich. *The Impact of a New State Commitment Law on Psychiatric Patients' Careers*. Hosp. & Commun. Psychiatry 31 (1980): 745–51.

Havel, R. W. *A Punishment Rationale for Diminished Capacity*. UCLA L. Rev. 18 (1971): 561–80.

Hermann, D. *Preventive Detention: A Scientific View of Man and State Power*. U. Ill. L. R. 1973 (1973): 673–99.

Hiday, V. A. *Arrest and Incarceration of Civil Commitment Candidates*. Hosp. & Commun. Psychiatry 42(7) (1991): 729–34.

Hiday, V. A. *The Attorney's Role in Involuntary Civil Commitment*. N. C. L. Rev. 60 (1982): 1027–56.

Hiday, V. A. *Civil Commitment: A Review of Empirical Research*. Behav. Sci. & L. 6(1) (1988): 15–43.

Hiday, V. A. *Court Decisions in Civil Commitment: Independence or Deference*. Int'l J. L. & Psychiatry 4 (1/2) (1981): 159–70.

Hiday, V. A. *Judicial Decisions in Civil Commitment*. Law & Soc. Rev. 17 (1983): 517–30.

Hiday, V. A. *Reformed Commitment Procedures: An Empirical Study in the Courtroom*. Law & Soc. Rev. 11 (1977): 652–66.

Hiday, V. A. *The Role of Counsel in Civil Commitment: Changes, Effects, Determinants*. J. Psychiatry & L. 5 (1977): 551–69.

Hiday, V. A. *The Sociology of Mental Health Law*. Sociol. & Soc. Res. 67(2) (1983): 111–28.

Hiday, V. A., and R. R. Goodman. *The Least Restrictive Alternative to Involuntary Hospitalization, Out-Patient Commitment: Its Use and Effectiveness*. J. Psychiatry & L. 10 (1982): 81–96.

Hiday, V. A., and S. J. Markell. *Components of Dangerousness: Legal Standards in Civil Commitment*. Int'l J. L. & Psychiatry 3 (1981): 405–19.

Hiday, V. A., and T. L. Scheid-Cook. *The North Carolina Experience with Outpatient Commitment: A Critical Appraisal*. Int'l J.L. & Psychiatry 10(3) (1987): 215–32.

Hoffman, P. B., and L. L. Foust. *Least Restrictive Treatment of the Mentally Ill: A Doctrine in Search of Its Senses*. San Diego L. Rev. 14 (1977): 1100–54.

Hogarty, G. E., N. R. Schooler, R. Ulrich, et al. *Fluphenazine and Social Therapy in the Aftercare of Schizophrenic Patients*. Arch. Gen. Psychiatry 36(12) (1979): 1283–94.

Hoge, S. K., et al. *Limitations on Psychiatrists' Discretionary Civil Commitment Authority by the Stone and Dangerousness Criteria*. Arch. Gen. Psychiatry 45(8) (1988): 764–69.

Hoge, S. K., P. S. Appelbaum, and A. Greer. *An Empirical Comparison of the Stone and Dangerousness Criteria for Civil Commitment*. Am. J. Psychiatry 146(2) (1989): 170–75.

"Homeless in America," *Newsweek*, January 2, 1984, p. 21.

Homelessness in America: Hearings Before the Subcommittee on Housing and Community Development of the House Committee on Banking, Finance, and Urban Affairs, 97th Cong., 2d sess., 1982.

Homelessness in America-II: Hearings Before the Subcommittee on Housing and Com-

munity Development of the House Committee on Banking, Finance, and Urban Affairs, 98th Cong., 2d sess., 1984.

Hopper, K. *Homelessness: Reducing the Difference*. New Eng. J. Hum. Serv. 3(4) (1983): 30–47.

Horowitz, D. L. *The Courts and Social Policy*. Washington: Brookings, 1977.

Horowitz, D. L. *The Judiciary: Umpire or Empire?* Law & Hum. Behav. 6 (1982): 129–43.

"Insane Risk", New York Times, April 15, 1987, p. A26, col. 1, editorial desk.

The Insanity Defense in New York: A Report to Governor Hugh L. Carey. New York State Department of Mental Hygiene, 1978.

Insanity Defense in Criminal Trials and Limitations of Psychiatric Testimony. Report of the Board of Trustees, American Medical Association, 1983.

Insanity Defense in Federal Courts: Hearings Before the Subcommittee on Criminal Justice, House Judiciary Committee. 97th Cong., 2d sess. (1982).

Isaac, R. J., and V. C. Armat. *Madness in the Streets*. New York: Free Press, 1990.

Isaacson, E. R. "Insane on All Counts; After Tortuous Deliberations, Jury Acquits John Hinckley," *Time*, July 5, 1982, p. 22.

Johnson, A. B. *Out of Bedlam*. New York: Basic Books, 1990.

Joint Commission on Mental Illness and Health. *Action for Mental Health*. New York: Basic Books, 1961.

Kalven, H. *Insanity and the Criminal Law*. U. Chi. L. Rev. 22 (1955): 317–404.

Kass, J. "Teen Trap: Treating Adolescents in Psychiatric Clinics: More Profit Motive Than Actual Concern?" *Seattle Times*, July 9, 1989, pp. K1–2.

Katz, J. *The Right to Treatment—An Enchanting Legal Fiction*. U. Chi. L. Rev. 36 (1969): 755–83.

Kaufman, I. R. "The Insanity Plea on Trial," *New York Times Magazine*, August 8, 1963.

Keilitz, I. *Researching and Reforming the Insanity Defense*. Rutgers L. Rev. 39 (1987): 289–322.

Keilitz, I., and J. P. Fulton. *The Insanity Defense and Its Alternatives: A Guide for Policymakers*. Williamsburg, Va.: National Center for State Courts, 1984.

Keilitz, I., and T. Hall. *State Statutes Governing Involuntary Outpatient Civil Commitment*. Mental & Phys. Disability L. Rep. 9(5) (1985): 378–400.

Kemna, D. J. *Current Status of Institutionalized Mental Health Patients' Right to Refuse Psychotropic Drugs*. J. Legal Med. 6 (1985): 107–38.

Kiesler, C. A. "Mental Hospitals and Alternative Care: Noninstitutionalization as Potential Public Policy," in *Mental Health Care and Social Policy*, ed. Phil Brown. Boston: Routledge and Kegan Paul, 1985, 292–315.

Kiesler, C. A., and A. Sibulkin. *Mental Hospitalization: Myths and Facts About a National Crisis*. Beverly Hills: Sage, 1987.

Kittrie, N. N. *The Right to Be Different: Deviance and Enforced Therapy*. Baltimore: Johns Hopkins University Press, 1971.

Kozol, J. *Rachael and Her Children: Homeless Families in America*. New York: Crown Publishers, 1988.

Kramer, M. *Psychiatric Services and the Changing Institutional Scene*. Rockville, Md.: U.S. Dept. of Health, Education, and Welfare, Public Health Service, Alcohol, Drug Abuse, and Mental Health Administration, 1977.

Krash, A. *The Durham Rule and Judicial Administration of the Insanity Defense in the District of Columbia*. Yale L. J. 70 (1961): 905–52.

Kristol, I. "What Is Neoconservative?" *Newsweek*, January 19, 1976, p. 87.

Kuh, R. H. *The Insanity Defense—An Effort to Confine Law and Reason.* U. Pa. L. Rev. 110 (1962): 771–815.

La Fond, J. Q. *The Case for Liberalizing the Use of Deadly Force in Self-Defense.* U. Puget Sound L. Rev. 6 (1983): 237–84.

La Fond, J. Q. *An Examination of the Purposes of Involuntary Civil Commitment.* Buff. L. Rev. 30 (1981): 499–535.

LaFave, W., and A. Scott. *Criminal Law,* 2d ed. St. Paul, Minn.: West Publishing Co., 1986.

Lagos, J. M., K. Perlmutter, and H. Saexinger. *Fear of the Mentally Ill: Empirical Support for the Common Man's Response.* Am. J. Psychiatry 134(10) (1977): 1134–37.

Laing, R. D. *The Divided Self.* Baltimore: Penguin, 1960.

Lamb, H. R., and J. A. Talbott. *The Homeless Mentally Ill: The Perspective of the American Psychiatric Association.* J. Am. Med. A. 256(4) (1986): 498–501.

Lamb, H. R., and M. J. Mills. *Needed Changes in Law and Procedure for the Chronically Mentally Ill.* Hosp. & Commun. Psychiatry 37(5) (1986): 475–80.

Langdon, J. K., and M. A. Kass. *Homelessness in America: Looking for the Right to Shelter.* Colum. J.L. & Soc. Probs. 19 (1985): 305–92.

Lebensohn, Z. M. *Pilgrim's Progress, or the Tortuous Road to Mental Health.* Comprehensive Psychiatry 16(5) (1975): 415–26.

Lefelt, S. L. *Pretrial Mental Examinations: Compelled Cooperation and the Fifth Amendment.* Am. Crim. L. Rev. 19 (1972): 431–64.

Lerman, P. *Deinstitutionalization and the Welfare State.* New Brunswick, N.J.: Rutgers University Press, 1982.

Levitan, S., and C. M. Johnson. *Beyond the Safety Net: Reviving the Promise of Opportunity in America.* Cambridge, Mass.: Ballinger, 1984.

Levy, L. W. *Against the Law: The Nixon Court and Criminal Justice.* New York: Harper & Row, 1974.

Lewin, T.H.D. *Psychiatric Evidence in Criminal Cases for Purpose Other than the Defense of Insanity.* Syracuse L. Rev. 26 (1975): 1051–1115.

Limiting the Insanity Defense: Hearings Before the Subcommittee on Criminal Law, Senate Judiciary Committee. 97th Cong., 2d sess. (1982).

Lipsius, S. H. *Judgment of Alternatives to Hospitalization.* Am. J. Psychiatry 130(8) (1973): 892–96.

Litman, J. *A Common Law Remedy for Forcible Medication of the Institutionalized Mentally Ill.* Colum. L. Rev. 82 (1982): 1720–51.

Livermore, J. M., and P. E. Meehl. *The Virtues of M'Naghten.* Minn. L. Rev. 51 (1967): 789–856.

Luckey, J. W., and J. D. Berman. *Effects of a New Committment Law on Involuntary Admissions and Service Utilization Patterns.* L. Hum. Behav. 3 (1979): 149–61.

Luskin, R. D. *Compulsory Outpatient Treatment for the Mentally Ill.* Report to the American Psychiatric Association Task Force on Involuntary Outpatient Treatment (March 1983).

Mahler, H., and B. T. Co. *Who Are the "Committed"?: Update.* J. Nervous & Mental Disease 172(4) (1984): 189–96.

Matter of Josiah Oakes. Law Rep. 8 (1845): 122–29.

Matthews, A. R. *Mental Disability and the Law.* Chicago: American Bar Association, 1970.

McGarry, A. L. *Pathological Gambling: A New Insanity Defense.* Bull. Am. Acad. Psychiatry & L. 11(4) (1983): 301–8.

McGarry, A. L., R. K. Schwitzgebel, P. D. Lipsett, and D. Delos. *Civil Commitment and Social Policy: An Evaluation of the Massachusetts Mental Health Reform Act of 1970*, Final Research Report. National Institute of Mental Health, Center for the Studies of Crime and Delinquency, U.S. Dept. of Health and Human Services, 1981.

McGreevy, M. A., H. J. Steadman, and L. A. Callahan. *The Negligible Effects of California's 1982 Reform of the Insanity Defense Test*. Am. J. Psychiatry 148(6) (June 1991): 744–50.

McNeil, D. E., and R. L. Binder. *Violence, Civil Commitment and Hospitalization*. J. Nervous & Mental Disease 174(2) (1986): 107–11.

McNulty, F. *The Burning Bed*. New York: Harcourt Brace Jovanovich, 1980.

Mechanic, D. *Correcting Misconceptions in Mental Health Policy: Strategies for Improved Care of the Seriously Mentally Ill*. Milbank Q. 65(2) (1987): 203–30.

Mechanic, D. *Mental Health and Social Policy: Initiatives for the 1980s*. Health Affairs (Project Hope) 4 (1985): 75–88.

Meisel, A. *The Rights of the Mentally Ill Under State Constitutions*. L. & Contemp. Probs. 45 (1982): 7–40.

Menninger, K. *The Crime of Punishment*. New York: Penguin Books, 1968.

Mestrovic, S. *Admission Patterns at South Carolina's State Psychiatric Hospitals Following Legislative Reform*. J. Psychiatry & L. 19 (1982): 457–69.

Miller, R. D. *Involuntary Civil Commitment of the Mentally Ill in the Post-Reform Era*. Springfield, Ill.: Charles C Thomas, 1987.

Miller, R. D., and P. B. Fiddleman. *Changes in North Carolina Commitment Statutes: The Impact of Attorneys*. Bull. Am. Acad. Psychiatry & L. 11(1) (1983): 43–50.

Miller, R. D., and P. B. Fiddleman. *Emergency Involuntary Commitment: A Look at the Decision-Making Process*. Hosp. & Commun. Psychiatry 34(3) (1983): 249–54.

Miller, R. D., and P. B. Fiddleman. *Involuntary Civil Commitment in North Carolina: The Results of the 1979 Statutory Changes*. N.C. L. Rev. 60 (1982): 985–1026.

Miller, R. D., R. M. Ionescu-Pioggia, and P. B. Fiddleman. *The Effects of Witnesses, Attorneys, and Judges Upon Civil Commitment in North Carolina: A Prospective Study*. J. Forensic Sci. 28 (1983): 829–38.

Mills, M. J. *Civil Commitment of the Mentally Ill: An Overview*. Annals Am. Acad. Pol. & Soc. Sci. 484 (1986): 28–41.

Milstein, E. S., S. Elliott, and K. D. Snyder. *PTSD: The War is Over, The Battle Goes On*. Trial 19(1) (1983): 86–89.

Monahan, J. *Risk Assessment of Violence Among the Mentally Disordered: Generating Useful Knowledge*. Int'l J. L. & Psychiatry 11 (1989): 249–57.

Monahan, J., and D. B. Wexler. *A Definite Maybe: Proof and Probability in Civil Commitment*. Law & Hum. Behav. 2 (1978): 37–42.

Monahan, J., and H. J. Steadman. "Crime and Mental Disorder: An Epidemiological Approach," in *Crime and Justice: An Annual Review of Research*, ed. M. Tonrey and N. Morris. Chicago: University of Chicago Press, 1982.

Monahan, J., C. Calderia, and H. D. Friedlander. *Police and the Mentally Ill: A Comparison of Committed and Arrested Persons*. Int'l J. L. & Psychiatry 2 (1979): 509–18.

Monahan, J., M. Ruggiero, and H. D. Friedlanger. *Stone-Roth Model of Civil Commitment and the California Dangerousness Standard*. Arch. Gen. Psychiatry 39 (1982): 1267–71.

Moore, M. S. *Law and Psychiatry: Rethinking the Relationship*. New York: Cambridge University Press, 1984.

Morgan, R. *Disabling America: The "Rights Industry" in Our Time*. New York: Basic Books, 1984.

Morris, G. *The Insanity Defense: A Blueprint for Legislative Reform*. Lexington, Mass.: Lexington Books, 1975.

Morris, N. *Psychiatry and the Dangerous Criminal*. S. Cal. L. Rev. 41 (1967–8): 514–47.

Margulies, P. *The "Pandemonium Between the Mad and the Bad": Procedures for the Commitment and Release of Insanity Acquittees After Jones v. United States*. Rutgers L. Rev. 36 (1984): 793–836.

Morrissey, J. P., and H. H. Goldman. *Care and Treatment of the Mentally Ill in the United States: Historical Developments and Reforms*. Annals Am. Acad. Pol. & Soc. Sci. 484 (1986): 12–27.

Morrissey, J. P., and H. H. Goldman. *Cycles of Reform in the Care of the Chronically Mentally Ill*. Hosp. & Commun. Psychiatry 35(8) (1984): 785–93.

Morrow, W. R., and D. B. Peterson. *Follow-up on Discharged Offenders—"Not Guilty By Reason of Insanity" and "Criminal Sexual Psychopaths,"* J. Crim. L., Criminology & Police Sci. 57 (1966): 31–34.

Morse, S. J. *Crazy Behavior, Morals, and Science: An Analysis of Mental Health Law*. So. Calif. L. Rev. 51 (1978): 527–654.

Morse, S. J. *Diminished Capacity: A Moral and Legal Conundrum*. Int'l J. L. & Psychiatry 2(3) (1979): 271–98.

Morse, S. J. *Excusing the Crazy: The Insanity Defense Reconsidered*. So. Cal. L. Rev. 58 (1985): 777–836.

Morse, S. J. *The Twilight of Welfare Criminology: A Reply to Judge Bazelon*. S. Cal. L. Rev. 49 (1976): 1247–68.

Morse, S. J. *Undiminished Confusion in Diminished Capacity*. J. Crim. L. & Criminology 75 (1984): 1–55.

Mosteller, R. P. *Discovery Against the Defense: Tilting the Adversarial Balance*. Calif. L. Rev. 74 (1986): 1569–1685.

Moynihan, D. P. *Maximum Feasible Misunderstanding: Community Action in the War on Poverty*. New York: Free Press, 1969.

Moynihan. D. P. *The Politics of Guaranteed Income: The Nixon Administration and the Family Assistance Plan*, 1st ed. New York: Random House, 1973.

Munetz, M. R. *Pennsylvania's Commitment Law: Problems in Implementation, Differences in Interpretation*. Hosp. & Commun. Psychiatry 32 (1981): 283–84.

Munetz, M. R., K. R. Kaufman, and C. L. Rich. *Modernization of a Mental Health Act I: Commitment Patterns*. Bull. Am. Acad. Psychiatry & L. 8 (1980): 83–93.

Munetz, M. R., K. R. Kaufman, and C. L. Rich. *Modernization of a Mental Health Act II: Outcome Effects*. J. Clin. Psychology 49(2) (1981): 333–37.

Myers, J. K., et al. *Six-Month Prevalence of Psychiatric Disorders in Three Communities*. Arch. Gen. Psychiatry 41(10) (1984): 959–67.

Myths and Realities: A Report of the National Commission on the Insanity Defense. Arlington, Va.: National Mental Health Association, 1983.

Nagel, R. F. *Separation of Powers and the Scope of Federal Equitable Remedies*. Stan. L. Rev. 30 (1978): 661–724.

National Organization for Victim Assistance. *Victim's Rights and Services: A Legislative Directory*. Washington, D.C.: NOVA, 1984.

Newman, D. F. *In Defense of Prisons*. Psychiatric Annals 4(3) (1974): 6–17.

Newman, K. S. *Falling from Grace: The Experience of Downward Mobility in the American Middle Class*. New York: Free Press, 1988.

Nicholson, R. A. *Correlates of Commitment Status in Psychiatric Patients.* Psychological Bull. 100 (1986): 241–50.

Packer, H. L. *The Limits of the Criminal Sanction.* Stanford, Calif.: Stanford University Press, 1968.

Page, S. *Civil Commitment: Operational Definition of New Criteria.* Canadian J. Psychiatry 26 (1981): 419–20.

Pantle, R. L., R. A. Pasewark, and H. J. Steadman. *Comparing Institutionalization Periods and Subsequent Arrests of Insanity Acquittees and Convicted Felons.* J. Psychiatry & L. 8 (1980): 305–16.

Parry, J. *Youngberg and Pennhurst II Revisited—Part I.* Mental & Phys. Disability L. Rep. 10(3) (1986): 154–258.

Pasewark, R. A. *Insanity Plea: A Review of the Research Literature.* J. Psychiatry & L. 9 (1981): 357–401.

Pasewark, R. A., and D. Seidenzahl. *Opinions Concerning the Insanity Plea and Criminality Among Mental Patients.* Bull. Am. Acad. Psychiatry & L. 7 (1979): 199–202.

Pasewark, R. A., and H. McGinley. *Insanity Plea: National Survey of Frequency and Success.* J. Psychiatry & L. 13 (Spring-Summer 1985): 101–8.

Pasewark, R. A., and J. L. Pantle. *Insanity Plea: Legislators' View.* Am. J. Psychiatry 136(2) (1979): 222–23.

Pasewark, R. A., and P. L. Craig. *Insanity Plea: Defense Attorneys' Views.* J. Psychiatry & L. 8 (1980): 413–41.

Pasewark, R. A., D. Seidenzahl, and J. L. Pantle. *Opinions About the Insanity Plea.* J. Forensic Psychology 8 (1981): 63.

Pasewark, R. A., M. L. Pantle, and H. J. Steadman. *The Insanity Plea in New York State, 1965–1976.* N.Y. St. Bar. J. 53 (1979): 186–89, 217–25.

Pasewark, R. A., R. L. Pantle, and H. J. Steadman. *Characteristics and Disposition of Persons Found Not Guilty By Reason of Insanity in New York State, 1971–1976.* Am. J. Psychiatry 136 (1979): 655–60.

Pasewark, R. A., S. Bieber, K. J. Bosten, M. Kiser, and H. J. Steadman. *Criminal Recidivism Among Insanity Acquittees.* Int'l J. L. & Psychiatry 5 (1982): 365–75.

Pepper, B., and H. Ryglewicz. *The Role of the State Hospital: A New Mandate for a New Era.* Psychiatric Q. 57(3–4) (Fall/Winter 1985): 230–51.

Perlin, M. *Mental Disability Law: Civil and Criminal.* Charlottesville, Va.: Michie Company, 1989.

Perlin, M. "Other Rights of Residents in Institutions," in *Legal Rights of Mentally Disabled Persons*, vol. 2, ed. P. Friedman. New York: Practicing Law Institute, 1979.

Perlin, M. *The Supreme Court, the Mentally Disabled Criminal Defendant, and Symbolic Values: Random Decisions, Hidden Rationales, or "Doctrinal Abyss"?* Ariz. L. Rev. 29 (1987): 1–98.

Perlin, M. *Whose Plea Is It Anyway? Insanity Defense Myths and Realities.* Philadelphia Medicine 79 (1983): 5–10.

Peterson, I. "Warm Season Masks but Doesn't End Problem of the Homeless," *New York Times*, June 3, 1983, p. A16, col. 1.

Petrila, J. *The Insanity Defense and Other Mental Health Dispositions in Missouri.* Int'l J. L. & Psychiatry 5 (1982): 81–101.

Phillips, B. L., and R. A. Pasewark. *Insanity Pleas in Connecticut.* Bull. Am. Acad. Psychiatry & L. 8(3) (1980): 335–44.

Pierce, G. L., M. L. Durham, and W. H. Fisher. *The Impact of Broadened Civil Commitment Standards on Admission to State Mental Hospitals*. Am. J. Psychiatry 142 (1985): 104–7.

Platt, A. M. *The Child Savers: The Invention of Delinquency*, 2d ed. Chicago: University of Chicago Press, 1977.

Pope, H. G., P. E. Keck, and S. L. McElroy. *Frequency and Presentation of Neuroleptic Malignant Syndrome in a Large Psychiatric Hospital*. Am. J. Psychiatry 143 (1986): 1227–33.

Poythress, N. G. *Psychiatric Expertise in Civil Commitment: Training Attorneys to Cope with Expert Testimony*. L. & Hum. Behav. 2 (1978): 1–23.

President's Commission on Law Enforcement and Administration of Justice. *The Challenge of Crime in a Free Society*. Washington, D.C.: U.S. Government Printing Office, 1968.

Rabkin, J. *Criminal Behavior of Discharged Mental Patients: A Critical Appraisal of the Research*. Psychological Bull. 86 (1979): 1–27.

Rachlin, S. "The Influence of Law on Deinstitutionalization," in *Deinstitutionalization*, ed. Leona L. Bachrach, vol. 17, *New Directions for Mental Health Services*. San Francisco, Calif.: Jossey-Bass, 1983, 41–54.

Rachlin, S. *When Schizophrenia Comes Marching Home*. Psychiatric Q. 50(3) (1978): 202–10.

Rachlin, S. *With Liberty and Psychosis for All*. Psychiatric Q. 48 (1974): 410–20.

Reagan, R. *The Creative Society*. New York: Devin-Adair, 1968.

Reich, R. B. *The Next American Frontier*. New York: Times Books, 1983.

Research & Forecasts, Inc. *The Figgie Report on Fear of Crime: America Afraid, Parts I, II and III*. Willoughby, Ohio: A-T-O, Inc., 1980.

Resnik, J. *Failing Faith: Adjudicatory Procedure in Decline*. U. Chi. L. Rev. 53 (1986): 494–560.

Reynolds, S. E. *Battle of the Experts Revisited: 1983 Oregon Legislation on the Insanity Defense*. Willamette L. Rev. 20 (1984): 303–17.

Rhoden, N. K. *The Limits of Liberty: Deinstitutionalization, Homelessness, and Libertarian Theory*. Emory L. J. 31 (1982): 375–440.

Robinson, D. N. *Psychology and the Law: Can Justice Survive the Social Sciences?* New York: Oxford University Press, 1980.

Rock, R., M. Jacobson, and R. Janepaul. "Police Participation in Initiating Hospitalization Procedures," in *Hospitalization and Discharge of the Mentally Ill*. Chicago: University of Chicago Press, 1968.

Rodriguez, J. H., L. M. LeWinn, and M. Perlin. *The Insanity Defense Under Siege: Legislative Assaults and Legal Rejoinders*. Rutgers L. J. 14 (1983): 397–430.

Rofman, E. S., C. Askinazi, and E. Fant. *The Prediction of Dangerous Behavior in Emergency Civil Commitment*. Am. J. Psychiatry 137(9) (1980): 1061–64.

Rogers, J. L., and J. D. Bloom. *Characteristics of Persons Committed to Oregon's Psychiatric Security Review Board*. Bull. Am. Acad. Psychiatry L. 10(3) (1982): 155–64.

Rogers, J. L., and J. D. Bloom. *The Insanity Sentence: Oregon's Psychiatric Security Review Board*, Behav. Sci. & L. 3(1) (1985): 69–84.

Rogers, J. L., W. H. Sack, J. D. Bloom, and S. M. Manson. *Women in Oregon's Insanity Defense System*. J. Psychiatry & L. 11 (1983): 515.

Rose, S. M. *Deciphering Deinstitutionalization: Complexities in Policy and Program Analysis*. Milbank Memorial Fund Q. 57 (1979): 429–60.

Rosenstein, M., H. J. Steadman, R. MacAskill, and R. Manderscheid. *Legal Status of Admission to Three Inpatient Psychiatric Settings, United States (1980)*, Mental Health Statistical Note No. 178. Washington, D.C.: U.S. Dept. of Heath and Human Services, 1986.

Rossi, P. H. *Down and Out in America: The Origins of Homelessness*. Chicago: University of Chicago Press, 1989.

Rossi, P. H., J. D. Wright, G. A. Fisher, and G. Willis. *The Urban Homeless: Estimating Composition and Size*. Science 235 (1987): 1336–41.

Roth, D. J., and G. J. Bean. *New Perspectives on Homelessness: Findings from a Statewide Epidemiological Study*. Hosp. & Commun. Psychiatry 37 (1985): 712–14.

Roth, D., G. J. Bean, and P. S. Hyde. *Homelessness and Mental Health Policy: Developing an Appropriate Role for the 1980s*. Commun. Mental Health J. 22(3) (1986): 203–14.

Roth, L. H. *Mental Health Commitment: The State of the Debate, 1980*. Hosp. & Commun. Psychiatry 31(6) (June 1980): 385–96.

Rothman, D. J. *Conscience and Convenience: The Asylum and Its Alternatives in Progressive America*. Boston: Little, Brown and Co., 1980.

Rothman, D. J. *The Courts and Social Reform: A Postprogressive Outlook*. Law & Hum. Behav. 6 (1982): 113–19.

Rothman, D. J. *The Discovery of the Asylum: Social Order and Disorder in the New Republic*, 1st ed. Boston: Little, Brown & Co., 1971.

Rothman, D. J., and S. Rothman. *The Willowbrook Wars*. New York: Harper & Row, 1984.

Rothstein. T. L. "Care Denied to Mentally Ill," *Seattle Post-Intelligencer*, Sept. 28, 1978, p. B3.

Rubenstein, L. S. *APA's Model Law: Hurting the People It Seeks to Help*. Hosp. & Commun. Psychiatry 36(9) (1985): 968–72.

Rubin, A. H. *Beating the Odds: Compulsive Gambling as an Insanity Defense—State v. Lafferty*. Conn. L. Rev. 14 (1982): 341–67.

Rubin, B. *Prediction of Dangerousness in Mentally Ill Criminals*. Arch. Gen Psychiatry 27 (1972): 397–407.

Rubin, L. C., and M. J. Mills. *Behavioral Precipitants to Civil Commitment*. Am. J. Psychiatry 140(5) (1983): 1061–64.

Sales, B., and T. Hafemeister. "Empiricism and Legal Policy on the Insanity Defense," in *Mental Health and Criminal Justice*, ed. L. Teplin. Beverly Hill, Calif.: Sage Publications, 1984, 253–78.

Sallet, J. B. *After Hinckley: The Insanity Defense Reexamined*. Yale L. J. 94 (1985): 1545–57.

Saltzburg, S. A. *Privileges and Professionals: Lawyers and Psychiatrists*. Va. L. Rev. 66 (1980): 597–651.

Salzburg, S. A. *Foreword: The Flow and Ebb of Constitutional Criminal Procedure in the Warren and Burger Courts*. Geo. L. J. 69 (1980): 151–209.

Santiestevan, H. *Out of Their Beds and Into the Streets*. Washington, D.C.: American Federation of State, County and Municipal Employees, 1975.

Sauer, R. H., and P. M. Mullins. *The Insanity Defense: M'Naghten vs. ALI*. Bull. Am. Acad. Psychiatry & L. 4 (1976): 73.

Scheingold, S. A. *The Politics of Rights: Lawyers, Public Policy and Political Change*. New Haven: Yale University Press, 1974.

Schneider, J. W., and P. Conrad. "The Medical Control of Deviance: Contests and Consequences," in *Research in the Sociology of Health Care*, vol 1, ed. J. Roth. Greenwich, Conn.: JAI Press, 1980, 1–53.

Scull, A. T. *Decarceration: Community and the Deviant—A Radical View.* Englewood Cliffs, N.J.: Prentice-Hall, 1977; rev. ed., 1984.

Scull, A. T. *A New Trade in Lunacy: The Recommodification of the Mental Patient.* Am. Behav. Sci. 24(6) (July/August 1981): 741–54.

Sheridan, E., and L. A. Teplin. *Police-Referreed Psychiatric Emergencies: Advantages of Community Treatment.* J. Commun. Psychology 9 (1981): 140–47.

Shore, J. H., W. Breakey, and B. Arvidson. *Morbidity and Mortality in the Commitment Process.* Arch. Gen. Psychiatry 38 (1981): 930–34.

Simon, R. J., and D. E. Aaronson. *The Insanity Defense: A Critical Assessment of Law and Policy in the Post-Hinckley Era.* New York: Praeger, 1988.

Singer, A. *Insanity Acquittals in the Seventies: Observations and Empirical Analysis of One Jurisdiction.* Mental Disability L. Rep. 2 (1978): 406–17.

Singer, R. G. *Essay—Abolition of the Insanity Defense: Madness and the Criminal Law.* Cardozo L. Rev. 4 (1983): 683–707.

Slobogin, C. *The Guilty But Mentally Ill Verdict: An Idea Whose Time Should Not Have Come.* Geo. Wash. L. Rev. 53 (1985): 494–527.

Slovenko, R. *Civil Commitment in Perspective.* J. Pub. L. 20 (1971): 3–32.

Slovenko, R. *Psychiatry and Law.* Boston: Little, Brown, 1973.

Smith, W. F. *Limiting the Insanity Defense: A Rational Approach to Irrational Crimes.* Mo. L. Rev. 47 (1982): 605–19.

Sobeloff, S. E. *Insanity and the Criminal Law: From M'Naghten to Durham and Beyond.* A. B. A. J. 41 (1955): 793–96, 877–79.

Spece, R. G. *Preserving the Right to Treatment: A Critical Assessment and Constructive Development of Constitutional Right to Treatment Theories.* Ariz. L. Rev. 20 (1978): 1–47.

Splane, S., J. Monahan, D. Prestholt, and H. D. Friedlander. *Patients' Perceptions of the Family Role in Involuntary Commitment.* Hosp. & Commun. Psychiatry 33(7) (1982): 569–72.

Steadman, H. J. *Beating a Rap? Defendants Found Incompetent to Stand Trial.* Chicago: University of Chicago Press, 1981.

Steadman, H. J. *Empirical Research on the Insanity Defense.* Annals Am. Acad. Pol. & Soc. Sci. 477 (1985): 58–71.

Steadman, H. J. *Insanity Acquittals in New York: 1965–1978.* Am. J. Psychiatry 137 (3) (1980): 321–26.

Steadman, H. J. *Mental Health Law and the Criminal Offender: Research Directions for the 1990's.* Rutgers L. Rev. 39 (1987): 323–37.

Steadman, H. J. *Some Evidence on the Inadequacy of the Concept and Determination of Dangerousness in Law and Psychiatry.* J. Psychiatry & L. 1 (1973): 409–26.

Steadman, H. J., and J. Braff. "Defendants Not Guilty By Reason of Insanity," in *Mentally Disordered Offenders*, ed. J. Monahan and H. J. Steadman. New York: Plenum, 1983, 109–29.

Steadman, H. J., and J. J. Cocozza. *Selective Reporting and the Public's Misconceptions of the Criminally Insane.* Pub. Opinion Q. 41 (1978): 523.

Steadman, H. J., et al. *Factors Associated with a Successful Insanity Defense.* Am. J. Psychiatry 140(4) (1983): 401–5.

Steadman, H. J., J. J. Cocozza, and M. E. Melick. *Explaining the Increased Arrest*

Rate Among Mental Patients: The Changing Clientele of State Hospitals. Am. J. Psychiatry 135(7) (1978): 816–20.

Steadman, H. J., L. A. Callahan, P. C. Robbins, and J. P. Morrissey. *Maintenance of an Insanity Defense Under Montana's "Abolition" of the Insanity Defense.* Am. J. Psychiatry 146 (1989): 357–60.

Stefan, S. *Preventive Commitment: The Concept and Its Pitfalls.* Mental & Phys. Disability L. Rep. 11(4) (1987): 288–304.

Steinfels, P. *The Neoconservatives: The Men Who Are Changing America's Politics.* New York: Simon and Schuster, 1979.

Stone, A. *Recent Mental Health Litigation: A Critical Perspective.* Am. J. Psychiatry 134(3) (1977): 273–79.

Stone, A. A. *The Commission on Judicial Action of the American Psychiatric Association: Origins and Prospects—A Personal View.* Bull. Am. Acad. Psychiatry & L. 3 (1975): 119–22.

Stone, A. A. *Law, Psychiatry, and Morality.* Washington, D.C.: American Psychiatric Press, 1984.

Stone, A. A. *Mental Health and the Law: A System in Transition.* Washington, D.C.: National Institute of Mental Health, 1975.

Stone, A. A. *A Response to Comments on APA's Model Commitment Law.* Hosp. & Commun. Psychiatry 36(9) (1985): 984–89.

Stromberg, C. D., and A. A. Stone. *A Model State Law on Civil Commitment of the Mentally Ill.* Harv. J. on Legis. 20 (1983): 275–396.

Sullivan, R. "Ferry Slashing Report Assails Hospital for Freeing Suspect," *New York Times*, July 12, 1986, p. A1, col. 1.

Szasz, T. *The Myth of Mental Illness.* New York: Hoeber-Harper, 1961.

Talbott, J. A. *Response to the Presidential Address: Psychiatry's Unfinished Business in the 20th Century.* Am. J. Psychiatry 141(8) (1984): 927–30.

Talbott, J. *The Death of the Asylum.* New York: Grune & Stratton, 1979.

Teplin, L. A. *The Criminality of the Mentally Ill: A Dangerous Misconception.* Am. J. Psychiatry 142(5) (1985): 593–99.

Teplin, L. A. *The Criminalization of the Mentally Ill: Speculation in Search of Data.* Psychological Bull. 94 (1983): 54–67.

Teplin, L. A. *Criminalizing Mental Disorders: The Comparative Arrest Rate of the Mentally Ill.* Am. Psychologist 39(7) (1984): 794–803.

Teplin, L. A., W. Filstead, G. Hefter, and E. Sheridan. *Police Involvement with the Psychiatric Emergency Patient.* Psychiatric Annals 10(5) (1980): 202–7.

Tonry, M. H. *Sentencing Reform Impacts.* Washington, D.C.: National Institute of Justice, 1987.

Torrey, E. F. *Nowhere to Go: The Tragic Odyssey of the Homeless Mentally Ill.* New York: Harper & Row, 1988.

Treffert, D. A. *Dying With Their Rights On.* Am. J. Psychiatry 141 (1981): 1041.

Treffert, D. A. *The Obviously Ill Patient in Need of Treatment: A Fourth Standard for Civil Commitment.* Hosp. & Commun. Psychiatry 36 (1985): 259–64.

Tribe, L. H. *American Constitutional Law*, 2d ed. Mineola, N.Y.: Foundation Press, 1988.

Trombetta, J. "Criminals Beware: The Screen Avengers Are Coming!" *L.A. Times*, July 12, 1981, "Calendar" section, p. 1.

United States President's Task Force on Victims of Crime: Final Report. Washington, D.C.: The Task Force, 1982.

United States Sentencing Commission. *Federal Sentencing Guidelines Manual, 1990 Edition*. St. Paul, Minn.: West Publishing, 1989.

Van den Haag, Ernest. *Punishing Criminals: Concerning a Very Old and Painful Question*. New York: Basic Books, 1975.

Vogel, W. *A Personal Memoir of the State Hospitals of the 1950s*. Hosp. & Commun. Psychiatry 42(6) (1991): 593–97.

Von Hirsch, A. *Doing Justice: The Choice of Punishments, Report of the Committee for the Study of Incarceration*. New York: Hill and Wang, 1976.

Waelder, R. *Psychiatry and the Problem of Criminal Responsibility*. U. Pa. L. Rev. 101 (1952): 378–90.

Walker, L. E. *The Battered Woman*. New York: Harper & Row, 1979.

Walker, L. E., R. K. Thyfault, and A. Browne. *Beyond the Juror's Ken: Battered Women*. Vt. L. Rev. 7 (1982): 1–14.

Walker, N. *Crime and Insanity in England*, vol. 1. Edinburgh: Edinburgh University Press, 1968.

Walker, N., and S. McCabe. *Crime and Insanity in England*, vol. 2. Edinburgh: Edinburgh University Press, 1973.

Walkover, A. *The Infancy Defense in the New Juvenile Court*. UCLA L. Rev. 31 (1984): 503–62.

Wanck, B. *Two Decades of Involuntary Hospitalization Legislation*. Am. J. Psychiatry 141 (1984): 33–38.

Warren, C.A.B. *Court of Last Resort: Judicial Review of Involuntary Civil Commitment in California*. Chicago: University of Chicago Press, 1982.

Warren, C.A.B. *Court of Last Resort: Mental Illness and the Law*. Chicago: University of Chicago Press, 1982.

Warren, C.A.B. *Involuntary Commitment for Mental Disorder: The Application of California's Lanterman-Petris-Short Act*. Law & Soc'y Rev. 11 (1977): 629–49.

Warren, C.A.B. *The Social Construction of Dangerousness*. Los Angeles: University of Southern California Press, 1977.

Weihofen, H. *The M'Naghten Rule in Its Present-Day Setting*. Fed. Probation 17(3) (1953): 8–14.

Weihofen, H. *The Urge to Punish: New Approaches to the Problem of Mental Irresponsibility for Crime*. New York: Farrar, Strauss and Cudahy, 1956.

Weinstein, J. B. *The Effect of Austerity on Institutional Litigation*. Law & Hum. Behav. 6 (1982): 145–51.

Weithorn, L. A. *Mental Hospitalization of Troublesome Youth: An Analysis of Skyrocketing Admission Rates*. Stanford Law Review 40(3) (1988): 773–838.

Wenger, D. L., and C. R. Fletcher. *The Effect of Legal Counsel on Admissions to a State Mental Hospital: A Confrontation of Professions*. J. Health & Soc. Behav. 10 (1969): 66–72.

Werner, P. D., et al. *Hostile Worlds and Assaultive Behavior on an Acute Inpatient Unit*. J. Nervous & Mental Disease 171(6) (1983): 385–87.

Wexler, D. *Mental Health Law: Major Issues*, Perspectives in Law and Psychology Series. New York: Plenum Press, 1981.

Wilbanks, W. *The Make My Day Law: Colorado's Experiment in Home Protection*. Lanham, Md.: University Press of America, 1990.

Wilson, J. Q. *Thinking About Crime*. New York: Basic Books, 1975.

Winnick, B. J. *Competency to Consent to Voluntary Hospitalization: A Therapeutic Jurisprudence Analysis of Zinermon v. Burch*. Int'l J. L. & Psychiatry 14 (1991): 169–214.

Winnick, B. J. *Psychotropic Medication and Competence to Stand Trial*. Am. B. Found. Res. J. 1977(3) (1977): 769–816.

Wooton, B. *Crime and the Criminal Law: Reflections of a Magistrate and Social Scientist*. London: Stevens, 1963.

Yesavage, J. A. *A Study of Mandatory Review of Civil Commitment*. Arch. Gen. Psychiatry 41 (1984): 305–8.

Yesavage, J. A., P. D. Werner, J.M.T. Becker, and M. J. Mills. *The Context of Involuntary Commitment on the Basis of Danger to Others*. J. Nervous & Mental Disease 170(10) (1982): 622–27.

Yesavage, J. A., P. D. Werner, J.M.T. Becker, and M. J. Mills. *Short-Term Civil Commitment and the Violent Patient: A Study of Legal Status and Inpatient Behavior*. Am. J. Psychiatry 139(9) (1982): 1145–49.

Zeisel, H., and A. Gallup. *Death Penalty Sentiment in the United States*. J. Quantitative Criminology 5 (1989): 285–96.

Index